TEEN EARTH MAGIC

AN EMPOWERMENT WORKBOOK

Welcome to our book – here's a few ways to get started!

- **Read** the Teens Roundtables and hear directly from TEM campers – (pages 17-24, pages 86-89, and more).
- **Skim** the Table of Contents (pages 10-11) or Ye Olde Index (pages 352-356) for an overview of the book.
- **Play** Reclaiming chants while flipping through the book (see pages 111-113 for online links).
- **Jump** to the chapter on Magical Activism for some quick inspiration (page 148).
- **Listen** to an online ritual with Starhawk while reading (see page 115).
- **Do Bibliomancy** (divination from a sacred text) – open the book at random and start reading!

Want to do a ritual without reading the whole book?

- Read the Ritual Skills intro and outline (pages 44-45) and Sacred Space: Quick Ways (pages 49-51).
- Select a core working from the Workings chapter or another that interests you.
- Choose a few chants that fit your theme and mood (pages 111-113).
- Let the magic begin!

A word to parents & other teachers

Please see page 9 for a special welcome and more information about Reclaiming and Teen Earth Magic.

You can contact us at: TeenEarthMagic@gmail.com and Quarterly@Reclaiming.org.

TEEN EARTH MAGIC

Raven,
here's some magic for all ages!
Silver RavenWolf

TEEN EARTH MAGIC

AN EMPOWERMENT WORKBOOK

From California's Pagan Youth Camp

by Luke Hauser

Co-Created by Teen Earth Magic Campers & Teachers
in the Reclaiming Tradition

Foreword by Starhawk

Reclaiming Quarterly
San Francisco / Ohlone Territory

Reclaiming Quarterly

Published by Reclaiming Collective

San Francisco

Our Founder

This book is produced and published by Reclaiming Quarterly in cooperation with Teen Earth Magic. Both work cells are part of Bay Area Reclaiming Collective.

Reclaiming Quarterly and Newsletter were published in print from 1980 to 2011, totaling more than 100 issues.

Today we publish online as well as books and recordings.

Back issues are available free at WeaveAndSpin.org/back-issues

Reclaiming Quarterly (1997-2011) was descended from Reclaiming Newsletter (1980-1997), itself a distant offshoot of Ye Olde Gazetteer & Reclaymer (1613-1776). The latter traced its roots to neolithic petroglyphs in western Anatolia, before which RQ's past is shrouded in mystery.

Views expressed in articles, graphics, interviews, advertisements, and miscellaneous marginalia belong to the authors, not to the Reclaiming community or the RQ production cell. Some of us don't even like some of the stuff we print.

RQ is a volunteer effort. You don't need to be in the Bay Area to help! Contact us at:

ReclaimingQuarterly@gmail.com

WEBSITES

Reclaiming.org
ReclaimingQuarterly.org
WeaveAndSpin.org
DirectAction.org
CampfireChants.org
TeenEarthMagic.org

Reclaiming Quarterly
San Francisco / Ohlone Territory

©2019 Reclaiming Quarterly. All rights reserved.

Hauser, Luke
Teen Earth Magic: an empowerment workbook

ISBN: 978-1719074216
LCCN TBA

Designed and published via volunteer labor in California, Planet Earth: No Borders!

Reclaiming Quarterly / Reclaiming Collective
PO Box 14404
San Francisco CA 94114

Thanks to: Witchlets in the Woods, Redwood Magic Family Camp, Bay Area Reclaiming groups and the Wheel, CRAFT teachers cell, GroundWork, Camp Epic, Mendocino Woodlands, Yuba River, Laura, Starhawk & Charles & Demetra at Golden Rabbit Ranch, Thalia & Lucy & Rhys & Cyris, Jamie & Ivory Fly, Meg & Jamie & Laurel & Owen, MoonCrone, Luz, Nicola & Mike, Susan & Brian, Paul & Natalia & Alexa, John & Kim, Catherine & Kirin, Paul Eaves, Copper, Dawnstar, Rosalie, Elka, Jada & Frank & Ezra & Keegan, Dress & Kala, Marg & Elaine, Jonathan, Ruby, Seed, Feather, Robin, Rock, Marie-Laure, Ewa, Bob, Marian, Bill, Rose, Joe, Nancy, Macha, Spiraleena, Irisanya, Justin, Gwydion, Heidi, Lore, Eric, Rahula, Tigris, Tarin, Patti, Gwion, Stas, Jax, Adissa, Rich, Beverly, Keith, Max.

Love and appreciation to the late April Cotte, our Witchlets and Redwood Magic Family Camp co-teacher. April's xeroxed book of exercises (available on our website) inspired us to create this expanded workbook, and her spirit is forever felt in our work. What is remembered lives!

Teen Earth Magic teachers and organizers: Allison, Riyana, George, Jason, Seneca, Jude, Abel, Aaron, Meagan, Captain, Eddy, Trillium, Karo, Fly, Lindsey, Vesper, Penskee, Jacin, Lyra, Rachel, Briar, Aja, Mykel, KaeliMo Valkyrie, Ingrid, Hilary, Sequoia, Athena, Ari, Maeve, Margaux.

Copy editing and magical consulting by Laurie Lovekraft.

Cover photo: Teen activism workshop with Starhawk and Dress. Photo by George Franklin.

Photos: Reclaiming Quarterly, Luke Hauser, George Franklin, Michael Rauner, Alla Irwin, Stephen Readmond, and as identified in text. All photos used with permission and ©2019 Reclaiming Quarterly. Photographers retain all further rights beyond Reclaiming publishing.

PUBLISHER'S NOTICE

This is a work of journalism. It reports activities from Teen Earth Magic, remembered to the best of our abilities. We make no further claim to originality, nor accept any further responsibility for the use, application, modification, etc of these workings after publication.

The author sifted through many years' notes and interviewed numerous participants in an effort to ensure the accuracy of the information contained in this book. Notwithstanding this commendable effort, all responsibility for errors, inaccuracies, omissions, inconsistencies, less-than-felicitous phrasings, and/or regrettable puns – as well as any and all issues that might arise from the application of this material – lies entirely with the author, not others cited, the copy editor, the publisher, Reclaiming, or the readers.

Photos are from TEM and other Reclaiming events. Connections between photographs and text may be coincidental, and do not necessarily depict the working described or the people involved in that working.

Over the years, Teens Path workings have been borrowed from many places, and we have reworked exercises and rituals to suit our work. We may have borrowed and/or refashioned a working that you helped create – and we may have forgotten or never known the source. If you feel that a working is particularly your creation or specialty, let us know and we will try to update the credits in future editions.

DOWNLOADS & PRINT EDITIONS OF THIS BOOK

Download of PDF: TeenEarthMagic.org • ReclaimingQuarterly.org • WeaveandSpin.org
Print Edition: Amazon.com

CONTACT

TeenEarthMagic@gmail.com • ReclaimingQuarterly@gmail.com • Quarterly@Reclaiming.org

Also by Luke Hauser
Direct Action: An Historical Novel
Being & Nothingness: An Epistemological Murder Mystery

Writing as Dixie W. Franklin
The Hardy Girls: The Mystery of Rafferty's Farm
The Hardy Girls: The Mystery of the Derailed Train
More Titles TBA

Info at DirectAction.org
google above titles for info and downloads
print editions at amazon

More from Reclaiming
Reclaiming.org – International Home Site
WitchCamp.org – International WitchCamps
& Family Camps
WeaveAndSpin.org – Current Posts
WeaveAndSpin.org/back-issues – Archives & Back Issues
WeaveAndSpin.org/resources – Resources & Freebies
Starhawk.org – Starhawk's website

A full-color PDF of this book is available on our website.
TeenEarthMagic.org

PDF version is good for printing single pages –
plus most of the photos are in color!

INTRODUCTION

Welcome to Teen Earth Magic!

"Welcome to Teen Earth Magic!"

Each year, these words open our camp.

With this book, we welcome you to our circle. We prepared this book of rituals, exercises, and spells so that you could do the same magical workings we do at our camps – alone, or with a circle in your home area.

Reclaiming-style magic can be done in large groups, small circles, or alone. You'll find a section of the Introduction that talks about Circles and Solitaries, and most workings include a Solo section.

Getting Started – Several Ways

Read the Introduction and Ritual chapters. You'll hear directly from participants in our camps – What is Earth magic? Why and when do we do rituals? How do we take magic into our daily lives? What do we (or don't we) believe about magic and spirituality?

Jump straight into one of the rituals. The Rituals chapter has several rituals that you can do alone or with a small circle – there's even a drum-trance ritual guided by Starhawk that you can find online. Read the Intent for each ritual to find one that calls to you. There's also a section on how to create your own rituals using workings from this book or ones you invent.

Flip through the Workings chapter and find one you like. Each working can stand alone – although you'll probably want to start off by reading Ritual Skills: Sacred Space: Quick Ways, which shows how to create a magical circle as a container for other workings.

Make up more ways. In Reclaiming we say: "Each person is their own spiritual authority." Each of us creates our own best ritual and magic. The purpose of this book is to share some basic skills and tools and to help you discover what works for you.

Blessings on your work. Welcome to the magic!

Who Can Attend Teen Earth Magic?

Teen Earth Magic is a retreat for young people from Reclaiming Tradition and their guests.

We welcome new folks at our family and all-ages camps – a great place for young people to get involved and meet TEM participants and teachers.

Visit WitchCamp.org, or contact us with questions – see emails on next page.

More about our camp – see page 16.

INTRODUCTION

A Word to Parents & Other Teachers

A word from TEM Teachers to Parents

Thank you for sharing this book with your teen!

Whether you are Pagan yourself, or are reading this to support your kid, we're glad to have a chance to share a word with you – and we invite you to contact us if you have questions or feedback (see bottom of this page).

Reclaiming is an Earth-based spiritual teaching and grassroots organizing collective with local communities and networks around the Americas, Europe, and Australia. Find out more later in this chapter, and at Reclaiming.org and WeaveAndSpin.org.

Teen Earth Magic, created in cooperation with Starhawk, offers retreats, workshops, and resources for young people interested in Earth-based practices.

What About Teachers?

This book is designed for young people working alone or with friends, or at Reclaiming Tradition camps. We're also honored to have other teachers adapt it for their use.

Unless you are formally trained in our tradition, please do not teach this material under the name "Teen Earth Magic" or "Reclaiming." Reclaiming has a teacher-development process. Teen Earth Magic also has its own process.

Bring TEM to your retreat! TEM teachers can anchor youth and adult classes, workshops, and rituals, bringing fresh inspiration and Earth energy to your event. Email us!

No Grooming or Recruiting – this book is not to be used to recruit youth for circles or classes apart from knowing and communicating with their families. No Reclaiming material is ever to be used to groom young people. Contact us with questions or concerns – email below.

Teens, Adults – & Young Adults

Teachers and campers have developed deep and long-lasting connections as they have returned to camp.

Some folks have aged-out of TEM, yet want to stay involved. Our Mentors path is a way for people 18 and up to stay a part of camp while gaining teaching and organizing skills. (See Organizing: Mentors in the final chapter.)

Contact Teen Earth Magic

Contact us at TeenEarthMagic@gmail.com and Quarterly@Reclaiming.org.

Paganism & Other Religions

Some practitioners of Paganism are also deeply involved in other spiritual traditions.

Some Reclaiming folks are active in Buddhist, Jewish, and Unitarian congregations or groups. Jewish folks and allies have held JeWitch Camp some years in Northern California.

Others combine Earth-based and Christian spirituality – Francis of Assisi and environmental ethics are bridges.

What about Satanism?

Are Pagans connected to Satanism? Perhaps somewhere – but in many Pagan groups, Satan is seen as part of a different religion. We honor many goddesses and gods, but Satan wasn't part of any Pagan pantheon, and has probably never been invoked in a Reclaiming ritual.

Fire Safety

This book avoids indoor fire magic. But we can't guarantee how practices might be adapted by creative practitioners.

Magic isn't the only reason that teens light candles. Here's a chance to do some fire-safety preparation:

- flat, non-flammable altar spaces – dresser tops, end tables, marble, brick, or ceramic tiles...
- glass jar candles (can you buy a case?)
- curtains and fabric at a safe distance or tied back
- smoke alarm tested (and not right above an altar)
- water-pressure fire extinguisher (test it outside – it's fun)

Witchlets in the Woods and Redwood Magic are all-ages family camps, where adults, teens, and kids share collective and age-based magic in a magnificent setting. More info at Witchlets.org and RedwoodMagic.org.

INTRODUCTION

Table of Contents

Welcome to Teen Earth Magic!.. 8
A Word to Parents & Other Teachers.. 9
Foreword: An Interview with Starhawk 12

Introduction

- Teen Earth Magic: On Indigenous Land...15
- Teen Earth Magic: About Our Camp..16
- What Is Magic? – Teens Roundtable..17
- What Do Teen Pagans Believe? – Teens Roundtable 23
- Covens, Circles, & Solitaries..26
- Etiquette, Hexes, Boundaries, & Safety...27
- Agreements: Building Trust..32
- About Reclaiming & Our Principles of Unity 34
- Gender Complexities – Interview with Mykel Mogg.................38
- Cultural Appropriation – Interview with Rahula Janowski......40

Ritual Skills

Ritual Skills..43
- Outline of a Ritual & Wheel of the Year...45
- Ritual: What / Why / When – Teens Roundtable.........................47
- Creating Sacred Space: Quick Ways..49
- Honoring First People..58
- Grounding – Teens Roundtable & Exercises................................62
- Casting a Circle – Teens Roundtable & Exercises.......................68
- Invoking – Teens Roundtable & Exercises....................................77
- Invoking Elements & Ancestors..84
- Invoking Deities, Allies, & Energies – Teens Roundtable..........86
- Goddesses, Gods, Mysterious Ones, & Energies 90
- Planning a Ritual & Ritual Arc 93
- Magical Themes, Myths, & Stories from Our Camps................98
- How to Lead a Spiral Dance 106
- Chants Resources Online...111

Sample Rituals 114
- Way to the Well: An Online Ritual with Starhawk....................115
- A Grounding Ritual & An Affirmation Ritual............................116
- Labyrinth Challenges & Stations Ritual Formats 125
- A Water Ritual (from Elements of Magic class) 133
- Opening Night at Witchlets..140
- Crafting Your Own Rituals..145

INTRODUCTION

Table of More Contents

Magical Activism

Magical Activism: Reclaiming's Unique Synthesis 148
- Activism & Magic – Teens Roundtable 149
- Student Activism – Teens Roundtable 151
- Magical Activism: Introduction & Resources 152
- Our Commitment to Nonviolence 156
- Finding Your Own Activism 158
- Preparing for Action: Skills for Street & Forest 160
- Workings: Street Theater, Chalking, Mystery Posters 166
- Activist Allies & Kindred Spirits 170

Workings

Exercises & Workings – Complete Alphabetical List 172
- Tips & Techniques for Teachers 175
- Book of Shadows 202
- Boundaries 203
- Divination & Oracles 214
- Labyrinth Workings 230
- Liberation Circle 234
- Magical Writing 239
- Mirror Workings 241
- Pentacle Magic 249
- Shadow Work 259
- Spell Crafting 271
- Tarot: A Key Magical Tool 285
- Tools of Magic / Wands 303
- Trust Exercises 312

Organizing & Resources

- Organizing Family & Youth Camps 325
- Teaching Magic To Teens: Early Experiments 328
- Mentors: Young Adults & Student Teachers 335
- Ethics Agreement & Organizing Tools 337
- Reclaiming Resources, Chants, Books, & Publications 342
- Connecting with Teen Earth Magic & WitchCamps 350

Index & Guide to the Book 352

Revolutionary Pagan Workers Vanguard 357

INTRODUCTION

Foreword: An Interview with Starhawk

Author of The Spiral Dance & The Earth Path

Author Luke Hauser and Reclaiming co-founder Starhawk have been comrades and co-agitators since the early 1980s.

In this interview, we look back at how Paganism has evolved from the days when each of us (often as adults) had to discover Earth-based spirituality on our own, through the early days of Pagan parenting, to today's Reclaiming family and youth camps and communities.

Luke: You grew up Jewish – was that an important part of your younger years?

Starhawk: Yeah. I went to Hebrew schools, and I was Bat-Mitzvah'd. I went to Hebrew high school and after-school programs. If I'd been a boy, I'd probably have grown up to be a rabbi. But in that era – it's not just that there were not women rabbis – it never even crossed my mind as a possibility.

What led you to Paganism and the Goddess?

I always loved fairy tales. I loved the idea of magic. I especially loved the kinds of stories where ordinary, modern-day kids discovered magic in the modern world. I always longed for magic.

When I got to be a teenager, it was the 60s. It was all sex, drugs, and rock & roll – its own kind of magic! I felt like I was having direct spiritual experiences, especially with nature. Judaism didn't say much about that, especially at that time. So I began exploring.

My friend Patty and I eventually met some witches who said they believed that the Earth is alive, that the sacred Being is the Goddess, that sexuality is sacred, that women can be leaders. And I was like, yes!

Was this an organized Pagan group?

It was the American Celtic Tradition. We studied with them for a while, then drifted away. At that point in my life I wasn't very good at following a discipline!

Back then, it was really hard to find out anything about witches. There was very little to read. Sybil Leek, Raymond Buckland. We read Joseph Campbell and other Jungians.

"Young people give me a lot of hope – even when I'm butting heads with them!"

When we met our teachers, Fred and Martha, they recommended that we read Robert Graves' book, The White Goddess – which is a pretty heavy read when you're 17.

I was really taken with his idea that there is this underlying Goddess tradition behind all of European culture.

You and I are part of a generation that had to seek the Goddess on our own. Now we see kids being raised as Pagans.

When we started Reclaiming in the late 70s and early 80s, it was mainly young, single people. There were some families, and as the community grew and matured, more people had kids.

But most Pagan parents did not grow up Pagan – it was a break with their family and their traditions.

I felt there was a need for a book about raising Pagan kids, if we want the tradition to carry on, and not just be, "Oh yeah, that's something my weird parents did back then."

But I didn't have any kids. Both Diane [Baker] and Anne [Hill] had kids, so it seemed like we would be a good combination to write Circle Round (see page 14).

Witchlets in the Woods started in 2001, and Redwood Magic Family Camp in 2013 – over the years, a lot of Reclaiming kids have been raised on that book.

I'm really grateful that people started those camps. It's really important for kids to have a spiritual community with other kids who have the same kinds of weird parents!

You've worked with a lot of young people in your Earth Activist Trainings and other Permaculture work. What have been your hopes and goals?

When it comes right down to it, I'm a pretty practical person. And Permaculture is the practical side of believing the Earth is sacred – really knowing what to do about it.

I've always loved gardening and loved being with nature. And I've also been an environmental activist all my life. It seems like Permaculture is the positive program, as

continued on next page

INTRODUCTION

Foreword: Interview with Starhawk (pg 3)

Author of Dreaming the Dark & Circle Round

we used to be. It's exciting to see younger people wanting to step up.

What about younger people coming into Spiral Dance or WitchCamp organizing?

It's great, although now that I'm older, I see the value in Native American traditions that say, "Honor your elders. Treat your elders with respect and care."

Good luck with that!

Yeah. Empowerment is great, but elders actually do know some things, which we've discovered through trial and error. Youth don't need to be condemned to making the same mistakes all over again. They can learn from our experience.

Part of creating the Teen Earth Magic Workbook is passing along lessons and ways of looking at things.

That's so important. Inside and outside of Reclaiming, young people are grappling with questions around gender, around diversity, all of these issues – trying to contend with not fitting into the roles that society offers.

I think it's wonderful to empower youth to create their own rituals, their own camp – to give them the skills and tools and see what they do with them. Reclaiming and especially Teen Earth Magic have been a supportive space for that work.

This book is an amazing magical resource for teens – and everyone. I really appreciate the work people have done to gather all of these resources for the next generation.

It's pretty impressive what people in Reclaiming have done – the number of authors and books, the music and chants and rituals – it's been a very creative space!

What gives you hope?

Getting to teach young people Permaculture. Seeing the Parkland [Florida] teens start a whole movement following the violence at their school. That makes me feel hopeful.

Young people in Reclaiming give me a lot of hope – seeing them so passionate about things. Even when I'm butting heads with them, the fervor and life force that they bring to bear is beautiful.

Books by Starhawk

- The Spiral Dance: A Rebirth of the Ancient Religion of the Goddess
- Dreaming the Dark: Magic, Sex, & Politics
- Truth or Dare: Encounters with Power, Authority, & Mystery
- The Twelve Wild Swans: A Journey to the Realm of Magic, Healing, & Action
- The Earth Path: Grounding Your Spirit in the Rhythms of Nature
- Webs of Power: Notes from the Global Uprising
- The Pagan Book of Living and Dying (with M. Macha Nightmare)
- Circle Round: Raising Children in Goddess Traditions (with Diane Baker & Anne Hill)

Novels

- The Fifth Sacred Thing
- Walking to Mercury
- City of Refuge
- The Last Wild Witch (picture-book for kids and everyone)

More resources from Starhawk and Reclaiming – pages 342-351.

INTRODUCTION

Teen Earth Magic
Is Held On Indigenous Land

Teen Earth Magic and most North American Reclaiming events are held on land stolen from Indigenous People.

We participate in a society built on genocide and theft.

In our rituals we acknowledge this debt and participate in the magical deconstruction of this abuse.

In our activism we seek to support Indigenous organizing, and to understand and heal the ways settler colonialism has and is influencing our efforts.

We take time to learn about the Indigenous People whose land we gather on, and how to support their ongoing efforts for recognition, autonomy, and healing.

We are engaged in a continuing process of listening, learning, and practicing.

So mote it be.

Acknowledging Indigenous People in our ritual practice – see Ritual Skills: Honoring First People – page 59.

INTRODUCTION

About Teen Earth Magic

Teen Earth Magic is a retreat for young people in the Reclaiming Tradition* of magic and activism. Our camp is co-created by teens, young adults, and WitchCamp teachers, and is supported by parents from Witchlets in the Woods and Redwood Magic Family Camp.

TEM began near Nevada City CA in 2008, as an offshoot of the Teens Path at Witchlets in the Woods. TEM weaves Earth-based ritual, empowerment and awareness workings, activism, and community.

TEM is a member of Reclaiming's WitchCamp Council, and TEM youth participate in Bay Area activist organizing and in events such as the annual Spiral Dance ritual.

TEM teachers and young adults have anchored paths at Witchlets, Redwood Magic Family Camp, Vermont WitchCamp, Loreley WitchCamp, Free Cascadia WitchCamp, Free Activist WitchCamp, and Winter WitchCamp, as well as co-teaching San Francisco Bay Area classes and workshops.

For more about TEM, see pages 334-341.

Who Can Attend Teen Earth Magic?

Teen Earth Magic is open to young people from Reclaiming Tradition* groups and their guests. Visit our website for more information – TeenEarthMagic.org.

We welcome new folks at our family and all-ages camps – a great place for young people to be part of an Earth-based circle and meet TEM participants and teachers.

Visit WitchCamp.org for camp contacts, or email us with questions – TeenEarthMagic@gmail.com or Quarterly@Reclaiming.org.

* - for more about Reclaiming, see page 34 and visit Reclaiming.org.

INTRODUCTION

What Is Magic? – Teens Roundtable

Magic is one of those words that means something different to everyone who uses it. Whether or not we "believe in magic" or "do magic" often depends on what we mean by the word.

Here's what TEM participants think about magic. As you read, you might want to get out your journal and answer some of these questions for yourself. (See page 25.)

What does magic mean to you?

Dusky: Magic is intentionally creating your own reality. I don't mean that in a delusional sense. It's like if you wake up in the morning and say, "I'm going to be happy today" – there's a pretty good chance you'll actually be happy. When I do magic that tries to affect the world outside me, that's when the lines get blurry. I've always struggled with my scientific mind arguing against my magical self – is this real, or is this just me convincing myself?

Meagan: Magic is the ability we have to influence reality in non-linear ways, to generate energy for an outcome and transfer it through non-physical means. It's intuitive, not rational. It can't be fully explained. It's mysterious.

KaeliMo: It's super vague – it's a mystery! It's different for everybody, which is part of what's cool – it's a no-pressure way to learn and work things out, to figure out what I'm trying to do in the real world.

Miranda: I think magic is different for every person. Many

times it's within you, mental, or something within your heart, your intuition. It's not like fairy magic, like a book or TV show. Magic is not going to just make something happen for you. Things will happen, but you have to help it through.

Mykel: It's the ways that our beliefs and intentions fundamentally change the world. Something about myth/story, and how telling a different story about yourself changes your situation.

Rhys: Magic is energy. I think it exists in everything we do and everything we are. It's difficult to put into words. I think I'm still defining the word.

What is the link between magic and energy?

Ola'i Wildeboar: To me, magic is the energy of the Earth that flows all around us. It's the little miracles we experience every day and the good

Magic can be flashy and physical (top right) or quiet and contemplative (lower left).

continued on next page

INTRODUCTION

What Is Magic? – Teens Roundtable (pg 2)

Teen Earth Magic 2008 campers celebrate our first year of camp!

feelings that make us light up inside. We are all capable of magic – from the little voice in our head that tells us right from wrong, to the compassion we feel for a friend in need – it's all magic. Our living, breathing, consciously loving souls are magic.

Lucy: Magic is the energy created when thought or time or practice is put into something. I believe that everything we do, say, or think sends out vibrations and energy into the universe – to me, that is magic. Practicing magic is the focus on exactly *what* energy you are sending into the universe and why.

Ingrid: What I call magic is moments in time – the quality of the day, walking down the street and it's perfectly sunny and warm, a slight breeze – I don't know how to explain it, but I'm pretty sure everyone knows what I mean, and has felt like that. It's a feeling of, to be completely cheesy, "wholeness" – why isn't there a better word? More than just the moment – all-encompassing.

How does magic work?

Meagan: Magic creatively changes individual or group consciousness. By being present with an intention in ritual, a situation and desired outcome are dramatized, which opens up new ways of relating to the situation. It frees up brain cells and makes new neural connections, which allow for ideas and solutions that wouldn't otherwise be thought of.

Mykel: For me, magic is something you do, a process – but it's also a thing that just exists in everything, without us "doing" anything. Part of doing magic is opening up to that – that magic is in everything.

Max: Magic entails knowledge and use of science, universal laws, art, and mystery. Magic is wisdom and love woven into an art form of personal development and transformation.

Dusky: It's making an intentional choice, then constantly reaffirming and renewing that choice – also sometimes having some little ritual you work around it. It's like self-hypnotism in a way. That's probably the main way I practice magic – intentionally telling myself how I'm going to experience the world. It really changes things.

Ola'i Wildeboar: It's something that happens within the thoughts and emotions, and the energy within us. It's slower, more internal – not something that can be seen so easily with our eyes.

continued on next page

Teen Earth Magic 2012 campers pay homage to the Chinook Salmon, whose magic inspires our camp.

INTRODUCTION

What Is Magic? – Teens Roundtable (pg 3)

Talise: I think that magic is about self-reflection, and reflection in general. There are a lot of ways to do that, like meditation, or working through things in a ritual – focusing on something and thinking about how it is in your life or in the world and maybe making a specific change. Magic is actively manifesting change.

How is magic different from things like meditation or seeing a counselor?

Miranda: In meditation, you get to know, like, this is a part of me I didn't know, or this is something I want to change. With magic, it's more like making charms, spells, rituals – it's making the change itself. Meditation shows you what you might want to do. Magic can help you on the journey.

Talise: Yeah, magic helps you make change – not just to realize what needs to be done. You do an exercise and start the change.

How have your ideas about magic or spirituality changed?

Rhys: When I was a child, I thought of magic as a physical power. As I got older I realized that it exists more within myself and what is around me. It cannot be held, but felt.

Ola'i Wildeboar: When I was little, I thought if I worked hard enough I could learn to fly or shoot lightning out of my fingertips. And I thought that with whatever spell I

was doing, the results would be immediate. I realize now that although some magic can be visible or physical or immediate, that's not all magic is, and that is not usually how magic works.

Lucy: For me, the realization that most magic doesn't produce a result in a day. Some of the most powerful work I've seen and done is long-term. Thinking of magic as a journey has helped me progress as a spiritual being.

Ingrid: I used to like being identified as a Pagan or a witch. I was happy to have these basic guiding Reclaiming principles. Lately, I just want to love nature – it's all I care about. Seriously, I'm sure I believe there's something larger, deities and such. But the idea of deities has been less important to me. I've been exploring interacting with the natural world, figuring out how to integrate my daily life so I can be out in nature more – in the forest, the mountains.

Dusky: Over the years, I have been able to incorporate magic into my inclined-toward-science mind. That's powerful to me, that I never have to choose between magic or science – it could be both. Magic is the science we haven't yet "scienced," that we haven't yet been able to quantify.

Photos – *Some years we've visited the Yuba River, one of numerous California rivers where Salmon once swam freely. Today, activists work to restore the Salmon runs.*

INTRODUCTION

What Is *Earth* Magic? – Teens Roundtable

What is "Earth" magic?

Sequoia: It's funny – I have this reaction that we're on our hands on the ground, we're directly in contact with the Earth, and we're speaking the names of plants. It's a visceral type of magic that immediately comes to mind. It's so easy to get into this esoteric world of spells and song and poetry – I think Earth magic is specifically rooted in things that we can see and touch and speak to. Even when it appears in esoteric ways, it's grounded, quite literally, in the real world.

Hilary: It's the idea of Earth as divinity, the energetic engagement with this being that we reside on. It's the connection to the mystery of the bones of the spells.

Dusky: What I believe is that the Earth and everything alive on it is connected, and there is some greater consciousness existing through that – something greater than the sum of its parts.

Hilary: It's a wisdom that we both know and don't know. It speaks to our bodies – to our energy bodies and our community bodies, our collective bio-diverse experiential bodies – it's that web of connection, that interweaving of deity and plant and animal and mineral and unnamed mysterious cauldron – that's what makes it "Earth" magic.

Sequoia: Earth magic is about recognizing the life and magic in the plants and animals we're interacting with, and recognizing it as collaborative and interactive magic.

What do you mean when you say that Earth magic is collaborative?

Sequoia: There's an older idea of magic as control over the elements – it's a manipulative type of magic. In Reclaiming, we talk about the concept of power-over versus power-with – Earth magic is very much a *power-with* experience, allowing our concept of sentience to spread across beings that we can't share words with.

Hilary: If you are invoking a deity, you are invoking the stories of the people who created them, the fragments of the stories that are lost and are held in the rocks and the drops of water at that place. If you invoke a tree, you invoke the idea of a tree, but you're also invoking what the tree has to say, beyond metaphor. Even science – you look at a leaf and see that there's not enough water, the edges are dryer, and you know what that means for the ecosystem of the forest – that's also Earth magic. It's not just imagining and personifying Butterfly or Bee or Salmon – it's listening to what their Earth-bodies are telling us.

A living relationship with the Earth, you could say?

Hilary: I can't help thinking about the chant we just sang in ritual:

We must let the land shape us
Let water carve canyons in us
Let the wind build and break us
Let fire remake us*

The song speaks to what Earth magic is – a dialectical relationship. It's not "mastery over."

It's about learning skills of interaction and skills of community. It's not like, "I now have taken Elements of Magic, so I get to level-up!"

It's about collectivity.

* – song by Nicole, Lindsay, & Clarice / Free Cascadia WitchCamp.

Teen Earth Magic gets down to the nitty-gritty with our 2018 theme: Mushrooms & Fungi. Artwork by Aja. Photo by Pavani.

INTRODUCTION

Who Are We (and what do we call ourselves?)

Take our survey and see how your answers compare to TEM campers! See the next page for TEM results.

Words	Call myself	Don't call myself but OK if others do	Don't use or like	Huh?	Notes
Pagan/Paganism					
Neo-Pagan					
Witch/Witchcraft					
Magic					
Wicca/Wiccan					
Reclaiming					
New Age					
Alternative Spirituality					
Spells/Spellcrafting					
Goddess-based					
Earth-based					
Spiritual					
Religious					
Agnostic					
Atheist					
Skeptic					
Anarchist					
Activist					
Radical					
Artist					
Woo					
Hippie					
Other:					

COMMENTS:

INTRODUCTION

Who Are We (and what do we call ourselves?)

What do Teen Earth Magic folks call ourselves? What terms do we use to describe what we're doing at camp?

Here are results from our non-scientific poll taken at Teen Earth Magic (see previous page for survey questions).

The most common self-description words

Magic
Witch/Witchcraft
Artist
Earth-based

Other words that people like – but more folks say, "I don't use it about myself"

Activist
Spiritual
Pagan
Reclaiming
Spells/Spellcrafting

Terms that get high marks, but also a few negatives

Anarchist
Radical
Woo
Goddess-based

Mixed reviews (half positive/half-negative)

Alternative Spirituality
Hippie

Terms that most people are indifferent about or don't like

Neo-Pagan
Religious
New Age
Wicca
Skeptic
Agnostic
Atheist

And a few write-ins that we'll ask next time

Super-Awesome
Redneck
Free-Thinker
Off-Gridder

Photos

Teens create body art illustrating some of our camp themes:
- *Top: Journey of the Monarch Butterfly (2012)*
- *Middle: The Bard's Journey (2011)*
- *Left: Pentacle of the Great Turning (2010 & 2017)*

TeenEarthMagic.org

INTRODUCTION

Teens Roundtable: What Do We Believe?

How do you refer to your spiritual involvement? Are there names you use?

Ingrid: Up till a few months ago I would have labeled myself "Pagan." Recently, my favorite expression is, "I find myself in nature." I could go on for hours and hours trying to explain it, but if there's one phrase that says what I feel right now, that's it.

Dusky: I've been trying to find a word for the entirety of my spiritual existence. I even fluctuate between whether I refer to myself as a spiritual or religious person. Finding a concise word is not easy. I'm usually like, "I'm Wiccan-ish, I'm Pagan-ish."

What about 'witch'?

Mykel: I love the word "witch." I like that it's about being a powerful, purposeful person instead of being attached to any one religion. I don't identify as a Wiccan because I associate that word with more theologically-rigid traditions that emphasize the gender binary.

Ingrid: I like "witch," although it requires more explanation, and a lot of people look at you and do this weird smile.

Dusky: I like "witch," even if I don't literally believe what witches believed when the word first came into being. But I really identify with witches.

What does 'witch' mean to you?

Dusky: Being a rad, bad-ass feminist. Witches are spunky chicks. Witches weren't afraid to be different, and that's a really big part of my self-identity – that I'm okay with being weird and wackadoo and all that stuff. It's part of my spirituality to be weird.

Mykel: The word "witch," to me, means that a person practices the art of doing magic, instead of focusing on any particular theology.

Were you raised in a spiritual tradition?

Ari: I was raised Christian, and taught that using magic was evil. But I was allowed to check out other religions. My dad was a Pagan and with him I attended rituals and Witchlets, where I began to look into Paganism. Both parents had a respect for each other's religions and never put them down.

Ola'i Wildeboar: My mother was raised strict Catholic but chose Native American and Wiccan practices in her early adulthood. My dad's family was agnostic but occasionally practiced magic. Wicca especially resonated with me, so I chose to go deeper.

Damien: I was born into Reclaiming and went to rituals and camps when I was young. I created an altar on my bookcase and followed my own path in my early teen years. I enjoy our traditions and some of the practices. I've bought many tarot decks, magic stones, and pendulums.

Peter: At birth I was a multitude of stitched-together spiritualities. I attended Sunday school, led by my mother, at a small Methodist church where we would watch the Sun rise on Solstice. I was baptized over a Mayan fire for peace and unification of the Earth. As I grew older we settled into Reclaiming and the Red Road.

Meagan: I was raised by a mom who used to pray for hours a day, pouring her woes to Jesus and saying Amen ten times at the end. She also taught me about astrology,

Photo – *Solstice in the Streets, San Francisco, June 2011.*

continued on next page

INTRODUCTION

Roundtable: What Do We Believe? (pg 2)

and she avidly believed in reincarnation, seeing family members in every animal we came across. Now I attend a Quaker church. Quakers advocate "no dogma," and offer many interpretations of traditional Christian texts and myths that are more resonant with my current worldview.

Mykel: My friend was involved in the Unitarian Church and they have a Pagan Interest Circle that does moon circles. I'd come along, and I was super into that from the beginning. It still feels good and natural to do that. I don't think I have another part of my practice and identity that has stayed with me as long as this has.

KaeliMo: When I was young, our dad took us to a bunch of different traditions. We'd go to UUs (Unitarians) one week, then go meditate in a yurt, then the next week we'd go with our friends to a Catholic service. For a while in high school I practiced Orthodox Judaism. Partly because I've experienced a lot of different traditions, I kind of identify as an agnostic, Unitarian type of person.

How is it to follow in your parents' tradition?

Peter: I always followed in my mother's spiritual path because it felt right. I loved the empowerment of the Reclaiming community, and value the ethics and manners and the recognition of equally valuable traditions from the Red Road.

Ola'i Wildeboar: Both my parents are open to all religions but especially to Earth-based ones. My parents have supported and taught me what I needed to know.

Lucy: My parents felt very strongly about raising me so that I would be free to choose any spiritual path, including none at all. While I am immensely thankful for that decision and the opportunities it has presented, I remember being very confused as a child.

What specifically was confusing?

Lucy: Most of my friends were Christian and I remember having a lot of struggle with being taught about the unknown, particularly about life after death. Fearing death as a child and fearing it being the end of everything has shaped my personality in a positive way and given me a really thankful feeling toward every day of life.

What has drawn you to work with Teen Earth Magic and Reclaiming?

Miranda: Teen Earth Magic is a camp where a bunch of teenagers get to hang out, do a lot of different types of magic, learn about each other – and have a lot of fun. You learn a lot about how others do magic. And everyone was so welcoming. By the end, I really knew everyone and was completely part of the group.

Ingrid: I appreciate the activism, and the inclusive nature – wanting to accept and value being diverse. I love that about Reclaiming, that we make space for and value diversity in every sense.

Maeve: One of the things I remember about Witchlets is when I was eight and got to have a ritual role, and got to be around a bunch of other people who were doing roles, people of all different ages. I got to learn by watching and being treated like I was on the same level as the others.

Dusky: When I'm in a Reclaiming camp or group, I don't feel like I have to be any one way. I initially thought I was supposed to be super magicky, super spiritual. But I realized pretty quickly that wasn't the case, that there would be someone in the community that would want to join me in whatever goofball activity I wanted to do.

Sequoia: My first year at Witchlets, I was eleven, and I was finally getting to learn from people who knew about magic! Now I'm 25. In some ways that sense of mysticism is so normal for me now that I take it for granted.

What keeps you coming back?

Natasha: A big part of what brings me back is the people. They're my family, people I've grown up with. It's something I feel really lucky and blessed to have.

Sequoia: The experience of being a co-creator.

Maeve: The same for me. My first year at Witchlets I was three. It was new and exciting and unexpected at every turn – it was completely magical. Part of the role I now see myself in, as a Weaver and ritual planner and student teacher, is creating that magic again. There's a different kind of magic that comes from being behind the scenes. But also keeping that spontaneity and unexpectedness and discovery for people who haven't had the chance to experience this. It's one of the most gratifying things, to pass on that sense of wonder and excitement even as I move on and go deeper with it.

Charlotte: I love having a space for young people to do magic in nature, people who are there for the same reason, who want to do Earth magic. There's only so many teenage witches in your life!

INTRODUCTION

What Do *I* Believe (or Not)?

Here's a chance to meditate on your own beliefs and non-beliefs. You could do it while you're washing dishes or commuting to school or work – but why not take a little time and first create a magical circle?

PREP

Set aside 30 minute or more where you can be undisturbed.

Bring – Book of Shadows or journal and pen; water; comfortable, layered clothes; music player if you wish.

Music – Reclaiming's Labyrinth Meditation Music – on all streaming services. Put this 8-minute track on loop and settle in.

Sacred space – decide how you will do it. See the Rituals Skills chapter for ideas for quickly creating a circle (especially pages 49-51). You can also simply close your door, stand tall and relaxed, and take five deep breaths – one each for Earth, Air, Fire, Water, and Spirit. When you finish, say, "Blessed Be," and sit down to write.

WORKING

✪ **Book of Shadows** – Write for a few minutes about any of these topics that call to you. You may want to leave blank space after your answers for later additions.

What Is Magic?

- What do you believe about magic? Is magic "real"? What does *that* mean? How does magic work?

- What are a few things you believe about magic/spirituality? (Note – "scientific" people can answer this one too – what does "magic" mean to you?)

- What are a few things that you do *not* believe about magic? List a few things you've heard about magic/spirituality that just don't make sense to you. Can you say why?

- When and why might you do magic, a ritual, a spell, etc?

- What is the point of ritual? Why would you or anyone else take part in a ritual?

- Does the word "sacred" or "spiritual" or a similar word have meaning to you? What does it mean in your life and your practice?

- What does Goddess/God/Deity/Divinity mean to you? Do you have relations with or attraction to any specific deities? What would you say you get from relating to these beings? (Or what might you wish to get)?

Your Involvement and Commitment

- Do you presently see magic and ritual as something you do or wish to do alone ("solitary")? With a small circle? Only when someone else organizes it? With a community of people who gather regularly? What draws you to one or another way?

- What were a couple of pivotal moments in your realizing you are (or might be) a Pagan/anarchist/witch/whatever?

- Do you consider yourself to "belong to" or to "be a part of" Reclaiming or another group? If so, what does this mean?

- What's something you wished you got from your involvement in Paganism and/or Reclaiming? What's something you could give/offer that you have not yet found the occasion? Any thoughts on your next steps?

More Meditations on Beliefs and Practices

See Starhawk's books: The Spiral Dance, The Twelve Wild Swans, and Truth or Dare.

INTRODUCTION

Covens, Circles, & Solitaries

Circles & Covens

In popular lore, a coven is a secret circle of witches. For magical people, a coven can mean a committed circle, sometimes dedicated to a particular kind of magic.

Around Reclaiming, people tend more to say, "My circle is meeting tonight," or "I talked about it with my circle."

Used this way, a circle means around four to ten people who meet regularly as a closed group. Some circles do deep healing magic. Others are "play and pray" groups who meet to do spontaneous (and sometimes less than fully serious) ritual. Some gather to sing or chant, some share food. Some go to protests together.

How Do Circles Form?

Sometimes circles form when folks meet in Reclaiming classes or at WitchCamps.

Other times, a few friends join together. Some keep showing up, some drop out. New people are invited, until finally you have consistent group. Voila – a circle!

What if people show up sporadically, or they're always late? You'll have to decide – is the person's low level of commitment hurting the circle?

How Long Do Circles Last?

A few circles keep meeting for many years. One Bay Area circle that formed in the 1990s from an Elements of Magic class still meets regularly, and most of the members have become Reclaiming teachers.

Others meet for a year-and-a-day, or for a year-or-so. Some end gracefully, with a final ritual and much love. Some fizzle out when people stop showing up.

The good news is, once in a while a circle really jells – just like once in a while a street theater troupe or a hip-hop crew really coalesces and does something amazing. Keep trying – in the long run, the odds are in your favor!

If a person is leaving the circle, or the circle is ending, maybe you want to have a farewell ritual, to recall good times together and then formally end the relation.

Solitaries – Magic without a Circle

Solitaries – people who work magic alone – have long been part of the magical tradition. In fact, witches and magicians working in groups might be the exception, not the norm.

A circle practices protest tactics at a nonviolent activism training.

When we talked to people about this book, one solitary said, "I don't like doing magic with other people because I always wind up feeling silly." (Others said this was precisely why they *do* like group rituals.)

Some who love group magic also have a "personal practice" that they do alone – meditation, circle casting, tarot readings, etc.

It's like music – some people only play with others. Some do it alone. Many do both, depending on the situation.

In the long run you'll discover what works for you. We hope this book helps.

Meanwhile, work with what's available. If you have some friends who want to explore magic, try a circle.

If not, guess what? You're a solitary until further notice!

Solo Workings in this Book

Many rituals and workings in this book include a Solo Working section for one or a few people. Some are actually "solo work" even in a larger group – tarot readings, labyrinth walks, altars – you do the working on your own whether you're a solitary or part of a 30-person group.

Social Magic – For Real!

For workings that need a group, we sometimes suggest trying it with friends – at a birthday party, with a youth group, or on a rainy afternoon. A lot of the workings in this book are fun and powerful whether or not you're doing a ritual. Try Lifting Each Other Up or a Blessing Circle.

INTRODUCTION

Magical & Ritual Etiquette

Observe these simple guidelines and you'll be welcome in open circles!

Reclaiming and the greater Pagan community share a few practices and a basic etiquette that students of the Craft should be aware of.

These guidelines are always in flux and being renegotiated. If you are meeting with a circle, take time to discuss these issues and other agreements (see Introduction: Agreements).

- Don't "out" other people as Pagans or witches. Even as times change and Paganism becomes more widely accepted, understanding and tolerance is not universal. Some people need to protect their identity as Pagans and witches in order not to compromise themselves in other parts of their lives.

- Each person has the right to be addressed by the name and pronoun they request. Some circles begin by sharing preferred names and pronouns, which might be different than what we assume, or how the person identifies in other parts of their lives. We can honor the diversity of our circles by listening and respecting these requests.

- A magical circle is not for observers – it is participatory and experiential. In a ritual, all participants are expected to conduct themselves in a manner respectful to the Goddess and to support the magical workings. If you're not prepared to focus your attention and efforts on the ceremony, don't join the circle.

- Do not take photographs or video unless you have advance agreement with planners. The ritual, and memories of it, are to be carried in your heart. The exception is when a photographer has been designated ahead of time and is announced to participants. At public rituals such as the Spiral Dance or Beltane, photographing altars or the maypole before and after the ritual is also accepted.

- Craft ceremonies are not inviolably solemn, but they are serious in central purpose. Inappropriate talking, joking, laughing, etc are disrespectful and interfere with the ceremony. Our attitude, conduct, and energy should reflect both joyousness and solemnity. There will be time after the ritual for the sharing of food, drink, conversation, and merrymaking.

- Traditional lore teaches that consecrated objects easily absorb energy – do not touch anyone's magical tools, such as a wand, chalice, athame, jewelry, drum, or other ritual regalia, without the owner's permission.

- If you find it necessary to tend to personal needs after the circle has been cast, you can quietly leave and return to the circle. If you leave for good, let someone know.

- The use of alcohol or non-prescription, mind-altering drugs and substances shows disrespect and puts the user(s) on another wavelength than the nonuser(s).

- What occurs in circle is sacred and not to be talked about with those who were not part of the circle (exception – if you feel someone's safety or well-being is in danger – see Introduction: Agreements).

By observing these simple, common-sense guidelines, you'll find a welcome place in most open circles. And that could lead to invitations to smaller, more intimate private rituals!

Adapted from a Reclaiming Newsletter article by longtime TEM supporter M. Macha NightMare. Find all our back issues at WeaveAndSpin.org/back-issues/.

Magical etiquette – always ask permission before you lie down on Pagan laps.

INTRODUCTION

Curses, Hexes, & Negative Magic

So What About Curses?

Curses and hexes have a long and illustrious history in magic.

Greeks and Romans created "curse scrolls" – thin lead sheets inscribed with names and magical words, then rolled up and dropped into a well or creek, where they survived for millennia until discovered by modern archaeologists. Ancient people were serious about their magic!

Halloween brings us the most common image of a European witch – a hag who hurls crook-fingered curses.

And face it, who hasn't wished for the power to turn their adversaries – or their geometry teacher – into newts?

Asking for What We Want

When doing spells and magical workings, we state our intentions and desires in positive terms – focusing on positive developments we want in our lives and the world.

We avoid infusing magical energy into negative thoughts such as harm to adversaries or fears about how our lives might go.

For example, we ask to ace the exam or audition, rather than not failing. We ask the universe to fill our lives with love, rather than that we not feel lonely or rejected.

Notice how this connects to curses – when a co-worker irritates us, we don't ask that they "lose" their job – although we might wish that they "find" a different one.

The Law of Threefold Return

Unfortunately, as many of us learn the hard way, when we put negative energy into the world it has a way of returning on us.

In fact, it happens so often that we speak of the Law of Three-Fold Return, or simply the Law of Threes.

Three-fold isn't an exact calculation – but it's close enough that we may want to take care about the energy we're putting into the world!

With most people, it's easy – we can smile, say a kind word, hold a door, or pay a little extra on a bill – simple acts that send good energy into the world

But what about those truly aggravating people we come across? We all know them – people who we wish would move to Siberia and not stay in touch.

How do we "keep things positive" with them?

A Magical Shrinking Spell

Here's a handy skill – how to magically shrink someone's significance in your life.

Suppose a classmate is driving you crazy by their lousy attitude. Being around them is making you miserable, and it might even hurt your grades.

If you curse or hex the person and wish that they flunk out of the class, you risk having it return on you – you might get away from them by flunking out yourself.

What if instead you crafted a spell where you claim the class as your own? Imagine yourself thriving in class, with ideal allies and support. Make a list of the qualities you want and demand: cooperation, good humor, focus, showing up on time... Try to state them in positive terms (eg, ask for "intelligent discussions," rather than "no stupid comments.")

Once you list a half-dozen, say each word or phrase and take a breath, pausing to picture your ideal environment.

Empower your vision by singing along with a chant (visit WeaveAndSpin.org/playlists) – try Kore Chant (She Changes Everything She Touches) or Weave and Spin.

continued on next page

Transformational Tableaux – one way to deal with negative energy.

INTRODUCTION

Curses, Hexes, & Negative Magic (pg 2)

Will your aggravating classmate be there next time? Probably – but they may have shrunk a bit. The more we empower our own work and vision, the less important others' bad attitudes become.

What About Negative Energy?

Magic can change our hearts, minds, bodies, and spirits – it helps us to be more focused, grounded, and powerful.

Why spend time doing negative magic toward someone else, when we could be doing positive magic for ourselves?

But it's a two-way street. What if we feel someone is directing bad energy at us (sometimes subtly, sometimes not), or even doing negative magic toward us?

Shielding & Shadow Work

Shielding is a way to guard ourselves from specific energy while remaining open to the world.

Rather than dealing with difficult situations or negative energy by withdrawing or shutting ourselves down, we can craft a magical shield that allows us to fully engage with all parts of our lives.

Shadow work lets us get in touch with difficult sides of ourselves and our world. Sometimes it can be fun. Not always.

Why does shadow work matter?

Because when someone aggravates or angers us, it's often because they are "pushing one of our buttons." Their words and actions land right on one of our sore spots, and we hurt all over again.

If we look at difficult parts of ourselves in magical ways, maybe we can be more flexible in "real life."

See Workings: Boundaries and Workings: Shadow

Negative Energy In Rituals

If magic works, we may encounter energies that surprise, upset, and maybe even scare us. What's going on?

Magic, no matter how far-reaching and mind-bending, is always our own experience. No matter what other beings or energies we might encounter, the experience remains uniquely and completely ours, and is always in our power to challenge, to change – or to step away from.

Banishing Negative Energies

Suppose negative energies do show up during or after a ritual – now what? Here's a few magical techniques for reclaiming your power.

- Turn the lights on. You don't have to wait until the working is complete. If you don't like the energy, turn on a light. Open a door or window. Get some fresh air.
- Name the energies. Trust your intuition and name what you are feeling. Use the name to demand that the energy desist and depart. "Negativity, be gone!"
- Devoke quickly. End the working and quickly devoke what you called in. Open the circle.

Then move to another space and re-ground yourself. Have something solid to eat. Shift your attention – watch a movie, play a game, give your cat a bath.

For more ideas about changing and shifting energy, see Workings: Auras and Workings: Shadows.

Transformational Tableaux – a way to work with difficult energy. What if we act out the tensions and frustrations – then transform them into support and understanding?

INTRODUCTION

Drugs, Alcohol, Health, & Safety

Drugs & Alcohol: Our Agreement

Reclaiming has only a few things where we say, "Don't do this." One of those is showing up at rituals or classes after having taken drugs or alcohol.

What counts as a drug? Well, if it's illegal, or something you don't have a prescription or medical card for, it's probably a drug for our purposes here.

With substances like caffeine and sugar that are legal but also impact people's behavior and moods, we ask people at our rituals, retreats, and classes to use them in moderation and not use them to "get high."

What you do outside of rituals and classes is your own business. But if you do magic in the Reclaiming Tradition – and particularly if you invite others to join you – we trust you to remain free of drugs and alcohol before and during the ritual, camp, or class (this includes post-ritual socializing, which is still part of the event).

We can't enforce this – we don't have any police, and we don't have a horrible place to send your soul after you die.

Instead, we offer some reasons for asking this agreement:

(1) We're going on a journey together – let's start off from more or less the same place. Agreeing to show up and stay drug- and alcohol-free strengthens our group magic.

(2) Many people – of all ages – are in recovery from substance abuse, or are trying to avoid substances. Drug-and-alcohol-free rituals create a safer space and show solidarity with those committed to sobriety.

(3) Magic and ritual can be spiritually and emotionally challenging – in fact, the strongest magic always is. Would we get high and go scuba-diving or rock-climbing? Then why would we be so careless with our spiritual practice?

Magical Safety: Your Experience

Reclaiming magic does not involve "losing ourselves." Our practice is about *increasing* our awareness.

When we trance and do other consciousness-changing magic, we remain aware of what is within and around us.

It may seem exciting to lose ourselves in a ritual or trance, to let the magic completely take over. But magic actually involves becoming more aware, not less. Unless we deliberately ignore our bodies or surroundings, we always remain aware at some level of all that is going on.

At all times, we know if there is danger at any level. When necessary, we are able to quickly return to full awareness, to act and react as needed.

At the end of a magical working or trance, we

continued on next page

Yes, we worry about your health and safety – although that doesn't stop us from inviting you to climb 50 feet up a tree (an optional workshop offered some years at TEM). See more photos in the Activism section.

INTRODUCTION

Drugs, Alcohol, Health, & Safety (pg 2)

typically feel refreshed and filled with life. If we feel depleted, cranky, or bored, something isn't working.

Sure, anyone can feel cranky or bored *during* a ritual. It happens to the best of us. But if you feel that way afterward, when you can do anything you want – it might be time to try a new type of magical working!

Indoor Fire Safety

At our retreats, fire magic plays a major role. The opening teens ritual at Witchlets often involves casting flour into a bonfire to create a theatrical flash. Bay Area Brigid rituals often include a central flaming cauldron.

In our homes, fire is not a safe magical tool. Magic involves an altered state where we don't always notice mundane details like flammable clothes or curtains.

Don't do fire magic in a physically unsafe space – you'll feel that negative energy and it will undermine your work.

Most of the workings in this book do not involve fire. Those that do are for campfires, so unless you have an amazing back yard with a bonfire pit, you may need to wait for a special occasion.

If you burn candles indoors, avoid open flames. Magic can be distracting – stick with glass jar candles or an enclosed tea-light holder. Tell your parents that these are the safest kind and maybe they'll buy you a case.

Even with glass jar candles, take these precautions:

- Create a special candle altar from non-flammable material, sturdy and uncluttered, away from curtains, wall-hangings, clothes, stacks of paper, and cans of gasoline.
- Have a smoke alarm in the room and a water-pressure fire extinguisher handy. Neither is expensive, and they're good to have for any emergency – ask your parents' support on this. Test the alarm with real smoke, and test the extinguisher outside.
- When you leave the room even for a moment, extinguish all candles – make it a dedicated magical practice. Candles re-light easily!
- Never get in bed or fall asleep with candles burning. End your ritual and extinguish all flames.

Agreements: Ways We Work Together

Part of safety in sacred space is trusting the people we work with, and coming to some understandings about how we will treat one another.

On the following pages you'll find some agreements that we renew before each camp (modifying the list as we go).

Working with other people is never easy – toss in magic and the feelings it can stir up, and you can sometimes find yourself in a pretty hot cauldron!

Agreements can't guarantee smooth sailing – but they might reduce misunderstandings, and give you a place to reconnect when things get rocky.

Our Ethics Agreement

TEM teachers and young adult mentors also discuss and sign an Ethics Agreement regarding working with young people. See page 337.

Fire safety tip – never build a ritual bonfire in your bedroom!

INTRODUCTION

Agreements We Make

Why We Make Agreements

In our camps, paths, and classes, we've found it helpful to make some agreements – ways that we agree to treat one another and the group.

Agreements are part of Reclaiming's anarchist heritage. Anarchists say that there is no one above us to make rules – we have to come to agreements among ourselves.

The fewer rules, the more cooperative people tend to be. Group agreements take longer, and often come out differently than expected. But they make stronger circles.

At Teen Earth Magic, we start each year by looking at our past agreements, seeing if we want to change anything, then re-agreeing.

The list tends to grow – it's a great idea to make agreements about all sorts of things, from quiet times at camp, to respectful touch, to a commitment not to use drugs or alcohol while doing Reclaiming magic.

For this book, we've chosen several agreements that are important if you're doing magic alone or with others. If you think of other agreements you want in your group (or with yourself) – go for it.

Agreements for Using This Book

Confidentiality – what happens in the circle is discussed only among those present – and only when they are present (no gossip).

Not everyone wants to be "out of the broom closet." Not everyone wants others to know that they are doing magic, or that they are interested in spirituality.

Four Key Agreements

- Confidentiality / No Gossip
- Respect / No Put-Downs
- One Group / No Cliques
- Right to Pass / Self Care

We can always share our own experiences and tell others what we did in a class or circle. But we don't identify others who were present, or if they are already known, we definitely don't talk about things others did or said.

Exception – if you feel someone is in danger, it is always okay to talk to your parents or others you think can help. Remember – you only get one chance to break confidentiality with a person – they probably won't trust you again. Knowing that, make your best decision.

Respect / No Put-Downs – treating others as we want to be treated. Listening. Giving others your full attention during rituals and exercises. Learning to support differences and diversity in the group.

And especially – learning to talk and joke without put-downs. How amazing it is to be together for five days, and not hear people making fun of one another or trying to score laughs at another's expense.

We remember the Law of Three-Fold Return – the energy that we put out into the world comes back on us three times (see Intro: Curses & Negative Magic). Respect for others makes good magical sense!

One Group / No Cliques – focus on including everyone, especially new people. There is a relaxed, open feeling to a group that includes everyone – no one has to work at belonging!

People who've been coming to camp for a while are excited to be together again, to share memories and experiences. It can be tempting to circle with old

Agreements around respectful touch come in handy during a massage spiral – Teen Earth Magic 2009.

continued on next page

INTRODUCTION

Agreements We Make (pg 2)

friends, to eat together, hang out in the evening, etc.

But every time we gather is unique. We're happy to see old friends – but it may be the new people who best support, inspire, or challenge us in the present moment.

Our young adult mentors are especially adept at building group unity. Teens like being around young adults – if the young adults set a tone of "everyone is welcome," it spreads to the whole group.

At Witchlets and Redwood Magic, the dining hall is "teens space" at night – a place where teens can stay up late, and all young folks know they are welcome.

Right to Pass / Self Care – in our camps and classes, people always have the "right to pass" – they can sit out an exercise, or take part and then choose silence during the go-round afterward.

Teen Earth Magic is about creating your own magical practice – it's not about checking off a list of things you've done. With that in mind, if anything in this book doesn't fit, doesn't feel right, or you just don't want to do it – follow your intuition..

Of course, if you skip major pieces, your rituals might feel short or kind of underwhelming. Maybe you can find an alternative. Skim through the workings in the back of the book and see what calls to you.

Self care means things such as getting a drink of water when you need it, mentioning that you are cold – and also mentioning that you are uncomfortable with something that is happening.

In Reclaiming, we say: "Each person is their own spiritual authority." We might add "political and social authority" as well. Each of us is responsible for our own well-being.

In the end, each of us is responsible for discovering and creating the magic that works for us!

Some Other Agreements

• Lights out / quiet time (or not)

• Availability of sugar and caffeine

• Gender language

Reclaiming's Agreements

Reclaiming Tradition itself also has agreements. The Principles of Unity are a statement that unifies the community. Not everyone agrees with every word – but at least we have a starting place for discussions!

See more about Reclaiming and our Principles of Unity in the following pages and at the end of the book.

Agreements help build the trust that others will truly support us – Trust Fall at Teen Earth Magic 2009 (see pages 312-314).

TeenEarthMagic.org 33

INTRODUCTION

Who Is Reclaiming?

Teen Earth Magic is part of the Reclaiming Tradition network of camps, local communities, and intentional circles.

Reclaiming is an international network of people committed to changing the world through magic and activism. Our vision is rooted in the religion and magic of the Goddess, the Immanent Life Force.

We see our work as teaching and making magic: the art of empowering ourselves and each other.

In our classes, workshops, and public rituals, we train our voices, bodies, energy, intuition, and minds.

We use the skills we learn to deepen our strength, both as individuals and as community, to voice our concerns about the world in which we live, and bring to birth a vision of a new culture.

Founded around 1980 in the San Francisco Bay Area, the Reclaiming Tradition now includes several dozen regional communities across the Americas and in Europe and Australia.

A 501c3 nonprofit called Reclaiming Collective is based in San Francisco. Several other Reclaiming communities are also organized as nonprofits.

For our Principles of Unity, see page 37.

Questions, Fan Mail, Chocolate, Etc:

ReclaimingQuarterly@gmail.com

Quarterly@Reclaiming.org

CONTACTS & WEBSITES

International Contacts: Reclaiming.org/worldwide/

About Reclaiming: Reclaiming.org/about/

WitchCamps: WitchCamp.org

Family Camps: Witchlets.org & RedwoodMagic.org

Archives, Writings, & Music: ReclaimingQuarterly.org

Current Features & Music: WeaveAndSpin.org

International Elists including Int'l Pagan Cluster (Activism) Elist – see page 36 for elists!

Photos by Luke Hauser & Alla Irwin

Above: Climate Justice march, Oakland CA, 2015.

Right: Dancing the spiral at Witchlets in the Woods, 2018.

INTRODUCTION

WitchCamp & The Spiral Dance
Two Unique Reclaiming Activities!

Reclaiming WitchCamps

WitchCamps are extraordinary intensive retreats for the study of magic, ritual, and for building and renewing our commitment to each other and to world change.

WitchCamps include all levels of experience (some camps include all ages). Newcomers learn basic magical skills. Advanced paths offer chances to apply these tools. Participatory rituals weave community while building skills.

Camps are currently offered in Europe, Australia, and around North America. Some camps are family- and teen-friendly, and offer programs for various ages.

Many camps are geographically based, and help anchor Reclaiming communities in their region.

For information on Reclaiming WitchCamps, visit:

WitchCamp.org

The Spiral Dance

First held in 1979 to celebrate the release of Starhawk's book, the ritual is danced each year around Samhain – the New Year of the Witches and one of the San Francisco Bay Area's biggest magical gatherings of the year.

This participatory ritual has become a central event in the Wheel of the Year for the Reclaiming community and beyond, as hundreds gather to honor our ancestors.

In addition to year-round ritual planners, dozens of others come together in the weeks prior to create this amazing gathering – singing and playing music, creating colorful invocations, building altars and installations...

If you are in the Bay Area in late October, you can join us!

Tickets and volunteer information can be found at:

ReclaimingSpiralDance.org

Stilt-dancing invokers welcome Earth at the 2010 Spiral Dance. Photo by Michael Rauner – michaelrauner.com.

INTRODUCTION

Getting Involved In Reclaiming

Reclaiming is not a group you "join" – it's more like a spider web that links people and groups (and it's sometimes as messy as a bunch of cobwebs!). Here's how to get involved.

(A) Join our elists/facebook pages:

- RIDL – Reclaiming's international list.
- BARD – Bay Area Reclaiming (Local rituals, activism, and events).
- Living River (LivRiv) – Pagan Cluster activism.
- Many Reclaiming groups have facebook pages – search <Reclaiming> and scan the groups.

To join a list, email ReclaimingQuarterly@gmail.com.

(B) Visit our websites:

- Reclaiming.org – basic info, international contacts.
- WitchCamp.org – international listings, including family and youth camps.
- WeaveAndSpin.org – current posts and selected archive features for all devices.
- ReclaimingQuarterly.org – our original magazine site – back-issues, archives, plus dozens of online features.
- ReclaimingSpiralDance.org – hub site for the annual Bay Area Samhain/Halloween ritual – our largest gathering of the year!

(C) Read a book

- The Spiral Dance, by Starhawk – magic and rituals in the Reclaiming Tradition – weaves feminism, activism, and Earth-based spirituality into a powerful blend that helped spark Reclaiming.
- Elements of Magic, edited by Jane Meredith and Gede Parma – a 2018 anthology of magical theory and practice featuring contributions by writers from around the Reclaiming network.
- The Fifth Sacred Thing, by Starhawk – a gripping, post-apocalyptic novel embodying Reclaiming-style values and practices.
- Direct Action: An Historical Novel, by Luke Hauser – fast-paced story about the activist cauldron in which Reclaiming was born.

(D) Declare yourself part of the Reclaiming community

- Attend a ritual or WitchCamp; create an altar; visit our websites; read a book.
- Gather some friends for a ritual, circle, or study group – or do a solo working.
- Read our Principles of Unity on the next page and ask yourself if you accept and agree with these community statements.
- When you feel ready: Turn clockwise three times and say: "I am co-creating Reclaiming magic – I am a part of Reclaiming!"

(Bonus) Take a class – in person or online

When you feel that you're ready to take a Reclaiming class, visit Reclaiming.org/worldwide to locate a group near you – visit their website or email them to find out if they are offering classes.

WorldTreeLyceum.org offers online classes including Reclaiming core classes. Visit their site for current offerings.

If you are under age 18, please tell the teachers your age when you contact them, and tell your parent or legal guardian as well. Until you are 18, please do not contact Reclaiming teachers without informing your parent or guardian.

INTRODUCTION

Reclaiming's Principles of Unity

Our International Statement of Core Values

"My law is love unto all beings..."
  – from The Charge of the Goddess by Doreen Valiente

The values of the Reclaiming Tradition stem from our understanding that the Earth is alive and all of life is sacred and interconnected. We see the Goddess as immanent in the Earth's cycles of birth, growth, death, decay, and regeneration. Our practice arises from a deep, spiritual commitment to the Earth, to healing, and to the linking of magic with political action.

Each of us embodies the divine. Our ultimate spiritual authority is within, and we need no other person to interpret the sacred to us. We foster the questioning attitude, and honor intellectual, spiritual, and creative freedom.

We are an evolving, dynamic tradition and proudly call ourselves witches. Our diverse practices and experiences of the divine weave a tapestry of many different threads. We include those who honor mysterious ones, goddesses, and gods of myriad expressions, genders, and states of being, remembering that mystery goes beyond form. Our community rituals are participatory and ecstatic, celebrating the cycles of the seasons and our lives, and raising energy for personal, collective, and Earth healing.

We know that everyone can do the life-changing, world-renewing work of magic: the art of changing consciousness at will. We strive to teach and practice in ways that foster personal and collective empowerment, to model shared power and to open leadership roles to all. We make decisions by consensus, and balance individual autonomy with social responsibility.

Our tradition honors the wild, and calls for service to the Earth and the community. We value peace and practice nonviolence, in keeping with the Rede, "Harm none, and do what you will." We work for all forms of justice: environmental, social, political, racial, gender, and economic. Our feminism includes a radical analysis of power, seeing all systems of oppression as interrelated, rooted in structures of domination and control.

We welcome all genders, all gender histories, all races, all ages, all sexual orientations, and all those differences of life situation, background, and ability that increase our diversity. We strive to make our public rituals and events accessible and safe. We try to balance the need to be justly compensated for our labor with our commitment to make our work available to people of all economic levels.

All living beings are worthy of respect. All are supported by the sacred elements of Air, Fire, Water and Earth. We work to create and sustain communities and cultures that embody our values, that can help to heal the wounds of the Earth and her peoples, and that can sustain us and nurture future generations.

Teens Help Rewrite the Principles

Reclaiming's Principles of Unity were created by the original Reclaiming Collective in 1997. The Principles were intended to guide the broader, decentralized Reclaiming network and provide a baseline of agreement as new communities and camps formed.

The Principles can be amended and updated by the BIRCH council (Broad Intra-Reclaiming Council of Hubs), which has met at all-Reclaiming Dandelion Gatherings.

To date, the only change in the Principles has been to broaden the gender language. Empowered as reps by Teen Earth Magic, two teens and a teacher traveled to the 2012 Dandelion Gathering in Oregon and played key roles in discussions which led to the change.

INTRODUCTION

Gender Complexities

Key Issues for Reclaiming – an Interview with Mykel Mogg

Mykel has been involved in Witchlets and Teen Earth Magic for a decade, first as a camper and now as a teacher. He is a trans man, first coming out at TEM, and has been active in bringing awareness of trans issues to broader Reclaiming and Bay Area circles.

Interview by George Franklin.

What made TEM a safe space to explore gender?

The social dynamics of Teen Earth Magic were geared toward transformation. Everybody was consciously choosing to be in a transformative space, and the container was set up in a way where we all agreed to hold each other in a certain way that made it feel possible for me to explore who I was.

I first thought of myself as sort of being outside of gender at Teen Earth Magic, in a trance. I talked about it with people, and they were like, cool! So it felt like a very low-pressure space to explore things.

There's also something about it being a camp, where you're there for a week, and can try stuff on and decide you don't like it later. You're not changing your whole life, just changing your whole life for a week! You try something on for a week and see if you like it.

Teen Earth Magic was the first place I changed my pronouns. It was a very positive experience. It's scary, but I felt very safe and supported. I felt confident it would be held well. That made it possible for me to go forward into the rest of my life with a foundation that people are holding me this way. It makes it easier to talk to other people who might not react as understandingly.

What specifically did people do that let you know they were your allies – and what wasn't helpful?

Something that gave me confidence was the conscious setting of the container, with very strong norms about how people listen to each other at camp.

I don't think I'd ever heard anyone do a pronoun go-round when I first requested it. That was the first time.

"What's the role of the people who are crossing that line, or creating a porousness in that barrier?"

But we have these norms where when somebody tells you something about their life, you listen to them and hold them in positive regard. People didn't do a lot of questioning another person's truth about themselves. That helped a lot.

Having queer teachers who were setting the container and holding the space was really a positive thing.

The hardest things have been a lack of "infrastructure," for lack of a better word. If I wanted a pronoun circle, I had to request it and explain what you should do.

I felt this in my school life, too. I wasn't the first person to come out as trans at my school, but I felt like my teachers didn't know what to do, they didn't have structures set up for asking people their pronouns, so I really had to advocate for myself if I wanted people to use the right name and pronouns.

I had to advocate for gender-neutral bathrooms. I remember going to the Spiral Dance one year, and there were men's and women's bathrooms. So I made my own DIY gender-neutral signs and put them up.

It would be different for a trans person coming out now, because some people have already done the work to set up structures so you don't always have to be asking people to do a pronoun circle or have gender-neutral bathrooms. I think that kind of thing is slowly improving everywhere, where you don't always have to be building the next step for yourself.

What are Reclaiming's next steps?

I would love for Reclaiming to be a leader in trans issues in the broader magical communities. I think overall Reclaiming has made a lot of progress on things like what deities we invoke, and asking for people's pronouns – having these procedural things in place that support trans people coming forward.

I've thought in the past that we were in a place where we all agree that trans women are women, and should be included in women's rituals, and that we could be a voice for that in pan-Pagan spaces. That's turned out to be

continued on next page

INTRODUCTION

Gender Complexities (pg 2)

Key Issues for Reclaiming – an Interview with Mykel Mogg

less true than I thought it was. But I think that we can get there. It's possible for us to get our shit together and be stronger allies, to be advocates for trans people in other spaces that we go to.

What about the question of gender binaries – seeing gender as male versus female?

For a long time I've identified myself as a boy or a man, and that actually does fit into the gender binary on an identity level. But the way I move through the world, the way the world reads and treats me, doesn't fit into that binary. I try not to change the way I look or act to fit into an expectation of maleness. So I'm often read as a woman or as a "what's that?".

I'm thinking about gym class, and it's boys versus girls, and you've got the girls' team over here and the boys' team over there, and the boundary between them is heavily policed.

What's the role of the people who are crossing over that line, or in the middle, or creating a porousness in that barrier? They're doing a service to everyone in that room, to create more freedom and to make that barrier less real, and hopefully less policed.

It makes me think about having different types of people invoking gods, goddesses, etc.

There's been a lot of cool experiments. At last year's Spiral Dance I was asked to do the invocation of the God, which I was excited to do with two of my friends, one of whom is gender queer and very fem-presenting, the other a woman. It was something I hadn't personally seen before in Reclaiming. There are often men in the Goddess invocation – the Goddess is in everyone! But it felt cool to do a similar twist, finding a female archetype of the God and exploring that.

What has TEM meant for your own growth?

Teen Earth Magic has been a home for me within Reclaiming, and in general in my life. It's interesting that it actually only exists for like five days of the year – but I have this cohort of people that I grew up doing magic with, this really solid sense of genuine community.

There's a role it's played in bringing things into reality that hadn't felt possible before. When I was a teenager, Teen Earth Magic felt like this place totally outside my life, this wild, fantastical space that was not related to how I was with my family or my school or anything. As I grew up and got more engaged and more involved with organizing, and started seeing people outside of camp, it became more and more a solid part of my daily life. Now I organize with people I first met at Teen Earth Magic, and they're part of my life year-round.

Teen Earth Magic gave me a clear path to leadership within Reclaiming. It got me organizing things and advocating for changes I wanted to see.

There's something really cool about young people who are already growing and changing so much having a space that is really about transformation and change – in a community where people don't expect you to be the same all the time. People are willing to be like, "Oh, I dig how you're growing as a person," instead of expecting people to stay the same.

Any final thoughts?

Thinking about gender at Teen Earth Magic – it's been a political education for everyone, regardless of how they identify. Having queer and trans people around, having the social space to explore one's self – that's one of the most lasting and transformative things we've done at camp.

How to Understand Your Gender

A Practical Guide

by Alex Iantaffi & Meg-John Barker

This down-to-Earth guide covers biology, history, sociology, plus relations with friends and family.

An excellent guide for allies and anyone seeking to better understand the complexities of gender.

TeenEarthMagic.org

INTRODUCTION

Diversity & Cultural Appropriation

Key Issues for Reclaiming – an Interview with Rahula Janowski

Issues of diversity, inclusion, and cultural appropriation are among the most challenging we face in building a spiritual community and a movement for social change. They impact relations to the land where we hold camps and rituals, the stories and deities we work with, and connections to our local cities and communities.

Rahula Janowski is an organizer with Catalyst Project, based in San Francisco and Oakland. In Spring 2018, Rahula and co-organizer Lindsey Shively facilitated a workshop for TEM teens and teachers around issues of cultural appropriation, racism, and white supremacy.

Rahula is also an organizer with Witchlets in the Woods family camp. When she speaks here of "story," she is referring to the myth, story, or theme that gives shape and content to a camp's rituals and magic (See Ritual Skills: Theme and Arc).

Interview by George Franklin.

Tell us about the Catalyst Project.

The Catalyst Project is about movement building, building multi-racial movements led by people of color – for racial justice, economic justice. Our particular focus is working with white activists and organizers around white supremacy, working with people who are already in motion, already engaged in work to change the world in a positive way,

We can't get the world we want unless we destroy white supremacy. We can't have a world that's ecologically in balance, we can't have a world where people aren't exploiting each other, if we don't address systemic white supremacy.

Reclaiming and some other grassroots groups are mostly white folks, but there are people of color strongly involved. What issues do you see coming up with these types of groups?

I think what you can see is an overwhelmingly white culture, also called white-privilege culture, where white is the norm, and people who are white have no idea that it's even happening, while people of color are very aware.

It can be very alienating when white people say or do things that are racist, not knowing that they've done it – for a person of color, speaking up about that can be exhausting. It can also have an impact on your position in the community if you're the one who is constantly pointing out the ways that people have messed up.

When you have white folks who are really committed to building a better world, and they are told, "You are being racist, or you did a thing that's racist, or you're supporting white privilege," or whatever – some people get really defensive. They make it all about themselves and their feelings instead of the ways they are actually perpetuating racism, even though they don't mean to.

A lot of the time people mean well, but they aren't *doing* well.

We talk a lot about intention, but we don't talk much about impact. Whatever your intent, your *impact* is real, and you have to address that.

Even if you meant well, if you hurt someone you still have to recognize the harm, offer to make amends, and figure out how not to do it again.

As a Witchlets organizer, what issues do you see coming up?

In the years I've been a Weaver [ie, a core camp organizer], when it's time to talk about story, we always talk about cultural appropriation, and we never resolve anything. We generally don't work with stories or myths coming from non-European cultures. Part of the reason for that is that most people in the weaving team are from European backgrounds, who are identified or would be identified as white. So we don't have many cultural connections to stories from other places.

When people bring up a story from another region, I have questions like, "What do we know about the context of this story? What do we know about what the story means to people who have told it? Are there deities, and what do we know about them?"

continued on next page

> "We talk a lot about intention, but we don't talk much about impact."

INTRODUCTION

Diversity & Cultural Appropriation (pg 2)

Say more about cultural appropriation and our camp organizing.

I think there are a lot of problems with taking stories and deities and magical concepts from cultures we don't know much about and assuming they are going to work the same way for us.

In the past I would have steered away from working with stories from outside the European tradition.

Talking to people of color around Reclaiming has shifted my thinking a lot – to be able to see yourself reflected in the stories we work, in the magic that we work, is a very important aspect of being part of the community.

How do we have stories that people can see themselves reflected in, while not doing all the things that white people typically do when they take things from a culture that they're not related to?

It's an issue of what comes first – do you need to have a critical mass of people of color to work with a story that comes from, say, the Americas or Africa or Asia? Or do you need to choose those stories to have people of color feel welcome in the community?

I think it will take a lot of work. We need to have some sort of relationship with somebody who has an authentic relationship with the story. We have to build the skills to have these conversations.

A parent at Redwood Magic Family Camp who is Latino said, "I want my daughter to hear stories from all of her ancestors, not just Europeans." How would you address this?

That's a question – who is initiating this, and why? If there's a person of color involved who says, let's do this story from my people, my inclination would be to have really open conversations about what the challenges are, and then support them if they still want to do it.

I can see us working with a story that the majority of campers are not culturally related to, and putting a ton of effort into educational work. Here's why we're doing this story. Here's how these deities are different than ones we've worked with before. Here's the colonial history of where this story is from.

Being really curious and really honest – I could see this making it possible.

What about using stories from our Mediterranean ancestors, like Egypt or Mesopotamia – ancient roots of our culture. These increase diversity – but to what extent is this just side-stepping the issues?

Side-stepping is not always bad! Sometimes it's a way to stretch.

I feel okay about Mesopotamia. With, say, the goddess Inanna – is it a living tradition? That's an important question.

Are we stereotyping people in the story based on racist and colonialist ideas? Are we extracting the parts that are useful for us, and dropping the bigger context?

What's the power balance? What's the history? Are we benefiting from the colonization of the people whose story we want to tell? If so, how are we making amends in the process? Are we working in an authentic and accountable way?

What about stories from nature or the land, such as TEM and Free Camp have used?

I think it's a great way to go. When you use a land-based story, or an animal's life cycle, that isn't going to alienate people based on culture and race – although it still might, depending on who is crafting the story. It's that thing where we have white-privilege stuff that we don't always know we're putting in there.

This offers a way to use stories in our workings and not go diving into the question of cultural appropriation.

I think there are also things that are lost, such as deity. There's a lot of power in old stories because they've been honed through the years – even though we re-hone them, usually to root out patriarchy!

"Is it possible to work with old myths and not work with patriarchy?"

"Can we tell any story about this land without talking about colonialism?"

continued on next page

INTRODUCTION

Diversity & Cultural Appropriation (pg 3)

This raises deeper questions. Is it possible to work with old myths and *not* work with patriarchy and colonialism?

Then again – for those of us coming from European backgrounds and living on this land – can we tell *any* story about this land without talking about colonialism?

What are some next steps for our camps?

I think having conversations about cultural appropriation that are strongly facilitated by someone who can hold a space for white people who are outraged at the idea that there's anything that they can't have, and other people who are outraged by *that* – all the polarities.

Building relations beyond the edges of our tradition is something we should be doing. Who do we want to build relationships with, and how do we do that?

Maybe coming up with some questions to ask when we choose stories or ritual intentions, like:

- Are there ways this could inadvertently be supporting patriarchy, or supporting racism or capitalism? Who could be hurt by this story?
- What do you want this story to *do*? Do we want a story that's going to propel us out with a purpose?
- Who's here – who are we? What are our connections to various stories, cosmologies, pantheons?
- If we want to work with a story that isn't an obvious choice based on who's in the room, what are we doing to address all of the questions about that?

Most of all, I think it's important to continue to talk about race explicitly, as much as possible, and to work to build the skills to have those conversations.

White people need to learn how to have these conversations both with people of color and without. I think people of color need to be able to opt in – or out – of majority-white space.

What is gained by building a diverse group and movement?

Thinking about people of color within Reclaiming and what they bring – not as "representatives of their race," but as the people they are – the witches that they are. We could lose them and everything they bring to our community, from the heart connections to the magic they bring.

Being in a multi-racial space calls us to that work. We see how damaging it is for people who are impacted on a daily basis. Energetically, politically, we're all impacted by that.

Every system that holds down anyone is holding down all of us.

"I don't think we can survive the ecological crisis without destroying white supremacy."

With the ecological and political messes we face, it seems like we need the participation and the wisdom of all sorts of people to change things.

It's kind of a truism from anti-racist thinking that the people who are most impacted have the best information about how to fight the thing. So people of color have the best information about how to fight racism.

In mostly-white spaces, we don't have enough information about what's happening, and how to change it.

I don't think we can survive the ecological crisis without destroying white supremacy. Which is daunting, since we're really far away from that.

What gives you hope?

I think that kids know a lot more about this than their elders do. Young people, in our tradition and broadly too, have access to a lot more information. They're learning what cultural appropriation is, they're learning about power and race.

I worry about people protecting our traditions too much, and not being willing to learn from kids – who can be kind of annoying and self-righteous sometimes, just like we were when we were young!

But they know a lot, and are starting out so much further along. Their leadership is so important!

Catalyst Project Website

For more about Catalyst Project, visit their website: collectiveliberation.org

RITUAL Skills

Ritual Skills

An Introduction to Basic Ritual Skills in the Reclaiming Tradition

- Outline of a Reclaiming Ritual 45
- Wheel of the Year 46
- Teens Roundtables – Interviews
    - Rituals 47
    - Grounding... 62
    - Casting a Circle................................ 68
    - Invoking 77
    - Deity, Allies, & Energies.................. 86
    - Magical Activism 149

- Creating Sacred Space: Quick Ways 49
- Sacred Space: A Longer Example 52
- Ritual Skills – Step by Step 58
- Ritual Planning 93
- Ritual Theme & Arc.................................. 96
- Two Classic Ritual Books........................ 102
- Chants Resources Online....................... 111

- Sample Rituals for Groups and Solo Work
  – complete index on page 114.

TeenEarthMagic.org

RITUAL SKILLS

Introduction
Rituals in the Reclaiming Tradition

Reclaiming rituals are literally all over the map – from California to Germany, from New England to Australia, from Spain to Brazil – and many points between. Find our various communities, WitchCamps, and contacts at Reclaiming.org/worldwide/.

Metaphorically our rituals are all over the map, too. Some are elaborate community gatherings like the annual Spiral Dance, with hundreds of participants. Some meet deep in the forest at WitchCamps. Some take place among a circle in a living room. And a lot take place alone or with a few friends.

Basic Structure of a Ritual

Whether it's a formal WitchCamp ritual or an impromptu home working, Reclaiming rituals share a basic outline, adapted from older magical traditions. Here's a quick summary – see the next page for a full outline:

(1) First we "create sacred space" – purify, ground, cast the circle, and invoke elements and allies. In a big ritual, creating sacred space might take half an hour or more. At home, it could take five minutes or less – it's up to you.

(2) Next we do "workings" – a meditation, walking a labyrinth, spellcasting, shadow exercises, etc – see the workings in the back of this book for many examples from our rituals and classes.

(3) After that, we "raise energy" by chanting, drumming, doing a spiral dance (or other dancing), and maybe raising a "cone of power" to charge our magic.

Circling up for a ritual at Teen Earth Magic.

(4) Then we "open sacred space" by devoking whatever we invoked and opening the circle – followed by snacks, socializing, drumming, dancing…

The next page shows a step-by-step Outline of a Reclaiming Ritual. The rest of this chapter goes into more detail about each step, as well as other ritual roles and skills such as teaching chants and tending a sacred fire.

Priestess – a Role, Not a Person

When we describe rituals and workings, we often refer to a priestess who does this or that.

Priestess is a role, not a person or gender. It's the word we use for anyone who fills a role at camp or a ritual, regardless of the person's age, rank, gender, etc.

Sometimes we use the word as a verb: "Who is going to priestess the cauldron working?"

Most rituals have multiple priestesses – fire priestess, invoking priestesses, spiral dance priestess, etc.

But Who's the High Priestess?

Reclaiming doesn't have "high priestesses." Ritual roles rotate among people, even at big rituals like the annual Spiral Dance. This keeps rituals fresh and nonhierarchical, and helps spread out responsibilities.

In classes and camps, anyone with a little experience can be a priestess. In solitary work and personal practice, each of us is our own priestess.

RITUAL SKILLS

Outline of a Reclaiming Ritual

Here is a one-page outline of a typical Reclaiming ritual like we do at camps, classes, and workshops. Even when a Reclaiming ritual is improvised, most follow this basic flow, which gives us a common language and structure.

Besides these roles, it helps to have a ritual wrangler who can remind people what is happening and in what order – especially when it comes time to devoke in reverse order.

Ritual Flow

BEFORE YOU START

- **Plan the ritual** – figure out what you're doing and what preparation is needed, assign roles, etc.
- **Purification** – sprinkle drops of salt-water with a wand of cut herbs as people enter, or brush people with elegant feathers.
- **Welcome** – a few words of greeting – share the ritual intention, tell folks where the restrooms are, turn off cell phones, etc.
- **Teach chants** – teach chants and songs for the ritual – sing them plenty of times so people feel confident.

CREATING SACRED SPACE

- **Honor First People** – acknowledge that our ritual is held on land taken from First People, with a commitment to work for justice.
- **Grounding** – often a guided meditation such as the Tree of Life. The aim is to get us present and centered.
- **Casting the circle** – inscribing a circle around the space. This can be done many ways, but often involves someone actually walking around the perimeter of the space and speaking words to each of the four directions, concluding with something like: "The circle is cast, we are between the worlds. What happens between the worlds can change all the worlds."
- **Invoking the elements** – calling in elemental energy, starting with Air/East, using song, movement, words....
- **Invoking deities and/or energies** – calling in magical support, often connected to the theme of the ritual, camp, or class.
- **Invoking and/or honoring allies** – calling in ancestors, the Fey, spirits of the land...

WORKINGS

- **Magical working(s)** – the heart of the ritual. This might be a guided trance to the Isle of the Ancestors, visiting and working at altars or stations, plunging into the ocean at Solstice, making a pledge at Brigid's flaming cauldron, doing a magical crafting project, etc. Many of the workings in the later part of this book can be used as the core of a ritual.
- **Raising energy / spiral dance / cone of power** – after the working(s), we chant, drum, and dance (sometimes a spiral dance, sometimes free-form) to stir up collective energy, which we focus in a cone of power and use to empower our magic.
- **Re-grounding after the cone** – by touching the Earth and breathing. A priestess might say a few wise words about anchoring the energy in our hearts.

OPENING THE CIRCLE

- **Devoking** – we thank and release all allies, energies, deities, and elements we have invoked, in reverse order. Devocations are short, ending in "hail and farewell" or "thank you."
- **Opening the circle** – a short, reverse version of the circle casting, ending with many people calling out these words: "The circle is open, but unbroken. May the peace of the Goddess go in our hearts. Merry meet, merry part, and merry meet again!"
- **Announcements** – at a community ritual, find a place for announcements and for passing the sacred donations hat.
- **Drumming and dancing** – the end of the ritual is the signal for music and dancing to begin. Sharing food is also popular.

RITUAL SKILLS

The Wheel of the Year

Reclaiming and many Pagans celebrate eight sabbats of the Wheel of the Year. The following order is for the Northern Hemisphere. Details are from Bay Area rituals. For events in your region (or around the world), visit Reclaiming.org/worldwide.

Samhain/Halloween

At Samhain, the veil is thin between the worlds of living and dead. We remember our ancestors, our Beloved Dead, and all who have crossed over. As we mourn those who have died this year, we also mourn the losses and pain suffered by the Earth, our Mother. Yet as we grieve, we honor the sacred cycle of life, death, and rebirth. We celebrate children born this year, and our own vital connections to the Earth and each other, in which we ground our hope.

Winter Solstice

This is Winter Solstice, longest night of the year. We watch for dawn, the return of the Sun, bringer of hope and the promise of Summer. This is the stillness behind motion, when time itself stops; the center which is also the circumference of all. We are awake in the night. We turn the Wheel to bring the light. We call the Sun from the womb of night.

Brigid/Imbolc/Candlemas

This is the feast of the waxing light. What was born at Solstice begins to manifest, and we who were midwives to the infant year now see the days grow visibly longer. It is the time of initiation, of beginning, when seeds that will later sprout and grow begin to stir from their deep sleep. We meet to share the light of inspiration, which will grow with the growing year.

Spring Equinox

This is the time of Spring's return, the seed time, when life bursts forth from the Earth. Light and dark are equal: it is a time of balance, when all the elements within us must be brought into a new harmony. Kore, the Spring Maiden, returns from the Land of the Dead with the scent of flowers on her breath. As She dances, despair turns to hope, want to abundance, and we sing the Kore Chant:

She changes everything She touches,
And everything She touches, changes.

Beltane/May Day/Int'l Workers' Day

This is the time when sweet desire weds wild delight. The green of the Earth meets the red and black of workers' rights in the greening fields, and we rejoice together under the warm sun. The maypole, the shaft of life, is twined with ribbons in a spiral web, and all nature is renewed. We meet in the time of flowering to dance the dance of life.

Summer Solstice

This is the time of the rose: blossom and thorn, fragrance and blood. Now on the longest day of the year, light triumphs, and yet begins to decline into dark. We set sail across the dark seas of time, searching for the isle of light that is rebirth. We turn the Wheel and share the Sun's fate, for we have planted the seeds of our own changes, and to grow we must accept even the passing of the Sun.

Lammas

We stand between hope and fear, in the time of waiting. The grain is ripe but not yet harvested. We have worked to bring things to fruition, but the rewards are not yet certain. The Mother becomes the Reaper, the Implacable One who feeds on life so that new life may grow. Light diminishes, Summer passes. We turn the Wheel, knowing that to harvest we must sacrifice, and light must pass toward Winter.

Fall Equinox

This is the time of harvest, of thanksgiving and joy, of leave-taking and sorrow. Day and night are equal, and we give thought to balance and flow within our lives. The Sun sails West, and we follow it into the dark. Life declines, yet we give thanks for that which we have reaped and gathered. We meet to turn the Wheel and weave the cord of life that will sustain us through the dark.

(A Note on Terminology)

Local communities use different names for some of the sabbats (Pagan holidays). Reclaiming Quarterly uses the neutral terms "Equinox" and "Solstice" to honor that these are holidays of the Earth Herself, not of any one culture. We often call the cross-quarters by Celtic names.

Descriptions adapted from The Spiral Dance – ©1979 by Starhawk

Wheel of the Year – the chant!

For an easy way to remember the sabbats, listen to Wheel of the Year on our Campfire Chants album. The song was written (as a joke) at a TEM retreat! See page 111 for links.

RITUAL SKILLS

Rituals: Teens Roundtable

"It's a place of intense connection with other humans who are open and accepting to that connection – people that you really want to connect with."

Why do you take part in rituals?

Rhys: Rituals are a fun but serious way to practice magic.

Ola'i Wildeboar: I think rituals can be helpful in every aspect of one's life. They help us learn to connect and interact with others, and to understand ourselves more deeply. Alongside that, it's a beautiful way to recognize and be in touch with the Earth. It also helps us learn how to use magic and how to build our own practices.

Lucy: I love being part of something so amazing and positive. I love feeling as though I am contributing to the massive amounts of magic that are being produced, and I love bringing that energy back out into the world.

Ingrid: When I do group rituals, I am coming together with a group of people with the desire to shift some aspect of our interaction with the world – or rather, first our interactions with ourselves and our relation to others.

KaeliMo: It's a supportive and safe format for understanding myself and the world. It's helpful that there are magical tools and structures and community in place. It gives a template for changing and exploring things.

Do you like group rituals?

Rhys: Yes. It's a way to be a part of the community. It is great to practice magic by yourself, but it is extremely powerful to be a part of a ritual and connect with other people.

Talise: I would say most of the magic I do is in a group setting. But I do some meditation.

Ingrid: Honestly, as much as I enjoy group rituals, I don't get that much out of them. I enjoy the community. I want to be surrounded by people who are okay with and understand where I'm coming from. I've gotten more out of going to a camp and doing a succession of group rituals.

Dusky: That's changed over the years. I don't necessarily believe literally in what we're doing in ritual. But it's still powerful. There's magic happening.

What sort of magic?

Dusky: It's a place of intense connection with other humans who are open and accepting to that connection – people that you really want to connect with. In modern society, connecting with other people is considered taboo. Opening up, being vulnerable and intimate, is kind of lost. Rituals are a place where I can be around beautiful magical people and share a connection with them. It's an opportunity to feed a side of myself that doesn't always get as much attention.

Do you do rituals and magic on your own?

KaeliMo: Yes – but I prefer working with other people more than being by myself a lot of the time – seeing how other people think and how their energy contributes is really helpful in finding new outlooks.

Damien: Magic is one of those things where if you don't have time, you don't have to do anything. It's more of a go with the flow thing and easy to pick up and drop. I enjoy practices like tarot, magic stones, and pendulums.

continued on next page

TeenEarthMagic.org

RITUAL SKILLS

Rituals: Teens Roundtable (pg 2)

"I don't sit down and go, 'I'm going to do this and this and this – then I'm going to do it backward, and we're going to be done!'"

Maeve: When I remember! I don't always remember in the hecticness of everyday life. I do more as I've gotten older. Having the baseline of what group ritual looks like has been really helpful, being able to pull out pieces that work for me. With time I've realized I don't have to do everything so formally when I'm by myself. It's like, "Oh, I need to ground myself," or "Hmmm, I need to just sit for a minute and breathe." But I don't have anything I do daily or regularly – which I kind of would like to do.

Ingrid: No. I don't sit down and go, "I'm going to do this and this and this – then I'm going to do it backward, and we're going to be done!" I would rather reconnect and balance myself to the best of my abilities. Maybe it's just hanging out and experiencing the moment, what's happening around me – experiencing the natural world.

Miranda: The magic I do on my own is more little things, less like full rituals. It's like a quick spell, like, "Today I want to try to make this happen!"

Sequoia: In my daily life, I do spells around mental health, spells around a job interview or school interactions. It feels like it's a constant thing. When I consciously create magic, when I sit down and say okay, we're going to make sure there's a space up, it's usually around life changes, new beginnings, or conclusions of life points.

Dusky: Every once in a while I will, but not very often. I feel like I don't live every day in a spiritual way. Some people do, some don't. But that spiritual side of myself is very present, very real. It's the side of me that I most strongly see as being my true self. And there isn't a lot of opportunity to feed my spiritual side in everyday life.

What do you do to feed that side?

Dusky: Not enough. I try to take a moment to slow my mind down and connect with myself and nature. But I don't do enough. I'd like to do it more often.

When you do a ritual alone or with a small group, do you do all the steps?

KaeliMo: It depends. Sometimes it's helpful to have the structure of sacred space already be there, and I can just do the work. Other times, playing with the structure of creating sacred space is part of what I'm doing. Sometimes the container needs to look different – especially if

it involves people who are not part of this tradition. I try to bridge that, to make their way of thinking part of the structure too.

Ingrid: I almost never do formal rituals. But recently I've done simple things like, when I'm going into a situation where I feel hesitant or scared, I do a practice where I'm making an aura bubble. I started off like, "Don't let anything in that's going to harm you." But I realized I don't want that, because what does harm mean? So I changed it to, "Only let in what is going to make me stronger."

What difference has that made to you?

Ingrid: It's helped me open up more as a person. It's helped me trust a little more. I'm a little more like, these interactions are going to be okay. Whatever is detrimental to me is not going to get through.

RITUAL SKILLS

Sacred Space - Quick Ways

INTENT

Sacred space means the overall magical container that we create by grounding, casting a circle, and invoking allies. Within sacred space we can do any sort of magical working. At the end, we open sacred space.

Sacred space can be a major part of the ritual – for example, the elaborate invocations at the annual Spiral Dance ritual. Other times – especially for personal magic – we might want to create sacred space quickly, so we can get on with the workings.

Let's start with some quick ways to create sacred space so you can jump right into the workings.

Later in this chapter, we'll show you in detail what the different parts of Reclaiming rituals might look and sound like.

Starhawk online – do you want to have Starhawk guide you through these steps? Listen to her Way to the Well meditation on iTunes, youtube, spotify, etc. The first ten minutes offer a simple way to create sacred space for yourself.

SPACE/TIME/SIZE

Once prep and planning are complete, you can create sacred space in five minutes or less. This will work for any number – with more people, spread out the roles and allow more time. Enough space for a comfortable circle.

PREP

No materials are necessary, but lots are optional – costumery, scarves, tarot cards, athames (sacred blades), cauldrons, twinkly faerie lights... Spontaneous magic is sometimes easier if you have a few props and tools at your disposal.

SACRED SPACE: QUICK WAYS (or invent your own!)

As with any Reclaiming practices, feel free to modify this and invent your own most effective ways.

Eventually you'll spend time with each of these skills. If this section is confusing, look further back in this chapter for details.

Honor First People – acknowledge the history of the land:
- Learn and acknowledge the names and cultures of tribes that have lived (and may still live) in your area.
- Learn about and mention a present-day campaign for justice for Indigenous people.

Purification – let go of the ordinary world as you begin:
- Sprinkle some drops of water over your head, onto your throat, and touch a drop to your heart.
- Light a match or lighter – gaze at it for a moment – blow it out.
- Fan yourself from top to bottom with a magazine or sheets of paper.

Grounding – take a minute or two to bring yourself fully present:
- Take deep, gentle breaths – on each exhale, let tension, worries, and negativity fall to the Earth – on each inhale, draw up Earth energy and fill yourself.

continued on next page

Purification? Grounding? Circle casting? Or just loosening up before the ritual starts?

TeenEarthMagic.org

RITUAL SKILLS

Sacred Space - Quick Ways (pg 2)

- Take five gentle breaths, watching your breath, without your mind wandering. If it wanders, begin again.
- Lie down on the ground/floor. Take some gentle breaths – on each exhale, let go of stress, worries, etc. Even though this is the "quick version," let yourself lie there as long as you wish.

Casting the circle – create a safe circle/sphere of magical energy within which to do your workings. In Reclaiming, there is no one way to cast a circle. The key is – do you feel that a strong container has been created? Here are some simple ways to try:

- Beginning in the North, face the direction, take a breath, and snap your fingers. Turn to the East, breathe, snap. To the South, snap. The West, snap. Turn again to the North to complete the outer circle and snap. Then face Center – breathe and snap above, then below. Say: "The circle is cast. We are between the worlds. Let the magic begin!"
- Close your eyes and breathe gently. Imagine that on each exhale you are inflating a beautiful soap bubble around yourself. Breathe into the bubble so it fills your space. Then take a breath and touch your center. Say: "Blessed be – let the magic begin."
- Use yarn to lay a circle around your space. Begin in the North and walk around the circle slowly, breathing steadily. When you complete the circle, face Center and take a breath. Say: "The circle is cast. We are between the worlds. Let the magic begin!"

Invoking elements – in a full ritual, we might call in each element – with words, theatrics, singing and dancing, and humor. Later in this chapter you'll learn lots of ways to invoke, and you can create more of your own.

Here are some quick, powerful ideas:

- Invoke with an all-elements song such as Air I Am – see Ritual Skills: Chants (pages 112-113).
- Face the direction, name the element, and say a few words of power that you associate with the element – North/Earth, East/Air, South/Fire, West/Water, and Center/Spirit.

"Everyone take a drink – welcome Water!"

- Face the direction, name the element (see above), and picture different ways the element appears in the world (in a group, you might speak these aloud).
- Face the direction, name the element (see above), and make a simple dance-movement (in a group, one person might start and others "flock" after them).

Invoking allies – this could be anything from deities to ancestors to energies to animals to plants to the Fey.

- Name a goddess or god who you feel would support the working you plan to do (the internet is good for quick research). Call them with words or a simple dance movement. Finally, welcome them by name.
- Call the mysterious ones – how will you welcome mystery and the unknown? With words? Movements? Silence?
- What kinds of energy do you want present? For instance, creativity, safety, powerful expression, support, etc. Name them, breathing after each. In a large circle, invite people to call out energies and breathe them in. (For more, see Ritual Skills: Invoking Deities vs Energies.)

continued on next page

RITUAL SKILLS

Sacred Space - Quick Ways (pg 3)

TRANSITION TO WORKINGS

You've now created sacred space, and are ready to do the magical workings in this book, or ones you invent for yourself. With practice, you will learn to create sacred space quickly, yet still have a strong magical container and strong allies.

At this point in a community ritual, we might ring a gong or bell, or sing a short song to let everyone know that the energy is about to change. A priestess steps out and guides us into the working...

OPENING SACRED SPACE: QUICK WAYS

At the end, devoke and open sacred space. Learn to do it quickly so when the workings are done you don't need a lot of time to wrap up the ritual. Even at big community rituals we devoke quickly so we can get on with snacks and socializing.

Devoke in reverse order from how you created sacred space.

Allies devoking – name any deity, beings, or energies you invoked. You can do this simply by naming and saying thanks – "Creativity, thank you and farewell." "Persephone, hail and farewell." If you feel called to say more, go for it – but briefly.

Elements devoking – you can simply say something like, "Water, thank you – hail and farewell," or a few more words. If you invoked the elements with a song, devoke with the same. Many chants have a devoking version – see our website for ideas (See Ritual Skills: Chants). Here's a TEM favorite – invoke elements with Air I Am. Devoke by changing to: Air We've Been...

Opening the circle – this is the final ritual act, since we don't "un-ground" or "de-purify." Do it similarly to how you cast the circle, only in reverse and more briefly. If you cast with yarn, roll it back up.

If you did snap-casting, skip the breaths – just snap to the six directions in reverse order and say: "The circle is open, but unbroken. May the peace of the Goddess go in our hearts. Merry meet, merry part, and merry meet again!"

Or turn to each direction and speak its name: Below... Above... North... West... South... East... Then say, "The circle is open..." as above.

You've got it! Time for snacks and socializing, writing in your journal, listening to music....

SPEED SPACE – finding our own quickest ways

At political actions we might create sacred space in a minute, so we can do our two-minute magical working and devoke before the march begins or the police arrive!

Back home, too, there are times when we might want to do a quick tarot reading and don't feel like spending five or ten minutes creating sacred space.

Each of us discovers our own best ways to quickly create sacred space. Practice is key.

Magical tools can sharpen a quick invocation or casting – a nice chalice practically invokes Water by itself. We'll offer more ideas in the following sections, and see also Workings: Tools.

✪ **Book of Shadows** – what is the fastest way you can truly ground? Cast a circle? Invoke an ally? Dedicate pages of your journal to a running record of your ideas.

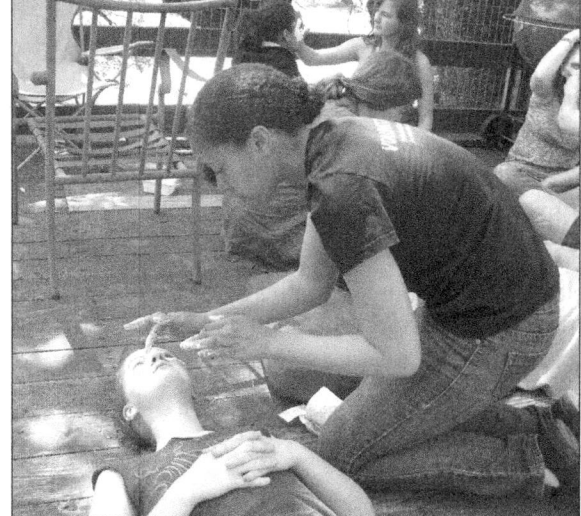

Photo – *after sacred space is created, we move on to a working – perhaps involving masks, such as this TEM ritual.*

RITUAL SKILLS

Sacred Space - A Longer Example

INTENT

Want to see what an entire Teen Earth Magic ritual looks like? Here's an example of an evening ritual. Camp occurs just before Summer Solstice, so there's still some dusky twilight as we get started.

This is just an example, not the "correct" way to do ritual. Every Reclaiming ritual that has ever happened has been unique – we couldn't do the same ritual twice if we tried! If what we suggest doesn't feel right for you – create something else.

PREP

Earlier in the afternoon, two teachers and a half-dozen campers got together and planned the evening's ritual, taking into account the ritual arc and intentions for the whole camp.

Since they wanted time for a couple of major workings, they decided that creating sacred space should take only about ten minutes. At the end they reviewed the prep still needed:

Sally and José agreed to arrive at the ritual circle early and bring a bowl of salt water and sprigs of greenery for the purification.

Sagewind offered to do a traditional circle casting, and suggested we used multi-gender pronouns (see Ritual Skills: Circle: Ye Olde Circle Casting – page 71).

Jeremy and Sharon volunteered to teach We All Come from the Goddess and Body of the Earth, and to review the words and melodies ahead of time.

Each day after lunch a circle of volunteers gathers to plan the evening's ritual.

Loreley offered to be Wrangler, keeping track of all the roles and the order of the invocations.

Affinity groups were asked to do short elemental invocations, and people were recruited for grounding and other invocations. Since we wanted to do the purification as folks arrived at the circle, we moved honoring First People after the welcome.

CREATING SACRED SPACE (an example)

Dinner and cleanup ran late, and dusk was settling as people dressed for the ritual and checked in with their invoking partners.

Ritual planners gathered outside the dining hall, reviewed the order of the ritual, and made sure all roles were filled. Finally, Loreley gave the signal to light the campfire and people began filtering down toward the circle.

Purification – Sally and José hurried down to the ritual circle ahead of the rest and used sprigs of greenery to sprinkle a bit of salt water over people's head, hands, throat, and heart as they arrived at the circle.

Welcome – after everyone gathered, Sharon rang a gong and welcomed us to the ritual, telling us a little about the evening's plans. Jeremy stated the intention of the ritual and the group repeated it three times:

"Feeling the winds of change, we empower our vision of a new world!"

Finally, the two of them taught the chants, so we would already know them for the ritual.

continued on next page

RITUAL SKILLS

Sacred Space - A Longer Example (pg 2)

Honoring First People

After a moment of silence, Sojourner stepped forward and said, "As we stand on this land, in this time and place – take a moment and remember that if we are in North America and are not Native American, we are on land that another People inhabited before us. A People who called this place home. We honor those who came before us, and acknowledge the injustices they suffered. We take a breath and renew our commitment to justice."

Grounding – The Tree of Life

Stacey stepped into the circle and took a breath. Then he closed his eyes and relaxed.

"Take a deep breath – and let it go," he said. "Grounding is the time to bring ourselves fully present. It's a chance to take some deep breaths, to relax our posture, to feel our connection to the Earth beneath our feet.

"This is called the Tree of Life. It is one of Reclaiming's basic groundings. We'll feel our personal roots sink deep into the Earth, draw up nourishment for our body, and send it up into our energetic branches."

He paused for a breath, then asked us to spread out arm's length apart. "Stand tall and loose, energy balanced, with your knees flexed. Breathe steadily and deeply.... Standing tall, let each breath gently float through your body.... On each inhale, draw in fresh air.... On each exhale, let yourself relax.... Breathe gently and steadily....

"Picture your spine as the trunk of a majestic tree.... As you breathe, let roots drop down from the base of your spine deep into the Earth... dropping down with each breath... dropping down till they reach the center of the Earth Herself.... Let your energy mingle with the fire at the core of the Earth.... And with a breath, let go of anything that you don't need, anything that is not of this time and place.... Let it go into the Earth...." He paused, and people's breathing could be heard in the stillness.

"Breathing deeply, begin to draw up power from the Earth.... With each breath, feel the energy rising through your tree trunk.... Feel the power rise up through your core... feel it filling and energizing your entire being with each breath....

"With steady breaths, draw this energy up through your body, up through your chest and neck and head.... And from the crown of your head branches sprout and reach toward the sky.... Let your arms rise like branches, and feel the Earth energy flow up through them.... Feel it drawing down the energy of the stars... feel the energy sweep through your branches and drop again to the Earth, returning to its source....

"Let the energy drop back to the Earth.... Now, from your own center, draw a deep breath, drawing in the energy of Earth and stars... Feel the Earth and stars mix and mingle in your center.... Breathe in all that you need.... Let it flow through you and back to the Earth."

Stacey paused for a moment. "And when you are filled with the energy you need, return any extra to the Earth." He bent down to touch the ground. Others did the same, or closed their eyes and touched their center. When it seemed like all were complete, Stacey finished: "Blessed be!" Then he rejoined the circle.

continued on next page

RITUAL SKILLS

Sacred Space - A Longer Example (pg 3)

Casting the Circle

Now Sagewind (who uses "they" pronouns) stepped into the circle. They planned to do the traditional circle casting and use multi-gender pronouns for the different directions (see Ritual Skills: Circle: Ye Olde Circle Casting – page 71-72).

They knelt and held their right hand toward the fire and took several breaths. Then Sagewind stood and moved out of the circle to the North, stopping a few steps outside the edge.

Facing North, they drew an invoking pentacle in the air, circled it, then "pushed" the pentacle out to mark the edge of the magical circle. Some people did the same, while others faced North with their palms open.

"By the Earth that is Her body," Sagewind declared.

Sagewind walked clockwise around to the East, where they drew an invoking pentacle and pushed it to the edge of the circle: "By the Air that is His breath."

They walked around to the South and inscribed a pentacle: "By the Fire of Their bright spirit."

And then to the West, where they drew a pentacle: "By the Waters of Our living blood."

Sagewind continued around the outside of the ring to complete the full circle to the North, then came to the Center.

Looking up, they drew an invoking pentacle in the air: "By all that is above."

Then they drew a pentacle toward the floor, pushed it down, and said: "By all that is below."

Finally Sagewind swept their arm in a full circle: "The circle is cast. We are between the worlds. And what happens between the worlds can change all the worlds. Let the magic begin!"

"So mote it be," some people called out.

Invoking the Elements

Although we begin our circle casting with North, Reclaiming begins elemental invocations with East, the direction of dawn and new beginnings. Age-based affinity groups were asked to invoke the elements, and had planned short invocations before dinner.

Practicing an invocation before a ritual at TEM 2012.

Invoking East/Air – The youngest group stepped out first. They seemed a bit tentative, but a couple of the mentors (young adults – see Organizing: Mentors) helped bolster them. All eight faced East and took a breath together. Then they started calling out words associated with the element of Air: "Inspiration! Clouds! New beginnings! Breaths! Gusts of wind! Clarity!" Other people around the circle supported them by tossing in their own Air words – some words made sense to everyone, and some seemed personal.

Finally, the invoking group made eye-contact with each other and called out: "Welcome East – Welcome Air!" The rest of the circle echoed it back. The invokers melted back into the circle.

Invoking South/Fire – The middle teens affinity group stepped out. People started rubbing their hands together or clapping them sharply. Others around the circle joined in. Then one invoker called out: "Hold your palms up and breathe in fiery

continued on next page

RITUAL SKILLS

Sacred Space - A Longer Example (pg 4)

energy of the stars... Hold your palms down and breathe in fiery molten Earth energy... Now place your hands on your center and breathe to the fire in your belly..."

After a moment, the affinity group clapped their hands sharply three times, then called out: "Welcome South – Welcome Fire!"

Invoking West/Water – The older teens affinity group came into the circle, each carrying an empty cup. One person carried a pitcher of water, which was poured into the cups. The invokers circled the fire and together took a drink. Then they fanned out, dipped their fingers into the water, and started flicking it at people, calling out: "Welcome West – Welcome Water!"

Invoking North/Earth – The mentors affinity group came into the circle and started the song that Jeremy had taught earlier: "We Are of the Body of the Earth / The Earth is of the body of the stars / We are stars that circle from life to death to birth." After three times through, the group ended on a harmony. Jeremy called out: "Welcome North – Welcome Earth!"

Invoking Center – For Center, Goldenrod started up a familiar song: "We are a circle, within a circle, with no beginning, and never ending." At the end, people called out: "Welcome Center – Welcome Spirit!"

Allies Invocations

We looked around, wondering what would happen next. Each ritual invokes different allies, and in different orders. Loreley, the ritual Wrangler for the evening, quickly looked at her notes, then leaned toward Sunflower: "Spirits of the land is first," she whispered.

Spirits of the Land – "Oh, right," Sunflower said, and took a step into the circle. "Please join me in honoring spirits of this place. Take a moment and think about the place we are standing right now.... Think about the rocks and underground waters.... the types of trees of flowers and animals you find here.... Think about the many kinds of life that have existed in this place...." Sunflower gazed down toward the Earth: "We thank the spirits of this land for hosting our ritual."

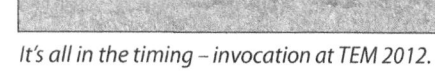
It's all in the timing – invocation at TEM 2012.

Honoring Our Ancestors – Sandra looked around the circle. "I invite you to take a moment and thank your ancestors – those of your own bloodline, and also all those whose work or writing or art has inspired you...Thank especially any ancestor who helped you arrive at this very time and place.... Blessed be."

Around the circle, people echoed, "Blessed be."

Then Loreley spoke again: "Finally, we invoke deity and energy to support our magic tonight!" (Note – you can find a lot more on this topic under Ritual Skills: Invoking Deity & Energies. Here, we will invoke one goddess and one type of energy.)

Invoking the Goddess – Randall, one of the mentors, stepped out and placed both hands on his center. The rest of us did likewise. "Breathe to your own center," Randall said, "and picture the beautiful blue ocean... Call to the ocean as the Mother... the power of birth and growth and every kind of creativity.... Feel how She speaks to us with Her tides, endlessly calling to us."

He took a breath and began singing: "We all come from the Goddess / And to Her we shall return / Like a drop of rain / Flowing to the ocean." Others picked up the tune, adding harmonies, until the song settled into a gentle final chord.

"Welcome Goddess!" Randall declared and people echoed.

continued on next page

RITUAL SKILLS

Sacred Space - A Longer Example (pg 5)

Invoking Creativity – Frida glided into the circle. "I call you to dance," she called out. "Dance like there is no wrong way! Dance like this is your world!"

Some people joined Frida in the circle. Others swayed a bit but stayed in the outer circle.

Frida called out: "Creative spirit of the universe – come to our circle today! We call to you with our voices! We call you as – "

Others joined her in calling out words of creativity: "Freedom! Courage! Inspiration! Color! Dedication! Excitement! Beauty!"

Finally Frida cried: "Welcome Creativity!" "Welcome Creativity!" the circle called back.

THE MIDDLE PARTS OF THE RITUAL

A gong sounded, and Sagewind stepped out to guide us into the first working....

Perhaps that evening we did an allies circle... or maybe we hiked down to the nearby meadow to walk a night labyrinth... maybe we did a trance journey to our place of power, then charged the working with fire and flour...

Whatever we did, we probably ended with a spiral dance around the bonfire and sang a high-energy chant like Weave and Spin or We Are the Rising Sun, chanting and toning until we built a whirlwind of magical energy.

DEVOKING & OPENING THE CIRCLE

As the energy settled back down, people took a deep breath. Some bent down and touched the ground, letting any excess or nervous energy return to the Earth.

Now it was time to devoke and open the circle. People felt tired and spacey, and we were glad to have a wrangler to keep track of who went in what order – especially since devocations go in reverse.

Devocations are usually short versions of the invocations – sometimes just a quick "thank you," or "hail and farewell." By this time of night, people are usually glad to wrap up and have something to eat.

Devoking/Thanking Allies

Thanking Creativity – Frida stepped forward. "Creative spirit of the universe – thank you for inspiring and challenging us in our magical workings and in our world. We ask that you travel with us and support us throughout this week. Thank you Creativity!" People echoed her final words.

Devoking the Goddess – Randall started singing We All Come from the Goddess. Others joined in, and he slowed the last line to show that he was ending. "Thank you Goddess," he said. "Hail and farewell."

Thanking your Ancestors – Sandra invited us each to whisper a few words of appreciation to our ancestors of blood and spirit. "Thank you, ancestors – hail and farewell," she concluded. The rest of us echoed her.

Thanking Spirits of the Land – Sunflower stretched out her arms. "We thank the land on which we stand – we thank the rocks and waters and living beings. Thank you for hosting our ritual, spirits of the land."

Devoking the Elements

Goldenrod, who was supposed to devoke Center, looked around. "Do we want to devoke all the elements with a song?"

People nodded, and Goldenrod launched into an easy chant that many people already knew:

The Earth, the Water, the Fire, the Air,
Return, return, return, return!

continued on next page

RITUAL SKILLS

Sacred Space - A Longer Example (pg 6)

Opening the Circle

The song faded, and Sagewind strode to the middle of the circle. They faced North, took a breath, and called out: "Earth!"

Turning counter-clockwise to the West, they called: "Water!"

Continuing to the South: "Fire!"

And finally to the East: "Air!"

They swept their arm around to North to complete the circle, then clapped over their head: "Above!" Reaching down, they clapped once more: "Below!"

Then Sagewind cried loudly: "The circle is open, but unbroken!"

Others joined in, voices rising through the final lines: "May the peace of the Goddess go in our hearts. Merry meet, merry part – and merry meet again!"

Applause and laughter burst out, as if we had just finished a successful dress rehearsal.

Gradually, people drifted into smaller conversations. Sharon sat down and wrote in her journal. José and Sagewind headed toward the dining hall. "Can you bring some dessert back?" Sandra called after them.

Sunflower picked up a drum and started playing a simple rhythm. Someone stacked a few more logs on the fire...

Ritual in the redwoods – fire circle at Mendocino Woodlands, home of Mysteries of Samhain, Witchlets in the Woods, Redwood Magic Family Camp, and California WitchCamp. Photo by Dawnstar.

Ritual Skills: Step-by-Step

Ideas & Inspirations for Each Part of a Ritual

- Honoring First People 59
- Purification 60
- Grounding 62
- Casting a Circle 68
- Invoking 77
  - Elements 84
  - Ancestors 85
  - Deity, Allies, & Energies 86
- Ritual Planning 93
- Ritual Theme & Arc 96
- Stories of the Land 99
  - Example: Journey of the Salmon 100
- Ritual Firetending 103
- Leading a Spiral Dance 106
- Teaching Chants 110
- Chants Resources Online 111

RITUAL SKILLS

Honoring First People

INTENT

Our intention is to honor the People who lived on this land before we did, and to acknowledge the history of genocide and dispossession that has displaced these People and continues to minimize their presence.

This is not about guilt – it's about awareness of history and a commitment to work for justice. This can be a complicated topic, depending on where you live and the ancestry of the folks in your circle. When this is done well, it can open a ritual on a note of resolution to work for justice.

See page 15 for a statement from Teen Earth Magic.

SPACE/TIME/SIZE

Any number, usually at or near the beginning of the ritual.

Allow the time needed. This might be a one-minute acknowledgment of First People and the history of expropriation, or it might be a longer explanation of a local campaign or other organizing efforts for Indigenous rights.

PREP

How will you learn about First People in your area? What resources are available?

What local organizing or gatherings are happening in your area? Maybe your ritual can tangibly support that work – for instance, by passing out flyers or collecting donations.

WORKINGS

This working can vary widely. Some Reclaiming groups honor First People at the opening of a ritual, before we cast our own circle. Someone involved with Indigenous organizing might update us on local actions and ways we can support.

In smaller circles, someone might acknowledge First People and the history of injustice.

Some years at the Spiral Dance in the San Francisco Bay Area, a member of an Ohlone tribe has honored the First People of the land we are on before we begin our ritual.

Honoring First People – A Shell Working

Here's a simple working from a Berkeley ritual. Ohlone People lived along the edges of San Francisco Bay for millennia before the arrival of Europeans. They harvested shellfish, and over the years created huge mounds of shells along the waterfront. Reclaiming groups including TEM have supported efforts to preserve local sacred sites threatened by development.

Space/Time/Size – space for a small altar and a circle of people. Each person will speak, so best size is 50 or fewer.

Materials Needed – a bag or two of small, plain seashells – enough for 2-3 per person at the ritual. Altar cloth, large bowl.

Prep – create a small altar with the shells already set out in a bowl. We chose an earth-colored cloth and some redwood twigs. We also had flyers for a local action/gathering on the literature table.

Working – priestess steps to side of altar and speaks words of acknowledgment and apology to the Ohlone People, then invites participants to step up to altar, take a couple of shells, and take a moment to think of one or two words of apology, commitment, power, hope, etc.

Finally, priestess invites people to place their shells back on the altar and speak their words – if more than 20 people, invite people to step up several at a time.

Finish – tone or sing over the shells, then say: "So mote it be!"

Afterward – invite people to take a few shells and put them in their garden or a sacred spot as a way of carrying our working into the wider world.

RITUAL SKILLS

Purification

INTENT

Purification prepares us to enter ritual space. The idea isn't that ordinary life is somehow "dirty" or "impure," but that it fills our days with annoyances and distractions that get in the way of entering sacred space and time. (Some people think we need a different word for this, but we haven't found it yet – stay tuned!)

In purification, we use elemental power such as flame, air, or salt water to clear away distractions and get ourselves ready to do ritual. Often it is simple – a sprinkle of salt water, a wafting with peacock feathers, the ringing of a bell...

Sometimes purification is part of grounding – near the beginning, we "let go of what we don't need and drop it to the Earth."

Other times it is done as we enter the room. At our Brigid ritual in San Francisco, priestesses stand at the door holding unlit taper candles. As someone approaches, a priestess steps forward and crosses candles over the person's heart.

At the Spiral Dance ritual, participants pass through veiled portals as they go from the lobby into the ritual room. Some years, priestesses greet people on the other side with salt water, sprinkling it over people with the words: "You are now entering sacred time – you are now entering sacred space."

In our daily lives we "purify" (or we're supposed to!) when we wash our hands before we begin the ritual of eating. At Teen Earth Magic, we chant a reminder before meals: "Witches wash your hands!"

SPACE/TIME/SIZE

Purification can be done at the edge of ritual space (as with the Brigid and Spiral Dance rituals described above), or as part of the grounding.

Any number – requires enough priestesses to keep the flow moving (standing in lines is one of those things we're washing away). Priestesses position themselves on the approaches to the circle.

Allow a few minutes. If done as people arrive, it won't take much time. Watch out for purifying one person at a time after everyone has arrived. No one wants to stand around and watch someone painstakingly waft air over each chakra of every person at a community ritual.

PREP

- Materials as needed – peacock feathers; bowl/salt/ sprig; hand-fan; candles/lighter; etc.
- Set up station and materials at edge of space.
- One or more priestesses to keep the purification moving quickly.

Could pre-ritual facepainting work as a purification? Try it out!

WORKINGS: SIMPLE PURIFICATIONS

Priestesses perform the purification, then silently gesture people forward, or say something like: "You are now entering sacred time – you are now entering sacred space!"

Saltwater and fresh greenery – need bowl of salt water and a sprig of greenery. As people approach, dip greenery into water

continued on next page

RITUAL SKILLS

Purification (pg 2)

and sprinkle a few drops on people, saying: "You are now entering sacred space. You are now entering sacred time."

Bowl of salt water for self-purifying – have a large, beautiful bowl filled with salt water. Welcoming graces invite people to purify themselves by dipping their fingers in the water and using it to touch their third eye, their heart, etc as they release energy and thoughts that don't serve them right now. End by saying, "Blessed be."

Feather wafting – get a few large, beautiful feathers that you can waft the air with. As each person approaches, invite them to stand with their eyes closed. Waft their aura, saying: "You are now entering sacred space, you are now entering sacred time."

Feather wafting with Wings – Graces sing Wings (from our album Second Chants – see Ritual Skills: Chants) as they waft people arriving at the ritual:

> Wandering in the deep of the night
> A thousand birds take flight
> And our dreams are borne on the wings of change
> We are weaving the world tonight

Shaking it out – this can be fun as the circle first gathers – before grounding or welcoming people, invite everyone to shake their bodies out, make noise, jump around, etc.

Games or silly songs – starting with a goofy game or a silly song can tap the nervous energy that we bring to the circle, stir it up a bit, and let it go. (Note – silliness doesn't work so well with younger teens, or with a group that doesn't know one another yet.)

Aura carwash – see Workings: Aura Carwash. We do this at the opening circle each year at

Pre-lunch handwashing is a key TEM purification – after which we form our food-blessing circle elbow-to-elbow.

Redwood Magic Family Camp. It's a fun way of purifying the entire group at once while building camaraderie – allow ten minutes.

Toning – invite people to use their voices to let go of what is not needed. Priestesses model free-form, wordless singing and release.

Star purification – see Workings: Purification: Star Purification. This is a longer personal purification for individuals or group.

Burning sage – in olden dayes, purifications were sometimes done by lighting a sprig of dried white sage and wafting it around people. More recently, concerns about cultural appropriation of this practice (often adopted from Indigenous Peoples) have curbed its use in our circles. Also, some folks may be allergic to the smell and/or smoke.

SOLO WORKING

Many of these ways of purifying work just as well for one person as 50. The star purification (See Workings: Purification) is designed for one person.

Try doing a quick purification (and grounding) before an exam, sports event, or job interview. What would help clear away your doubts and nervousness?

RITUAL SKILLS

Grounding: Teens Roundtable

"I remind myself that whatever happens, the Earth is always here for support. The Earth will always love me, and I can trust it."

Grounding is a word that covers a variety of ways in which we call our energy back to our own center and strengthen our connection to the Earth.

Sometimes grounding means getting into a deep, trancey space and preparing for prolonged introspective work.

Other times, being grounded means being alert and flexible, such as facing a row of nervous cops at a direct action – or a cranky teacher during an exam.

What does grounding mean to you?

Lucy: Grounding is centering myself in relation to the universe and the Earth.

KaeliMo: To me, it's about awareness – being ungrounded means not noticing what is going on around you.

Peter: Grounding is a connection to my inner self, outer self, and outer community, in equilibrium. I want to be grounded before facing conflict or a difficult topic. I feel that it allows for a smoother conversation and less miscommunication.

Ingrid: I think of grounding like balancing – connecting to a balanced, whole, authentic expression of myself.

Mykel: Grounding reminds me where I am in relation to the rest of the world. I can see the bigger picture of the Earth and the stars, so it becomes easier to drop my attachment to little stresses that I don't need to carry around with me. I can slow down, drop my center of gravity, and be aware of my body and my energy.

When do you find grounding helpful?

Ari: In everyday life, when I'm stressed out or need to be clear-headed in the midst of chaos, being able to ground and find my calm center – the eye of the storm within myself – is truly valuable in keeping high-risk situations safe and/or from escalating.

Ola'i Wildeboar: When life gets overwhelming and stressful and I feel myself fill up with worries and anxieties and unpleasant thoughts, I try to find a way to center myself. Often, grounding is that way. For example, when I feel myself freaking out, maybe even on the verge of a panic attack, I step out of whatever situation I am in and try to ground myself.

What do you do that helps?

Ola'i Wildeboar: If I can, I go to nature or a space that I consider magical. But often that isn't available, so I go somewhere quiet and sit. I try to align my spine and feel the ground beneath me. I remind myself that whatever happens, the Earth is always here for support. The Earth will always love me, and I can trust it. Once I become aware, I am usually in a calm state of mind and ready to move forward and make whatever decision I need to make.

Often we do a simple grounding when a circle gathers.

Lucy: One thing that works for me is visualizing a flower blooming into the space around me with roots in the Earth, pointing to the sky.

Dusky: I usually ground lying down or standing. Sitting feels kind of odd. I try to go somewhere quiet. I close my eyes and listen to my breath or to natural sounds around me. I turn down my thinking mind, stopping that constant rush of thoughts. To me, grounding is slowing myself down and feeling myself in touch with everything around me, feeling the connection that I have to other people and nature – tapping into Earth energy.

Natasha: A big part of how I feel grounded is feeling my body in the space – if there's sunlight on my face or air on

continued on next page

RITUAL SKILLS

Grounding: Teens Roundtable (pg 2)

"Oh, right, this is reality. Why do I spend so much time seeing only a fraction of things?"

my skin. Also checking in with energies going on internally and calming them, putting ones that aren't serving me at that moment aside so I can be really present and centered.

Charlotte: I feel most grounded when thinking about where I am in relation to the Earth. Wherever I am, I try to imagine myself being even more connected with the Earth and all its energies.

When is grounding difficult?

Charlotte: When you live in a city it's hard – cities have all this concrete and plumbing and electrical wires underground – but there's also soil. So I try to find myself connected to that somehow – trying to keep some sort of Earth awareness in my day to day life.

Damien: I don't ground. It's not something I generally need because I'm a really calm person and it's hard to get me uncalm. So when we ground in rituals, I end up either not grounding, or just doing something totally different.

Dusky: I don't interact in the world in a grounded way very often. I think I do that intentionally. I'm an energetic, bouncy person. When I've tried to be grounded, I get kind of bored. I like being fast-moving most of the time. But when I do that for too long, it gets exhausting. I recharge when I'm by myself, or when I'm with other spiritual people. That's when it's good to be grounded.

Meagan: Grounding is tough for me. Most of the guided grounding meditations I encounter, in Reclaiming rituals and elsewhere, leave me feeling *less* grounded, in the sense of centered, present, and comfortable in my body and in the moment.

So what does work for you?

Meagan: The most effective paths to grounding I've found are not formulaic, but involve a very subtle tracking of my emotional state, as well as my external environment, and the relation between the two.

Dusky: I like grounding near the ocean. The sound of the waves really helps ground me.

KaeliMo: Grounding is a personal process for me. I like to follow guided groundings, but I'm very much inside my own head. Touching my body helps – letting go of the situation for just a second, and looking inward to remember what is there. That's calming, and after that I can more easily be aware of the other things around me.

Deep pentacle grounding? Or maybe it's just nap time on the trampoline.

How can you tell you're grounded?

Dusky: My off-the-cuff cheesy answer is, it's kind of like being in love – you just know.

Ingrid: I feel really sure of myself. I often suffer from self-confidence issues, so it's a distinct feeling to me to feel that I have a little bit more power and confidence. I can definitely feel the difference.

Mykel: Often, when I ground, I'll feel a shiver up my spine of the Earth's energy moving through me. After I ground, I usually feel like, "Oh, right, this is reality. Why do I spend so much time seeing only a fraction of things?"

Practice Grounding with Starhawk

You can practice Reclaiming-style groundings and guided meditations with recordings by Starhawk on youtube, spotify, etc.

See page 115 for details.

RITUAL SKILLS

Grounding

INTENT

Grounding means something like "relaxing, calling my energy back to my center, letting go of thoughts and energy that I don't need at this moment, and feeling my connection with the deep core of the Earth."

In Reclaiming rituals, we often do a combination of purification, centering, grounding into the Earth, and drawing up Earth energy, and call the whole ensemble "grounding."

Grounding is a valuable personal skill as well. What if you could quickly ground and center yourself before a test, or before a stage performance or athletic contest? What if you could easily renew your sense of groundedness and self-confidence when someone upsets you or makes you angry?

Different people find different ways of grounding that work for them. When a priestess "leads a grounding" at the beginning of a ritual, some people just tune it out and do their own personal grounding.

So we can't tell you "how to ground." You'll figure that out for yourself. What we offer are some ways that Reclaiming folks do personal and group groundings, and then some workings that will help you explore various methods.

However you ground, you'll want to finish by returning the energy to the Earth afterward. When you finish the grounding, drop to your knees (or touch any solid object that is sitting on the ground). Place your hands on the ground. Let any excess energy drain into the Earth, where it can be renewed.

✪ **Book of Shadows** – grounding is a great topic for your journal or Book of Shadows. As you try out different ways of grounding, jot down notes about what works and what doesn't. Look back occasionally and notice any patterns and changes.

TEM teens perfect a tricky dual grounding as a witchily-attired mentor looks on.

Online samples – you'll find sample groundings from Starhawk online. See page 115 for more information.

SPACE/TIME/SIZE

There's no limit to the number who can do a grounding together except the ability to be heard. With a microphone, people lead groundings for large gatherings like the annual Spiral Dance. People have even tried it over TV or audiobooks!

On the other hand, trying to lead a verbal grounding at the ocean on a windy day can be a challenge even for a small circle. In that case, we try toning together, with experienced people modeling how we can use gestures to draw down calm, powerful, healing Earth energy to our centers.

continued on next page

RITUAL SKILLS

Grounding (pg 2)

Groundings typically take two to five minutes. This is our chance to draw healing Earth energy into our bodies and auras. Taking time and care to ground and come fully present can improve all of our magical – and mundane – work.

PREP

Usually a single priestess leads the grounding. This can be a good role for someone who did not help plan the ritual – they don't need to know the whole ritual flow to do a good grounding.

Grounding priestess – do whatever prep you need. You may want to practice ahead of time. Practice the pauses too... give people time for their own thoughts between your words....

In a small circle or alone, it's fine to read groundings from a piece of paper or play recordings the first few times. But have a goal of doing them spontaneously – once you understand what a grounding is and how it works in a ritual, you'll be surprised at how easy they are to invent!

In a group or circle – invite people to stand if they are able, with their weight evenly balanced and knees slightly relaxed. Standing in a relaxed position often makes it simpler to draw Earth energy up through our bodies rather than sitting or lying down.

WORKINGS: Some Ways of Grounding

Tree of Life

This may be the most common grounding in our repertoire – we envision ourselves as trees, exchanging energy with Earth and sky.

See Ritual Skills: Sacred Space: A Longer Example. You can also search on youtube for <Starhawk Grounding Meditation>.

Roots Down, Branches Up!

A super-fast version of the Tree of Life grounding – although its strength depends on having a regular practice of grounding that we can quickly call upon.

Campers practice their grounding skills during a break at TEM.

Stand tall, with your weight balanced and knees slightly bent.... Take a deep breath.... As you exhale, drop your roots down from the base of your spine to the center of the Earth.... On a second deep breath, exhale and throw your arms upward as branches.... Breathe life energy from the core of the Earth to the tips of your fingers and beyond....

Call out: "Roots down, branches up!"

✪ **Book of Shadows** – try this exercise, then ask – does this grounding actually work for you? What might make it stronger?

continued on next page

TeenEarthMagic.org

RITUAL SKILLS

Grounding (pg 3)

Ground with the Ground

Does it work to lie down on the ground to ground? Try it out. Try different positions. Uncross your arms and legs. Draw deep breaths. Does it work for you? What's different than standing?

✪ **Book of Shadows** – how do you know when you are grounded/centered? Or not? What makes a difference?

Star Purification & Grounding

See Workings: Purification: Star Purification (page 256) – this working can be turned into a grounding by adding one piece at the end – when you have completed the purification, take three more breaths, letting your aura be filled with Earth energy, connecting you to the center of our planet. Let it mingle with the Star energy.

Speak or sing the words to the chant, Body of the Earth: "We are of the body of the Earth / The Earth is of the body of the Stars / We are stars that circle from life to death to birth."

Running The Pentacle
Pentacle Magic – see page 249

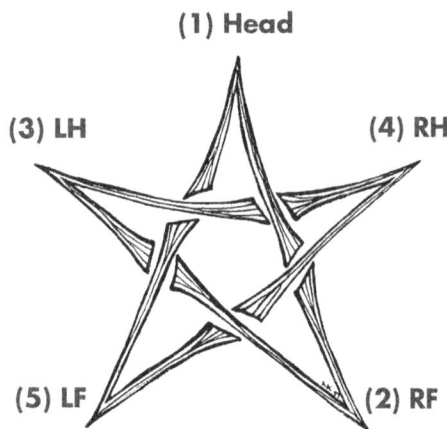

(1) Head
(3) LH   (4) RH
(5) LF   (2) RF

Stand as a relaxed star. Take a breath to your center. Let that energy rise gently to a point just above your head.

Begin at the top. Run the pentacle three times as shown (1-2-3-4-5-1), returning to the top to complete it.

Then trace a circle around the star (1-3-5-2-4-1), again finishing at the top.

Let the energy rest there for a moment, then drop gently back to your center for completion of the cycle.

Pop Quiz – compare this to the invoking pentacle on page 72. Why is the invoking pentacle a mirror image of the "running" pentacle?

See page 250 for one possible answer!

Pentacle Grounding

This grounding runs pentacle energy to ground us. (For more pentacle magic, see Workings: Pentacles – page 249).

Stand like a star, legs spread, arms stretched loosely to sides. Close your eyes and take a deep breath, letting your energy come together in your own center. Breathe again to your center.

Now, on a breath, let your energy rise gently above your head and rest there, glowing like a bright ball of light. Breathe to this energy.

Let the energy drop diagonally through your body to your right foot. Breathe and let your energy rest there, glowing like a bright light.

Continue in this order, resting for one breath at each point:

- Head
- Right Foot
- Left Hand
- Right Hand
- Left Foot
- Return to Head

Run the pentacle three times, finishing above your head. Take a breath..

Now gently run the energy once around the circle in this order:

- Head
- Left Hand
- Left Foot
- Right Foot
- Right Hand
- Return to Head

Take one more breath. Then let the energy drop gently back to your center. Anchor it there with three breaths. Say: "Blessed be!"

continued on next page

RITUAL SKILLS

Grounding (pg 4)

Instant Grounding

How quickly can I go from ungrounded to grounded? What helps me do this?

Try doing a personal grounding that helps you feel centered, calm, and present. Hold this feeling for a moment. Now touch a part of your body – perhaps your "center." Draw your grounded attention into that center. Perhaps you can visualize an object such as a rose or a crystal in that spot.

When you finish, set a timer for an hour or so. Now go back to your daily life – anything except more magic.

When the timer sounds, see if you can re-ground simply by touching your center (or whatever spot you chose) and calling up the image you visualized. Can you call back your groundedness with a breath? With three breaths?

Practice helps – try this a few times in different contexts. Try it at a retreat where you feel especially grounded. Try different images until you find one that really resonates. See if instant grounding can become a skill you develop, and not just an exercise you did this one time.

Note – instant grounding depends on a steady practice of grounding. Then when you need it, you're in practice.

✪ **Book of Shadows** – where are three places/situations where you could benefit from instant grounding? What would make it difficult or awkward? What would make it more possible?

Group Personal Grounding – "Come Back Grounded"

For group ritual at a camp or class. This works well when folks have already done other types of groundings at prior classes or rituals. Use a bell or drum to call people back.

When it's time to do the grounding, invite people to spread out a bit. "Give yourself some space. You'll have a few minutes. When the bell rings, come back grounded." Allow 3-4 minutes.

Moveable Grounding

Can you ground while walking? Or – can you stop and ground, then move without losing it?

Try it out. Try grounding while you walk. What makes it different than standing still? Does walking in a circle help?

Can you move after grounding and still maintain your grounding? Would anchoring the feeling in your body help? What if you envision a crystal in your heart – so whenever you touch your heart, you recall the crystal and the grounding it symbolizes?

✪ **Book of Shadows** – after trying some moveable groundings, take a few minutes and write your impressions. What might make moveable groundings work better for you?

Invisible Grounding

When we ground in public, we may not want everyone to notice what we're doing. What are some simple, "invisible" ways that you can ground? Is it essential to get a bit of private space? Can you ground with people around you? With your eyes open?

SOLO WORKING

Grounding is one of the most basic magical skills, in some ways the foundation of all the rest. Maybe that's why we do it at the beginning of rituals!

Try different ways of grounding as above, including the online recordings from Starhawk, and invent some of your own.

✪ **Book of Shadows** – keep a running commentary in your Book of Shadows. What works in which situations? What changes do you see as you gain skills? When has grounding particularly worked for you? Where and when has it been most difficult to stay grounded?

RITUAL SKILLS

Circle Casting: Teens Roundtable

"I've come to see circle casting as a way to hold an intention. It contains the energy we are working with until we are ready to release it or further direct its path."

What is a magical circle?

Mykel: I love being in circles of magic, whether I cast by myself or in a group. It changes the space – the air feels physically different once we set it aside as sacred. It reminds me of being in temples, churches, and other buildings of worship because of the reverence and openness they make me feel. The "walls" we build help to define the feel of a space and protect us in the vulnerability of doing magic.

Miranda: A magical circle is sacred space that's created so that the magic you do stays within the circle unless you specifically choose to bring it out. It's kind of like a barrier – you're safe within it. Nothing you need with you will go away, and nothing harmful will come in. It gives you a good space to work in.

Talise: I think that a circle is a container for magic. It also helps set the tone for your magic. It helps you set the intention that you're going to do magical working in that space.

Why exactly do you cast circles?

KaeliMo: It's a way to separate yourself from outside stressors and create an intentional physical and mental space to safely do what you're doing.

Ingrid: Okay, so I guess this is when I admit that for a long time I had no idea what it actually meant to myself (or others) to cast a circle. It just seemed to be something you "should" do when creating sacred space.

What do you find puzzling about it?

Ingrid: Sometimes, after casting the circle with pretty words (at this point the variations on "By the Earth..." are so numerous and so lovely that I want a list just to read them all again and again), I get the distinct feeling that I missed something. Where was that circle again? As much as I want to feel the newly-created circle holding us in our work, I just don't. I love the poetry, I appreciate the idea, my heart soaks in the intention. But let's face it, I feel slightly less than "between the worlds".

What do you think might work for you?

Ingrid: At our last camp, I started asking what exactly I was hoping to create when I helped cast a circle. I've come to see circle casting as a way to hold an intention. It contains the energy we are working with until we are ready to release it or further direct its path.

Do you cast circles on your own?

Miranda: Very rarely – maybe once.

Ingrid: Yes, or I'd fret if I didn't – haven't you heard at least one story of strange energies taking over a ritual for lack of a "circle of protection?" There are times when I've flat out forgotten to cast a circle, or I've

The circle gathers.

continued on next page

RITUAL SKILLS

Circle Casting: Teens Roundtable (pg 2)

"In the moment our circle is cast, we breathe into the fullness of our edges, into the vast presence of each other's being, and into the woven body of our circle."

gotten halfway through invoking the elements and say, "Wait! Hold up! I totally want to bask in your radiance, Fire, but first let's get the circle cast!" And there are other times that I just decide not to cast a circle.

KaeliMo: I cast a circle for myself when I first got to college. College is a really intense place, and I figured it would be good to go into it with intention, holding my own boundaries. I still haven't closed it – it's there until I leave, or I feel that this portion of my work is done. When I feel like things are getting difficult or out of my control, I put some extra intention into it and let myself have the space I need. One of the things I'm working on is being away from my family and home, and still going about things in a safe and productive way, holding myself accountable and being a good support system for myself.

Growing up, did your family provide grounding and a circle for you?

KaeliMo: Yeah, a combination of family and friends and my various communities I grew up with – these have provided a lot of grounding for me. When I went away to school, I only knew a couple of people. People are coming and going all the time, it's chaotic – that's part of what's so cool about it too! – but it's important to have something steady there, to deal with all the moving stuff.

Do you have a favorite way to cast a circle?

Ingrid: If I had to pick a favorite – one that speaks to me every time – it would be "Hand to Hand and Heart to Heart" (see page 73). When we bring each heart into the circle, there is some sort of spark created. In the moment when our circle is cast, we breathe into the fullness of our edges, into the vast presence of each other's being, and into the woven body of our circle, holding us gently in this transitional space. I love that way of casting. It never gets old for me.

Meagan: Last year I started coming up with fun new ways to cast circles that would help me feel energized and take people by surprise. One of them is a Duck, Duck, Goose style casting in which everyone sits down and someone starts walking around tapping heads saying, "Earth, Earth, Earth, Earth.....Air!" They are then chased around by that Air person who afterward takes over with, "Air, Air, Air, Air....Fire!" And so on. I received really mixed reviews on this. Some people seem to enjoy more serious castings, while others found this to be delightful mischief. (See page 75.)

Talise: I like when people gather the energy by doing something like passing a seed around, or picking up a rock in your hand and each person touching it to their heart.

Miranda: It's much easier to visualize if there is a physical circle – if everyone is holding hands in a circle, or one person walking around the circle, It's like, "Oh, we have a circle!" That's easier than if someone says, "Now we're going to imagine there's a circle here."

Mykel: I like the traditional circle casting structure, because it feels stable, balanced, secure. I also like experiments that play with different combinations of physical and energetic aspects, like making a circle around us with rope or physical objects, or physically taking each other's hands.

Each morning path and evening ritual at Teen Earth Magic begins by casting a circle.

RITUAL SKILLS

Circle Casting

INTENT

Magical circles are part of the ancient lore of witches, occultists, and magicians. A circle can protect us from malignant energy, or summon and hold positive energy. In old stories such as the Legend of Dr. Faustus, terrifying demons can be invoked and controlled if one has cast a strong enough circle.

Whether anyone ever did such things, or they just make good stories, it illustrates the power of magical circles.

Even in the mundane world, a circle brings a group of people together on equal footing – unlike sitting in rows facing a lectern. Being in a circle gives us a sense of belonging and of being separate from anything outside our circle. Whether or not we name it, that's magic!

Casting a circle is a useful skill anywhere from a ritual, to a direct action protest, to walking down the street. You might even want to cast a circle when you're by yourself, as a way of concentrating and collecting your energy.

There's no one correct way to cast a circle. Sometimes it can be theatrical and poetic. Other times it can be five seconds of focusing on your boundaries. Sometimes it's serious, other times playful or goofy.

Ask – is this way of casting this particular circle likely to create a powerful container that suits the work that you (and other participants) hope to do here and now? If so – go for it!

The important thing is that you can *feel* the circle around you. All of the fine words don't mean much if they don't produce a feeling of being in a strong circle. Experiment with different ways of casting your own personal circle. What works for you?

✪ **Book of Shadows** – what are some reasons/times/places you might want to cast a circle? What are some simple ways you discover to quietly create a circle for yourself (see end of this section for some ideas)?

SPACE/TIME/NUMBERS

Circles are important for groups of every size, including solo work. Different ways of casting work better for different numbers and situations.

Poetic, theatrical castings work well in community rituals, weddings, workshops, etc – especially places where "casting a circle" is a new concept for many people.

Playful and participatory castings work well at camps and ongoing classes – places where people will experience multiple circle castings over several successive rituals, and you want to mix it up.

Each of us will discover (and create) ways that work best for us when we are alone or with a few friends.

PREP

For some ways of casting, you'll need props, or you'll need to recruit a few people to help. If you use Ye Olde Circle Casting, you'll want to decide on which pronouns to use (see next page).

Handy magical skill – learn a few simple ways to cast circles for groups of different sizes, so if you're called on, you're ready!

¡Caution! ¡Danger! ¡Cuidado!

Beware the never-ending circle casting. In larger groups (50-plus), beware of having each person do something one at a time (for example, see Heart-to-Heart below). Ten seconds per person times fifty people equals close to ten minutes. If the casting takes more than a few minutes, people are going to lose focus, and you'll wind up spending a long time casting a weak circle. Save one-by-one participation for smaller circles, or for small group workings within the larger circle.

Beware the unfinished circle. In castings where you turn to each direction and name it (common in Reclaiming), start in the North, proceed to East-South-West – then be sure to return to North to complete the circle before moving to Center.

continued on next page

RITUAL SKILLS

Circle Casting (pg 2)

Finishing the Circle Casting

However creatively you cast, it often makes sense to finish by declaring something like: "The circle is cast, we are between the worlds – and what happens between the worlds, changes all the worlds. Let the magic begin!" These traditional words put a "seal" on the circle casting and bring it to a crisp close. It's also something everyone can say together.

End of Ritual – Opening the Circle

However you cast, at the end of the ritual, after all allies and elements are devoked in reverse order, you are responsible for "opening" the circle – often by doing a short version of your casting. See Ye Old Circle Casting just below for an example. This is the final act of the ritual, so keep it short and focused.

When you finish, it's "traditional" to say these words, with others joining in:

"The circle is open (clap hands once sharply), but unbroken. May the peace of the Goddess* go in our hearts. Merry meet – and merry part – and merry meet again!" (* Some say mysterious ones, or "peace and justice," etc.)

WORKINGS: Some Ways To Cast a Circle

What's the best way to cast a circle? This is Reclaiming – you can cast a circle any way you like. There are as many ways to cast a circle as there are rituals. By practicing, you'll learn what works for you in different situations.

Here are some castings we've done over the years.

Ye Olde Circle Casting

Creative circle casting is exciting. There is also power in "traditional" ways. This formula comes to us from the Feri Tradition (and perhaps other magical traditions from the mid-twentieth century).

This is a good way to cast big circles. One priestess leads this, and everyone else either listens or repeats after the priestess, so it's great for newcomers.

Prep – ahead of time, read through these words a few times until you can feel the rhythm of the poetry. Then decide which pronouns you are going to use – in a group, discuss it with other organizers so you are in agreement.

The words outside the parentheses are the version that was common in the early years of Reclaiming and WitchCamp. The parenthetical "God" text was added in the 1990s.

>   By the Earth that is Her body (by the Grove that is His home)
>   By the Air that is Her breath (by the Wind that is His song)
>   By the Fire of Her bright Spirit (by the Heat of His blazing passion)
>   By the Waters of Her living womb/blood (by the Dew that is His sweet tears)
>   By all that is above
>   By all that is below
>   The circle is cast – we are between the worlds
>   What happens between the worlds changes all the worlds
>   So mote it be (or: Let the magic begin!)

Honoring Gender Diversity

More recently, some people (including Teen Earth Magic campers) have challenged the idea that every person fits neatly into one – and only one – of two possible genders. Some circle castings have substituted the words Our or Their in place of Her/Him. Try saying the above lines using Our or Their in each line.

continued on next page

Ritual Skills

Circle Casting (pg 3)

Here's a creative circle casting from an Ocean Beach Solstice ritual around 2013:

> By the Earth that is Her body
> By the Air that is His breath
> By the Fire of Their bright spirit
> By the Waters of Our living blood
> By all that is above...

What Do You Do While You're Saying This?

Step to the center of the space. Bend and touch your writing hand (or point your athame or wand) to the Earth. Take a breath, gently pulling Earth energy into your hand or the tool. Stand and walk to the North edge of the space so you are a bit outside the circle of people, facing out.

Facing North, use your writing hand (or magical tool) to draw an invoking pentacle (see drawing) and then circle it clockwise. After it is drawn, "push" the pentacle out to the edge of the space. If you're outdoors or in a large room, decide where the edge of the circle will be. In a group, invite others to draw the pentacle with you and help push it to the edge of the space.

Facing North, say: "By the Earth that is Her body" (or "His/Our/Their body" – decide pronouns beforehand – see above).

Walk around the edge of the space to the East. Draw an invoking pentacle and push it to the edge of the circle.

Facing East, say: "By the Air that is Her breath."

Walk around the edge of the space to the South. Draw an invoking pentacle and push it to the edge of the circle.

Facing South, say: "By the Fire of Her bright spirit."

Walk around the edge of the space to the West. Draw an invoking pentacle and push it to the edge of the circle.

Facing West, say: "By the Waters of Her living womb." (Some say "living blood.")

After West/Water – remember to walk back to North to complete the outer circle before coming to the Center.

Step into the Center. Draw an invoking pentacle in the air above you and **looking up, say**: "By all that is above."

Draw an invoking pentacle toward the floor – push it down below the floor – **looking down, say**: "By all that is below."

Conclude by saying: "The circle is cast. We are between the worlds. And what happens between the worlds can change all the worlds. Let the magic begin!"

(No other words are needed before the East/Air invocation begins – allow a short pause as circle priestess leaves the circle.)

Opening Ye Olde Circle – at the end of the ritual, after all allies and elements are devoked in reverse order, open the circle with a short version of the casting – priestess steps to the Center and leads everyone in the basic poem. "By the Earth that is Her body, and by the Air that..." – we often use female pronouns here, to remind us that our tradition is rooted in Goddess spirituality. Of course, this is Reclaiming Tradition – it could change at any time!

Invoking Pentacle

Face outward from the edge of your circle

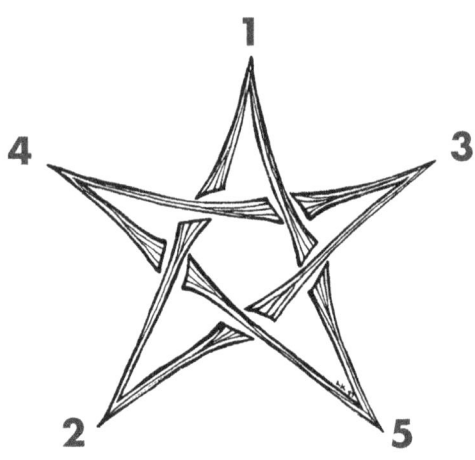

Face North. Take a breath.

Begin at the top. Crisply draw the pentacle as shown (1-2-3-4-5-1), returning to the top to complete it.

Then trace a circle clockwise around the star (1-3-5-2-4-1), again finishing at the top.

Take a breath. Gently push the pentacle to the edge of your space and a bit beyond.

Say, "Welcome Earth!"

Proceed to East...

continued on next page

RITUAL SKILLS

Circle Casting (pg 4)

Bare-Bones Circle Casting

Here's a stripped-down version of the Ye Olde Circle Casting – good when time is limited (for instance, at a street protest or when it's raining), when it's hard to hear (eg, a windy day at the beach) – and also simply for the impact of minimal words.

Face North. Hold your writing arm out like a sword and point. Take a breath and say: "North – Earth!"

Pause for a moment, then swing your sword-arm to the right, facing East. Take a breath and say: "East – Air!"

Swing your sword-arm to the right, facing South. Take a breath and say: "South – Fire!"

Swing your sword-arm to the right, facing West. Take a breath and say: "West – Water!"

Swing your sword-arm back to the North to complete the outer circle. Then turn to face the middle. Take a breath and say: "Center – Spirit!"

Take a breath and feel the circle of energy all around you. See if you can picture it as a band of colored light.

Now say: "The circle is cast – we are between the worlds! And what happens between the worlds changes all the worlds! Blessed be."

A shady spot on a sunny day helps gather a quiet circle.

Snap Casting – fastest casting ever!

Here's the fastest circle casting ever, courtesy of a Witchlets teacher.

Step to Center. Shake your body and arms so you're loose and can move quickly.

Face North – snap! Turn to East – snap! Turn to South – snap! Turn to West – snap! Turn again to North, then face Center – snap above, snap below. Say: "The circle is cast!"

✪ **Book of Shadows** – see how quickly you can cast while actually being aware of each of the directions as you snap. Does it feel like a strong circle was created (this will vary for each person)? Would going more slowly make a difference? What else might quickly strengthen this circle?

Hand to Hand and Heart to Heart

This might be the #1 favorite Witchlets and TEM circle casting of all time! We've also used it for the opening circle at JeWitch Camp.

This works for about 25-30 people. After that it may run too long. (In that case, try Taking Hands and Toning, below.)

This casting works better later in the class or camp, or with a group that already knows one another – the hand-on-heart part could be challenging for some people (even though it's just the back of the hand).

continued on next page

RITUAL SKILLS

Circle Casting (pg 5)

Stand in a circle without holding hands. First person reaches out with left hand and takes right hand of neighbor, saying: "Hand to hand (then lightly touching the backs of their locked hands first to their own heart and then to their neighbor's) and heart to heart, the circle is cast." Leave locked hands over neighbor's heart – they then reach out to next person and repeat, around the circle.

Beware – this takes about 10-15 seconds per person, and may lose focus in groups of more than 25 people. We tried it once in a San Francisco ritual of a hundred people, and the focus was lost early on. Result – it took a long time to cast a weak circle.

Opening the circle – everyone joins hands. Circle priestess looks to right (counter-clockwise), meets next person's eyes, and releases their two hands. Nod to that person to indicate that they do the same for the next person, until it's gone all the way around and all hands are released. Priestess begins and others join in: "The circle is open, but unbroken..."

Taking Hands and Toning

A quick way to create a circle for larger groups (20 or more).

Circle casting priestess needs to be confident holding a tone until others join in.

Once folks are grounded, priestess brings people into a circle, then says: "We are going to cast our circle by building a tone. I will begin by singing a tone and taking the next person's hand. That person will join the tone, then take the next person's hand, and so on."

The priestess pauses and takes a deep breath. Begin a tone (any tone you wish, just hold it steadily). After a few seconds, take the hand of the person to your *left* (clockwise). Look at them so they join your tone, then nod so they take the next person's hand. After that it will probably continue on its own. (You might want a friend at your left to help get things started.)

When the tone comes all the way around and all hands are joined, slowly raise your arms together and let the volume rise. Let the toning peak and come back down in synch with your arms.

When it's silent again, the priestess speaks: "The circle is cast. We are between the worlds. What happens between the worlds can change all the worlds. Let the magic begin!"

Opening the circle – everyone joins hands. Priestess explains: "We will all begin toning, then as we release hands counter-clockwise, each person drops out." Priestess begins by looking at person to their right, letting go of their hand, and letting her voice fade. That person will do the same, and so on. If toning wavers, priestess can subtly join back in and be the last to stop.

When all hands are dropped and toning fades, priestess speaks (and others join in): "The circle is open, but unbroken (all clap sharply). May the peace of the Goddess go in our hearts. Merry meet, merry part – and merry meet again!"

Broomstick Casting

You can use a broomstick to draw the pentacles as you cast in Ye Olde Way. And here's a further twist on the old broomstick:

At one of the early years of Teen Earth Magic, two of our older teens came up with this magical and hilarious circle casting, then matched it with their opening of the circle at the end of camp (see photos on next page).

Prep – two people, two brooms; witchy garb such as pointy hats, striped socks, etc – or any costumes.

Witches begin in the North, mount their brooms, and race around the circle clockwise three times (or race in opposite directions three times, finally meeting again in the North). Then fly to Center, whirl around, and say: "The circle is cast, we are between the worlds..."

Opening – same witches begin in North and use brooms in the ordinary way, to sweep up the circle counterclockwise (or in opposite directions). Then say, "The circle is open, but unbroken..."

continued on next page

RITUAL SKILLS

Circle Casting (pg 6)

Earth-Earth-Air! (Duck-Duck-Goose!)

Works well for 20-50. After that the size of the circle may get clumsy. Most will recognize Duck-Duck-Goose. Don't give the joke away.

Prep – four secret priestesses spread out around the circle so they are in the North, East, South, and West.

Once people are grounded, North priestess invites all to kneel or crouch in a circle. Priestess begins in North and goes clockwise around outside of the circle, tapping heads and saying, "Earth, Earth, Earth..."

When the priestess reaches the secret East person, tap them and cry: "Air!" North priestess runs, and East priestess jumps up and chases – never quite catching up before first priestess completes the circle and takes the East spot.

East priestess resumes with, "Air, Air, Air..." until they reach the secret South priestess, whom they tap and cry: "Fire!"

After their chase, South taps secret West priestess and yells: "Water!" West chases South, and finally continues around and takes the spot where North priestess began, completing the outer circle.

For Center, all four priestesses come to the middle, meet eyes, and say together: "Center, Center, Center, Center, Center!"

North priestess speaks: "The circle is cast. We are between the worlds. And what happens between the worlds, changes all the worlds. Let the magic begin!"

Note – by ending with these traditional lines, we can anchor a funny and high-energy circle casting, weaving the circle more strongly as we speak the familiar words.

Opening circle – what's a simple way to open this circle?

Broomstick casting – the witchiest circle casting ever!

Here's an idea – priestess steps to middle, faces North, and says: "Earth!" Turns to West: "Water!" To South: "Fire!" To East: "Air!" Face Center: "Above! Below!" Then conclude with the traditional words (see above): "The circle is open, but unbroken..."

Speaker & Pentacle-Inscriber (good when it's difficult to hear)

Try this at a big ritual where it can be hard to hear (for instance, at the beach, or on a hilltop when the wind is blowing). You'll need two priestesses – a speaking priestess and a drawing priestess.

Speaking priestess steps to middle of circle where they can best be heard. Drawing priestess, wielding a tall staff with ribbons and feathers, steps to Center too – then dramatically strides to the North, through the circle, and ten feet beyond.

Facing outward, drawing priestess inscribes a big pentacle in North. Speaking priestess calls: "By the Earth that is Her Body!"

Drawing priestess strides around to East, inscribes a pentacle. Speaking priestess calls: "By the Air that is Her breath," and so on.

continued on next page

Circle Casting (pg 7)

Drawing priestess – remember to complete the circle after West/Water by circling back to the North, then stride to Center.

Drawing priestess inscribes a big pentacle above. Speaking priestess says: "By all that is above," and so on.

Finish by calling out: "The circle is cast, we are between the worlds…"

Take Hands and Start Singing

Here's a fast and easy casting for when a group is already well-established, so it builds off earlier circles.

With no words, priestess simply takes the hands of the person on either side and starts singing: "We Are a Circle Within a Circle." Or simply start a tone that others pick up. Let a few people know you are doing this, so they will join hands right away.

Packing & Unpacking Circles

If the circle will soon be re-cast (like at WitchCamp or a weekend intensive, where we open the circle at night and re-cast the next morning), we sometimes "pack up the circle" at the end of the night ritual – everyone helps gather it like a big tablecloth and pack it into the center, then perhaps tuck it under an altar, or toss it into the air with instructions to come back the next day.

The next time we cast, everyone helps unpack/unroll the circle. Then a priestess might go around, beginning with North, and "peg down" the directions, stating them aloud as they go. End by saying, "The circle is cast, we are between the worlds…"

At the end of the final ritual or class, do a full circle-opening (perhaps Ye Olde Way, or a creative way).

Invisible Circle Casting (casting without being seen)

Casting a grand, poetic circle is great at a community ritual or behind the closed doors of your bedroom.

But there are times when you might want a strong circle, yet you don't have the luxury of calling out the directions and elements as you turn and inscribe pentacles in the air. You might even want to cast a circle without anyone else noticing.

Maybe you're on a bus or in a crowded hallway and want to feel stronger boundaries. Maybe you have to meet with a teacher and want to remind yourself of your own center and intentions. Maybe it's exam time and you want to block out distractions.

Each of us will discover our own best ways of quietly creating a circle. Here are a few ways you might try:

- Close your eyes and imagine facing North. Take a breath for Earth. Imagine turning to the East. Take a breath for Air. Imagine South and breathe for Fire, then West and breathe for Water. After you've done it a few times – can you take one deep breath and simultaneously inhale and exhale one-quarter in each direction?
- With eyes closed, imagine a spiral of energy radiating from your belly and wrapping around your body. Gradually expand the spiral until it's a comfortable distance from your body. Change the spiral into a circle and feel the energy around you.
- Front-to-back, side-to-side – draw a breath to your center – let it flow slowly forward from your center, then backward, like a pendulum swinging gently through your body. Take a second breath and let the pendulum swing side to side. Now – can you feel it move out in all four directions at once, then gently back till they meet in your center? Can you feel the balance?
- ✪ **Book of Shadows** – what works? Which ways of casting actually help you feel your own strong circle? What gets in the way?

Circle Workings

See the alphabetical Workings chapter for some ways to strengthen circles (pages 208-210).

- **Workings: Circle Blessing** – use the circle to share blessings and strengthen your connections for future workings.
- **Workings: Circle: Pass the Knot** – this quick game can be repeated to strengthen your circle. Great for a younger group.
- **Workings: Circle: Yarn Web** – a fun way to weave a strong circle. Good for the opening day of a class or camp.

RITUAL SKILLS

Invoking: Teens Roundtable

"Calling on energies and beings greater than myself for support or wisdom."

What does Invoking mean to you?

Ari: To me, invoking means welcoming, inviting, or calling something to share sacred space with you.

Rhys: Invoking is a way we both honor and ask for help from whatever we want to be present. It helps create the circle and raise the energy level of the magic.

Ingrid: It sounds so formal when you say you invoke, like I'm only allowing this energy to be with me right now. I think of it less as invoking than reconnecting, integrating – coming back into focus.

KaeliMo: I like to think of it more as inviting, not expecting them to be there. It's weird for me to think about a relationship where it would be, "You're here if I want you to be here." It's good to have boundaries where you can say, "Here's where you're not welcome." But it's also like, "Now my door's open, if you want to come in, it's cool."

Natasha: Invoking means bringing a request for deities or energies to be present. It means calling on energies and beings greater than myself for support and wisdom

Dusky: When I invoke, what I'm really doing is connecting with something that is already there – remembering it, getting back in touch. I've always identified closely with water, so when I invoke Water what I'm doing is more poignantly establishing my connection to water.

Why do you do invocations?

Lucy: Invoking the elements and spirits and so on creates a container for great magic to be done. It's necessary because once that energy is created it needs somewhere to go – the things we invoke can help us send that energy into the world.

Dusky: The times that I do what I'd more specifically call "invoking" are when I'm working with something that isn't as close to me, that isn't an ally. If I were going to invoke a deity, or something more abstract that I'm less familiar with, that's when I would do a ritual, get some pageantry involved, and invoke that thing into myself or into the circle I'm working in.

Ola'i Wildeboar: Invoking is a way to honor and to receive energy from something. When invoking, whether you consider it to be a higher power or deity or even just an idea, it's a way to honor and acknowledge something other than yourself. And it's a useful way to gather the brilliance that these things can offer.

Some invocations are spontaneous, some are rehearsed.

Do you do any kinds of invocations on your own?

Ingrid: As a personal practice, "invoking" is not a very useful term. It works for me sometimes. When I think about invoking the elements, I think of it like honoring this energy. We're bringing it into our minds more presently.

Dusky: I think I do more "invoking" in my daily life than I do ritual. A good example is my spirit animal. As far as I'm concerned, he's always with me. He's a companion. But sometimes I go for days without thinking about him. When I do think of him, I get in touch with him, send out little connection threads.

Would you say you 'invoke' your animal ally, or is it just there with you?

Dusky: No, he's just there with me. If I say I invoke him, it's really just that I would be sending out connections, affirming connections with him. I do the same with everything else in my life that I'm close to.

continued on next page

RITUAL SKILLS

Invoking: Teens Roundtable (pg 2)

"When I do an invocation at the Spiral Dance, I invoke it for myself before I invoke it for everyone else."

At the annual Spiral Dance, you've danced elemental and deity invocations. What would you say you're doing there?

Dusky: Well, it's complicated. I guess I'm being a medium. When I do an invocation at the Spiral Dance, I always invoke it for myself before I invoke it for everyone else. I think of it as opening myself up as a channel. To me, that's a really powerful experience. When I did the Water invocation, I tried to become Water – I opened myself up as a conduit to Water. It's like aspecting.

Charlotte: Dancing an invocation feels like trying to embody and honor the element, the energy of Water or Fire. It's a powerful way to try to connect with something bigger than yourself. With such big concepts as the elements it's hard to put them into words.

What makes for a powerful invocation?

Sequoia: In a big group, a powerful collective invocation is going to invite participation from everyone – more of a collective effort than just a witnessing.

Charlotte: I am a big fan of moving during invocations. With dancing invocations, it's all through the body, using the body as a way to honor or respect or call forward the element. Even if I'm doing a spoken invocation I try to be moving, to align myself better with what I'm invoking.

Maeve: When there's space for spontaneity, that makes invocations powerful for me personally. I want to have some sense of what I'm going to do and what the intention of the ritual is. But really, I let myself wait till I'm in the circle to feel out what seems to be the right thing. There's an aspect of invoking that's the magic of the moment.

Sequoia: I think my favorite invocations are ones that don't go as planned. There are so many instances where I've had this poetry all planned out to invoke some deity or element, and when I get into the circle it all goes out the window. If the thing wants to be there, I think it will show you how it wants to be invited in.

What shows that an invocation has worked?

Rhys: It's pretty easy to tell when it has *not* worked because something feels off. If an invocation works, you can feel how powerful it was after the ritual is over and you understand that the invocation was part of that.

Lucy: When an invocation has worked I can feel it in my center. Especially at the end of a ritual, if I feel exhausted or am in tears I know the invocations (and the rest of the work) were successful.

Miranda: It's in your mind, your heart, your soul. Did you feel that it really came in? There's no sudden moment where you see this thing that comes up: "Oh, there's Earth!" It's just going to be, "I feel it." That's all you really have.

Talise: One way I know the elements are really invoked is when I can feel them in the presence around me. It helps to notice the air, the ground beneath you. They come to life, they stand out. Other times, someone might be talking about the elements, but it doesn't resonate with me. I get a little lost.

KaeliMo: When you're listening and you start getting answers, or you get more questions, or some kind of response. And part of it is being okay with *not* getting a response.

Ola'i Wildeboar: When something has been successfully invoked, you often aren't aware of it until the ritual is complete because you get so lost in the flow of the ritual. It is often more apparent when something has *not* been successfully invoked because you are left feeling weird, unbalanced, like something is missing. Which is opposite to the settled, balanced, complete and full feeling of a successful invocation.

Altars are good places for personal invocations and workings.

RITUAL SKILLS

Invoking

INTENT

Along with grounding and casting the circle, invoking is one of the three main things we do to "create sacred space."

The goal of this section is to help you figure out who/what/where/when/why/how you might want to invoke various spirits, beings, and energies, and to help you gain skills to use in rituals and in your personal practice.

✪ **Book of Shadows** – keep a running record of invocation ideas in your magical journal – it will help you track your magical growth, and remind you of great ideas you've tried or seen.

What Is Invoking & Why Do We Do It?

Invoking literally means "in-calling." Sometimes we say, "I'm calling in Air." When we invoke, we are calling energies, elements, deities, ancestors, magical allies, etc into our circle to assist and support us in our work.

Invoking can be serious or goofy, simple or elaborate, heart-felt words or a pre-planned skit. Sometimes invocations are rehearsed, with props and costumes. Other times they are spontaneous and tailored to suit the moment. See below for many possibilities.

Invoking is sometimes the most colorful and festive part of a ritual. People sing, dance, chant, do skits, call out spontaneous poetry – with the support of the whole circle. It's not exactly a performance, but it can be a chance to play with those kinds of skills.

Before We Start – A Note on Devoking

At the end of a ritual, we usually "devoke" anything we invoked – this is handy to know ahead of time!

Devoking means releasing anything we called in, thanking energies and entities that have worked with us. In Reclaiming and other traditions, we wrap up rituals by devoking whatever elements/energies/allies we called in, usually in reverse order.

However, at WitchCamps and retreats, we often invoke elements and allies for the entire event. At the end of each ritual, we go through the devoking order, but instead of saying, "Hail and Farewell," we say, "Thank you and goodnight." The next ritual, we re-invoke and welcome them again. At the final camp ritual, we fully devoke everything (the wrangler reminds us – see below).

A quick rehearsal helps craft a crisp invocation.

Devocations are usually short, and echo the invocation – if you invoked with a song, devoke with two lines. Speed things up by devoking all five elements with one song (such as When We Are Gone – see Ritual Skills: Chants Resources).

Ritual Wrangler keeps track of invocations and reminds people when it's their turn to invoke or devoke. At a week-long WitchCamp, the wrangler may be the only person who remembers everything that got invoked through the week.

continued on next page

RITUAL SKILLS

Invoking (pg 2)

Who/What Gets Invoked?

Who and/or what are we calling in? That's up to each ritual and each person.

Elements get invoked at almost every ritual – often individually, but sometimes all together with a song.

At many rituals, spirits of the land are honored – we thank the place where we are holding our ritual. The Fey (faeries) are often honored as well (although not always "invoked" – see below regarding "what we don't invoke.") And at Redwood Magic Family Camp we make sure to invoke (ie, to honor and welcome to our circle) the redwood trees all around us.

Goddesses, gods, and ancestors are often chosen because they can help with the specific working we plan. If we are using a myth as a camp theme (for instance, the myth of Inanna's Descent to the Underworld), we would probably invoke various deities involved in the story (eg, Inanna, Erishkegal, Ninshubar, Enki...).

For a harvest ritual we might invite Demeter (Mediterranean goddess of grain). For a Spring Equinox ritual we might invoke the Green Man or Flora or the maiden goddess Persephone.

We also sometimes invoke natural beings like the Sun or the Ocean, and energies such as Commitment or Justice.

Invocation rehearsal, or a game of magical charades? Maybe both?

Gender Complexities

In ye olden dayes (ie, before the early 2000s), Reclaiming and other traditions tended to "balance" gender energy by invoking one goddess and one god. This was sometimes seen in an alchemical sense of uniting "opposite" energies.

More recently we have discovered that gender is a lot more complicated than binary, male/female oppositions, and our invocations have reflected that (see Intro: Gender).

When we worked with Theseus and Ariadne and the Labyrinth, we invoked the Minotaur so we'd have other options besides male-female – in one version, Theseus marries the Minotaur while Ariadne sets up a thread shop on Naxos.

Do People Really Believe This Stuff?

Are deities – gods and goddesses – real? It depends on what you mean by real...

Some people think of gods and goddesses as independent beings that we invite to assist us for a specific working.

Others say they are archetypes, or parts of ourselves that we call forward (so Loki might stand for trickster energy within me).

Still others see deities as names for energies in the world (so Aphrodite might represent the spirit of romantic love).

And honestly, a lot of people don't give it much thought, period.

Sometimes people wonder – if I don't believe in deities, is it okay to work with them? Sure, but be careful – they may not take kindly to you not believing in them! (Anyway, ask yourself – can I really "not believe" in a deity if it might simply be seen as a name for a type of energy?)

At teen retreats, we have explored invoking "energies" rather than deities. If we want playfulness in our ritual, why not call it directly instead of calling a god like Pan? If we want to honor the Sun at Solstice, why not invoke it directly instead of calling on Helios or Amaterasu? The answer is up to each person and each ritual (see below, Ritual Skills: Invoking Deity and Energy).

continued on next page

RITUAL SKILLS

Invoking (pg 3)

What about the elements? Some say we are calling elements and their qualities into our circle – others say, "No, they're here all along, and all we are doing is acknowledging them." Some see the elements as guardians of our magical circle.

In Reclaiming, we find all these and other views. Reclaiming doesn't have an official thealogy that tells us what we are supposed to believe. We each have to figure it out on our own. Or not.

A fun way to explore these issues is to do spectrums, which let us see the range of experiences and opinions in our community (see Workings: Spectrums of Belief). Sometimes we start a camp or class with this working as a way of recognizing the diversity of views within our circle.

What Don't We invoke?

Is there anything we do not invoke? Generally we're careful about invoking deities and ancestors from traditions where we don't have ancestry and/or training. With some traditions we want to avoid "cultural appropriation" – borrowing practices from other cultures. This is the case, for example, with African American or Native American traditions, which have been oppressed and appropriated in many ways by the dominant society we live in.

We're careful about invoking deities and ancestors and then not working with them in the ritual. If we invoke Cerridwen and Her Cauldron of Death and Rebirth and then don't mention her during the rest of the ritual, we may be asking for trouble.

In recent years, some WitchCamps including Teen Earth Magic have moved away from invoking traditional gods and goddesses at every ritual. In particular, we mostly no longer invoke one god and one goddess – an older Neo-Pagan pattern that implies that there are only two gender options, and we need one of each to have a complete ritual. We especially try to avoid stereotypical gender prejudices such as "gods are rational and adventurous, goddesses are intuitive and nurturing."

For more on these topics, see Intro: Gender and Intro: Cultural Appropriation. For more on invoking various sorts of deities, allies, and energies, see the following pages.

The Fey – we don't "invoke" the Fey unless we're sure we want faerie energy running unpredictably through our circle – sometimes we *honor* the Fey, setting a bowl of honey or shiny coins some distance from the ritual circle as an offering.

When Do We Invoke?

In Reclaiming and many other traditions, invocations happen just after the circle is cast. First we ground ourselves and cast a circle – then we invite allies and energies to assist our work.

Having a standard invoking order makes it easier to do group ritual. No one needs to be in charge – we all know that Fire follows Air, and that allies come after elements. When doing your own magic, you can do it in whatever order works for you.

Here is the invocation order for a typical Reclaiming ritual, beginning after circle casting. We start with the elements:

- East/Air
- South/Fire
- West/Water
- North/Earth
- Center/Spirit
- Allies: spirits of land / ancestors / Fey / deities / energies (order can vary)

continued on next page

RITUAL SKILLS

Invoking (pg 4)

Where Do We Invoke?

We usually invoke within a sacred circle that has just been cast. The circle holds the deities and energies that we summon, and helps keep out unwanted energies during the ritual. That way, we can call Demeter for a harvest ritual without getting the entire Greek pantheon tagging along.

In old tales, legendary magicians called in angels and demons from within a magical circle which protected them from the awesome powers the spirits might unleash. If the magician dared to step out of the circle (tempted by the demons, of course), their soul could be lost forever.

Lost souls have not proven to be a major concern in Reclaiming rituals. For us, it's a question of focus, of choosing which energy we want in a particular ritual. By invoking specific deities and energies within a sacred circle, we get a more focused working.

How Do We Invoke?

The Sufi poet Rumi says there are hundreds of ways to kneel and kiss the ground. There are nearly that many ways to invoke.

Each person will have ways of invoking that work for them. Some like to chant, some to dance. Some like spontaneous poetry, some want to plan every word. Try different methods and find what works for you – see the following pages for ideas.

Each ritual or class will have its own mood – one might be playful, another somber. A ritual at a street protest might be quick and crisp, while a Fall Equinox ritual may be relaxed. The invocations will help set this tone.

In a group – invoke in a bold, loud, clear voice. When someone begins too softly, we call out: "Say it, sister/brother/comrade!"

Ask for help – before invoking, take a deep breath and think of what you are invoking. If it's Fire, ask Fire for assistance – "Help me call you into the circle with power and grace!" Let yourself flow with Fire energy as you invoke.

Re-ground yourself after you finish an invocation (or any ritual working).

Practicing Invocations

- Watch experienced people invoke. What do you notice that is different than when you do it? Sometimes it's simply a matter of confidence – they step out with no apologies or mumbled excuses – they just take a breath and dive in.
- Practice invoking an element such as Air which is already present – try closing the door and "singing Air" or "dancing Air" – relax and do whatever your body or spirit wants to do when you think of Air.
- Learn (or invent) an Air chant – sing it over and over, until you're singing it without thinking. What else comes into your mind? How do you feel when you move as you sing?
- Play with Air (or another element) – hold your breath, then exhale as loudly as possible. Breathe quickly, calling out an Air-word between each breath. Use a notebook to waft air over your face.
- Try invoking qualities or moods. Can you invoke a good mood? Can you summon creativity, or relaxedness, or sharp focus?
- At the end of this article are a bunch of ideas for ways to invoke. Try a personal "invocation lab" and see what appeals to you.
- Sometimes in a class or path we practice invoking each element in a different way. Here's an outline from a Witchlets path:
  - Air = circle-poem (go around three times, with each person saying one word each time to create a poem).
  - Fire = group movement with no words – how does Fire move?
  - Water = personal check-in plus the chant, (The Ocean Is the) Beginning of the Earth.
  - Earth = look around and name one Earth-object you see – at the end, welcome them all.
  - Center = human knot game ending in a group hug.
- ✪ **Book of Shadows** – after invoking, do you notice anything different? What ways of invoking work better for you? Are there any that didn't seem to work for you, but still intrigue you? What might help?

continued on next page

Invoking (pg 5)

Ways to Practice Invoking

- **Dance/movement** – spontaneously dance or move for each element – can you dance a quality (anger, peace, confidence)?
- **Sing or rap** a song or chant (See Ritual Skills: Chants later in this chapter for lots of ideas).
- **Pop songs** – find a pop song for each element (use your intuition to match them) – play each one for a minute or so, letting yourself listen, dance, space out, or whatever you want while it plays. At the end of each song, say welcome to the element.
- **Flocking** – someone makes sounds and movements related to the element, others pick it up. This is a simple way for others to show support for a new person doing an invocation.
- **Draw a tarot card** from the related suit and enact it (eg, for Air, draw a sword-card and act out the image – Swords = Air, Wands = Fire, Cups = Water, Pentacles = Earth, Majors = Center).
- **Tools of the elements** – use a Blade to invoke Air, a Wand for Fire, a Chalice for Water, and a Pentacle for Earth. Center is a challenge – what tool or object would invoke Center for you? (See Workings: Tools for more on this.)
- **Props** – a simple prop can amplify your actions – a blue scarf for Water, a peacock feather for Air...
- **Scavenger invocations** – explore your space and find an object for each element, beginning with Air – use your intuition to tell you what fits. When you find it, stop and look at it, touch it, etc. Then say welcome to the element, leave it, and move on.
- **Invoke in silence** – especially when working alone or in a small group. Name the element, allow a minute of silence, and then quietly say welcome.
- **Snappy invocations** – practice crisp invocations. If you're speaking, what are the fewest words that can do the job?
- **Science brain** – think about each element, starting with Air – ask yourself what you know about that element from science classes, the internet, etc. Think or speak about the element for a minute, then say welcome and move on.
- **Create a skit** that shows/welcomes an element or ally. How might you welcome compassion, self-expression, or confidence?
- **Goofy invocations** – how much energy can you raise by invoking in goofy ways? What if small groups each do the craziest element invocation they can come up with? How will you work with this energy once you've stirred it up?
- **Write a really good invocation** – then set it aside and speak spontaneously. Afterward ask – did the advance-writing help?
- **Go online and read about gods and goddesses** – Wikipedia is a good place to begin. When you find a deity you want to learn more about, stop and invoke them before reading further – ie, ask the deity to help you learn about them. When you finish, remember to thank (devoke) the deity.
- **Participation** – can you find ways that others can participate in your invocation, rather than you "performing" it alone? Can you invite people to call out words, to make sounds or movements?
- ✪ **Book of Shadows** – write about your invoking experiments – if you're in a circle, compare notes when you get together.

A Few Notes for Youth Teachers

- Teachers and older teens can model different ways of invoking.
- Don't push teens to step out alone unless they want to.
- Involve teens in invocations for path or rituals by pairing a couple of young people with a teacher/mentor.
- Ask small groups (maybe affinity or check-in groups) to do an invocation.
- Ask for volunteers ahead of time – then circle up for a few minutes and brainstorm ideas – let people inspire each other.
- Try invoking energies in place of deities and see what happens – see Ritual Skills: Invoking Deities & Energies.
- Have a fast way of invoking – a "short form" – that you can use when energy for circle casting seems low. A simple song that calls all of the elements can sometimes lift spirits more than laboring through five spoken invocations.

RITUAL SKILLS

Invoking Elements

Elemental magic – working with Earth, Air, Fire, Water, and Spirit – is the basis of Pagan rituals. Reclaiming shares with many other traditions the practice of anchoring our magical circles by invoking sacred elements for each quarter (and Center too).

In some traditions, elemental "guardians" are summoned to stand watch at the edges of the circle. An echo of this practice can be heard in The Guardian Song on our Let It Begin Now album.

Other folks see invoking the elements as a way of honoring the material world in which our ritual is taking place. What better way of anchoring our work in the real world than to take some time to notice the air around us, the fire of the Sun, etc.

Then again, some people just like the chants we sing when we invoke elements. Nothing gathers our invoking voices quite like Sweet Water or The Welcome Flame.

An Entire Book & Elements Chants Too!

We could write an entire chapter, or even an entire book, about invoking and working with the elements.

Fortunately, some other Reclaiming folks already did!

You can immerse yourself in elemental magic by reading Elements of Magic: Reclaiming Earth, Air, Fire, Water, Spirit, edited by Jane Meredith and Gede Parma. For more info, see page 102.

And it may not surprise you to learn that Reclaiming folks have written and/or recorded more than a few chants honoring various elements.

Some, like Air I Am or Earth My Body, quickly summon all of the elements. Others, like Rise with the Fire or Born of Water, devote a whole song to one element.

Elements chants: WeaveAndSpin.org/playlists.

Working with the Elements

Invoking the elements is a great place to begin practicing invocations. After all, it's pretty hard *not* to have Air present in our circle. It's more a matter of honoring and acknowledging the element than laboring to bring it present.

Sometimes an Air invocation can be magnificent poetry – what's more airy than words and ideas?

Other times it can simply mean taking a moment to notice and appreciate a fresh breeze wafting through the meadow where we've gathered.

Make friends with the elements – they are one ally that will always be there for us!

✪ **Book of Shadows** – look at the list on page 83 and try invoking Air in various ways.

Which ways work for you, and which are empty actions? What helps you feel the presence of Air (not just "air," but "Air")?

How would you help a group invoke Air together?

Tools of the Trade

In Reclaiming and other traditions, each element is associated with various other "magical correspondences," such as tarot suits, colors, and compass directions.

Each element also has a corresponding magical tool, such as the athame or the chalice – for more on magical tools and correspondences, see Workings: Tools of Magic.

Elements of Magic - Classes Online

Elements of Magic is Reclaiming's intro class. Some regions offer local classes, and World Tree Lyceum teaches online:

Bay Area & North Bay: BayAreaReclaiming.org/classes

Worldwide contacts: Reclaiming.org/worldwide

Online classes: WorldTreeLyceum.org

RITUAL SKILLS

Invoking Ancestors

Ancestor work is at the core of many magical and spiritual practices. In some traditions, knowing and honoring your ancestors is one of the first steps on your spiritual journey.

In Reclaiming, our biggest ritual of the year, the Spiral Dance, is held at Samhain – the time when the veil is thin between the worlds of the living and the dead.

Some ancestors are related to us by close genetics – by "blood," we say.

Others have raised us, or helped shape the culture in which we have lived and grown.

And some ancestors are just downright difficult....

Ancestors of Your Bloodline

The most familiar ancestors are members of your own family who have crossed over. Maybe it's a grandparent who taught you a favorite recipe or a vanishing skill, or a beloved aunt or uncle who took you camping.

Some have lost members of our immediate family. Others have never known our blood family or ancestors.

Regardless of which relatives we know, all of us have an ancestral line stretching back through history to the beginnings of our species (and beyond).

Known and unknown, these ancestors made us who we are.

The bodily presence of our ancestors may have passed. But their spirit can be very present to us. Remembering their love for us can be a great support in difficult times.

With practice, we can learn to summon them into our circle, to converse with their spirits and gain the strength and wisdom – and hopes and challenges – they have to offer us.

How will you invoke a grandparent whom you clearly recall?

How will you summon the spirit of a more distant family ancestor whose name you do not know?

What things about your family background (known or imagined) call you to learn more?

Ancestors of Craft & Culture

Do you have a favorite author from the 1800s? A playwright from 1600 that you think is the greatest? A jazz singer from the 1920s that you sometimes just have to hear?

Or maybe it's an unnamed wise woman and healer from the fifteenth century, or an alchemist from ancient Egypt?

People from our cultural past are our ancestors. Some, like Jane Austen or Will Shakespeare, we know by their own words. With Bessie Smith, we can listen to her recordings.

With others we may have only a vague idea about who they were and what they did – yet we yearn to know more.

The internet can be a powerful magical tool. So can casting a circle and invoking the ancestor's presence.

How would you call Jane Austen into your circle? How would you create a channel for her spirit to reach out to our realm? Readings? Food? Music?

How would you summon an herbalist who healed many neighbors, but died without leaving an enduring trace? Maybe it would involve gathering and smelling various herbs, drinking tea, visualizing a flowering meadow....

Invoking a beloved ancestor can be as simple as saying their name and a few words of appreciation. Remember to say thank you (ie, devoke) at the end of your working.

Invoking and working with difficult forebears may be the beginning of the healing.

The Unquiet Dead

Calling beloved ancestors of your family or culture can be rich work – although even the most amazing and delightful ancestor might present us with an unexpected challenge.

But other spirits are more problematic.

What about ancestors who participated in genocide and slavery, or who colluded in atrocities such as the witch hunts?

What about the ancestor who abandoned their family, or the great-grandparent who abused their children?

These, too, are our ancestors – the unquiet dead.

They, too, have shaped our lives. They, too, have lessons for us. They call to us, not only to avoid their errors, but to help heal the damage and pain they left behind. This may be part of our work in this lifetime.

Invoking and doing thoughtful magical work with these difficult forebears may be the beginning of the healing.

Altars & Workings

Do you have family photos? Prints of old artworks? Dried herbs or flowers? Words that remind you of someone? Tending your altar might be a way for you to connect with your ancestors – and a way for them to reach out to you.

RITUAL SKILLS

Invoking Deities, Allies, & Energies

A Teens Roundtable

One of the ongoing discussions and experiments at Teen Earth Magic, Witchlets' Teens Path, and other youth camps is our relations to deities – gods, goddesses, and mysterious ones – and the myths and stories that have grown up around them.

Some WitchCamps work with myths and deities from older traditions. Does this speak to you?

KaeliMo: Yeah! Sometimes I get the feeling with Reclaiming, when we research deities and stories that go back a long time – Celtic and Greek mythology and things like that – it is really an ancient practice. We might be doing something really differently than was originally done with it, but it appeals to me.

Charlotte: I don't think at TEM we've ever invoked a specific deity, have we? I don't work with deities that often. I find it hard to connect with deities except within a workshop space with a mentor, someone who has worked with this deity in the past. That's helped me connect with a wisdom or other energy.

Dusky: I don't believe in deities in a literal fashion. I work with deities in a metaphorical way. Using Pan as an example – nature is a huge part of my belief, but I don't believe in Pan as a god that exists as we've heard about him. But there's a flip side to that – if enough people believe in something, in some way it becomes manifest – not physically, but in this psychic, spiritual way.

Mykel: I love old stuff. If I wasn't already a Pagan and I wasn't already gay, I'd probably run away and become a monk – because of the discipline and the structure of it, that feeling of an unbroken lineage of lives of purpose. I think there's a lot of meaning in going back and looking at traditions and what people have been doing for a really long time, and reconstructing that in some way.

What does it mean to reconstruct an older tradition?

Mykel: I feel like Neo-Pagan ideas are connected in spirit to things that have been happening for a long time. But the idea that witchcraft could possibly mean the same things to us that it did to people in Europe hundreds of years ago – I don't think that's true – and I don't think we need that to have legitimacy. You take what works and leave what doesn't, and really own that we're creating something new – it's about self-determination.

What is your relation to the Goddess or deity?

Mykel: I don't work with "the Goddess" specifically, but sometimes if I'm freaking out, I have a sense of something big and powerful and universal supporting me, holding me – that's my experience of the Goddess.

Ingrid: At first deity was easier for me to understand than invoking "nature." You see gods and goddesses represented in books with human features – it was an easier way to have a first step toward interacting with energies – they have their stories. Whether or not we believe they are true, we attribute qualities to them.

Dusky: For me, deity is *not* human. Why should deities that govern all of nature be humanoid? That doesn't make sense to me. A lot of deities are humanoid, though, so working with them always seems a little odd. And when you do invoke a humanoid deity, they are, like people, complex. Pan is a nature god. But if we invoke Pan, we're also invoking a lot of other things like sexuality into our ritual, and we don't necessarily want that.

Ingrid: When I think of deities like Pan I think of everything I've read when I've gone to Pagany websites. Deity may be beyond human – but at the same time deity has a fair amount of qualities that are very human. And I find humans really confusing! So I'm way happier to chill out with nature. It's much less confusing at this point in my life.

Sequoia: I like having deity-specific rituals. I think they make me feel the most Pagan – I love those "Stonehenge moments!" But I find deities to be tricky. It's easy to get kind of academic about a deity. I start to go through a list, like what do I know about their energy, what are they like, what are ways I can interact with them? It prevents any kind of energetic exchange. I'm trying to "know" too much, and not allowing space to feel and interact.

Do you ever invoke the Goddess?

Mykel: As far as invoking, Spiral Dance is probably the only place I've been where we invoke "the Goddess" – it's pretty different than what we usually do at Teen Earth Magic. But I always love the Goddess invocations (at Spiral Dance) – they're always so big and joyful.

continued on next page

RITUAL SKILLS

Invoking Deities, Allies, & Energies

A Teens Roundtable (pg 2)

KaeliMo: It makes sense because of the scale of the Spiral Dance. With so many different people, invoking "the Goddess" makes sense as a unifying thing. But if I were doing my own ritual, invoking the Goddess might seem really intense and not exactly what I was looking for.

What about specific deities?

Maeve: It's a mixed bag for me, depending on the ritual. If I have more time to prepare for an invocation, or have spent time working with a story that has a specific deity, I really love doing deity invocations. Something about the complexity of deity and the spontaneity – you don't know what aspect of that deity is going to show up!

Miranda: I used to do it more when my mom was part of a coven that did a lot of work with them. I like working with them because they have a specific purpose, like "I am the Goddess of Love!" – a very specific purpose that they can help with.

Talise: I haven't done much work with deities, but I have enjoyed it in a group setting. I agree with Miranda, they have certain qualities that you can work with.

KaeliMo: I work sometimes with the Fey, and with Pan and Hecate. With a deity, I think of what they might represent to me at that time, and I focus on that – that's my way of opening the door. I say, "This is why I am interested in exploring things you might have to share."

What's difficult about working with deities?

Ingrid: Invoking a specific energy, deity, whatever? I feel like I'm less specific in my practices. Less organized might be a way to put it.

Charlotte: I feel like I don't know enough about deities. I don't know if I'm in the position to be working with them or if I am doing this deity justice by invoking them and asking their guidance. Is this the right energy for what I need? I get kind of caught up in the semantics of it.

Mykel: I'm not comfortable invoking a deity I'm not already tight with. I feel like I don't know a deity if I just have one person's version – like, "This is the Goddess of the Sea." I feel like where I really get the essence of a deity is when I hear different people's versions – what they all have in common, or the gaps – that tells me a lot more about them than a detailed explanation.

Natasha: I feel like deities are further away from everyday life than ancestors or energies, which have more of a place in the greater society. Deities are a lot of the time written off. We have less acknowledgment of their power, which for me makes it harder to connect without guidance – a class or working with other people in on it.

Charlotte: It's easier to feel more connected with something like the elements. You can be walking down the street and see the ocean or feel rain, and you're like, "Oh, Water!" But you're not often walking down the street and go, "Ah, Hecate." Unless you're crossing the street, I guess!

KaeliMo: I'm more inclined to invoke allies than deities, especially deities I don't already have a relationship with in my personal practice. When I'm sorting out personal or emotional issues I'm more likely to invoke allies that I have already created relations with.

What sorts of things do you mean?

KaeliMo: Usually it's animals or plants – on my own I tend to create space and work with one thing like a plant and sit there and listen and see what I can learn from it. I feel like at TEM we do more with spirits of the land or the Fey than with deities – things that are smaller, so you have a more personal experience. Things which are more specific to you and your place.

What's an example of a spirit of the land?

KaeliMo: Redwoods have incredible significance to me. I have a personal and tactile relationship with redwoods. I've done a lot of magic in the redwoods, and we call the same places home. They have an intense physical presence – it's like they hold the rest of the forest. It's one of the profound connections I've discovered. I've invoked them at college in Ohio, because the redwoods aren't there. There's a kinship with redwoods, a home feeling.

What's it like to invoke an animal or plant ally?

KaeliMo: With plants, I find that working with them takes a lot of patience – things are a lot slower and more detailed. It's never occurred to me to invoke a plant when I'm moving. I don't tend to do it with words – it's a non-verbal communication. Then I notice whatever feeling I might get in response to that.

continued on next page

RITUAL SKILLS

Invoking Deities, Allies, & Energies
A Teens Roundtable (pg 3)

Ingrid: I feel like Reclaiming lends itself to exploring deity and interpersonal relationships, but I haven't worked out how well it works for me to connect with nature. You want me to invoke a tree? I like that idea, but I have no idea what it means. I'm sitting here and it feels like there's nice energy coming out of the tree. I enjoy it, it's calming – that's my experience.

Do you work with other allies like ancestors of blood or craft?

Hilary: Sometimes I do it without thinking about it. I show up for a grieving friend, and I may not "cast a circle," but there's a circle there, and allies are there. There are some allies that I work with formally and have altars to, plant allies or ancestor allies that came to me in some trance a million years ago. And I'll be standing next to someone I dearly love, and they're going through something, and I'll feel this energy come up behind me, and I'll be like, "Oh, I see what this person needs right now!"

Sequoia: I think the most powerful allies are ones that are physically with us in the space. Like here with these trees that have witnessed so much, I get some of the deepest connections I can have in any space. Calling creatures that are here, and ancestors of the land – those are often the most potent allies.

What about invoking a specific energy like groundedness or perseverance?

Ingrid: Invoking a certain energy has definitely worked for me.

Dusky: Invoking a specific energy or emotion or idea – that's internal magic. When I invoke perseverance, I'm telling myself I'm going to persevere. And that works really well. Having a group of people do that together strengthens that commitment, because you're not only committing to yourself – you're committing to everyone else.

An invocation at Solstice in the Streets. See page 148.

Maeve: I love invoking energies that are simply named, like invoking our "innocent brave hearts" the first night at Witchlets this year. By combining what those words mean to us – "innocent, brave, heart" – it creates something that you wouldn't have been able to imagine if you hadn't connected the words.

Sequoia: I think invoking something like "innocent brave heart" allows for an individual experience within the ritual. It's not as definite as a character in a story. It sets up an energetic intention. That's what we do when we create sacred space – we build this "church" that we then energetically customize. It's a space that's more about personal journeys and growth than worship.

What is the difference between invoking a goddess of love, versus simply calling 'love' as an energy?

Miranda: I think calling in "love" is a very broad term. There's so much to love – romantic love, I love my best friend, I love my parents and sibling, I love the Earth, I love doing an activity. But if you call on Aphrodite, she has a more specific type of love. I think most deities have a more specific purpose – they usually help with a specific purpose within this big giant bubble of "love."

Talise: I agree. All around the world are different deities that have to do with love, yet they all are slightly different. It's about bringing that unique deity into the circle.

Pop Quiz: Who Is the Goddess, Really?

Who is the Goddess, really? Find our answer by listening to the chant by Moonrise – part of our Spiral Dance playlist at WeaveAndSpin.org/tem-chants.

RITUAL SKILLS

Invoking Deities – Gender Issues

A Teens Roundtable (pg 4)

In ye olden Neo-Pagan tymes, such as Reclaiming rituals prior to around 2000, people aimed to "balance" magical energies by invoking one goddess and one god.

Around 2010, the Spiral Dance ritual added a trans deity invocation, and also an "activist goddess." The 2018 ritual invoked Justice for the deity invocation, along with a song for the Egyptian goddess Ma'at.

The journey continues!

It seems like gender is a complicated part of working with deity.

Sequoia: As a non-binary person, it sometimes irritates me that gender is where all the energy goes. I think it dissipates the energy. If we want to invoke a specific goddess, why do we need a god every time? Or if we're trying to have an interaction with a god, maybe the goddess needs a break. Or maybe we're having an interaction with a genderless deity. That's great, too.

Maeve: I've moved away from the need to have a binary counterpoint. It feels too attached to gender being the only balance-point. If you want to counter-balance, why not have a different energy, or focus on aspects of a deity's nature that are not their gender.

Sequoia: It's essentialist.

Maeve: Yeah, it's essentialist. So I appreciate being in a space where we can challenge older traditions that say, "We must have a goddess, we must have a god."

We ask, what is the purpose of this magic? Maybe this particular ritual doesn't need a deity, it just needs an energy. Maybe in this particular ritual we are going to engage with the land at a really visceral level, and that is the magic, that is sacred.

That brings up the idea of working with stories of the land, or nature-based stories.

Mykel: I find that working with non-human stories is more bendy – it bends a lot of our binary ideas around gender, and also identity – one's identity as an individual, even. There's the approach that Free Camp and Teen Earth Magic have taken, not so much working with pre-existing folk tales, but focusing on the land and life cycles of beings in nature – stories that are more grounded in "right now," and not so much engaged with archetypes and folklore.

I'm excited about taking these modes of engaging into any story – looking at modern myths and stories that have not passed into folklore yet. It has the potential to open up all sorts of stories, and not just the kinds we've explored so far.

To bring questions of gender and power and relation to the land into all kinds of stories?

Mykel: Yes, I think there's really interesting stuff that can happen in all these spaces. It's interesting to explore the wisdom in finding women's agency in a story where it has not been told that way, or finding the queer and the trans and other things where you don't usually see it. It shifts the story, or shifts your perspective. It's the work of finding the power in the story that didn't seem to have anything there for you.

Sequoia: It allows each person to value and experience deity in the way it comes through for them.

It means treating myths like they're living stories – asking how they're alive for us.

Mykel: I think that's part of how Reclaiming approaches stories – there's faith that there *is* something in the stories for you, no matter who you are.

Interviews by George Franklin.

Gender, Deity, & Power: Persephone

One of the stories I think about is Persephone and Hades. I've heard conversations asking where is Persephone's power – as a survivor, or as somebody who has chosen Hades?

Different people might have different ideas about what pieces of the story have power and for whom, but the conversation is never, *is* there a place for Persephone's power in this story?

– *Mykel*

For more on gender issues, see Introduction: Gender – an interview with Mykel Mogg.

TeenEarthMagic.org

RITUAL SKILLS

Invoking Deities, Allies, & Energies

INTENT

In Reclaiming and many other Neo-Pagan groups, it is traditional to invoke one or more deities – gods, goddesses, or mysterious ones – as allies for a ritual.

Deities are sometimes part of a myth featured in a ritual or camp; sometimes they seem especially suited for the work at hand; sometimes they have seasonal or sabbat associations; and sometimes they just strike the planners' fancy.

Deities can carry multi-layered associations – cultural history, psychological challenges, interpersonal dynamics…

They bring myths and tales which can be fashioned into the "arc" of a WitchCamp or class (see Ritual Skills: Theme and Arc). By building a series of rituals around a story such as Inanna's Descent to the Underworld, our workings become a mythical journey.

Extra Baggage: Gender, Violence, Appropriation…

Deities bring a lot of baggage! Old versions of myths, stories, and fairy tales often involve unchallenged hierarchies, assumptions, and oppressions. Many deities are fitted into male/female pairs, and their stories revolve around stereotypical gender roles – men are active and enterprising, women are passive and/or malevolent, and no other options exist.

Myths often involve deceit, cruelty, and violence against women and children.

Some stories and deities carry issues of cultural appropriation – what does it mean to "borrow" a myth from an African American or Native American tradition from which the dominant culture has already stolen so much?

Reclaiming and others have worked to "reclaim" our cultural heritage and re-shape it for today. Gender-bending roles, unexpected alliances (eg, Ariadne and the Minotaur), resistance to violence and oppression, and creative solutions to age-old challenges have refashioned some myths for our time.

Other times, we've explored ritual and magic without invoking traditional deities and myths. Approaches have involved invoking the mysterious ones, energies, and spirits of the land.

For more on these topics, see Intro: Gender, and Intro: Cultural Appropriation.

Invoking the mysterious ones puts us outside the traditional male/female, god/goddess binary systems.

It allies us with all those who live their lives outside of usual expectations and boundaries, and it strengthens those parts of each of us that yearn to break free.

The Mysterious Ones

Who or what (or where or when) are the mysterious ones? Some say they are aspects of deity and spirit that transcend human understanding. They might be beyond species, gender, age, race…. beyond all of our usual categories. When we call the mysterious ones, we acknowledge that divinity is a mystery that human consciousness cannot fathom.

Invoking the mysterious ones puts us outside the traditional male/female, god/goddess binary systems. It allies us with all those who live their lives outside of usual expectations and boundaries, and it strengthens those parts of each of us that yearn to break free.

How do we invoke the mysterious ones? It's up to each person. How would you call "mystery" into your circle and your life? How would you show that you honor parts of reality (and of yourself) that you do not understand?

Deities vs Energies

At one of the early TEM camps, we invited teens to help plan a ritual (a step forward at that time!). People signed up to cast the circle, invoke elements, teach songs – but when we asked what deities they wanted to invoke, we drew a blank.

continued on next page

RITUAL SKILLS

Invoking Deities, Allies, & Energies (pg 2)

We tried reframing the question – what *energies* would you want to invite into the circle for this ritual? Presto! Everyone had ideas: playfulness, commitment, journeying, soul-sharing…

We could have said, "You want playful energy? Let's invite Pan. You want a journey? Let's invoke Inanna." But it didn't connect with the magic of our circle. Why not just directly invoke the energies we want?

Sometimes we choose a couple of specific energies and create invocations for them. We invoked playfulness by having small groups do ridiculous elemental invocations – it worked!

Other times we invited everyone to call out types of energy they wanted to see in the circle, then stirred them all together.

At Bay Area rituals in recent years, it's not uncommon to invoke a deity alongside an energy, such as Demeter and Compassion, whereas in years prior we might have invoked a god and a goddess.

Who knows what we (and you) might be invoking in another 20 years?

Spirits of the Land

Some ask: Why are we invoking gods and goddesses instead of directly working with nature?

At an early Redwood Magic ritual, seeking deep magical allies, we invoked the World Tree, the Green One, and Artemis the Huntress – but someone had to interrupt to remind us to pause and honor the actual redwood trees encircling us.

While planning a Witchlets tarot working, someone asked: "Why not send people to sit with a tree and do nature divination? If we can read a picture on a card, why can't we read the bark of a living tree?" (See Workings: Divination: Nature Readings.)

At TEM, we've moved toward working with stories of the land rather than older Pagan myths. The life cycle of the Chinook Salmon or the Monarch butterfly have provided the framework for our rituals. (See Ritual Skills: Theme and Arc.)

We also try to remember to invoke and/or thank the actual beings of the land we are on – trees, plants, animals, rocks….

Cultural Appropriation: Challenges for Magical Activists

An ongoing topic in Reclaiming and other grassroots groups is cultural appropriation. We are inspired by and want to honor other traditions and cultures, while not cherry-picking stories and practices for our rituals.

Broadly speaking, Reclaiming rituals tend not to invoke deities from traditions that have historically been oppressed by the dominant culture, such as Native American and African-Caribbean traditions. Folks drawn to those traditions are encouraged to seek and learn from experienced practitioners rather than inserting bits and pieces into Reclaiming events.

For more on this topic, see Introduction: Cultural Appropriation.

What Works?

What works for a given group? There is no single template, but here are some thoughts:

• Invoking energies rather than deities works with a younger group or when people are resistant to "religion" and deity.

• Working directly with nature and stories of the land are a good fit for outdoor retreats.

• Traditional deities make sense at certain rituals – a flaming cauldron ritual may call out for an invocation of Brigid or Vulcan.

• One way we move beyond gender dualities is to have various people do invocations – folks of various genders might invoke a god or goddess, people of various genders, ages, and physical abilities might dance together to welcome Aphrodite, etc.

• At Beltane we've had a diverse group of people collectively invoke the goddess – each proclaiming as they dance into the circle, "I am the Queen of May!" (Of course, in San Francisco, "Queen" can mean anyone who dares to step into the role!)

For TEM and Reclaiming, invoking is an ongoing experiment. What worked yesterday might not work today. And what we dream up today might never have been possible before this moment!

RITUAL SKILLS

Invoking Allies: A Pop Quiz!
Discovering My Own Allies

✪ **Book of Shadows** – here's a chance to do some reflecting and writing. Given all of the options, who might some of your best allies be? Consider different types of allies, and write about each.

You could even invoke them before you write. It's as simple as thinking about something, naming it, and saying "Welcome!"

Don't forget to devoke when you finish: "Such-and-such, thank you for working with me today. Hail and farewell!"

Kinds of Allies

For each type, consider whether there is one particular being which you might invoke as an ally. For example, for ancestors of your culture, you might choose a favorite author from the past. For deities, you could choose a goddess that your intuition tells you might be helpful. And for types of energy, couldn't all of us benefit from invoking a bit more patience or understanding?

- Elements (magical, chemical, culinary, quantum...).
- Gods, goddesses, mythical beings, magical beings, imaginary beings.
- Ancestors of your own bloodline.
- Ancestors of your culture.
- Animal allies – favorite animals, scary or challenging animals.
- Spirits of certain places (a favorite place, your place of power, a place you want to travel, etc).
- Trees, plants, vegetables, etc.
- Astronomical bodies such as Sun, Moon, stars, planets, planetoids that used to be planets, large asteroids....
- Types of energy such as Creativity, Perseverance, Justice, Passion, etc.
- And so on!

Reflections On Your Allies

- Why (and when and where) might they be a good ally to you – what calls you to them?
- What are some favorite things about this ally?
- What do you want/need to learn about this ally?
- What is something this ally might expect from you (for instance, learn about them, follow through on commitments, etc)?
- What are some ways that you could invoke this ally:
    - (A) In a private, personal ritual?
    - (B) In a circle of like-minded people?
    - (C) When you are in public and don't want to be noticed?
- What songs, tarot cards, colors, etc remind you of this ally (and might be useful in invoking them or feeling them present)?
- Is there a word you can speak, or a place on your body you can touch, that will quickly call back this ally when you need them?

My Own Best Ally

And let's not forget our closest ally, the one that's always right there when we need support – our self!

See Workings: Allies: My Own Best Ally.

RITUAL SKILLS

Ritual Planning

INTENT

Planning a ritual can be exciting, magical, fun – and sometimes a lot of work! Planning often takes as long as the ritual itself.

Words of wisdom for all occasions: Keep it simple. Even after you've planned the ritual – go back and simplify.

Before we start planning, we sometimes do a go-round where people share why they are called to plan this ritual, what this season or ritual means to them, and any inspirations they have. This will often lead into a brainstorm about ritual actions and intentions.

Take notes. At the end of the meeting, read back through what people have volunteered to do. Then give the notes to the ritual wrangler or email them to the planning group.

What if it's a personal ritual? You can still plan carefully. Take some time to think about the magic you intend to do. Write the outline in your journal or Book of Shadows. Have it handy in case you get off track during the ritual and have to wrangle yourself.

Group Process & Consensus

Reclaiming meetings often operate by consensus. This doesn't mean that all of our decisions are unanimous – it means that when we disagree we keep trying to find something that works for all of us, or at least something we can all live with.

There is no built-in hierarchy – everyone's voice is heard, and no one can out-vote or "pull rank" over someone else (although we often leave the details to folks who will actually carry out the decision).

Sometimes when we're stuck in a decision-making process we have to compromise – but other times a new inspiration will burst out that excites the whole group. This is consensus at its best!

For more on consensus and group process, see the handbooks at DirectAction.org/handbook.

Intentions – What Is a Ritual Intention?

A ritual intention is a short statement of why we are doing the ritual and what we hope to accomplish. The intention reminds us of the challenges we face and the action we will take. Often a priestess reads the intention during the welcome at the start of the ritual, and then the whole group repeats it three times "to make it a spell."

Some years at California WitchCamp, each day's intention is inscribed in beautiful calligraphy and posted outside the dining hall. At the week's final ritual, a priestess re-reads the intentions one by one and offers them to the fire.

Intentions are sometimes a sentence stating what is at stake and what change we want. Here's the intention from the 1981 Spiral Dance:

"Remembering the dead and the threatened Earth, we reclaim the power of magic to transform despair into hope and action."

Sometimes the intention is short and to the point – the shortest ever for a San Francisco Reclaiming ritual was at Summer Solstice 2011: "Rekindling."

Here are a few more examples of ritual intentions:

- From scarcity to abundance, we share the possibilities of our harvest (see Workings: Harvest Stations)
- Celebrating the diversity of our dreams
- Reclaiming the Commons and its bounty as our birth rite (and our birthright)
- With our ancestors, we weave the web of connection to protect and regenerate life's resilience
- Unite and press on!

continued on next page

RITUAL SKILLS

Ritual Planning (pg 2)

Intentions – first or last?

Some people say that when you plan a ritual, the first thing to do is come up with the intention – then find the workings that fit. This is especially true for one-time, focused rituals such as political actions, coming-of-age rituals, or healing rituals. For instance, activists planning a ritual as part of a protest often know the political intention of the action beforehand.

Other times, we start by talking about what sort of working we want to do – maybe we collectively envision a bunch of people in a sunny meadow, milling about and sharing magical thoughts, going on a journey, then talking in small groups. After we know what we're doing, we craft a verbal intention that fits our ritual.

Teen Earth Magic rituals are part of our magical arc for that year (for examples, see Ritual Skills: Theme & Arc), and we determine ahead of time what the general intention of each ritual will be – for example, we decide whether a particular ritual calls for "seeking allies and community" versus "journeying into the deep unknown" versus "making a commitment."

Sometimes we build the ritual around specific workings: an ally circle, a night hike, transformational theater...

Whichever way we start, in the end we want two things: (1) a clear idea of the magical work people will be doing during the ritual, and (2) a clearly stated intention.

Planning the Tofu

The core of our ritual will be the magical workings, or the "tofu," as it is sometimes called (in ye olden tymes it was known as the "meat" of the ritual sandwich – today we honor our vegetarian roots).

Usually the tofu is one major working, sometimes paired with a second, shorter working. So we might do a meditation that leads us to a question or challenge, followed by an Overflowing Cup Spell that reminds us of the abundance of our resources.

At TEM, we sometimes begin with specific ideas of workings we want to do – a trust walk, a night sit, or a labyrinth working – and our task is to weave these workings into the ritual arc as best as we can.

You'll find dozens of ideas for ritual tofu in the Workings section of this book – and inspiration to create your own.

Keep It Moving

Use small groups, milling, wagon wheels and stations to keep energy moving (see pages 175-179).

Remember to balance active exercises, games, etc with quiet bits. Use songs and chants as transitions from one activity to another. If there's enough room and people, do a spiral dance after the main working to empower the magic.

Things to Remember

See next page for some ritual roles you'll need. You'll also need to decide how to create sacred space.

Figuring out how to create sacred space is often the last thing we do. Since the outline is the same at most Reclaiming rituals, we already know many of the roles we'll need to fill – grounding, casting the circle, invoking elements, etc.

What about deities and other allies? Think about what magical support your specific ritual needs – goddesses and gods, energies such as creativity or sustainability, allies such as a local animal or plant.

Balance – think about your group or community and its special interests and needs – in the Bay Area, we've learned that the old-style "gender balance" of invoking a goddess and a god excludes an increasing number of people who identify outside of binary genders. Recently some Reclaiming groups have begun invoking the mysterious ones as a way of honoring deities who don't fit into the "god versus goddess" box (see Ritual Skills: Invoking Deities and Energies).

Depending on the workings, we might want a really strong circle, or need to save time by invoking the elements with a song.

continued on next page

RITUAL SKILLS

Ritual Planning (pg 3)

Ritual Roles

Priestesses – priestess is a role, not a person or gender. It's the word we use for anyone who fills a magical role at camp or a ritual. Most rituals have multiple priestesses – we might speak of a fire priestess, invoking priestesses, a spiral dance priestesses – even a cleanup priestess.

Ritual roles rotate, so in classes, camps, and community rituals anyone with a little experience can take a priestessing role. In solitary work and personal practice, each of us is our own priestess.

Sometimes we use the word as a verb: "Who is going to priestess the cauldron working?"

Sometimes priestesses lead a working – usually by guiding or suggesting rather than imposing their will on others. Rather than saying, "Everybody close your eyes," we might say, "I invite you to close your eyes."

Other times, priestesses hold space while participants do their own work. A priestess at a Water station (see Rituals: Stations Format) might wear a veil and repeat a watery phrase over and over as people come and go from the altar.

Graces – magical ushers who help things flow smoothly. Graces might welcome people with a purification by sprinkling drops of water from a bundle of herbs, or slip out of the circle and hide Ostara eggs at Spring Equinox. They also help in subtle ways like joining in group invocations, taking hands for the final spiral, etc. Some people prefer this role to being a priestess.

Dragons – in some public rituals we have a few people who watch the circle's boundaries – letting passersby and bystanders know that they can join us, that we are drug and alcohol free, discouraging photographers, etc.

Deep Anchor – this is an advanced role. In some rituals, one or two people act as deep anchors. They sit silently to one side of the circle, usually veiled, and meditate, tapping into the deep flow of the ritual's energy. Sometimes they will later report back to the planners about what they noticed. After their time as anchor is complete, a wrangler or tender will help them devoke that role and return fully to themselves. (Sometimes we also call logistics priestesses "anchors" – and they may need tending too!)

Wrangler – we use this term in two ways.

(1) Someone who helps a deep anchor prepare for their role, and helps the anchor fully return to the mundane world afterward – they wrangle the anchor's energy. This role is also called a tender.

(2) A person who keeps track of roles, songs, and timing in complicated rituals. The wrangler quietly cues people – especially for devocations, when people are tired and have to remember their places in reverse order. In a big ritual, this person should not have any other roles. You are basically the magical stage manager!

Other roles to remember:
- Ritual space prep/set-up/beautification
- Who will bring tables and maybe a pop-up canopy for outdoor rituals?
- Teaching chants (see Ritual Skills: Chants: Teaching Chants)
- Firetending (see Ritual Skills: Firetending)
- Pass the hat (at community rituals)
- Holy sacred clean-up crew

Step Into the Flow

One of our favorite chants (by Ana Moffett) goes, "Step into the flow and then I let it go..." – a good guide for ritual priestessing!

Just before the ritual begins, all priestesses gather, ground, and do a quick talk-through – the wrangler reminds us as needed Then we take a breath, step into the flow, and let it go...

RITUAL SKILLS

Ritual Theme & Arc

INTENT

The goal of a ritual theme and arc is to weave together a series of rituals, workings, and exercises into a journey that lasts the length of the class, camp, or retreat.

For many camps and classes we choose to work with a myth, fairy tale, or natural theme. Witchlets in the Woods has tended to use classic myths and fairy tales (see following pages).

Teen Earth Magic has favored nature-based and activist themes. We've based our camps on the life cycle of the Salmon (a native species of our region), on the journey of the Monarch butterfly, and on the Pentacle of the Great Turning (see Workings: Pentacle of the Great Turning).

Redwood Magic Family Camp has taken nature-based themes and crafted kid-friendly stories – "myths" for our times.

Whatever the basis of our camp theme, the "arc" divides the story into a half-dozen segments that follow the outline of the narrative. The segments inspire the themes of the rituals and morning paths – so when the protagonists go on a journey, we do a journey ritual. When they face an inner obstacle, we do shadow workings.

Walking the labyrinth – Ariadne, Theseus, and the Minotaur – Witchlets 2012.

For instance, with the Journey of the Salmon, segments included birth, swimming downstream, exploring the mystery of the ocean, and hearing the call to return home. Can you see how these could be the basis of a series of rituals and workings? Which do you think was the "deepest" working? (See the end of this section for the full Journey of the Salmon story.)

PREP – CHOOSING A THEME

It's great to have wide participation when choosing the camp story. Witchlets has several discussions before making the final decision. TEM sometimes has a gathering where locals can take part in discussions, and out-of-towners can email suggestions.

Before we begin debating the merits of various stories, we talk about what we want in general from our camp theme or story. People might suggest things like "liberating our society," "no gender stereotypes," "a journey of some sort," or "a series of challenges." Then we think about stories we know (or can imagine) that have some of these attributes.

Once we have some ideas, we take a break – sometimes a month or more between meetings – and let the ideas percolate. People can do additional research, talk about why they like one story or another, share problems they see, etc.

And they can start suggesting "ritual arc" ideas for a story. People say things like, "this story has a journey to the underworld, which will make a good trance," or "this story includes a labyrinth, which we could use for a major ritual."

Finally planners and teachers choose the story for the coming year – sometimes with a little bargaining about future years.

PREP – CREATING THE ARC

Once you've chosen the theme for your retreat or class, delegate a small group to draft an arc. This is a good job for three or four people, not a big group. Then bring it back to the planning group, get feedback, and hopefully everyone can consense on it.

continued on next page

RITUAL SKILLS

Ritual Theme & Arc (pg 2)

Some things we think about:

- A ritual arc should deepen the magic, not be a rigid structure. Let the story inspire you, not shackle you. Adapt the story and arc to the work you want to do.

- The opening ritual helps people feel welcome and included in the circle, and begins to immerse us in the entire story. For the Salmon story, the opening ritual focused on our awakening into a "school" of fish, all starting the journey together.

- Morning paths are good times for discussions, nature explorations, and projects. Night rituals are good for mystery, allies work, and trances. Arc planners think about this back-and-forth flow.

- At a camp with four or five nights, we often leave the last night for the talent show – a nice way to begin to transition back to our daily lives. This means our most intense ritual – the journey into the deepest mystery, the working we expect to be most challenging – is the second-to-last night. Arc planners keep that in mind as they look at the story.

Facing the "Minotaur" at the center of the labyrinth – Witchlets 2012.

PREP – GENDER, VIOLENCE, & WEIRD ENDINGS

What do we do about issues such as gender (male/female fairy tale couples whose life-goal is to get married and live happily ever after), or the violence and abuse (often against women or young people) that is central to many stories?

In a word – we "reclaim" the stories. We realize that myths and fairy tales are living stories. They have existed in many forms in the past, and we have the power to reclaim and reshape them for our times.

Roles can change. Genders can change. Characters can act differently – and can question or challenge their "fate," just as we can in our own lives. In our camps – and in our world – we can write the latest versions of the old stories.

Example: Ariadne, Theseus, & the Minotaur

In the ancient Greek story, Theseus (archetypal adventurous male hero) comes to the island of Crete to slay the horrible Minotaur (archetypal monster) who is imprisoned in cruel King Minos' labyrinth. Minos' daughter Ariadne (archetypal damsel is distress) longs to escape from Crete. She falls in love with Theseus and helps him navigate the labyrinth. Theseus kills the Minotaur, and the lovers escape King Minos' clutches together (although in the old versions they do not live happily ever after...)

We really like the labyrinth (who doesn't?), the call to fight injustice, and the way Theseus and Ariadne need one another as allies to have any chance of success.

But we weren't so happy with the Minotaur getting killed without getting to tell its story. We also wanted Ariadne to take a more active role, such as coming up with the plan and persuading Theseus to join her, not just assisting him.

We asked – Do Theseus and Ariadne have to fall in love? Do they need to be hetero? Must they even be male and female? Or could they simply be two young people who make an alliance to fight injustice?

Do they need to kill the Minotaur? Is the Minotaur really a monster after all? What is our personal "Minotaur" that we find when we travel to the center of the labyrinth? Maybe no one has to kill anyone! Maybe there's a creative way to outfox King Minos. Can Ariadne, Theseus, and the Minotaur find a win-win-win solution?

continued on next page

RITUAL SKILLS

Ritual Theme & Arc (pg 3)

THEMES & STORIES – Examples from Teen Earth Magic & Family Camps

Our California family and teens camps have worked with all sorts of stories and myths. Themes at Witchlets have ranged from ancient myths such as Demeter and Persephone, to Medieval romances like the Grail or Thomas the Rhymer, to fairy tales such as Sleeping Beauty or The Twelve Wild Swans.

Themes at TEM have included the life cycles of local species such as the Salmon and the Monarch butterfly, and magical workings such as the Pentacle of the Great Turning and Journey of the Bard. Each of these themes was built into a "ritual arc" to help shape the rituals of that year's camp (see preceding pages).

Sometimes the camp story is told in great detail – this is common at Witchlets and Redwood Magic, where a portion of the story is told each day. Other times the story provides a structure for rituals, but is not fully narrated. The pentacle themes don't have stories, and some people miss this part of the magic.

Myths & Stories from Teen Earth Magic, Witchlets in the Woods, & Redwood Magic Family Camp

TEM 2008	Savitri & Satyavan (Hindu)		WITW 2001-03	Probably no theme for first few years
TEM 2009	Journey of the Salmon		WITW 2004	Thomas the Rhymer
TEM 2010	Pentacle of the Great Turning		WITW 2005	Quest for the Grail
TEM 2011	Journey of the Bard		WITW 2006	Rowan Hood
TEM 2012	Journey of the Monarch Butterfly		WITW 2007	Sleeping Beauty & the Thirteenth Fairy
TEM 2013	Life of the Redwoods / World Tree		WITW 2008	Amaterasu
TEM 2014	Sweet Magic of the Bee Hive		WITW 2009	Baba Yaga
TEM 2015	Journey of the Salmon		WITW 2010	Sir Gawain & the Green Knight
TEM 2016	Bears!		WITW 2011	Demeter & Persephone
TEM 2017	Pentacle of the Great Turning		WITW 2012	Ariadne, Theseus, & the Minotaur
TEM 2018	Mushrooms & Fungi		WITW 2013	The Twelve Wild Swans
			WITW 2014	Burd Jan & Tam Lin
Redwood Magic 2013	Earth: Redwoods & World Tree		WITW 2015	The Last Wild Witch
Redwood Magic 2014	Air: Raven		WITW 2016	Cerridwen & the Cauldron of Inspiration
Redwood Magic 2015	Fire: Butterfly & Phoenix		WITW 2017	Brighid & the Cailleach of the Snows
Redwood Magic 2016	Water: Journey of the Salmon		WITW 2018	The Red Mare
Redwood Magic 2017	Center: Gossamer the Spider			
Redwood Magic 2018	Earth: Randy Raccoon			

Teens Workshop Fall 2007	Labyrinths: Ariadne, Theseus, & the Minotaur
Teens Workshop Spring 2011	Nonviolent Activism Weekend with Starhawk & Dress
Teens Workshop Spring 2012	Pearl Pentacle Weekend with Seed
Teens Workshop Spring 2018	Diversity & Anti-Racism Work with Rahula & Lindsey

A Cycle of Themes

Redwood Magic Family Camp took the idea a step further by planning a cycle of elemental themes relating to native species that stretched over the first five years of camp.

The 2013 Redwoods & World Tree theme was Earth. The Raven legend for 2014 was an Air story. 2015's Fire story was Butterfly & Phoenix. And see the following pages for our favorite Water story!

continued on next page

RITUAL SKILLS

Ritual Theme & Arc (pg 4)

STORIES OF THE LAND – Examples from Our Camps

Many Reclaiming WitchCamps work with myths and traditional tales. Myths of Inanna, Persephone, Freya, or Cerridwen, and tales like Sleeping Beauty, Thomas the Rhymer, or Tam Lin have formed ritual arcs for many camps over the years.

Several newer and younger Reclaiming camps have focused more on stories of the land, including Free Cascadia WitchCamp, Teen Earth Magic, and Redwood Magic Family Camp. These camps have had some overlap of teachers and campers, and have swapped camp themes back and forth.

Teen Earth Magic teachers developed the Journey of the Salmon for our 2009 camp (see next page). The story was used at Free Cascadia Camp, Redwood Magic, and also in a local Bay Area class taught by TEM and Free Camp teachers.

The ritual arc for the Journey of the Monarch was crafted at Free Cascadia Camp, and brought to TEM by FCWC teachers. The Pentacle of the Great Turning was also created at Free Camp (based on Joanna Macy's work) and later brought to TEM.

Other nature-based themes were developed at Redwood Magic, which in its early years wove stories rooted in the Northern California ecosystem combined with magical beings such as the World Tree and the Phoenix (see previous page for complete list).

Here are notes on a few stories of the land we've used, plus the full Journey of the Salmon story.

Journey of the Monarch

Monarch butterflies migrate through many areas including Northern California. Their intuitive navigation and their transformation from caterpillar to butterfly (with the mysterious period in between) mirror our own deep desire to burst free, and the beauty of what comes forth results in rich themes for magical workings.

Life of the Redwoods / World Tree

Redwoods are a communal species. Many trees spring from common roots, and the entire forest interweaves its roots and canopy. For the World Tree, a myth common to various cultures, we worked with the Norse idea of the Lower, Upper, and Middle Worlds. This allowed us to interweave nature and mythical magic.

Journey of the Salmon

Ritual planning table amid the redwoods at Witchlets.

Salmon are born in the upper reaches of many West Coast rivers. Soon they migrate downstream, eventually transforming from fresh water to salt water breathers. Salmon travel vast distances through the ocean, then at some point feel a "call" to return to their fresh water homes and give birth to a new generation.

As you'll see from the following narrative written for TEM 2009, our goal was to divide the story into a half-dozen segments, each of which could be the basis for a distinct magical working.

For instance, our journey downstream as young Salmon led to workings that explored our hopes and dreams. The transformation to salt water and the journey into the vast ocean were rituals of mystery and unknown changes. The urge to return home was our call to our own deepest truths and dreams, while the journey upriver, swimming against obstacles and strong currents, was seen as our struggles to bring our dreams to birth in the real world.

As you read the Journey of the Salmon (next page), see if you can follow the magical arc of the story. Then see our brainstorm notes on the following page for ways that we've woven the story into our camp.

RITUAL SKILLS

Ritual Theme & Arc (pg 5): An Example
Journey of the Salmon

This story was crafted for TEM 2009. See preceding pages for discussion of how this story can be worked as a "ritual arc" – the paragraphs correspond to a series of rituals and morning paths (and see our brainstorm notes on next page).

We begin far to the North, in the pristine mountain streams surrounded by madrones and manzanitas and round gray boulders with unnaturally smooth, alabaster-like surfaces.

In this sanctuary, the Salmon come to life, born out of the eggs left in these cool streams. Like the Salmon, we gather to create a sanctuary, a pool where we can come together to bond and share our stories.

When the time is right, the Salmon begin their journey downstream. Growing with every little rivulet and fin-stroke, we learn that each new estuary that might seem like a turning away from the path, or a period of stasis, is completely necessary in order for us to have accumulated the skills and stature that we need in order to make it through the challenges ahead of us. We dive into the flow of our journey and experiment with new identities, ideas, and ways of doing things.

Once the Salmon reach the delta, this period of experimentation takes on a more urgent timbre. As waves and waves of unbreatheable salt water merge with the sweet fresh waters of the rivers, they find themselves in a place of intense transformation. Their bodies change rapidly in order to prepare for the next chapter of their lives, preparing them to go out into the deep darkness of the ocean's depths. We learn to understand cycles, to investigate how our bodies transform and grow, and how to navigate the tricky brackish waters of transition.

The ocean is a place of mystery. No one really knows where the Salmon go or what they do as they undertake the long journey across thousands of miles of uncharted sea sand. This is a time of testing, of self-sufficiency and empowerment. We delve into the shadows and the unseen, learning to trust ourselves and our intuition. And in doing so we begin to hear a call from far away, yet one that also rises from deep within ourselves. It grows and grows within us until it becomes impossible to ignore. We turn and follow the song of our destiny, of the legacy of our ancestors, of our own hearts.

The song continues to lead us, mile after mile, back to the rivers from which we came. As we return to our communities, we bring with us the lessons and nourishment of the ocean, all that was once thought to have been lost downstream. We return abundance to the wider community of bears, madrone and manzanita trees, people, osprey, and the river herself. We find ways to engage our fully empowered selves into the healing of the Earth.

We swim unerringly through the labyrinth of streams and rivulets, upstream and over dams. We return to our true homes – whether it is the place of our birth or a place in our heart – and take the steps needed in order to leave a legacy of healing and connection to the circle of life for future generations.

Created by Riyana & Jason Scarecrow for Teen Earth Magic 2009. In addition to being reprised at TEM in 2015, this story has also been worked at Free Cascadia WitchCamp and at Redwood Magic Family Camp.

RITUAL SKILLS

Ritual Theme & Arc (pg 6)
Details of the Salmon Story: A Brainstorm

Here's our brainstorm for the various rituals and paths, based on the Journey of the Salmon theme.

Sanctuary (Saturday night ritual)
- Schooling up – who am I? What called me here?
- Milling exercise
- Creating sacred space, the sacred container
- Group altar
- Group agreements
- Questioning and uncertainty
- Getting acquainted / bonding / name games

Swimming Downstream (Sunday morn path)
- Skills building exercises
- Stations exercises – multiple challenges
- Team building
- Experimentation
- Building confidence
- Trying things on / possibility and potential
- Masks / identities / projections

The Delta (Sunday eve ritual, Monday path)
- Transformation
- Gender – body changes and transformation
- Physical changes necessary for the next stage of life
- Salt-water trickery
- Salt-water scrying
- Getting ready to step into the unknown
- Mirror work during the day time
- Where do we end on Sunday night – leave it as a question, unresolved: "What do you need to do to be ready to swim into the deep unknown depths of the ocean?"
- Feature transformation part of story at evening ritual, and the preparation to head into the depths during the day on Monday, plus the first part of the ocean topics.

At the River (Monday afternoon field trip)
- Magic with water, healing the waters, healing ourselves
- Calling back the Salmon
- Salmon altar
- Dams / environmental destruction of the Yuba River

The Ocean (Monday night ritual)
- Power and self-sufficiency, testing ourselves, going into the great unknown
- Nature sensing or attuning (nature divination, awareness, tracking, etc)
- Authentic voice exercises, learning how to hear it
- What are my special talents?
- Dams and watershed issues
- Overcoming disempowerment — ally circle, group work
- Night sit, leaving them one at a time to do meditation
- Ending with the call, gathering teens with a conch, then reinforce that the Salmon (and we, too!) hear the call from deep within as a subtle yet undeniable knowing.
- Trusting ourselves and our intuition.
- Question for teens as we collect them from their solo meditation: Are they ready to answer the call?
- Emotional response to environmental situations
- Truth Mandala from Joanna Macy (at night)
- Moving through, not around, our shadows
- Being seen and not seen, like the Salmon who are dark on the top and light on the bottom

Swimming Upstream (Tuesday morn path)
- Activism, returning the abundance to the community
- Moving through adversity
- Writing a letter to politicians or local Water Boards about river issues
- Scrub-jay lines
- Physical games, teams
- Stations ritual with activist activities, other activities
- Affirmations
- Group art project

Renewal (Tuesday night ritual)
- Spawning, new life, next steps
- The world we want to leave for future generations – our legacy

Closing ritual (Wednesday final ritual)
- New Salmon going out into the world, the beginning of a new cycle, personal intention setting

RITUAL SKILLS

Two Classic Ritual Texts
plus online Reclaiming classes!

You'll find lots of books by Reclaiming authors in the Resources section at the end of this book.

Here are two key texts – one from 1979, the other from 2018 – that share basic Reclaiming magical practice.

Elements of Magic

Reclaiming Earth Air Fire Water Spirit

Edited by Jane Meredith & Gede Parma

Writers from across Reclaiming survey basic magical theory and practice in this anthology from 2018.

Echoing the structure of Reclaiming's Elements of Magic class, chapters feature meditations, essays, and practical workings around each magical element.

Reclaiming Classes Online

World Tree Lyceum offers Reclaiming classes

World Tree Lyceum offers basic and advanced magical classes online, including many Reclaiming classes.

Here's a chance to connect with others studying and working magic in our tradition.

Visit WorldTreeLyceum.org.

If you are under age 18, please tell teachers your age when you contact them, and tell your parent or legal guardian you are contacting them.

The Spiral Dance

A Rebirth of the Ancient Religion of the Great Goddess

by Starhawk

The foundational text for Reclaiming Tradition – the first Spiral Dance ritual at Samhain 1979 was the book release party.

The book, revised and updated in 1999, begins with chapters on Goddess religion and the world view of (modern) witchcraft, then moves on to discuss creating sacred space and ritual, invoking and working with deity and energy, initiation, and more.

Other Starhawk books that cover practical ritual skills for groups and individuals include:

• The Twelve Wild Swans
• Truth Or Dare

RITUAL SKILLS

Firetending Magic

INTENT

A ritual fire is more than the center of our ritual, more than the warmth and light of our hearth. Well-tended, the fire flows with the energy of the ritual – low and spooky during meditation and trance, roaring during the cone of power. Working the magic of the fire adds an extra energetic dimension to the ritual.

Firetending is a unique ritual skill – you're a priestess with a single task that lasts for the entire ritual – not to mention the time you spend gathering wood and building the fire.

Firetending for rituals is not necessarily a role for "fiery" people – a ritual is (usually) not a fire performance. Let fiery types invoke Fire, while "earthier" types do the actual tending.

Firetender is a role for one or two people. Here, we'll speak of it as one person – but two can trade off if they are in close touch. Recruiting more wood-gatherers and choppers helps spread the work out.

COMMITMENT

If you take the role of firetender, you commit to prepare, build, and tend a fire for each ritual during camp. This is a sacred commitment to the camp, to your fellow campers, and to the Goddess (and/or whatever other energies you wish to invoke as witness).

Like kitchen anchor, we usually consider this a role for the whole length of a camp. Even if you invite more people to help tend during rituals, the main firetender always anchors the fire from start to finish.

The firetender is responsible for the fire, from the gathering of the wood, through to the extinguishing of the fire at the end of the night, and everything in between. You are responsible for tools such as lighters, fire-starters in damp climates, back-up wood supplies, safety water access and buckets, etc.

Ideally, at the beginning of camp, we do a short ritual of commitment where the firetenders step into the circle, speak their commitment, and are seen and supported by the whole circle.

The first year or two, you will probably assist someone with more experience. Watch, learn, and be ready to step in on a moment's notice. The Goddess sometimes calls us quite unexpectedly, and we want to be ready to lend a hand! Ask questions – and when you think you're ready to tend for a ritual, ask to do it.

FIRE PREP – PRE-CAMP

Talk to the ritual planners and learn where the firepit will be, how big fires should be, and how long they will burn each night. All of this information will affect how much and what sorts of wood you will gather.

Confirm whether plenty of firewood (including kindling if you're not in the woods) will be at site, or you and others need to bring or gather wood (for instance, we have to bring our own wood to Solstice bonfires at Ocean Beach). Ask if there is a budget for supplies ($10-20 should do it unless you need to buy wood).

Materials – non-toxic campfire starters (very handy in damp areas); lighters and/or matches; fresh, dry newspaper and kindling (and a plastic bag to keep it dry); a large splitting axe and a small hatchet if needed; wheelbarrow to haul wood.

continued on next page

RITUAL SKILLS

Firetending Magic (pg 2)

PREP – RESEARCH DESIGNS

Even if you know how to build campfires, do a little online research. There's always something to learn.

We like "log cabin" fires because they tend to collapse inward rather than falling over like a "teepee" design. Build them with heavy base-logs and you'll have a long-lasting structure to feed wood into.

At California WitchCamp, Dawnstar and other firetenders have experimented with "Stonehenge" fires – eight-sided bases with a "tower" in the center. The layout creates fantastic multi-layered fires, but it can be hard to tend after a while, as a large mound of coals builds up.

FIRE PREP – AT CAMP

Visit your fire circle and consider doing your own mini-ritual – an offering to the fire faeries, to Vulcan, to the trees that gave their wood, etc. Magical help never hurts!

Prep – Things to Figure Out

- Figure out how big your fire will be and how much wood you will need. Then double your estimate! If it's a multi-day camp, gather enough wood the first day for two fires, just to be sure you have plenty.
- Where will wood come from? Figure out a back-up stash – where can you find extra wood quickly if you run low?
- Are there wheelbarrows or carts? A good axe? Review axe safety with any helpers, and put away axes when not in use.
- What is the emergency fire plan? Where is the all-camp alarm and phone? Where is water, hose, bucket? Where is first aid?

Prep – Things to Do

Allow time for wood-gathering and chopping. Ask for help – and let helpers know exactly what you need so they don't waste their time. Gather wood and build the fire early so you get a pre-ritual break before you light it.

Sort extra wood by size and have it handy – we stack it around the fire to create a little "firetenders' zone." Gather plenty of smaller wood too – handy for quick bursts of flame.

Keep newspaper in a plastic bag – in the woods, old news gets damp fast.

Most important – always have lighters handy! Carry a couple in your pocket all the time. Hide a couple near the ritual circle for emergencies. Stick a few extras in your pack.

continued on next page

RITUAL SKILLS

Firetending Magic (pg 3)

FIRE MAGIC – TENDING THE FIRE

Our goal – to build the fire up and down with the energy of the ritual. It's not hard to build a big fire – just use more wood. The trick is having it rise and fall with the magic.

Build a solid log cabin frame with lots of smaller "stuffing." It will flare up at the outset, then burn down. Keep feeding it during the opening invocations until you get a good hot bed of coals. Then you can let it burn lower as you reach the trance or other "spookier" parts of the ritual.

Number one firetending trick – when adding wood, lean new logs and sticks at angles so air can circulate under them. Laying logs right onto the coals just makes them smolder. If you remember this simple trick – angle sticks against one another and leave space for air under them – you'll be surprised how well your fire burns.

Steady feeding = steady fire – feed smaller amounts of wood more often to maintain a steady fire.

More light – sometimes we want light so we can see one another. Small and medium sticks make more and faster light. Have lots of small stuff on hand, because it will burn fast.

Flaring – If you want the fire to flare high (for example, during the cone of power), add a bunch of medium sticks – then take a big handful of twigs and put them on top – they'll flare up dramatically. But they'll burn down quickly – so don't peak too early, and/or have plenty of small wood ready.

Lighting the fire – check with ritual planners, who may want the fire lit at a special moment. If it's to be lit midway through the ritual, use non-toxic fire starters and plenty of fresh newspaper for a fast, sure light.

If they leave the lighting to you, here's a magical way:

Phantom fire lighting – ahead of time, place non-toxic firestarters at each end of the fire with plenty of newspaper and kindling a few inches above. When people aren't paying attention, quietly light the starters and step away – after a minute or two, the fire will seem to spontaneously combust.

POST-RITUAL FIRE MAGIC

After the ritual ends, folks might like to hang out around the fire. See Workings: Campfire Activities for some magical games.

Firetending after the ritual can be less formal – others can feed the fire. However, the main firetender is responsible for the fire until it is put out.

DEVOKING THE FIRE

At the end of the evening, the last people "devoke" the fire – we hold hands around it (sometimes in a horseshoe to avoid the smoke). Maybe we go counter-clockwise and each person says one thing they appreciated that day. Then we say thank you to the fire and blessings on all who gathered around it.

The firetender remains until the end and puts out the fire.

A classic "Stonehenge" campfire layout.

END OF CAMP

Clean up fire area – if it's not always a fire circle, return it as close as possible to its former condition. Stack or return wood.

Devoke and/or thank any faeries, allies, or energies you called on the first day. Thank the hearth for warmth and light and for being the center of the circle. Touch the hearth, then touch your hand to your center. Breathe in the fire magic to carry with you.

RITUAL SKILLS

Spiral Dance: How to Lead

INTENT

The spiral dance is our most magical way to wrap up a ritual (or a street protest, handfasting, birthday party, etc). During this simple dance, every person passes face-to-face with every other person.

The dance is usually done to an upbeat chant – see pages 112-113 for chants you can hear online.

The following are directions for the single-led spiral that we do at WitchCamps and local rituals – it works for about 30-200 people. The larger double-spiral done at the annual Spiral Dance ritual has different turns.

SPACE/TIME/SIZE

25-30 people minimum – you can do it with fewer, but the "spiral" will resemble a snake looping back on itself.

A flat, clear space large enough to make a loose circle. A central bonfire or altar is great. Takes about five minutes.

Folks who can't or choose not to do the dance can take part by sitting with the drummers in the center.

The closing spiral dance at Teen Earth Magic – under the World Tree.

LEADING A SPIRAL DANCE

Three Things To Remember

(1) Always move to your left.

(2) Always turn to face the person behind you.

(3) Once you turn, follow the line of faces to its end.

Spiral Priestess

The lead spiral priestess helps set the tone of the dance and the way people interact as they pass one another. At a camp or community ritual, we look for someone who will radiate warmth and enthusiasm – not hard to find at a teens camp!

Either the spiral priestess knows how to lead, or someone who knows the turns can go second and guide by tugs on the lead priestess's hand. If you have this role, tell the leader not to look back at you: "Keep meeting eyes, but listen to what I whisper."

Set-Up

Important – any people/stuff/obstacles must be moved to the very center or completely outside the circle. The spiral shifts unpredictably, and can't wrap around lawn chairs, trees, etc. Dogs and little kids should not be underfoot, since many dancers are not paying attention to where they are stepping. Holes in the ground should be filled.

Remind dancers to make eye contact, and to move slowly and gently. "The spiral is a stately dance," someone once said.

Chants – see pages 112-113 for spiral dance songs. This is not a good spot for a new, untested chant, or one with more than four lines. Teach song at the top of the ritual so people are ready when the time comes.

Drummers

Try to work with experienced ritual drummers, and practice the chant ahead of time. Ask new drummers to wait until after the ritual to join in the drumming. Urge ritual drummers to come to the middle – if they stand outside the circle, the energy gets lopsided. Don't have a drummer lead the spiral – leader should be someone who can focus on steady eye contact.

continued on next page

RITUAL SKILLS

Spiral Dance: How to Lead (pg 2)

The Dance

Start in a circle, all holding hands.

Sing the song through one or two times before you start moving to build some energy.

Spiral priestess frees her left hand, so the person to her left becomes the tail – a good place for an experienced priestess.

Always move to your left – clockwise as you spiral inward – always to the left.

Move slowly – your first steps will set the pace for the dance. Spiral toward the center longer than you think – with enough people, a good approach is to wait until part of the circle is three rows deep before you turn. Turning early creates a crescent and lets energy escape (sometimes unavoidable with fewer than 50 people).

A Reclaiming-initiated spiral dance at Occupy Oakland, Fall 2011.

First turn – and every turn – turn to face the person following you. This is the easiest way to remember the turns for the single-led spiral. *Always* turn to face your follower. (This is different than the double-spiral at the Spiral Dance ritual!)

Spiral back out. Keep passing faces until you reach the end of the line – you will have passed every person. Spiral priestess is now facing outward, away from the circle, moving to the left.

Continue around outside of circle, facing outward, for about one-third of the circle. Turning early creates a traffic jam.

Final turn – when spiral priestess has gone about one-third around the outer circle, she turns – as always, turn to face the person behind you. You will again be passing each person in the line.

Keep passing people, one by one. After a short while, spiral priestess will suddenly face a "fork in the road" – two double-lines are moving past one another. You may be tempted to swing outside and avoid the congestion. Don't do it!

Remember – always follow the line of faces, one by one. This will lead you back into the spiral and take you toward the center. It may seem like a narrow opening, but just keep tracing the line of faces and you'll find your way.

The Peak of the Spiral

When you pass the last person and reach the center for the second time, you're almost done – however, if it is a small group or there is a lot of energy, you may want to spiral out and back again.

Once the spiral priestess reaches the center for the final time, look over your shoulder – the end of the line will still have their backs to you, spiraling out. Keep singing and spiraling slowly inward until the entire tail has turned and everyone is facing inward. To avoid "tightening" the spiral – move slowly and keep the same person roughly behind you.

Once all spiralers are facing inward, spiral priestess and others drop hands and start clapping. Center-dancer types move inward. Energy wranglers drift outward and work the edges. All keep the chant going strong. Drummers drive the beat.

Cone of Power

Now, if the magic is right, we raise a "cone of power" – we bring the music and energy to a peak, then focus and send it to the Earth and sky – and finally draw it back into our own hearts. (See the next section for more on Cone of Power.)

Whether or not there is cone, the toning finally fades. Hold silence for a moment. Then a wise priestess can say something like, "Hear our voices echo. Breathe the power of our working. When your heart is full, return some to Mother Earth. Blessed be."

RITUAL SKILLS

Cone of Power

INTENT

Toward the end of many Reclaiming rituals, we sing a high-energy song. Maybe we do a spiral dance, or maybe it's free-form dancing around a fire. The drums drive the rhythm higher and higher, then suddenly release the beat. Singers let loose of the lyrics. The tones soar to a peak, then settle into a beautiful tone.

A cone of power is not a wild melee, nor is it perfect polyphonic chanting. It's somewhere in between.

The goal is to use our collective voices as a powerful magical tool that can raise and focus the group's surging energy, gather it in the center of the circle, and then send it off to places that need power, beauty, and healing. At the end, each participant gathers some of the energy into their own heart for personal healing and empowerment, and shares some with the Earth.

This ecstatic "cone of power" is one of the things that make Reclaiming rituals different than many other Pagan and Wiccan rituals, as well as the more traditional mainstream religions many people were born into.

Someone poking fun at different Pagan groups once called Reclaiming the "Pentecostal Pagans" – and as far as the energy of our rituals, this comparison might not be far off.

The cone can be seen as empowering our work and providing a climax to the ritual.

In small circles and classes, it may be difficult to raise a cone – especially if most people haven't ever been part of one. If so, let the singing fade gently. You can still "ground" the energy at the end – it just won't have the ecstatic quality of the cone.

Attending a WitchCamp or the annual Spiral Dance or Beltane rituals in the San Francisco Bay Area is a way to experience a cone of power. Once you've been part of a cone, it makes it easier to show others how to do it.

The cone of power at the end of the final spiral dance at the 2006 all-Reclaiming Dandelion Gathering in Massachusetts.

You can get an idea of a cone of power by listening to the last minute of the song Rise with the Fire on our Chants: Ritual Music album. Imagine the chaotic voices settling into a long, rich harmony, and you've got it. Links at WeaveAndSpin.org/playlists.

For more information, read The Spiral Dance by Starhawk.

SPACE/TIME/SIZE

Any number of people can do a cone, although under 20 may be difficult. More than a thousand people have been part of the annual Spiral Dance ritual, which culminates in a beautiful cone of power that reverberates for several minutes.

PREP

Clear the space of debris, backpacks, etc if you're doing a spiral dance – see Ritual Skills: How to Lead a Spiral Dance.

If you're circling around a fire, let the firetender know you want flames leaping during the cone (see Ritual Skills: Firetending).

Chant – the choice of the chant is important. Since this is the climax of the ritual, the words should connect with the theme. You'll want a short, easy-to-learn song – it's hard to raise energy when people are struggling to remember the words.

continued on next page

108   TeenEarthMagic.org

RITUAL SKILLS

Cone of Power (pg 2)

Many chants are beautiful, yet don't raise energy. How will you know? Get a few people together ahead of time to sing the song. Or if you have a recording, sing along. Start clapping to the beat. Do you get any momentum, or are you struggling to keep it going?

Here are a few proven energy-raisers from our albums (see pages 112-113 for links to these and more online chants):

- Weave and Spin
- We Are the Rising Sun
- Sweet Water
- Kore Chant (She Changes Everything She Touches)
- Let the Beauty We Love
- Let It Begin Now
- Harvest Chant (Our Hands Will Work)
- Rise with the Fire of Freedom
- We Are the Power in Everyone
- We Are Alive

WORKING – Cone of Power

This assumes you are already doing a ritual, and have grounded, cast your circle, and invoked allies. Your main working is done, and you're ready to raise energy and empower the working.

Gather in a circle and start the song. Drummers let the singing begin on its own before starting a rhythm. If you're doing a spiral dance, sing the song a couple of times through before beginning the dance.

As the song builds, drummers play stronger and fuller. Eventually people drop hands and begin dancing and clapping. Some voices let go of the words and freely tone the melody, then drift into harmonies and discords, creating a mash-up of sound. We look for a balance between singing whatever we feel, yet somehow blending with our neighbors – collectively lifting the energy higher and higher.

As the energy grows, people can help gather it by swirling it clockwise – use your hands to sweep the energy around the circle. In a larger circle, some people might start skipping or dancing clockwise around the outside of the circle.

As the singing and dancing reach a peak, the drummers (perhaps signalled by a priestess) suddenly cut their rhythm down to a simple pulse. The voices leap out. Everyone lets go of the words and tones freely.

People's arms often rise spontaneously to form a cone shape around the center of the circle. Some people might hold their arms downward to form a second cone toward the Earth.

Gradually the voices settle into a rich harmony – this may take a while in a large group. When the voices settle into a chord, let it ring as long as it will, then fade to silence.

Now – hold the silence. After a long moment, spiral priestess may quietly say: "Listen – hear our voices still ringing..."

Finally a priestess says something like: "Breathe in the power of our voices and our intention. Anchor that power in your own center and drink deeply. When you are full, return the rest to the Earth."

People often touch their own center for a moment, then kneel, ground their energy, and bless the Earth.

What's next? Usually the cone of power follows the final working of the ritual. The food blessing and devocations begin when people are finished re-grounding. At the annual Spiral Dance ritual, the chorus sings a gentle hymn while the crowd relaxes for a couple of minutes.

SOLO WORKING

Doing a solo cone of power will depend on your ability to do a spiral dance and sing three-part harmonies by yourself!

If that sounds daunting, you have some choices. You could attend a family camp or WitchCamp, or a San Francisco Bay Area ritual. Visit WitchCamp.org and BayAreaReclaiming.org for more information.

You can also do the musical Let It Begin Now ritual later in this chapter. When the title song comes up late in the ritual, join in as we sing a slow, stately chant and use harmonies and rhythms to raise a lot of magical energy. While it lacks the final peak, you can start to feel the power of weaving our voices together.

TeenEarthMagic.org

RITUAL SKILLS

Chants: Teaching Chants to a Group

No one is born knowing how to teach Pagan chants. It's a skill we learn.

It doesn't especially matter how good a singer you are. It's about being able to clearly communicate words and melody to a circle of people ranging from operatic divas to shower singers.

Anyone who can carry a tune can do it, regardless of how "good" your voice sounds. Teaching chants and songs is not about having a pretty voice, but about singing clearly and with confidence.

Of course, that's easier said than done!

Singing in front of others is one of the hardest things people in our culture can do – and yet our voices are basic to who we are.

Later in this book you'll find a working called Voice Magic – some ways we can release tension and old hurts regarding our voices. Counseling and emotional-release work around our voices can help as well.

Don't be surprised if it takes you a while to get comfortable teaching chants. Here are some tips we've learned along the way.

TIPS ON TEACHING SONGS & CHANTS

Choosing the Perfect Chant

- Look for chants whose lyrics and mood connect to the theme of the ritual. See the following pages for resources.

- We might introduce a new or more complicated song for an invocation or food blessing – whereas for a spiral dance or to raise energy at the end of a ritual, we want a simple chant that a lot of people already know, or that is very easy to learn.

- If a chant is longer than four lines, it's hard for people to learn quickly enough to raise energy. Consider using just part of it.

Be Ready When You Step Out

- Practice a lot. Know a song in your sleep before you teach it – if you have to look at the words or think about the tune, you're not ready. Sing it fast, slow, high, low, serious, funny. Sing it looking into a mirror. Sing it with a friend teasing you.

- Teach a song alone – having two people do it together may seem reassuring, but unless you are pros, no two people sing a tune exactly alike. Hearing two voices just confuses those trying to learn the chant.

- Find a way to get your starting pitch. One way is to know which is the highest line of the chant, and sing that line to yourself in a comfortable range right before you teach it. That will keep you from starting too high. (You could also get a pitchpipe.)

- If the chant is longer than two lines, sing the entire chant alone once so people can hear it, then come back and teach it one line at a time, call and response. Then go back and sing two lines at a time, call and response.

- Finally, have people sing the song 5-10 times so the group really knows it when it comes up during the ritual. Most people enjoy singing – let's get good and warmed up!

Hecklers & Helpful Friends

- When you're teaching a song, people in the circle who already know it may join right in – ask them not to sing yet: "Let people hear one voice – it's easier to learn the tune that way."

- Someone with a loud voice may say: "You're singing too high/too low." Politely remind them that human voices are spread all over the scale, and what works for some won't work for others. If they persist, ask for a show of hands of those who found your pitch difficult to sing – only a few will do so, and you can move on. Offer to check in with dissenters after the ritual.

Here's the good news – the more chants you teach, the easier it gets!

RITUAL SKILLS

Chants: Resources Online

Chants & Songs for Rituals

Music is a key part of Reclaiming rituals and magic. Many of the workings in this book include suggestions for songs and chants. You can use any songs that seem right for your workings and rituals – when the occasion demands, we use everything from pop hits to old folk favorites.

Often we use chants written by Reclaiming teachers or like-minded people. From the earliest years, Reclaiming teachers and priestesses have crafted chants and simple songs to use in our rituals and classes. Many of our favorites are included on Reclaiming albums.

In particular, Chants: Ritual Music and Campfire Chants include many of our most popular chants. Several people from TEM sang on Campfire Chants!

Reclaiming Chants – Listen Free Online!

Many chants mentioned in this book are on Reclaiming albums. If you're doing a solo working or a small circle, play the chants and sing along with us.

Listen free on all streaming services. Search <Reclaiming Chants> and <Campfire Chants>. Downloads at CDBaby, iTunes, Amazon, etc.

Playlists for spotify & youtube: WeaveAndSpin.org/playlists

Playlists for workings in this book: WeaveAndSpin.org/tem-chants

Reclaiming chants are written by many people, including Starhawk, Suzanne Sterling, and T. Thorn Coyle. There's even one song written by Teen Earth Magic – Wheel of the Year, on Campfire Chants!

You'll find these Reclaiming albums online – with more to come:

- Chants: Ritual Music
- Second Chants
- Let It Begin Now (Music from the Spiral Dance)
- Witches' Brew: Songs From the Reclaiming Cauldron
- Campfire Chants: Songs for the Earth

Reclaiming Albums – Directly From Our Magical Circles!

Reclaiming's albums come directly from our circles. Although some have been recorded in professional studios (and others in converted garages...), the sound is intended not to win production awards but to draw you into a circle of magical song.

Chants: Ritual Music carries the sound of a Reclaiming circle or class.

Let It Begin Now features the ensemble sound of the band and chorus for the annual Spiral Dance ritual.

Campfire Chants catches the relaxed harmonies and acoustic music of a late-night WitchCamp bonfire.

Each of our albums will give you ideas for your own rituals, circles, activist marches, handfastings, birthday celebrations – and of course for singing in the shower!

continued on next page

RITUAL SKILLS

Chants: Resources Online (pg 2)

Reclaiming Chants – Whodunnit?

Our albums have been recorded by different groups of singers and writers, with some overlap. Maybe you'll help record the next one!

Chants: Ritual Music was recorded around 1990 and released as a cassette tape. Legend says that a small chorus rehearsed for a while, then recorded the entire album in one day.

Campfire Chants (2016) was recorded by folks from Witchlets and Redwood Magic. It took longer than one day. Free Lyrics & Lore booklet at CampfireChants.org.

Suggestions for Rituals and Workings

Stream on youtube, spotify, etc. Downloads at iTunes, Amazon, etc

Search <Reclaiming Chants> – or search by album titles

Playlists for youtube and spotify – WeaveAndSpin.org/playlists

Playlists for this book – WeaveAndSpin.org/tem-chants

Gathering the Circle
- Weave and Spin
- Sweet Water
- Air I Am / Earth My Body / Air Moves Us
- We Are the Flow
- We Are the Power in Everyone
- Circle Round the Balefire
- Rising of the Moon
- Wake Again

Personal Commitment
- My Soul
- Let the Beauty We Love
- Let It Begin Now
- Weave and Spin
- Kore Chant (She Changes Everything She Touches)

Earth / Activism / Empowerment
- Sweet Water
- Harvest Chant (Our Hands Will Work For Peace and Justice)
- We Are the Power in Everyone
- We Are Alive As the Earth Is Alive
- Body of the Earth
- Rising of the Moon
- We Are the Rising Sun

Invoking Elements and Allies
- All of our elements chants: WeaveAndSpin.org/playlists

Best Spiral Dance Songs (some of them!)
- We Are the Rising Sun
- We Are the Power in Everyone
- Weave and Spin
- Harvest Chant (Our Hands Will Work for Peace and Justice)
- She Changes Everything She Touches (Kore Chant)
- Sweet Water
- Body of the Earth
- Let It Begin Now
- Rise with the Fire
- We Are Alive

continued on next page

RITUAL SKILLS

Chants: Resources Online (pg 3)

Favorite Non-Reclaiming Chants

Find these chants and more on our "Non-Reclaiming Faves" playlist on youtube and spotify – WeaveAndSpin.org/playlists

- We Are a Circle Within a Circle
- Earth My Body
- The Earth Is Our Mother
- The River She Is Flowing
- Spiraling Into the Center – *good spiral dance/energy-raiser*
- Step Into the Flow – *good spiral dance/energy-raiser*
- Sweet Surrender – *good spiral dance/energy-raiser*
- She's Been Waiting
- The Earth, the Air, the Fire, the Water, Return
- May the Circle Be Open

Chants for the Streets

Many favorite chants were written for street actions – we sang some of these at the 2018 Rise for Climate Justice march in San Francisco.

All are recorded on Campfire Chants except Rise with the Fire from Chants: Ritual Music. For links, see WeaveAndSpin.org/playlists

- We Are the Rising Sun
- Sweet Water
- Rising of the Moon
- Rise with the Fire
- We Are the Power in Everyone
- Weave and Spin
- Harvest Chant (Our Hands Will Work)

Best Sing-Along Chants

The idea for our latest album, Campfire Chants, came from late-night singalongs. Chants sound different when we're relaxing around a fire with guitar and ukulele. Some work as call-and-response sing-alongs.

- My Soul – *call-and-response*
- Let the Beauty We Love
- The Welcome Flame (Spark Blaze Ember Ash)
- We Are the Rising Sun
- Cycles of the Moon
- Wheel of the Year – *call-and-response*
- Barge of Heaven (Pour It Out For Me) – *call-and-response*
- When We Are Gone – *call-and-response*
- Goodnight Sweet Witches

Two Trance Recordings – Free Online

- Way to the Well – a ritual trance journey with Starhawk
- Labyrinth Meditation Music – perfect for rituals

Find links at WeaveAndSpin.org/tem-chants

Reclaiming Chants & Songs – free online!

Listen free to our chants on all streaming services. Search for <Reclaiming Chants> and <Campfire Chants>. Downloads at CDBaby, iTunes, Amazon, etc.

Playlists for spotify & youtube: WeaveAndSpin.org/playlists

Proceeds benefit Reclaiming organizing, archives, publications, and future recordings!

RITUALS

Sample Rituals

- Way to the Well – an online trance journey with Starhawk 115
- A Ritual for Grounding & An Affirmation Ritual – two typical rituals 116
- Let It Begin Now – a musical journey with Reclaiming 124
- Labyrinth Challenges – a ritual of personal commitment 125
- Stations – building a complex ritual 130
- A Water Ritual – from Reclaiming's Elements of Magic class 133
- Opening Night At Witchlets – our original teens ritual 140
- Crafting Your Own Rituals – creating spells and workings using this book 145
- After the Ritual – around the WitchCamp fire circle! 147

The grandmama of all Reclaiming rituals – the annual Spiral Dance. The first ritual, held at Halloween 1979, was the book-release party for Starhawk's book of the same title. People liked the ritual so much they did it again, and again... and as we say in Reclaiming: "Twice is nice – and thrice makes it a tradition!" The ritual continues to this day. TEM teens have played strong roles in the ritual for the past decade, creating powerful invocations, circle castings, and altars. Visit ReclaimingSpiralDance.org. Photo from 2010 ritual, by Michael Rauner.

RITUALS

Ritual: Way to the Well

A Trance Journey with Starhawk

Let's begin by accompanying one of Reclaiming's founding priestesses, Starhawk, on a trance journey.

You'll experience the flow of a ritual – and see how simply she creates sacred space and gets on with the working!

Way to the Well – free online

Free on youtube, spotify, etc – search <Starhawk Way Well>

Way to the Well is a 45-minute drum-trance ritual in the Reclaiming Tradition. Starhawk and singers Anne Hill and Suzanne Sterling help you create a personal magical circle and explore magical wells of power, healing, and challenge.

Set aside an hour in a space where you can relax and not be disturbed. Turn off your phone ringer.

You may want to lie down or sit in a comfortable spot. (If you fall asleep, no problem – just rewind the recording and start again when you're ready.)

Have your journal and water handy, and some healthy snacks for afterward (nuts, fruit, bread).

Once the recording is ready, press pause. If you're using a computer, put a scarf over the screen.

Take three breaths and bring yourself present at this time and place. When ready, press play, and begin the journey.

At the end, take a breath, then journal for at least a few minutes before breaking the energy.

End with a breath, and say, "Blessed be" to your journey.

A Grounding Meditation

The Tree of Life Grounding by Starhawk

The Tree of Life is one of the basic grounding meditations we use in Reclaiming.

By visualizing yourself as a tree with deep roots and tall, striving branches you can anchor yourself to the Earth.

Feeling yourself grounded, steady, and fully present makes a difference anywhere, from magical circles, to personal relationships, to sports and games, to final exams.

The importance of a daily practice

Starhawk: "If you want to practice the craft – if you want to be a witch – it's important to have a personal practice, something that you do every day.

"In some traditions there's a meditation that you do, or a particular prayer that you say. In Wicca, we encourage people to *find* the practice that works for them.

"This, for me, is the basic thing that I do every day, and I find especially useful in dangerous or tense situations. It's called 'grounding.' Basically what it is, is connecting your energy to the energies of the Earth."

Youtube – search <Starhawk Grounding Meditation>.

Also on Starhawk's Way to the Well – all streaming sites.

Other Recordings by Starhawk

Available on amazon/audible and elsewhere.

Wiccan Meditations by Starhawk
• Grounding: 1:30 / Place of Power meditation: 16:38

Earth Magic – meditations and exercises for building sustainable relations with ourselves and our planet.

The Fifth Sacred Thing – Starhawk's classic novel about the troubled birth of a new world – now an audiobook.

TeenEarthMagic.org

RITUALS

A Ritual for Grounding

INTENT

Here's a simple ritual you can do alone or with some friends or your circle to strengthen your sense of grounding – of being fully, clearly, strongly present in the world. All you need is a youtube connection and some red yarn.

We invite you to do this ritual for yourself or your circle early in your practice. It might be your first working – as it sometimes is in our introductory Elements of Magic classes.

If it looks long (five pages!), that's because we're printing it all out like a script. Feel free to improvise, shorten, skim, etc to suit your own needs.

The main working is a **red cord spell** – but before doing a grounding spell, you'll want to *feel* truly grounded. We've included a link to a grounding meditation by Starhawk, or you can read the printed meditation below (or both – whatever helps you feel calm, present, strong, etc).

This ritual can help you feel what it's like to be strongly grounded in a certain moment, even if you don't feel that way all the time (who does?). Once you've done this spell, you can call it back by touching the red cord, or your own center. To strengthen it, you can repeat the meditation as often as you wish. Some people do a grounding meditation or exercise every day.

Gradually you may notice that it takes less effort to feel grounded, and more disturbance to throw you off balance.

So mote it be!

✪ **Book of Shadows** – before you create the ritual, take some time and write:
- Why are you doing this ritual at this time?
- What do you hope the ritual will accomplish?
- Are you ready to follow through and work on getting more grounded?
- What will be difficult about following through? What changes will you need to make? What sort of support might you need?

SPACE/TIME/SIZE

This is meant for one to about 15 people with enough room for a comfortable circle. Allow about an hour including some journaling time afterward.

PREP

Craft your intention – what do you hope the ritual will accomplish? Can you state this in one sentence? Write it down.

For a group – ask each person to come up with their own intention or commitment.

Materials needed – journal or Book of Shadows; red yarn or embroidery floss (3 feet per person); this book to read the grounding below and/or an internet link to listen to Starhawk's Tree of Life grounding (see previous page); healthy snacks for post-ritual.

Ritual space – a space where you can close the door or be undisturbed.

Create a small altar either in the center or on one side, on which you can place the red yarn. The altar can be as simple or elaborate as you wish.

Creating sacred space – let's keep it simple for this ritual. There are plenty of complicated rituals later in the book! Read ahead for simple ideas for grounding, casting your circle, and invoking – feel free to change and substitute as you wish. See the beginning of the Ritual Skills chapter for lots of ideas for quickly creating sacred space.

continued on next page

RITUALS

A Ritual for Grounding (pg 2)

Chants – WeaveAndSpin.org/tem-chants/
If you have internet access during the ritual, have our Grounding Ritual youtube playlist cued up. It has the music and meditation in the order you'll need them. You can choose either to use the recorded grounding by Starhawk or read the meditation below.

If no access during your ritual, download the music ahead of time – you'll find the songs listed below plus plenty of other choices. Or you can substitute songs of your own choice (including pop songs that seem to fit the mood).

Either way, have your music player and/or lyrics handy when you start.

Priestessing – for a group, decide who will priestess (lead) each part. For solo work, you are your own priestess.

RITUAL

When your plans and the space are ready, step out of the room. Get a drink. Turn off your phone.

Before re-entering, take a breath and state your intention to yourself. Step into the space.

Rock magic is another way to do a grounding spell!

Gathering Song – Air I Am (Song #1 on the Reclaiming Grounding Ritual youtube mix).

Honoring First People – take a moment and remember that if we are in North America and are not Native American, we are on land that has been taken from another People. We honor those who came before us, and renew our commitment to justice for their descendents.

Grounding – two options (do one or both)

(1) Standing (or lying or sitting with good posture) – listen to the Tree of Life Grounding meditation on the youtube mix.

(2) Read this meditation slowly, breathing deeply yet gently. Pause for a moment when you see three typed dots...

"Take a deep breath – and let it go. Grounding is the time to bring ourselves fully present. It's a chance to take some deep breaths, to relax our posture, to feel our connection to the Earth beneath our feet...

"This is called the Tree of Life. It is one of Reclaiming's basic groundings. We'll feel our personal energetic roots sink deep into the Earth, pull up nourishment for our body, and send it up into our energetic branches...

"Stand tall and loose, energy balanced, with your knees flexed. Breathe steadily and deeply... Standing tall, let each breath gently float through your body... On each inhale, draw in fresh air... On each exhale, let yourself relax... Breathe gently and steadily...

"Picture your spine as the trunk of a majestic tree... and as you breathe, let roots drop down from the base of your spine deep into the Earth... dropping down with each breath... dropping down until they reach the deep, molten center of the Earth Herself... Let your energy mingle with the energy at the core of the Earth... and with a breath, let go of anything that you don't

continued on next page

RITUALS

A Ritual for Grounding (pg 3)

need... anything that is not of this time and place... let it go into the Earth...

"With your breath, begin to draw up power from the Earth... feel the energy rising through your tree trunk... Feel the power rise up through your core... feel it filling and energizing your entire being with each breath...

"With steady breaths, draw this energy up through your body, up through your chest and neck and head... And from the crown of your head let branches sprout and reach toward the sky... let your arms rise like branches, and feel the Earth energy flow up through them... feel it drawing down the energy of the stars... feel the energy sweep through your branches and drop again to the Earth, returning to its source...

"Let the energy drop back to the Earth... now, from your own center, draw a deep breath, drawing in the energy of Earth and stars... feel the Earth and stars mix and mingle in your center... breathe in all that you need... Let it flow through you and back to the Earth...

"When you are filled with the energy you need, return any extra to the Earth..."

Allow 30 seconds – then however you have done this meditation, stop and take a deep, relaxed breath and say: "Blessed be!"

Casting the Circle – let's use a traditional formula:

Face North and say: "By the Earth that is our (my) body."

Turn to the East: "By the Air that is our breath."

Turn to South: "By the Fire of our bright spirit."

Turn to West: "By the Waters of our living blood."

Turn back to the North to complete the circle, then turn to face Center. Look up: "By all that is above."

Look down: "By all that is below."

Now say boldly: "The circle is cast – we are between the worlds. And what happens between the worlds, changes all the worlds! So mote it be."

Invoking the elements – how about a song? Try Air Moves Us on the youtube mix. Or see suggestions on pages 112-113.

Invoking an ally (or several) – if you want to invoke a deity or an ancestor, welcome them in any way you wish.

You might also want to invoke a quality such as "groundedness" or "calm presence" that will help strengthen your magical working. How will you do that? It's up to you to invoke in a way that the quality (or goddess, etc) feels present. For more on this, see the sections on invoking in the Ritual Skills chapter.

Chant – Who Is the Goddess? We Are! – on the youtube mix (and also on spotify etc), find the song Who Is the Goddess from our Witches Brew album (sung by Moonrise). You can sing it here to invoke deity into your circle.

Red Cord Spell

Priestess explains a bit about spellwork. Here's the short version – see Workings: Spellcrafting for more.

"A spell is a combination of your intention plus a physical working. When doing a spell, strike a balance between (A) being clear and specific, and (B) leaving the Goddess/universe room for creativity.

"Some cautions – in general, be careful what you ask for (you just might get it!). Beware of doing spells that affect another person – these can misfire and/or return on you, according to the Law of Threefold Return (see Intro: Curses). Put an end-term on a spell. Treat and dispose of spell materials carefully and with clear intention."

continued on next page

RITUALS

A Ritual for Grounding (pg 4)

Music – start Labyrinth Meditation Music (optional – on youtube mix).

Priestess hands out threads. Invite people to play with the string and feel it in their fingers as they meditate.

Priestess leads short meditation, touching on these points (leave short pauses after each phrase):

"What is your foundation?... Start with your body... Where is your own physical center?... Where is your body strong?... Feel your body and your senses as your unique connection to the material world...

"Tie a knot into your cord for that connection...

"Feel your connection to the Earth. Feel the pull of gravity... Breathe into your connection to the Earth... Feel the energy move up and down between you and the Earth...

"Anchor this experience by knotting it into your cord...

"Think about what gives you a sense of stability, belonging, and connectedness in your life... Is it your home?... Your family and friends?... Your work?... Tie a knot for each thing that gives you this sense of stability...

"Do you have a connection to the Goddess or to spirit?... Do you have a daily spiritual or magical practice?... Meditation? Prayer? Exercise? Gardening? Walking?... Think about ways that you are connected to the divine, and tie a knot in your cord for each way....

"For everything that helps you feel connected, that calls you back to your groundedness, that strengthens your foundation, make a knot in your red cord..."

Priestess holds silence for a few moments as people complete their knots. Then invite people to hold the cord in their hands and draw up Earth energy into it with their breath. "Feel the physical substance of the cord. Feel the knots that signify your groundedness."

Begin a low toning. In a group, others join in. Tone until it fades – keep it low, not raising energy here.

Completing the spell

Priestess says:

"Breathe in the strength of this circle and state to yourself a simple affirmation of your own groundedness...

"You may want to fasten the cord somewhere on your body. If so, fasten it with a final knot while holding in mind your affirmation to strengthen your grounding.

"If you choose to wear the thread – decide how long you will do so. Will it be for the length of this camp/class, for a moon cycle, until you go to bed tonight, until it falls off? State this aloud to yourself.

"If you do not intend to wear the cord, tie a final knot to create a circle. Decide what to do with it – will you place it on an altar, bury it in your garden, carry it in your pocket? Decide for how long."

Song: Weave and Spin – "This is how the work begins!" (on youtube mix).

Binding the Spell

Priestess leads group in call-and-response spell-binding:

> By all the power of three times three
> This spell bound round shall be
> To cause no harm nor return on me
> As I do will, so mote it be!

continued on next page

RITUALS

A Ritual for Grounding (pg 5)

Priestess reminds people: "When the spell is complete – whenever you have decided – dispose of the string magically. Thank it for its work, declare it returned to being just a piece of string, and bury or burn it.

"If you decide to remove the string before the time declared, do it magically and intentionally."

Devoking and opening the circle

We end the ritual by devoking whatever we invoked, in reverse order. Devocations can be as simple as naming what you are devoking and saying, "Thank you – hail and farewell!" If a song was used to invoke, we might sing it one more time to devoke.

Goddess – say aloud: "Who is the Goddess? I am! Hail and farewell, Goddess!"

Qualities, allies & ancestors – if you invoked any allies or qualities, now is the time to name them and say some words of appreciation and respect, ending by saying, "Hail and farewell."

Devoking the elements – let's sing one of the all-time favorite Reclaiming chants, When We Are Gone, from the youtube mix. When the song ends, say: "Earth, Water, Fire, Air, and Spirit – thank you – hail and farewell!"

Opening the circle – a simple way is to repeat the poem that cast the circle. Since it's a poem, we don't typically reverse the order of the elements and directions, but some people do:

By the Earth that is our (or my) body
By the Air that is our breath
By the Fire of our bright spirit
By the Waters of our living blood
This circle is open (clap hands once) but unbroken
May the peace of the Goddess go in our hearts
Merry meet – merry part – and merry meet again!

AFTER THE RITUAL

Now is the time for some healthy, grounding snacks – nuts, fruits, bread.

Music – you can play Labyrinth Meditation Music again if you wish. Or play our Campfire Chants album.

✪ **Book of Shadows** – this is a good time to journal for a while. If you're in a group, allow 5-10 minutes for writing and personal reflection before you start socializing.

The 24-Hour Rule – we've learned the hard way not to "evaluate" a ritual for at least 24 hours afterward. It's great to say you liked it, to compliment someone on their role, etc. But save critical or "helpful" feedback for later. Let people – especially ritual planners – enjoy the energy for a while before we start thinking about how to make it better next time.

Thankfully, there's always a next time – the wheel of the year keeps turning, and pretty soon here comes another ritual!

Blessed be.

Photo – an impromptu altar at TEM.

RITUALS

An Affirmation Ritual

INTENT

Here's a simple ritual that you (alone or with some friends) can do to affirm yourself and/or a decision you are making.

Maybe there's a project or task that you feel you could commit more time and energy to. Maybe there's someone you could try to be more communicative with.

Or maybe your affirmation is to believe that you are a good, brilliant, amazing, powerful human being! All of this is true – but sometimes it takes some work to recognize it in ourselves.

What do you want to affirm? What work calls to you?

We invite you to do this ritual for yourself or your circle whenever you feel ready. It might be your first working – or it could take place after a year-and-a-day of prep. Or maybe somewhere in between?

Before you create the ritual, take some time and consider:

- is this an affirmation that is about you and your life (not about another person whom you hope to change)?
- are you confident that it will not harm or manipulate you or others?
- are you affirming something that you are ready to follow through and work on?

✪ **Book of Shadows** – write about why are you making this commitment at this time. What will be difficult about following through? What changes in your life will you need to make? What sort of support might you need?

SPACE/TIME/SIZE

This is meant for one to about 15 people. Because each person will speak, more than a dozen may take too long. Space for a comfortable circle. Allow about an hour including some journaling time afterward.

PREP

Craft your intention – why are you doing this ritual at this time? What do you hope the ritual will accomplish? Can you state this in one sentence? Write it down.

For a group – ask each person to come up with their own intention (or commitment, etc).

Materials needed – journal or Book of Shadows; pitcher(s) of water – about one gallon for every four people (a quart per person); nice drinking cups; large bowl; towel for under bowl.

Ritual space – do you have a room where you can close the door? A garden where you won't be disturbed?

Create a small altar either in the center or to one side, on which you can place the large bowl. This can be as elaborate as you wish, or as simple as a colored cloth and a few special objects. Note – there may be some splashing water.

Creating sacred space – let's keep it simple for this ritual. There are plenty of complicated rituals later in the book See below for simple ideas for grounding, casting your circle, and invoking – feel free to change and substitute as you wish. See beginning of the Ritual Skills chapter for lots of ideas for quickly creating sacred space.

Chants – you'll find a playlist with chants for this ritual at WeaveandSpin.org/tem-chants/.

Priestessing – for a group, decide who will priestess (lead) each part. For solo work, you are your own priestess.

RITUAL: Overflowing Cup Spell

When your plans and the space are ready, step out of the room. Go to the bathroom. Turn off your phone.

continued on next page

An Affirmation Ritual (pg 2)

Before re-entering, take a breath and state your intention to yourself. Step into the space.

Gathering song – Born of Water (on ritual playlist).

Honoring First People – how will you honor the First People who lived on this land? How might you make or renew a commitment to justice for their descendants?

Grounding & Casting the Circle – two choices
- come up with your own ways to ground and cast your circle (for ideas, review the Ritual Skills chapter).
- refer back to the previous ritual (A Grounding Ritual) and use the ideas from that ritual.

However you do it, finish your circle casting by saying: "The circle is cast – we are between the worlds. And what happens between the worlds, changes all the worlds! So mote it be."

Invoking the Elements – how about a song? Try Air I Am (on ritual playlist). End by saying: "Air, Fire, Water, Earth, and Spirit – Welcome!"

Invoking an ally (or more) – try invoking a goddess or an ancestor. Welcome them in any way you wish.

You might also want to invoke a quality such as "commitment" or "dedication" that will help strengthen your magical working. How will you do that? It's up to you to invoke in a way that the quality (or goddess, etc) feels present. For more on this, see the sections on invoking in the Ritual Skills chapter.

Working – small group

Now that you've created the ritual container, it's time to affirm and bind your commitment.

Taking up your cups, gather round the bowl.

One by one, people step up and say: "I call into this cup _____ (such and such energy – eg, "I call into this cup awareness of the abundance of love around me," or "I call into this cup my own true power," etc).

Then the person holds their cup over the bowl and again names the energy they are invoking as the priestess begins pouring from the pitcher. As cup fills, priestess continues pouring and lets it overflow into the bowl until the person says, "Now."

Focusing on their commitment, the person drinks the cup of water. When the person finishes, all call out: "So mote it be!"

Song – when all have gone, bind the spell with a song: Born of Water, or Kore Chant (She Changes Everything She Touches).

Afterward – offer the surplus water to the Earth.

Working – solo

You can pour an overflowing cup for yourself. Set up a bowl and pitcher, and do each step slowly and with intention.

Begin with a meditation or tarot reading where you think about your life and what energy you would especially like to invoke.

Once you know what you want to call in, take your cup and name the energy you are invoking, then pour slowly and let the water overflow into the bowl. When you feel it's enough, focus on your intention and drink slowly from the cup.

End with a song – see ideas above.

Devoking & Opening the Circle

We end the ritual by devoking whatever we invoked, in reverse order. Devocations can be as simple as naming what you are devoking and saying: "Thank you – hail and farewell!" If a song was used to invoke, we might sing it through once to devoke.

Qualities, allies, & ancestors – if you invoked any allies or qualities, now is the time to name them and say some words of

continued on next page

RITUALS

An Affirmation Ritual (pg 3)

appreciation and respect, ending with, "Hail and farewell."

Devoking the elements – sing Air I Am three times, then end by saying: "Earth, Water, Fire, Air, and Spirit – thank you – hail and farewell!"

Opening the circle – the usual way to open the circle is a simplified "reverse" of the way we cast the circle – if I walked clockwise to cast, I walk (or swing my wand or hand) counter-clockwise to open the circle. Then we often say this together:

   This circle is open (clap hands once) but unbroken
   May the peace of the goddess go in our hearts
   Merry meet – merry part – and merry meet again!

AFTER THE RITUAL

Eat some healthy, grounding snacks. Journal for a while. In a group, allow 5-10 minutes for writing and personal reflection before you start socializing.

You may want to play our Campfire Chants album (WeaveAndSpin.org/playlists – the first tracks on the Chants Megamix).

At some point take the bowl of water to the garden or a tree, and offer it back to the Earth.

The 24-Hour Rule – try not to "evaluate" a ritual for at least 24 hours afterward. Just enjoy the energy for a while before thinking how to do it differently next time.

Blessed be.

Note – want to see this Overflowing Cup Spell as part of a more elaborate ritual? See A Water Ritual later in this chapter.

TEM teens limber up for deep magical workings.

RITUALS

Ritual: Let It Begin Now!

Someday we'll figure out how to re-create the annual Spiral Dance as a do-it-yourself Samhain/Halloween ritual, so people who can't make it to the Bay Area can take part.

Meanwhile, listening to the original music is a magical journey in its own right – and you can use the music along with this book to create a ritual in your home community.

Cue up the Spiral Dance playlist at WeaveAndSpin.org/tem-chants – and let the magic begin!

Doing the dishes versus creating ritual space

You could listen while doing the dishes or giving your cat a bath. You could listen on your way to work or school. We recommend all of these times and places.

However, you might want to create a more magical space. Lower the lighting (twinkly faerie lights always help!). Make yourself comfortable. Get your journal and a cup of tea.

New to rituals? The Outline on page 45 shows the overall flow.

Hear the Spiral Dance album and more on youtube, iTunes, etc – WeaveAndSpin.org/tem-chants

VISIONING THE RITUAL

Want to see what the annual Spiral Dance ritual looks like?

There are two youtube videos showing several minutes of highlights. Search for <Spiral Dance Ritual>, or find them at the end of the <Reclaiming Chants Megamix>.

Watch these videos, then close your eyes and imagine a community ritual that you help create. Play these songs and let your mind's eye see the ritual space.

Envision the most beautiful and powerful images that come to you – maybe someday you'll help priestess it!

Water invocation at the 2010 Spiral Dance. TEM teens often take part in invocations and anchor an altar. The Let It Begin Now album is music from the Spiral Dance ritual. Photo by Michael Rauner.

LYRICS to choruses

Lyke-Wake Dirge (first/last verse)
This ae nicht, this ae nicht
Every nicht and all
Fire and sleet and candle licht
May Earth receive thy soul

No End to the Circle / God Song
There is no end to the circle, no end
There is no end to life, there is no end

Set Sail
Set sail, set sail
Over the spray where the waves grow white
Into the night, into the night

Let It Begin Now
Let it begin with each step we take
Let it begin with each change we make
Let it begin with each chain we break
Let it begin every time we awake

Join Us for the Spiral Dance!

You can be part of the Spiral Dance if you are in the Bay Area at the end of October. If you live here, you can help create the ritual, sing in the chorus, set up an altar, etc. Volunteers are always needed.

You can also use this book and music to create a Samhain/Halloween ritual in your own community. Let it begin now!

For more info, visit ReclaimingSpiralDance.org.

RITUALS

Ritual: Labyrinth Challenges

INTENT

This ritual evolved as a climactic working at Witchlets and other teen paths – a way to pull together different threads from the week into a final working. Teens enter the labyrinth one at a time and are met by a priestess who issues a series of challenges. Each time, the person gets further into the labyrinth, until on the final visit they reach the center.

The three labyrinth challenges can be changed and modified to suit whatever issues your group has been working on.

Solo Working – we've described the ritual as we would do it at camp, with some of the older teens helping with priestess roles. Following this description you'll find a modified version for one or a few people in a small space.

Labyrinth ritual at Witchlets in the Woods teen's path. The labyrinth is created from fallen redwood branches.

SPACE/TIME/SIZE

You'll need an open space at least 15 feet square for the labyrinth, plus more space for people to spread out and create altars and do their workings. In the woods we use a small clearing with lots of trees and ferns around it.

Works for six to 15 people (a few older teens can help with priestessing roles). A larger group will have stretches of time with people waiting to begin or for others to end.

One or a few can do this working – see Solo section below.

The working will take an hour or more for a group of 10-15. When we do this as part of a path, the only other things we do that day are create sacred space beforehand plus a short concluding working – the Overflowing Cup Spell is good way to wrap up the day.

PREP (lots of prep for this ritual)

In advance – lay out a three-circuit labyrinth in a mysterious spot – or in your basement or back yard. (See end of this article for directions.)

Find a magical location – or make it magical. At Loreley Camp we laid the labyrinth inside a little chapel. To enter, a person had to knock on a heavy wooden door. At Witchlets we laid it in a redwood grove. At Vermont WitchCamp it was in the middle of a wooded glade.

Plan three workings and gather materials needed. See Workings chapter for ideas and lists of materials needed.

For the labyrinth challenges as described here, you'll need a tarot deck plus a veil or cloak for the labyrinth priestess.

Get beads or another "reward," and a pouch to hold them (plus spool of waxed bead-string – see Workings: Bead Ceremony). Labyrinth priestess holds pouch. If indoors, determine materials to use for altars, or create a different first working.

Have some substantial food ready for afterward unless a meal is about to be served.

You'll need a nearby place to gather and a group activity at the beginning of the working, so people can approach the labyrinth one at a time – a quiet game works well here.

Also use this spot for the end, and have something to hold the energy until everyone is done (eg, fire-gazing, gentle music).

continued on next page

RITUALS

Ritual: Labyrinth Challenges (pg 2)

Priestesses (at least four)

- Labyrinth priestess with robe and veil – very mysterious. This person will get very trancey, and needs tending after the ritual.
- Facilitator near labyrinth entrance for traffic flow, questions, etc. Your task is to keep things moving, yet not have five people enter the labyrinth at the same time. You'll keep track of which challenge each person is ready for – a "scorecard" helps.
- Roving priestesses (two or three) wander, answering questions, witnessing workings, etc. Roving priestesses may hold tarot decks and other tools for challenges. A good role for student teachers or for older teens who've done the working before.
- Anchor priestess for the gathering circle at beginning and end.

Labyrinth Challenges Ritual

Create Sacred Space

- Welcome / teach songs
    - briefly explain how the labyrinth challenges will work and the priestess roles
    - let people know who they can ask for help or clarification (ie, roving priestesses or facilitator)
- Grounding
- Cast circle
- Elements
- Invoke deity / energies – possibly:
    - Theseus & Ariadne & the Minotaur (possibly invoke the Minotaur as "alternate possibilities"?)
    - energies such as openness, dedication, mystery

Transition – something to occupy time as people approach the labyrinth one by one. How about a simple game – see Workings: Games for ideas. Anchor priestess anchors this space until all have begun, and later welcomes people back as they finish (maybe with quiet drumming and fire gazing).

Labyrinth priestess, roving priestesses, and facilitator depart and take their positions. Facilitator can help priestesses drop into their magical role with a few breaths. Roving priestesses bring whatever "props" will be needed for challenges (a tarot deck in this example).

A few minutes later, anchor priestess begins sending people to the labyrinth one at a time, about 60 seconds apart. Once everyone has started, this priestess can become a roving priestess until the first people are nearly finished and you return to anchor the re-gathering.

Labyrinth Working (for Class or Workshop)

First visit – one at a time, people approach the labyrinth, about a minute apart. Let's say Chris goes first and enters labyrinth. Labyrinth priestess greets her at end of first circuit (see drawing on page 129) and says, "Stop!" Then gives her a challenge.

First challenge – take 10-15 minutes to build a personal altar using objects you find. Create a magical space where you can return to do a couple of short workings.

Chris goes back out of the labyrinth, finds a spot nearby, gathers leaves, stones, and twigs, and builds a small altar. When complete, she gets a roving priestess to visit it. Priestess asks her to take a minute and describe the altar.

When priestess says, "OK," Chris goes back for her second round (others may finish before her, so order may change – facilitator coordinates).

continued on next page

RITUALS

Ritual: Labyrinth Challenges (pg 3)

Second visit – enter labyrinth again. Facilitator lets labyrinth priestess know where the person is in the process: "Chris is entering for her second challenge." Chris enters, and this time gets to end of second circuit (see drawing on page 129), where labyrinth priestess again says: "Stop!" Then priestess gives second challenge.

Second challenge – go to roving priestess, draw three tarot cards, then go to your altar and do a simple reading for yourself about a question such as, "What is one change I would like to make in my life?" or, "What is my next magical step when I get back home?" (Presumes we taught intuitive tarot during camp – see page 289.)

Chris walks back out of labyrinth (possibly silently passing others coming in). Goes to roving priestess and draws cards, goes to altar and does intuitive reading.

When Chris finishes her reading, she goes back to the roving priestess and shares a bit about her "next step" (or holds silence). Priestess says, "Okay" or, "Work a little more on it."

Once complete, Chris returns to the labyrinth.

Third visit – enter again. Facilitator lets labyrinth priestess know where each person is in the process: "Chris is entering for her third challenge." Chris enters, and this time gets all the way to the third circuit before hearing: "Stop!"

Third challenge – go back to your altar and do a short personal ritual (including quickly grounding, casting a circle, and invoking whatever elements or allies you wish) that empowers your "next step" from your tarot reading. Create one phrase or sentence that expresses your commitment. Remember to devoke and/or thank your allies at the end.

Chris goes back out, goes to altar and does a 10-minute personal ritual, creates her commitment phrase, then shares it with roving priestess (aloud or silently). When roving priestess says "OK," Chris goes back to labyrinth one last time.

Final visit: Again, Facilitator lets labyrinth priestess know: "Chris has completed all three challenges and has returned."

Chris travels all the way to the center of the labyrinth, where the priestess asks if she has completed her challenges.

When Chris says, "Yes," labyrinth priestess invites her to reach into a pouch and draw a bead (or another gift).

Chris silently returns to the original gathering spot, where a priestess is drumming to hold energy till all have finished. People are journaling or quietly gazing at candles – focused and low-key. Bead string can be available.

Transition – when all have gathered, have everyone re-ground. Then go around and let each person share their phrase of commitment (aloud or silently). Or if time permits, you may want to use the phrases as part of an Overflowing Cup Spell.

Spiral dance – raise energy to empower the pledges by doing a spiral dance or some energetic singing and drumming.
  • Song Ideas: Spiraling Into the Center; We Are the Rising Sun; Welcome Flame

Devoke in reverse order and open circle.

Afterward – have something substantial to eat. Maybe it's meal time. If not, have some fruit, bread, cheese, etc.

Remember to tend the priestesses afterward. Especially the labyrinth priestess, who will keep saying, "I'm fine, no problem, everything's amazing!" Help the priestesses re-ground by removing any magical items, scarves, etc. Have them breathe deeply, say their own name three times, then look around and name some very ordinary things they see.

Following pages – Solo Working and How to Draw a Labyrinth

RITUALS

Ritual: Labyrinth Challenges (pg 4)

Solo or Small Group Working

You can do this working on your own – even if you don't have space to draw a labyrinth. You can use the above workings, combine any three workings from this book, or create your own. In this example we'll use the same workings as the example above – an altar, a tarot reading, and a short ritual that expresses a commitment in words.

Allow about an hour, plus some time afterward to relax, journal, etc.

You'll want a comfortable place to begin and end, and some water and healthy snacks for afterward.

Music – cue up Reclaiming's Labyrinth Music, created for a WitchCamp ritual and recorded by Crow for Reclaiming's album Witches' Brew. Put the 8-minute track on repeat. Free on youtube, spotify, etc – or download it at the usual sites. Search <Reclaiming Labyrinth Music> – or find it near the end of the Chants Megamix at WeaveAndSpin.org/playlists.

Drawing a Labyrinth – for your fingers?

If you have space, follow the outline for a three-circuit labyrinth on the next page.

If you don't have enough space, or want to do this work privately, create a finger labyrinth – a small version that you can "walk" by tracing the paths with your finger. (See Workings chapter, page 231.)

Carefully draw a three-circuit labyrinth on paper – maybe in your Book of Shadows. Drawing the labyrinth is part of the magic. One Reclaiming priestess outlined a seven-circuit labyrinth on heavy paper, then as a meditation carefully drew and colored dozens of little "stones" to outline the pathways.

When complete, place it on a table or altar where you can work with it.

Choosing Your Workings

Decide on three workings that you feel belong together in a ritual. Your intuition is your best guide. Browse the Workings chapter for inspirations – or make up your own. Gather whatever materials you will need.

If you follow our example – what materials will you have handy to create a personal altar? Perhaps you already have an altar in the space you're using? Great – think about how you will change it, spruce it up, or simply honor it as part of this working.

What will be your "reward" at the end – a small talisman that symbolizes completion of the work. At camp we use beads. Choose some simple magical item that you will "receive" at the end of the working. Place it near the labyrinth, covered with a cloth.

Doing a Personal or Small Group Labyrinth Ritual

When all is ready, step out of the space you will be using. Get a drink, use the bathroom. Before you re-enter, take three breaths. Step into the space and say: "I am (we are) now entering sacred space. I am (we are) now entering sacred time."

Your ritual follows the flow described for the camp ritual above. Create sacred space (for ideas, see Ritual Skills: Sacred Space: Quick Ways). Then follow the descriptions above, or three workings you choose.

Pause to breathe and perhaps write in your Book of Shadows between each working.

At the end, take three breaths and state that your working is complete. Then remove the cloth from your bead or talisman and pick it up with your non-dominant hand. Take a breath and blow the magic of your workings into the bead. Say: "Blessed be!"

One you have devoked and opened the circle, remain in the space for a while. Have some snacks, write in your journal, listen to music, color your labyrinth....

When you finally leave the space, stop and place your hand on your center and say thank you to yourself for the work.

Blessed be!

Ritual: Labyrinth Challenges (pg 5)

How to Draw a Three-Circuit Labyrinth

This is not a common layout, but we've found it perfect for our Labyrinth Challenges ritual.

Make the paths plenty wide for this working (the distance between the lines and the points in the first figure is the width of the paths).

Note that the cross is not the center of the space.

Draw this with chalk on pavement or floor. In dirt, use corn meal – you'll need 20 (yes, 20!) pounds of corn meal to make good thick lines. Start with a thin trace – once you have your outline, use the rest to thicken the lines.

Seven-circuit labyrinth – instructions for drawing a seven-circuit labyrinth as well as other ideas for labyrinth magic – see Workings: Labyrinth.

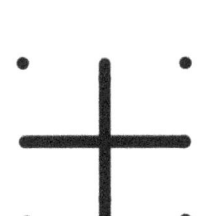
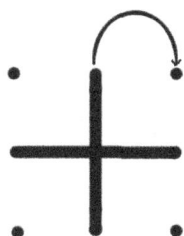

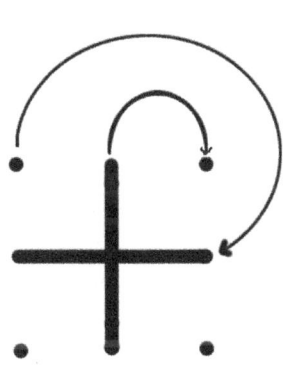
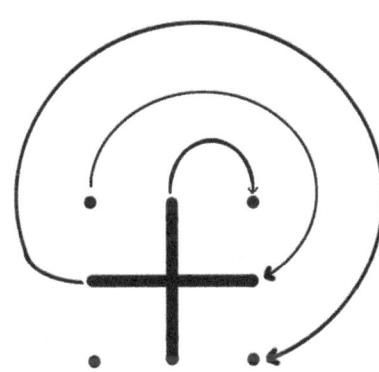
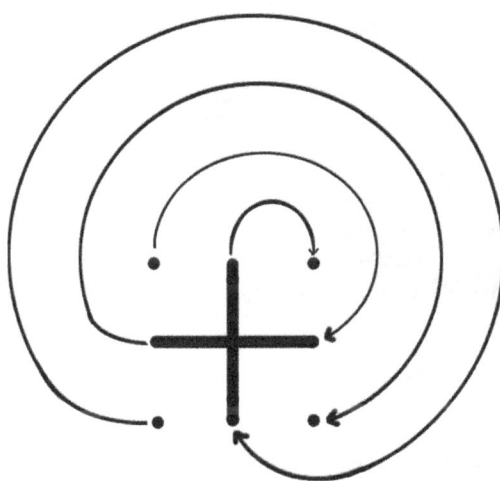

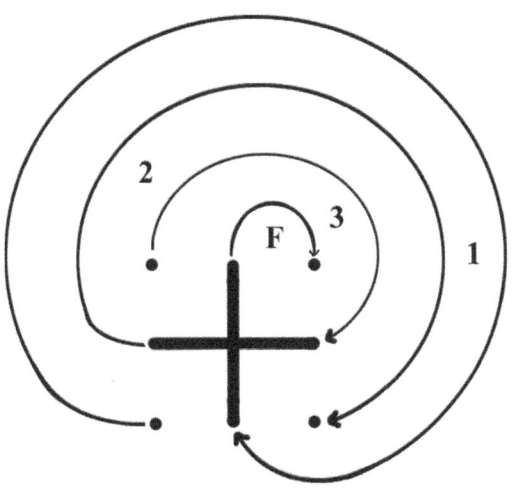

Left – Labyrinth Challenge positions

Numbers indicate position of Labyrinth Priestess for each of the three challenges plus the final position (F).

Ritual: Stations Format

INTENT

A "stations" ritual is a working in which individuals or small sub-groups rotate among several different exercises or workings. This format allows a large group to divide into smaller, more intimate groups and do exercises that require a tighter circle.

Many exercises work best in groups of about 8-12. At Teen Earth Magic we might have 20-30 people. On a stations day, we begin and end the path or ritual as one circle. For the specific workings, we divide into smaller groups and rotate among three or four workings.

Multiple workings requires more priestesses – ask older teens if they want offer or co-anchor a station.

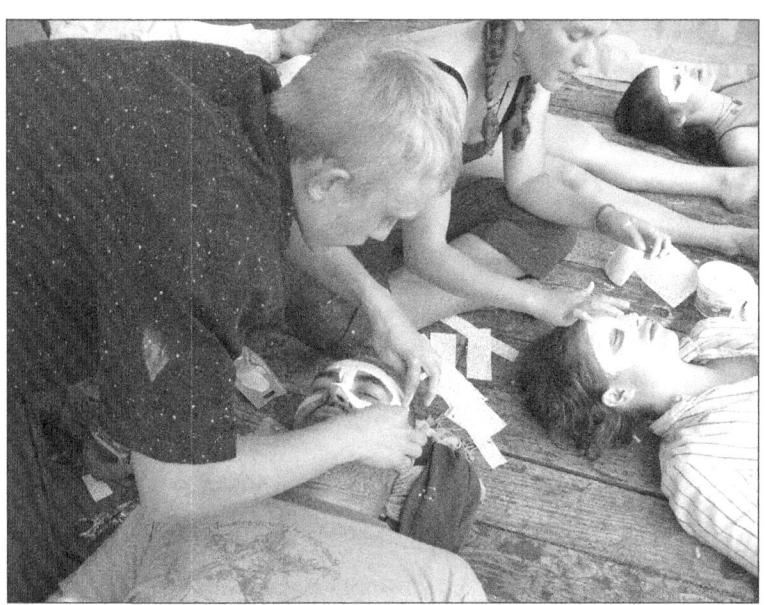

Mask-making workshop – a possible station at a camp ritual.

Group vs Optional Rotation

In this description, the groups rotate to each station at the ringing of a bell. Sometimes we do optional stations, where several simultaneous workings are offered, and participants choose for themselves which stations to visit.

The "optional" format has more of a workshop or drop-in feel. "Group rotation" allows deeper and more intimate workings.

The specific stations can be as varied as desired. A stations ritual is a good way to introduce magical skills to a new group, or to do a series of short, deep workings. Below are several examples of stations rituals – create one to suit your needs.

SPACE/TIME/SIZE

The overall size of the group determines the number and size of the stations. Three is a typical number, but you can have as many stations as there are interests and priestesses for. Under group rotation, each station will need to accommodate about the same number of people.

Time – at least two hours total – about 30 minutes per station including transitions (plus another 30 minutes for gathering, creating sacred space, and devoking at the end). If there are more than three stations, adjust accordingly.

Space – room for stations to spread out and not interfere – yet close enough for people to hear a bell and quickly rotate to the next station.

PREP

Whatever prep is needed for the various stations – some are simple, and some (like Permaculture) may take some research and a visit to a hardware or garden store.

Research your site, so you know where the activities can best be held.

A bell or gong to let people know it's time to rotate. If stations are "optional," perhaps do a short gathering in between rounds, where presenters can again remind folks what they are offering.

continued on next page

RITUALS

Ritual: Stations Format (pg 2)

WORKING: Stations Ritual Outline

Sacred Space

• Welcome / teach songs
  • briefly explain how rotation will work; form small groups if not already done
  • a bell or gong signals the changes
• Ground
• Cast circle
• Invoke elements
• Invoke deity / energies – think about which energies would be useful for the workings you are getting ready to do.

Transition – an active game is good if stations will involve sitting still – stations priestesses can leave to do their final prep.

Stations working – see next page for examples and/or create your own stations.

Recircle – go around clockwise and each person say one word about what you are feeling or have learned.

Spiral dance or upbeat song that weaves group energy: Weave and Spin; Sweet Water; We Are the Power in Everyone

Devoke in reverse order and open circle.

SAMPLE STATIONS WORKINGS

EXAMPLE ONE – Ritual Skills Stations

Small groups rotate among stations such as grounding, circle casting, and invoking, practicing skills and coming up with fun and creative ways to do these ritual roles. Each station is a mini-workshop, and together they teach the most common ritual skills.

Keep the work fun, embodied, and fast-paced. Prepare exercises at each station for beginning and advanced students. Consider inviting older teens to assist in the stations, sharing their experience with the younger folks.

Do this as a morning path one day. That evening, have the teens try out their new skills in a ritual.

EXAMPLE TWO – Permaculture Stations

At the first All-Reclaiming Dandelion Gathering in Texas (2004), Austin activists offered Permaculture stations one afternoon. There were several optional stations, each about an hour long:

• Rainwater Catchment – a fancy name for running rain from gutters into a collection barrel. In less than an hour, we fastened guttering onto an old shed, guided the water into a big blue plastic barrel, and affixed a spigot to the barrel for easy access.

continued on next page

Ritual: Stations Format (pg 3)

Add a few goldfish to control mosquitoes, and voila! – an instant fifty-gallon water storage container.

- Seed Balls – these little balls of dried clay, compost, and native-species seeds have a high rate of germination and give an extra boost to indigenous plants. They can be prepared at camp and carried elsewhere for guerrilla planting.
- Bioremediation (involving soil renewal after a gasoline spill) – we heard a short talk about the chemistry of petrochemicals and how they could be broken down into simpler, harmless molecules using ordinary fungi. Then we concocted a mix of mushroom spores which we later spread over the site of the gasoline spill on the retreat land (along with a ritual and much dancing!). As the mushrooms sprouted, they would begin to break down the petrochemicals and renew the land (Wikipedia has a good summary of this process under "Bioremediation").

EXAMPLE THREE – Listening Stations

One year on the opening morning of Teen Earth Magic we decided to focus on listening skills, which we hoped would be useful through the rest of camp. We broke into three groups of about 8-10 and visited three stations, each of which offered a short working followed by a discussion:

- Listening to Myself – a grounding and purification working – letting go of chattering voices, as well as tasks and concerns from "back home," etc – coming fully into this moment and listening to our own feelings, hopes, and desires.

- Listening to Others – practicing non-judgmental listening – listening to another person silently and with complete attention, with no attempt to give advice, fix anything, or even think about how the person's life might go better! This can be a strong challenge for some people, but many say they like it: "I'm not used to being listened to with that much attention." (See Workings: Non-Judgmental Listening.)

- Listening to Nature – people were invited to find a nearby tree and sit for 10-15 minutes with their back pressed against it, listening to the sounds and silences of nature.

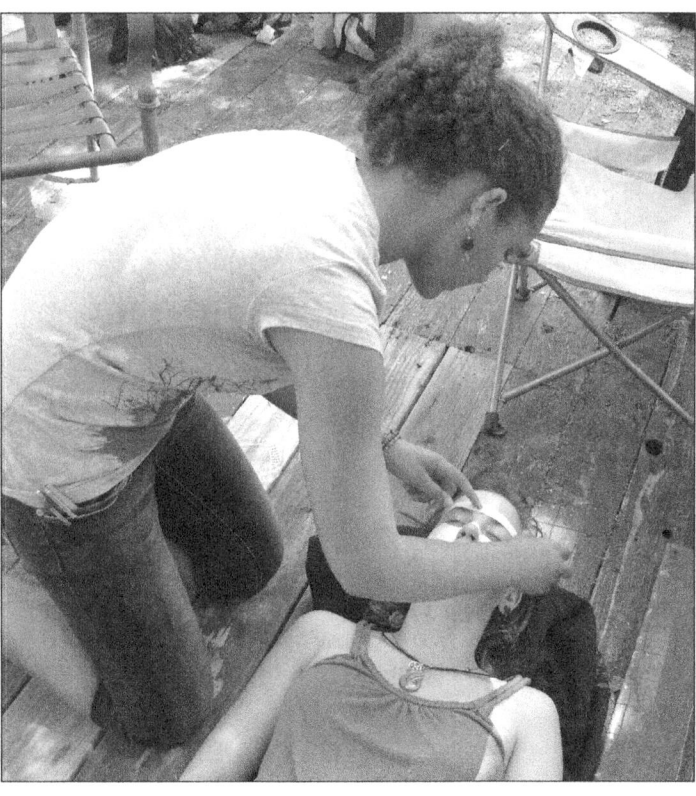

SOLO WORKING

The essence of a stations day is to link several related workings.

Solitaries can do stations, too. Listening to yourself and to nature can be done alone. How will you "listen to others" – in a way that they really feel listened to? Would you listen to youtubes and write supportive comments? Call a friend and really listen? The trick is to be fully present and not get caught up in your own thoughts. (See Workings: Non-Judgmental Listening.)

Maybe you want to do a personal (or small group) version of our magical skills stations – allot 5-10 minutes each to experimenting with new ways of grounding, casting a circle, and invoking the elements.

✪ **Book of Shadows** – before you open sacred space – write about any new ideas (or things you want to be sure *not* to do!).

RITUALS

A Water Ritual

INTENT

As part of Reclaiming's Elements of Magic class (offered in some camps, communities, and online – see page 351) we dedicate a session to exploring each element and practicing related magic. Here's a sample class/ritual for the element Water.

What is Water? Water is our dreams, our emotions. Water is the dripping of a faucet. Water is a simmering pot of soup. Water is the substance of our bodies. When we work Water magic, we become aware of the role of this element (with all its meanings) in our lives, and how we can learn to ebb and flow with its tides.

In this ritual, we'll include grounding, casting a circle, and invoking – but our main focus here will be on the "workings" – we'll do two full workings, including an intuitive tarot reading and the Overflowing Cup Spell.

We'll also pay attention to the transitions between the different parts of the ritual – the "flow" of the ritual. Some say that the true magic of a ritual lies in the transitions. We'll use a chime (or a glass jar with some water in it) to "ring" the transitions. See if you can do this with no words – just ring the chime and begin the next working.

Songs – this ritual has lots of music – the playlist makes good listening, too! Visit WeaveAndSpin.org/tem-chants

SPACE/TIME/SIZE

You can do this ritual alone or with friends. You'll need enough space to create a Water altar (in the West or the Center, as you wish). You'll use this altar for the Overflowing Cup working.

Allow two hours – 60-90 minutes for the ritual, plus prep time and some relaxing time afterward.

PREP

This ritual has a lot of prep. Look through the workings to see when you'll need things like cups, pitchers, bells, etc. In a ritual planning group, we call this role the wrangler – the person that keeps track of all the details. As a solitary or in a small group, you'll be your own wrangler.

Altar – using your intuition, make a Water altar in the West or in the middle of your space. The altar can be on the floor, or if you want to stand for the working, use a small table or a couple of milk crates. Decorate it as your inspiration calls – knowing that the Overflowing Cup working might splatter water on objects. What color cloth will you use? What sorts of objects will you want on a Water altar?

TEM teens know that careful preparation is the key to powerful Water magic!

Priestesses – if you're a group, decide ahead of time who will priestess each part of the ritual. That person carefully reviews the notes for that section, learns any songs, gathers materials, etc. For a solo working, you are your own priestess.

Things you'll need (set on or near your altar)

- Bowl of salt water for purification – set this outside (or just inside) your room.

- Bell, chime, or glass jar half-filled with water, etc – something that you can tap with a mallet or the butt of a knife to ring a tone. This will help with smooth transitions.

- Book of Shadows and a pen.

- Hand mirror for the Deity invocation (Who Is the Goddess).

continued on next page

RITUALS

A Water Ritual (pg 2)

- Working 1 – tarot deck – if you don't have a deck, use this online site: serennu.com/tarot/pick.php
- Working 2 (Overflowing Cup) – a large bowl; a towel; a pitcher full of drinking water (and a couple of extra jugs of water if you're a group); a nice drinking cup (or a magical chalice) for each person. You can set these on your altar, or on the floor in front of it.
- Water bottle or separate glass of drinking water (you might want a drink during the Water ritual!).

Songs – this ritual uses lots of songs – a different chant for every element. Find all of these songs, plus a grounding meditation, in a special youtube playlist: visit WeaveAndSpin.org/tem-chants, or search <Reclaiming Chants Water Ritual>.

- Born of Water (gathering song)
- Grounding with Starhawk (optional)
- Elemental songs (all-in-one, or one per element)
    - Air Moves Us (all elements in one song)
    - Wings (Air)
    - Holy Well and Sacred Flame (Fire)
    - Beginning of the Earth (Water)
    - Let the Beauty We Love (Earth)
    - We Are a Circle Within a Circle (Center)
- Ancestors: Never Lose Our Way to the Well
- Deity invocation: Who Is the Goddess
- Working 1: Labyrinth Meditation Music (optional)
- Working 1: The River She Is Flowing
- Working 2: She Changes Everything She Touches
- Devoking elements: When We Are Gone

WORKING: A WATER RITUAL

Reclaiming Chants & Magical Audio – Free Online
- *Playlists for rituals, workings, classes, and just plain listening*
- *Trances, groundings, audiobooks, & spoken word*

WeaveAndSpin.org/playlists • WeaveAndSpin.org/tem-chants

BEFORE YOU START

When all prep is done, step out of the space. Do any bio-tasks like visiting the restroom.

Take a drink of water and pay attention as you drink it.

Purification – step up to the bowl of salt water. Take a breath and call your energy to yourself. On the exhale, let go of any tensions or distractions into the bowl of salt water. Do this several times. Then, dip your fingers in the water. Let them soak up the purifying power of the salt. Then, touch your belly, neck, hands, heart, third eye, etc. When you are finished, speak these words: "I am now entering sacred space. I am now entering sacred time."

CREATING SACRED SPACE

Song for gathering: Born of Water.

Welcome – in a group, this is a time to welcome people to the space, explain a little about what to expect, teach songs, etc.

Honoring First People: Take a moment and remember that if you live in North America, other Peoples lived here before you, and were the first to know the waters of this place. They did not leave this land voluntarily. Take a breath in memory of those People. Take a second breath as a commitment to work for justice for all people, and especially for First Nations.

continued on next page

RITUALS

A Water Ritual (pg 3)

Grounding – if you are a group, one of you might lead the following grounding for the others. If you are working solo, you can slowly read the grounding below and follow the steps – or use the grounding led by Starhawk on our Water Ritual playlist.

Grounding priestess invite people to stand tall and loose. Speak the following meditation slowly and calmly – pausing for a few seconds wherever you see three dots...

"Take a breath, and rock easily back and forth until you come to rest balanced on both feet...

"As you breathe, notice the moisture in your mouth... On each gentle exhale, water vapor is flowing out from you, flowing like mist, like a tiny rivulet... meeting other rivulets and flowing together, always gently seeking the easiest way forward...

"And the rivulets flow together into a bubbling brook... into a rushing creek... into a winding river that makes its way past rocky rapids... joining other rivers to form a torrent rolling toward the sea...

"The river widens into a delta, the fresh and salt water mix... and the water flows into the great ocean, joining waters that touch every continent... the tides carrying the water back and forth, back and forth...

"And from the water rises a mist, a vapor, carrying the water upward to the sky... swirling in the winds, billowing as a towering cloud... floating back over the land, carrying the water back to its home... raining down on us, replenishing the Earth and all living things...

"Take a breath for the rains... breathe in the water vapor in the air... and complete the cycle of water...

"Touch your center and thank the water that sustains our life...

"Blessed be."

Casting the circle – let's use Hand to Hand and Heart to Heart to cast our circle. This is a favorite at Teen Earth Magic and Witchlets. Here's a group version and a solo version.

Group circle casting – stand in a circle without holding hands. First person reaches out with left hand and takes right hand of neighbor, saying: "Hand to hand (then touching the backs of their locked hands first to their own heart and then to the neighbor's) and heart to heart, the circle is cast." Leave locked hands over neighbor's heart – they reach out to the next person and repeat, on around the circle. When it comes all the way around, with hands still on hearts, first person speak these words: "The circle is cast. We are between the worlds. What happens between the worlds, changes all the worlds. Let the magic begin!"

Solo circle casting – step to the Center and take a breath. Face to the North. Clasp your hands together and say, "Hand to hand (touch clasped hands to your heart and then outward) and *from my heart*, the circle is cast." Turn to the East and repeat. Continue around. Remember to turn all the way back to North before turning to the Center. Repeat once more for Center: "Hand to hand and from my heart – this circle is cast. I am between the worlds. What happens between the worlds can change all the worlds. Let the magic begin!"

Invoking the elements – we'll invoke the elements with song. If time is short, you can use one song to invoke all the ele-

continued on next page

RITUALS

A Water Ritual (pg 4)

ments (we've included Air Moves Us in the playlist). But why not sing a special song for each one?

If you like singing, this is your ritual. You can sing each invoking song for as long (or as short) as you wish. If you're shy about your voice – read Workings: Voice Magic – then close the door, turn up the playlist, and start singing!

Each of these songs is on the Water Ritual playlist. Use either the "all elements" song, or skip it and do the other five.

Invoking all elements – sing Air Moves Us at least five times. At end, say: "Hail and welcome, elements!"

Invoking East/Air – Facing East, sing Wings. At end, say: "Hail and welcome, Air!"

Invoking South/Water – Facing South, sing Holy Well and Sacred Flame. At the end, say: "Hail and welcome, Fire!"

Invoking West/Water – Facing West, sing (The Ocean Is the) Beginning of the Earth. At the end, say: "Hail and welcome, Water!"

Invoking North/Earth – Facing North, sing Let the Beauty We Love. At the end, kneel and kiss or touch the ground and say: "Hail and welcome, Earth!"

Invoking Center/Spirit – Facing Center, sing We Are a Circle Within a Circle. At the end, say: "Hail and welcome, Center!"

Invoking spirits of this place – sing a simple tone as you call to mind the special qualities of the rocks, air, and waters of this place on Earth.

Invoking ancestors – sing Never Lose Our Way to the Well as you think about ancestors of your bloodline and your culture. When the song ends, name one or more ancestors and welcome them.

Invoking deity – take up the hand mirror. Gazing into it, sing along with the chorus of Who Is the Goddess (if you're a group, pass the mirror around as you sing, with each person holding it up for the next).

Transition – with no words, ring the bell or chime.

WORKING 1 – Intuitive Tarot Divination

Music (optional) – Labyrinth Meditation Music (put the track on loop for this working).

Intent (in a group, a priestess speaks these words and more as needed to guide the working): "Here's a chance to learn a simple tarot reading that you can do for yourself. We'll be reading intuitively, not by book-learning. If you already read tarot, set aside your knowledge and sink into your intuition.

"Whether you are new to tarot or already do readings, remember – with intuition, there are no right or wrong answers, only your unique inspirations.

"This will help us frame a commitment or affirmation that we'll charge with an Overflowing Cup Spell later in this ritual."

Working – priestess takes up the tarot cards. Others sit comfortably around the space. Solo – you'll be your own priestess.

First – the question – sit quietly for a few minutes and come up with a question. It might be quite specific, like: "Should I change my major this Fall?" Or it might be a broad query like: "Show me something new about my life."

✪ **Book of Shadows** – when you have your question, write it on a fresh page in your journal.

When people are ready, priestess speaks: "We're going to do a three-card, 'Past-Present-Future' reading. We will be reading intuitively, not by book-knowledge. Try to set aside anything you already know about the cards and open your intuition. When you look at a card, let go of judgments and expectations, and follow your first glimmers of thought. With intuitive tarot reading, there are no right or wrong answers, only questions and inspirations."

Priestess invites people to think again of their question, say it silently to themselves, then draw (using their non-dominant hand) three cards and lay them *face down* as Past, Present, and Future.

continued on next page

RITUALS

A Water Ritual (pg 5)

Turn over the Past card. In your Book of Shadows, write "Past Influences," and the number/suit of the card. Gazing at the cards, meditate on these four questions. After the final question, write your answer (and any other thoughts) in your journal.

1) Look at the image on the card. Focus on the picture. Describe several things you see with your eyes. Let go of stories and interpretations, and just describe things you see.

2) Quickly find one object or being in the card that is you. No need to know or say why. Simply feel that it's you.

3) Make up a simple one- or two-sentence story about what is happening in the card, including the object that is you.

4) Now say briefly – "Given my question and the fact that this card represents 'past influences' – what is the meaning for me?" Write your thoughts in your journal.

Turn over the Present card. In your journal, write "Present Influences," and the number/suit of the card. Repeat steps 1-4 above, taking a few minutes to write after step 4.

Turn over the Future card. In your Book of Shadows, write "Future Possibilities," and the number/suit of the card. Repeat steps 1-4 above, taking a few minutes to write after step 4.

✪ **Book of Shadows** – finally, lay all three cards side by side and see what patterns you notice. Take some time and write in your journal. Let the tarot images act as inspiration for wherever your imagination might go. Try automatic writing – start your pen moving and don't stop for a few minutes.

Finish by closing your Book of Shadows. Take a slow drink of water, paying attention to each sip.

Group – if you're a circle, you may want to get into groups of two or three and each person take a couple of minutes to talk about your reading – whatever you want to share. The others listen and hold space. Then come back to the circle and do a go-round where each person shares one word about what they gained from their reading.

Song – end this working by singing The River She Is Flowing for as long as you wish.

Transition – when the song comes to silence, priestess rings a bell, then begins the next working.

DISCUSSION – Magical Correspondences: What is Water?

In a group, a new priestess leads this part. Speak these words.

"While your journal is out, start a clean page and write this question: What Is Water?

"Now set your pen down. Make yourself comfortable and let the spirit of Water flow through your mind. Let ideas and images filter past without judgment or attachment.

"When we say Water, do we mean the stuff our body is made of? Deep healing energy? The place we go swimming? Flexibility? The secret ingredient of instant soup? A symbol for constant change?

continued on next page

RITUALS

A Water Ritual (pg 6)

"When I invoke Water, I might be calling in cool, refreshing energy. I might be honoring the whales, a not-so-distant relative of ours which lives in water. I might be invoking relaxation and washing away tensions and stress. I might be settling in for a long, watery trance....

"Here are a few Water correspondences to get you thinking." (Read list slowly, one word at a time.)

Water Correspondences (a few examples)
- Fluidity
- Steam
- Neptune (the god)
- Rapids
- Blue
- Dolphins

"Now ask yourself: what does Water mean to me? What does my intuition tell me? Write some words and ideas now, and add to your list over the next few days (or weeks).

"After you have written some words that mean Water to you, set your pen down and read the list to yourself. At the end, take a breath, then say to yourself: "These and much more are the gifts of Water. Blessed be!"

Transition – ring the chime and begin the next working.

WORKING 2 – Spell: Overflowing Cup (The Ace of Cups Spell)

Note – this working is explained in more detail in the back section – see Workings: Overflowing Cup Spell.

Prep – Set a large bowl in front of – or on – your altar. Set the pitcher full of drinking water next to the bowl. If you're a group, have a couple of backup jugs of drinking water somewhere nearby.

Explain – Priestess briefly explains how the spell will work – after a short meditation, each person declares what they are calling into their cup. Priestess pours and lets water overflow until the person says "Good." Then the person drinks the water.

Priestess invites people: "Remember your tarot reading. Look back at your journal if you wish... What was your question?... What past influences did you discover?... What did you learn about your present situation?... What future possibilities do you see?...

"Let the past, present, and future wash through your mind. Feel the possibilities.... And ask yourself – what energy do I need to invoke for myself to help me step into these possibilities?... What energy do I invoke to assist me in my work? Is there a type of energy that will especially support me?..." (For example, "awareness of the abundance of love around me," or "patience and understanding," or "focus and hard work" – whatever will support you.)

Give people time to think, then priestess invites people to take cups in their hands. One by one, people step up and declare (or silently think about) the energy they are invoking into their cup: "I call into this cup _____."

Priestess invites the person to hold their cup over the bowl. Priestess takes pitcher and begins pouring (solo – pour for yourself, with your attention on the cup, not the pitcher). Let the water overflow the cup and fall into bowl until person says, "Good." (Solo – pour until you feel that you have enough and then some!)

Person breathes, then drinks the water and with it the magical energy they invoked. As you drink, keep your focus on your commitment. When finished, take a breath, then say clearly: "So mote it be!" (If a group, everyone repeats this.)

When everyone has had a turn, set bowl of water aside. Afterward – offer any surplus water to the Earth.

Song – sing a song to complete and charge the working – Kore Chant (She Changes Everything She Touches)

✪ **Book of Shadows** – take a few minutes and write in your journal. What feelings came up during and after this working?

continued on next page

RITUALS

A Water Ritual (pg 7)

OPENING THE CIRCLE

We'll devoke quickly, recalling a few of the songs we sang to invoke (or you can sing the songs again if you want – is it ever possible to sing Way to the Well too many times?):

Devoking deity – gaze again into your mirror. Ask: "Who Is the Goddess?" Take a breath and answer: "I am!" (In a group, priestess models this, then passes mirror counter-clockwise so each person can do this). At end, say: "Hail and farewell, Goddess!"

Devoking ancestors – take a breath, recalling your ancestors (and naming again any you named earlier), then say something like this: "Ancestors, we will never lose our way to the well. We remember you. Hail and farewell."

Devoking spirits of this place – sing a simple tone as you thank the rocks and waters and spirits of this land.

Devoking the elements – let's devoke all the elements with one of the all-time favorite Reclaiming songs, co-written by Anne Hill and Starhawk: When We Are Gone. At the end, say: "Hail and farewell, elements!"

Opening the circle (group) – everyone joins hands, then circle casting priestess looks into the eyes of the person to their right – counter-clockwise – and releases hands. Indicate with a nod that they should continue their right. When it comes full circle, circle casting priestess begins and others join in: "The circle is open, but unbroken. May the peace of the Goddess go in our hearts. Merry meet, merry part, and merry meet again!"

Opening the circle (solo) – step to the Center, clasp your hands, and take a breath. Turn to the North, place your clasped hands over your heart, and say, "From my hands and from my heart, this circle is open." Turn counter-clockwise to the West and repeat. Continue around. Remember to turn all the way back to North before turning to the Center. Say: "From my hands and from my heart – this circle is open, but unbroken. May the peace of the Goddess go in my heart. Merry meet, merry part, and merry meet again!"

Announcements – at a community ritual, now is the time for announcements and passing the hat. In a class, this is a time to remind people what they'll need to bring to the next session and offer "magical home adventures" for people who want more.

Saying goodbye – if you're a group, goodbye hugs can be a nice way to end a class. Asking permission before hugging someone is always a good idea, especially when people have been doing deep personal work.

If you're doing a solitary ritual – hug yourself – and take some time to journal, listen to music, and have a grounding snack.

Afterward – offer any surplus water to your garden or a tree as a libation – pour it out as an offering onto the Earth.

CREATING MORE ELEMENTAL RITUALS

Reclaiming's Elements of Magic classes does ritual/classes like this for each element including Center/Spirit. The final session of the class is a student-planned ritual – sort of like a final exam before we turn you loose to do elemental magic in the world!

Now that you've seen a Water ritual, can you take the basic outline and create a ritual for another element?

The recipe is pretty simple, really: you take the outline at the beginning of the Ritual Skills chapter, add one or two workings that seem to fit with the element, mix in a few chants, wave your wand – and voila, instant Reclaiming ritual!

Workings – flip through the back of this book and let your intuition guide you. What workings make you think of Air? Fire? Earth? Spirit?

Chants – look over the chants on pages 112-113 – or better yet, go to the links below and give our playlists a listen. There's even a special elements playlist. Visit these web pages:

WeaveAndSpin.org/playlists • WeaveAndSpin.org/tem-chants • ReclaimingQuarterly.org/web/elements

RITUALS

Opening Night at Witchlets

NOTE – one-page summary of this ritual follows the full version

INTENT

Help folks arrive at camp. Begin to develop/strengthen group bonds. Dive head-long into some flashy magic.

Here's an opening ritual we've used at Witchlets for many years, and more recently introduced at Redwood Magic Family Camp. Returning campers like the familiar opening (and teachers like not having to reinvent the proverbial wheel).

This ritual developed so we could build and strengthen group bonds right from the start. Teens Path (aka Ursa or Ravens Path at various camps) gathers on opening night to establish our circle, welcome new folks, and jump into the magic.

We've found it important to have a separate "teens space" at Witchlets and other camps – a separate campfire that is just their space, and which the rest of the camp agrees to stay out of (sound familiar, parents?). At Witchlets, the teens fire circle is only 50 yards from the dining hall and the main fire ring – but it's through some trees and across a bridge/creek, so it feels more remote. (See Organizing: Teaching Magic to Teens for more on creating teens space – page 329.)

SPACE/TIME/SIZE

Any number of people – but over 25 may get long. If you're a bigger circle, maybe it makes sense to do some of the opening ritual in smaller groups? Allow at least an hour to gather and do a ritual, and also some hang-out time afterward.

PREP

Review ritual plans, make changes as needed. Ahead of time – ask experienced teens to take roles in the opening ritual.

Firetender gathers lots of wood and builds/tends the fire – don't wait until after dark to start! You'll need a lighter and some paper or fire-starters. Check on fire safety gear, nearby water, etc. Stay to the end and put fire out (see Ritual Skills: Firetending).

Beforehand – try to talk to all the teens as they arrive at camp, especially new folks, and make sure they feel invited. Young adult mentors gather teens at a designated time (after dinner or after all-camp opening ritual) and walk over to the teens space together.

Don't forget to let parents and camp organizers know your plan ahead of time.

Need:
- 5-pound bag of flour for every 10-15 people.
- strips of paper pre-cut (strips about 2 x 6 inches).
- magic markers (easy to write without a hard surface).
- basket to hold paper and markers.
- bell or gong (we have a Teens Path gong that attends some camps) – the gong means "something is about to happen!"
- list of agreements, announcements, etc. A list of teens will be handy to see if anyone is missing.
- have a couple of simple games and songs ready, to pass time until all arrive.
- fun snacks for post-ritual (not smores – something with less sugar – and remember vegans, gluten-frees, etc).

RITUAL

Firetender lights fire as group gathers, tends as needed.

If people are missing (especially new folks), send a runner back for one last look. To pass time, play a group game.

continued on next page

RITUALS

Opening Night at Witchlets (pg 2)

Circle up by starting a simple song: Air I Am, Earth My Body, Air Moves Us.

Let the song fade. Priestess rings gong or bell, welcomes people to the circle, and briefly describes what we'll be doing in the path, gathering time, etc – don't give away the magic, just give brief overview. Mention where closest restrooms and water are.

Teach any songs you will sing later in the ritual.

Name game – take some time and start to learn names and preferred pronouns. At the end of this part, ask: "Who can go around and name everyone?" Let a few people try and someone will get it, to the delight of the group!

Create Sacred Space

• Honor First People

• Grounding – keep it simple – focus on breath, feeling our bodies on the Earth

• Cast circle – this circle will stay cast for the whole camp, so take time and cast a strong circle

• Invoke elements – call each separately – good roles for experienced teens:
- East/Air
- South/Fire
- West/Water
- North/Earth
- Center/Spirit

• Invoke deities/energies/spirits.

• Invoke ancestors and allies as desired: Spirits of the Land, First People, Fey

continued on next page

Opening Night at Witchlets (pg 3)

Working: Burning Put-Downs

Each person gets a slip of paper and a marker.

Priestess: "Think of a time when you did not feel safe or welcome in a group. Think of something someone said to you that hurt you or made you feel less welcome or safe. Write it down in just a few words – print it so another person can read it. Don't include your or anyone else's name. When done, fold your paper."

Priestess gathers folded papers in basket. Group circles around the fire. Pass the basket and everyone draws one piece of paper – it doesn't matter if you get your own, just don't say so. This keeps the harsh words anonymous – these things could be said to any of us.

One by one (have an experienced teen go first), someone reads a "put-down" aloud, then wads it up and throws it into the fire. Whole group chants "Burn! Burn!" or hisses, boos, etc as it burns. Do this quickly, one after the other, so you build momentum.

Song: Letting Go; She Changes Everything She Touches (Kore Chant); Rise With the Fire of Freedom

Agreements

"Agreements" are an ever-expanding list of etiquette, understandings, and operating procedures that we have developed over the years. Some affect the whole camp experience, such as Quiet Time and No Drugs/Alcohol. Others are specific to one time in Teens Path.

Reaching consensus on a dozen agreements the first night can be an energy drain. Focus on ones that immediately impact how people treat one another in the circle, and do the rest the next morning. Set a time limit on the first night and try to stick to it. We've done it within sacred space at Witchlets, but before the first ritual at Teen Earth Magic – do what suits your group best.

Here are four key agreements we've developed – with a positive and a negative way of saying each. Someone reads a proposed agreement, then we ask a couple of returning campers to comment on why this has been an agreement. See if there are any questions or concerns. If so, have a short discussion. If not, test for consensus.

Four Key Group-Process Agreements

- mutual respect / no putdowns (Not making put-down jokes will be a new experience for some people. Invite people to have this intention, do their best, and not expect perfection.)

- one group / no cliques (There may be sub-groups of old friends, but we can set an intention of including everyone.)

- self care / right to pass (We are responsible for our own well-being, and we always have the right to pass when it's our turn – this means that someone can go to the restroom as needed, choose to sit out an exercise, or take part in a working but choose silence during a go-round.)

- confidentiality / no gossip (Talk about your own experience, not others' – but it's okay to reveal dangerous situations to teachers or parents.)

For more details, see Introduction: Agreements.

Working: Calling In What We Want and Charging It With Fire (& Flour)

Stand up, shake off the discussion. Priestess has flour ready. Firetender tends a steady fire – plenty of flames, not just coals.

Priestess invites people to close their eyes and envision something that they want to call into our circle – something they want to experience, to see happen, or to be part of while at camp – and find a way to say it in a few words. (Typical things people say are: Make new friends; Do deep magic; Learn about myself; Have fun with my friends; Do something unexpected.)

One by one, people are invited to step forward and take a handful of flour. They state their "invocation" for the group aloud (or silently) – then hurl the handful of flour into the center of the fire. The fire will flare brightly but harmlessly.

continued on next page

RITUALS

Opening Night at Witchlets (pg 4)

After everyone has a turn, some will want to do a second intention – if there's time and more flour, why not?

As energy winds down or flour runs out, gather the circle again. Go around and each person speaks their name one more time – and the whole group responds, "Welcome So-And-So!"

Song – a simple, upbeat song to charge the working: Weave and Spin ("This is how the work begins"); Kore Chant ("She changes everything She touches"); My Soul ("I am stepping out into the unknown").

Opening Sacred Space

Devocations – explain that we will leave this opening circle cast for the whole week, and will reinforce it each time we gather. For tonight, we will simply say thank you to what we invoked.

Say thanks in reverse order to all that we called in.

Perhaps use a song for elements:

    The Earth, The Water, The Fire, The Air
    Return Return Return Return...

To "open" the circle, priestess who cast the circle says something like this (and others join in):

"This circle remains cast, and is unbroken.
May the peace of the Goddess go in our hearts.
Merry meet, merry part – and merry meet again!"

Afterward

Pass out snacks and water! Remind people of starting time the next day and anything they need to bring.

Then start some music or a campfire game (see Workings: Campfire Activities).

One-page summary of ritual on next page

RITUALS

Opening Night at Witchlets (Summary)

One-Page Summary of Preceding Pages

PREP

Review ritual plan, make changes as needed. Ask some of the experienced teens to take roles in the ritual.

Try to talk to all the teens as they arrive or at dinner, especially new folks.

Need a 5-pound bag of flour for every 10-15 people.

Need strips of paper pre-cut, magic markers, a basket to hold paper and markers.

Bring a list of agreements, announcements, people's names. Have a couple of games and songs ready.

Gong or bell.

Firebuilder/tender (earlier prep needed).

Snacks.

Game and/or music ready for after ritual.

RITUAL

Circle up with a simple, easy to learn song – just start singing. Good songs: Air I Am, Earth My Body, Air Moves Us
 • priestess rings gong, welcomes people to circle – brief overview of path/camp plans; restrooms and water
 • teach songs (see below).

Name game & share pronouns – at end, ask: Who can go around and name everyone? Let a few people try.

Create sacred space

Burning put-downs

Song: Letting Go; She Changes Everything She Touches; Rise With the Fire of Freedom

Agreements – four key agreements
 • mutual respect / no putdowns
 • one group / no cliques
 • self care / right to pass
 • confidentiality / no gossip

Calling in what we want and charging it with fire (and flour)

At end, go around and each person speak their name – group responds, "Welcome So-And-So!"

Song – Weave and Spin; Kore Chant (She Changes Everything She Touches); My Soul (call-response verses, all sing chorus)

No devocations – thank any elements and allies we invoked.

AFTERWARD

Snacks! Music or a campfire game.

Remind people of starting time the next morning and anything they need to bring.

RITUALS

Create Your Own Rituals

Use this Book to Craft Your Own!

INTENT

Now that you've seen (and heard) some rituals, you can take the tools from the Ritual Skills chapter, combine them with one or two workings, and add chants. Stir vigorously, then let it stand for a while. There you have it – a Reclaiming ritual!

Although we love it when people come to our camps, classes, and community rituals, our goal in Reclaiming is to empower you to do your own magic – to do your own unique blend of invocations and workings for yourself or a circle.

You can make your rituals as formal or simple as you wish. Grounding, casting a circle, and invoking elements and allies can be major undertakings, or quick (yet powerful) ways to create a magical container for other workings.

Shortcut – you can use the invocations and music from the Grounding and Affirmation rituals earlier in this chapter, and substitute different workings, divination, meditations, etc.

Want a quick review? Listen to Starhawk's trance journey Way to the Well (see page 115). You'll see how simply she creates sacred space and gets on with the workings.

Not sure you're ready? Welcome to the club!

A lot of people felt that way when they did their first roles at a WitchCamp or as part of a community ritual, or did their first meditation or tarot reading on their own. Let the magic begin!

A ritual planning circle gathers during a teens Pearl Pentacle weekend workshop. Sometimes the best rituals are planned right before they happen – this allows us to shape ritual workings to fit the group's energy.

SPACE/TIME/SIZE

Any number of people, from yourself to a small circle to a community gathering. Allow an hour or more to do a ritual, and also some hang-out time afterward – even for a solo ritual.

PREP

Bookmark the Ritual Outline on page 45 – this reminds you of the typical flow of a Reclaiming-style ritual. Reclaiming rituals can be improvised, but most follow this basic flow, which gives us a common language and structure.

Plan your ritual – write down your ideas for creating sacred space, and decide on your working(s) – post-its are handy.

Find chants on youtube, spotify, or other source and "save/like" them – make a playlist of your favorites so they're handy. For ideas, see pages 112-113 and visit WeaveAndSpin.org/playlists.

continued on next page

TeenEarthMagic.org

RITUALS

Create Your Own Rituals (pg 2)

Use this Book to Craft Your Own!

Create an altar – it might be elaborate, or as simple as a cloth and bowl of water – whatever will help you feel that your space is sacred.

Materials needed – look over the instructions for your workings to see what prep and materials are needed. Put stuff by an altar or wherever will be handy. Bring your Book of Shadows as well.

Have water available, and have some healthy snacks ready for afterward – fruit, nuts, bread – food that will help you feel grounded. Save chocolate and soda for later.

RITUAL

Ready? You can always keep this book handy for quick inspirations!

Step outside your space. Turn off your phone. Ask family or roommates not to disturb you.

Step up to the entrance to your ritual space. Take a breath. When you are ready, enter and begin.

Go at your own rate – every individual or group has their own pace, their own sense of when "enough is enough." Trust your intuition – while giving things time to come to fruition. Sometimes a working starts slowly, then picks up momentum. Give it time.

✪ **Book of Shadows** – when the last ally is devoked and the circle is opened, take a bit of time and write about your experience, what worked (or not), lessons learned, etc. If you're a group, allow 5-8 minutes. Alone, take the time you need.

Congratulations! We hope you feel as satisfied as we do when the ritual is complete. If it wasn't perfect, remember – the Wheel of the Year never stops turning. There's always next time!

Small ritual circles gather in the meadow – TEM 2010.

RITUALS

After the Ritual...

Welcome to the WitchCamp Fire Circle!

Join us – by listening to Campfire Chants! Find the album on spotify, youtube, etc and have it ready when your ritual ends. There's also a downloadable Lyrics & Lore booklet available at CampfireChants.org – including guitar/ukulele chords.

Welcome to the WitchCamp fire circle. We could be gathered anywhere from Vermont to Queensland, from British Columbia to Germany.

On this evening, we're gathered among the redwoods of Northern California for our Teen Earth Magic camp.

The ritual is over. A few folks have headed to bed. Others pull up camp chairs or blankets around the fire ring. Snacks magically appear.

As people talk or gaze into the fire, a camper picks up a guitar and strums a Magnetic Fields song. Someone borrows the guitar and sings Joni Mitchell. Another plays Kimya Dawson on a ukulele. As the fire flares up, we sing The Welcome Flame.

We really do sing chants around the campfire. Not all the time. They're interspersed with Indigo Girls, Nirvana, Beyoncé, the Corries, and always another Beatles song. One Direction gets their due, along with Patsy Cline, Chuck Berry, and Bob Marley.

Still, nothing gets everyone singing more than My Soul or We Are the Rising Sun. And there's rarely a night that doesn't end with Goodnight Sweet Witches.

The ritual may be over – but the WitchCamp circle is cast for the entire week. Even around the campfire, we are still between the worlds. And what happens between the worlds, changes all the worlds.

Let the magic begin!

TeenEarthMagic.org

MAGICAL ACTIVISM

Magical Activism
Reclaiming's Unique Synthesis

From its earliest days, Reclaiming has blended practical magic with front-line activism – taking direct steps to change our world.

When we directly work for change, rather than expecting or demanding that someone else to do it – we are activists.

Whether it's volunteering with Food Not Bombs, organizing a community event such as a ritual or festival, or joining in nonviolent civil disobedience – we are taking direct action.

When we add magical skills, voila – magical activism!

Reclaiming: A History of Activism

In Reclaiming's early years, Pagan affinity groups took part in mass direct actions at sites such as Diablo Canyon Nuclear Power Plant, Livermore Nuclear Weapons Lab, and Vandenburg Air Force Base. Over the years the Pagan Cluster has been active at Nevada Test Site (late 1980s), Seattle WTO protests in 1999, anti-globalization protests of the 2000s, and as part of the Occupy actions in late 2011.

TEM continues the tradition. In Spring 2011, Teen Earth Magic did a weekend-long nonviolent action training with Starhawk, Dress, and others. Then in June we co-organized Solstice in the Streets, a colorful day of street theater at various locations around downtown San Francisco.

Welcome to Magical Activism!

This chapter shares tools for taking action in the world. We'll share stories, skills – and simple ways you and a few friends can take action starting right now!

Reclaiming's early affinity groups are described in Luke Hauser's book, Direct Action: An Historical Novel and Starhawk's Dreaming the Dark. Follow Pagan Cluster activism at WeaveAndSpin.org.

Photo – *Solstice in the Streets, San Francisco, June 2011.*

MAGICAL ACTIVISM

Magical Activism: Teens Roundtable

What's the connection between activism and Earth magic?

Ingrid: I don't see how you can teach people to respect the Earth if you don't teach them to love the Earth. If they don't feel connected, I don't see how they would consider changing their lives to help their fellow animals and plants. If you don't honestly love and care about and understand and know something, how are you going to commit to living your life in a new way?

I'm not saying you have to be Pagan. You just have to care about the Earth. If you come from a strong connection to the Earth, then activism is a given.

Miranda: It's an overlap, like a Venn diagram. You can be an activist and not be spiritual, or, spiritual and not really an activist. And then you can be both. If you do Earth magic and care for the Earth, you want to do something to take care of it.

Dusky: As someone who worships the planet, activism is extremely important to me. It was really powerful for me to find a group that unites the two.

I'd like activism to be a bigger part of my life. I'm sometimes bothered that I don't do more – getting involved in a physical sense in activism – going to protests.

You took part in our TEM tree-climbing workshop – is that activism?

Dusky: I wasn't thinking about activist prep at the time. I've always loved climbing – always wanted to be the one who climbed highest. Now that you mention it, though, it was good activist training!

I got to see [tree-sitting activist] Julia Butterfly Hill speak once. That inspired me. Tree-sitting is something I can imagine myself doing.

I don't know if it's something I can fit into my daily life -- which I'm not saying is a good thing. But it is feasible for me to go to protests, and that's something I would like to do.

What's your first step?

Dusky: It's taking the step of looking for that community.

Mykel: I have the impulse to teach and mentor people, and I can do what my impulse tells me the needs are – I feel like I'm filling a gap in the universe.

TEM teens magically soften the "Bankers' Heart," the local name for the massive granite blob at Bank of America plaza – San Francisco, 2011.

KaeliMo: My focus has been more on the interpersonal level – smaller-scale methods of problem-solving, listening skills, being aware of what my thoughts are and allowing them to change – that's something I can do, and know how to do.

Where does it get difficult?

KaeliMo: At a larger level, I don't know how to start. I don't feel like protests grab people's attention any more. And I don't feel like things are changing. The Occupy movement was so big and so cool – and it didn't change most of the core things they were talking about. I guess I'm still looking for things to do about it.

Mykel: It's weird to me what issues emotionally catch on with people – sometimes it seems kind of random. That doesn't mean I won't support people doing activism around it, or think that they are right. But I don't feel called to it, or in any way particularly alarmed about it.

Then when I do feel emotional about something, it's hard for me that others don't feel the same urgency as I do.

That speaks to how we all have different places where we fit in, different places we're called to help make the world a better place.

continued on next page

MAGICAL ACTIVISM

Magical Activism: Roundtable (pg 2)

How do rituals relate to activism? How does magic affect the world?

Talise: Magic is about making change – to have the intention to go out and make a change.

Ingrid: When I think of magic as a vehicle for change, I feel like I'm just starting to explore the possibilities. I've been to rituals where we've done magic to change the world, and I've felt incredibly moved. But I've always felt that [the power] is in the moment that we're doing it, and not the future.

Have you done spell-type magic around activism?

Sequoia: Yes, but when it's a mobile kind of situation, the spells are very informal. I don't employ tools, like physical objects. In some ways that makes it easy – if I need fire energy, or I need a grounding, I view my body as the vessel of my magic.

Maeve: I've been lucky enough to go to protests with witches, where we do stuff together – a brief grounding, maybe a pop-up circle that can travel with us. This can help contain and conserve our energy, instead of getting overwhelmed, which I can easily do in a big crowd when many things are happening all at once!

Hilary: In the last year, yes – and it's been a conscious effort. Quite frankly, there were fascists coming to San Francisco. And I was like, I'm freaking out and I feel helpless and I want to do something. So I called on my community, many of whom I met through Witchlets and Teen Earth Magic, and they were like yeah, I feel the same way. So we did a spell in the middle of a march through San Francisco.

You did the spell during the protest?

Hilary: Right – as we were navigating cops with giant machine-gun-looking things, guarding buildings for gosh knows what reason, and we're checking twitter feeds to find out where these [right-wing] people were – it was in-the-moment, a spell we did in the middle of the street. It doesn't often occur to me to do that!

What are ways you do activism in your personal life?

Hilary: When we were in a drought, I made a conscious effort every day, at some point when I was using water, to say thank you to that water. That was a result of a spell we did at Teen Earth Magic around water. We did a whole ritual as a gift to water. From there, I did a year and a day of gratitude to water.

Mykel: Recently I've been involved in a letter-writing group to get resources for prisoners to advocate for themselves. I have a pen-pal in a state prison. She's a trans woman. I feel like what I have to offer is that I can listen. It's a concrete way I can, not dismantle the system, but fight against the isolation it causes. I can relate to people and decrease isolation – that's something I know how to do, that fills this huge need. That feels really good.

TEM teens join an occupation of the downtown Bank of America lobby – Solstice in the Streets, 2011.

Ingrid: While I do believe we can change ourselves and our community through ritual, I feel like there's this other piece that Reclaiming has – a lot of us believe that there's personal steps we can take, too. It's about weaving together a state of living that allows us to be conscious and really engage with the environment and living on this planet – coming to a place where we really deeply care about reducing our impact.

Follow the Pagan Cluster at WeaveAndSpin.org.

MAGICAL ACTIVISM

Magical Activism: Roundtable (pg 3)

What About Student Activism?

Charlotte, Natasha, and some other TEM teens have attended the San Francisco School of the Arts (SOTA), and have been part of National Student Walkouts around gun violence.

SOTA students joined the National Walkouts?

Charlotte: Yeah, several of them. There was one on the anniversary of Columbine [a 1999 mass shooting at a Colorado school], and an earlier one around Sandy Hook [a 2012 school shooting in Connecticut]. They were student-organized, there were meetings at the public library.

Natasha: Maeve and I organized call-ins to representatives. We had posters in the halls with phone numbers of people who were giving money or backing up the NRA [National Rifle Association].

Also, one of our teachers helped us get students to Sacramento to join the protests in the capitol, to lobby representatives. Some teachers have helped make resources available to us, while still letting it be student-led, which is really important.

How was it to go to the capitol?

Natasha: Really stressful! But I felt it was really impactful to have a mix of direct action and people working within the system.

Have you made a difference?

Charlotte: I think different walkouts had different effects. We shut down Market Street, and when you do something that ends up in the news, you know you're getting somewhere. We let people know that young people are upset. It's really important that young people have their voices heard, and not just on the internet.

Natasha: I think every action makes a difference, even if it's really small. I'm not sure it led to any laws being changed, but we were outside the NRA offices, and I think making our voices heard by people in power is really important, even if nothing immediately gets changed. It always has a ripple effect.

Charlotte: Yeah, if it makes changes now, or makes changes down the line, it's worth it.

What gives you hope?

Charlotte: Other people. Sometimes activism can feel like you're going against the current. Having strength in numbers, knowing that other people have the same concerns, is really heartening. Even if it's a long way off, eventually there will be so many people that things will have to change.

Natasha: Yeah, seeing compassion and passion from other people is so inspiring – to see that other people feel the way I do. We're able to feel that spark of connection and communication. It lets me know that there is more to life than cars going down the street to buy gas and rich overlords trying to control us all!

Does that connection make activism easier?

Natasha: I think it's what makes activism possible. It's a lot of emotional labor to see what's wrong with the world and to try to fix it – to try to do it alone would be impossible, in my opinion. To have people who will support you when things get hard, who are willing to stand up with you, is so important.

Across the U.S., young people have inspired and led walkouts, rallies, lobbying, and civil disobedience to demand gun control. Photo by Luke Hauser/RQ.

MAGICAL ACTIVISM

Magical Activism: Intro

INTENT

Reclaiming is an "activist" tradition. When we say the Earth is sacred, we are willing to work to protect and heal our planet.

Activism means many things – it can mean taking part in a protest or occupation, and even risking arrest, as many Reclaiming people have done over the years.

It can mean volunteering in a soup kitchen – Reclaiming folks helped start Berkeley-Oakland Food Not Bombs, and in turn FNB activists created the North Altar for many years at the Spiral Dance.

It can mean dancing in the streets, as we did at Solstice in the Streets, Occupy Oakland, and many other events. It can mean rituals, silent vigils, festivals, and marches. It can mean writing letters or attending public hearings and city council meetings.

Activism also means how we live our daily lives. Are we reducing our carbon footprint? Do we recycle or collect rainwater? Take public transit? Practice nonviolent communication? Take an active role in our community (whatever that means to each of us)?

GETTING STARTED – Alone & With Others

Solitary Activism – What Can We Do Alone?

The personal is political – this wisdom comes from the feminist movement, reminding us that the ways we treat one another, ourselves, and our community – the ways we live our daily lives – are just as important as our efforts to change the wider world.

If we organize for peace but constantly fight with our fellow activists... if we work to protect the environment but drive everywhere we go... if we say our body is a living temple but feed it with junk food – we're out of balance with ourselves.

✪ **Book of Shadows** – personal-as-political – take five minutes or more and write in your journal about some ways you might want to change the way you live your daily life.

When you finish, look back and ask: "What is one thing I could do in the next week to begin to make these changes?" Write that down.

Take a breath and read it again. Does it seem right? Does it seem do-able?

If so, write the date and sign your name. If not, take a breath and release it for now.

Either way, inhale as you commit to continuing to look at your life, and exhale to seal the working. "So mote it be!"

Educate ourselves – we can visit Guardian.co.uk and other progressive sites and learn what is going on in the world. We can learn about alternative energy, new transit design, home gardening, etc. Hopefully our learning inspires us to take the next step and seek out like-minded people.

Permaculture – learning about and practicing Permaculture

Solstice in the Streets – TEM teens helped organize a day of activism and street theater in downtown San Francisco in 2011.

continued on next page

MAGICAL ACTIVISM

Magical Activism: Intro (pg 2)

(sustainable agriculture and social practices) is another step we can take on our own. The Earth Path by Starhawk is a good introduction, and you can visit Starhawk.org for her current workshops and writings.

Finding Others – Wherever We Live

Co-conspirators – beyond the "personal as political," though, activism needs co-conspirators. Trying to change the world alone is a great way to burn out and get discouraged and cynical. Having others – even a few – to share activism can make all the difference.

Sidewalk chalking – a low-risk way to take our message to the people. Radiation suit and faerie wings optional!

If you know people – friends, school comrades, folks at your church, temple, or synagogue, local activists you've met – you're in luck! With even one friend, you can do bannering, street theater, sidewalk chalking, and other actions. As you step out, others may come forward to join you.

As Pagans, we're keenly aware of the importance of community. A Pagan Cluster has been part of many direct actions, occupations, and encampments going back to the 1980s. A large and vibrant Pagan Cluster took part in the 1999 Seattle WTO actions, and at many other "convergences" – activist gatherings for protest, networking, and education.

Groups of Pagans have taken part in Bay Area actions, including Occupy actions in 2011. Reclaiming folks spiral danced at Occupy Oakland, did activist preps at San Francisco, and organized singalongs at Occupy Berkeley – TEM teens took part in all three cities. One Witchlets/TEM family even moved in at Occupy Berkeley.

What are groups doing in your area? Join in and start sharing your own inspirations. You just might be the new spark that's needed!

What If I Don't Know Others?

Don't know others interested in activism? Not to worry. No matter where you live, there are good-hearted people working to change the world.

Think about the issues you care about – then look around and find one that has already brought people in your community together.

By volunteering at a community garden you'll meet other caring, active people. Maybe there's a bike repair co-op where folks might be excited about making street theater props. Join a letter-writing circle, and you might find people interested in other activism as well. Unitarian and Quaker congregations as well as local eco-villages and environmental groups are good places.

Wherever we are, we can take the first step. Find people doing something you believe in, and ask to join in.

Taking the First Step

Do you know your next step? Do you know who you will contact and what you want to do? Go for it!

Looking for a little more clarity? Try an intuitive tarot reading (see Workings: Tarot) with questions such as: "What issues and types of activism call me? Where should I look for allies (and co-conspirators)?"

In making a commitment, consider a personal working such as the Overflowing Cup to add magical energy to your resolve.

continued on next page

MAGICAL ACTIVISM

Magical Activism: Intro (pg 3)

Internet Activism? Nope...

What about the internet?

Use the web to google activism in your hometown and see what you find – maybe a Food Not Bombs group or a soup kitchen, a health clinic looking for volunteers, anti-nuclear activists, a bike co-op, people working for the rights of women, gays, minorities, etc.

Use the internet to learn about issues – but see the next section for some thoughts on "the news."

Beyond that? Clicking a mouse isn't "Earth activism." All the "likes" in the world don't add up to one more forest saved.

Creating change comes from weaving our life energy, not sharing status updates. We spin world-changing energy not by typing words, but by chanting, spiral dancing, or laughing together, whether we're around a WitchCamp bonfire or in someone's living room.

Magic itself can be solitary. Depending on where we live and who we know, we may be doing our rituals alone right now.

But wherever we are, we can seek kindred activist spirits. Serving food together, picking up trash on a beach, co-tending a community garden – these connect us more than digital "chatting" ever will.

What About Following the News?

What about staying up on "the news"? Does it make us more effective activists and human beings to know up-to-the-minute facts about distant events?

Here's some thoughts.

Most "news" is entertainment in disguise. Its purpose is not to educate or empower you, but to sell the accompanying advertising.

The last thing "news" aims to do is empower us. The unspoken message of media reports is always that the "news" is happening somewhere else, and you are not involved. Your job is to watch and consume.

If there's a hurricane in your hometown, by all means, follow the news.

If something distant happens that demands your personal response, don't worry – your friends will text you about it!

What if we agreed that we will spend no more time looking at news than doing activism? What if for every hour we spend looking at media, we spend an hour cleaning up a hiking trail or going to a protest march?

What if we caught up on the news once a week, figuring anything important will stick around for a while, or we'll hear people talking about it?

Just asking.

News can be irresistible, like chocolate. When you need to indulge, try the UK Guardian.

UK Guardian (guardiannews.com)

If you are called to the news, bookmark The Guardian, a daily newspaper and website based in London.

It's the best source of English-language news on the internet, with lots of U.S. and world news.

Luke Hauser's historical novel tells the back-story of Reclaiming, placing the Pagan Cluster amidst California's vibrant activist scene.

Free download of PDF version – DirectAction.org

"Dramatically brings to life the experience of nonviolent direct action – a new generation of activists will learn from it."

– Daniel Ellsberg, author of The Pentagon Papers

MAGICAL ACTIVISM

Activist Resources

Activist Books by Starhawk

- Dreaming the Dark – visionary activist tools
- Truth or Dare – the personal and the political
- The Earth Path – building relations with our home
- Novels
  - Fifth Sacred Thing – a world in conflict and revolution
  - Walking to Mercury – activist-infused prequel to FST
  - City of Refuge – creating the new world
  - The Last Wild Witch – an activist parable

Reclaiming's Activist Backstory

- Direct Action: An Historical Novel by Luke Hauser – the activist roots of Reclaiming. Download at DirectAction.org.

Activist Handbooks

Free PDF downloads of direct action handbooks. Practical discussions of consensus, nonviolence, affinity groups, feminism, confronting oppression, and much more.

Visit: DirectAction.org/handbook/.

Chants for the Streets

Some of Reclaiming's favorite chants were written for street actions and marches. At the 2018 Rise for Climate Justice march in San Francisco, the Pagan Cluster sang (and sang...) these songs from our Campfire Chants album:

- We Are the Rising Sun
- Sweet Water
- Rising of the Moon

More good "marchers" from our albums:

- Rise with the Fire
- We Are the Power in Everyone
- Weave and Spin
- Harvest Chant (Our Hands Will Work)

See Ritual Skills: Chants Resources for links to our albums and playlists – pages 112-113.

Photo – *Reclaiming activists took part in this march and blockade in support of Indigenous resistance at Standing Rock – San Francisco 2017.*

Pagan Cluster Listserve

The Living River (LivRiv) is the Reclaiming Pagan Cluster's international activist list. Learn about upcoming actions, workshops, etc. Contact others and join the actions.

To join the Living River elist, or for questions, contact: ReclaimingQuarterly@gmail.com.

Websites for Magical Activism

- Starhawk.org – workshops, writings, resources.
- EarthActivistTraining.org – intensive retreats with Starhawk and others.
- DirectAction.org – free downloads of Luke Hauser's activist novel, plus handbooks, music, and more.
- WeaveAndSpin.org – current Reclaiming posts.
- ReclaimingQuarterly.org – includes photo-coverage of Pagan Cluster actions from about 2005-2016, plus front-line reports from Starhawk, Kate Raphael, Lisa Fithian, Juniper, and more.

Keep Us Posted!

If you're involved in activism in your area – and doubly so if you have a Pagan affinity group – let us know! Email ReclaimingQuarterly@gmail.com.

MAGICAL ACTIVISM

Our Commitment to Nonviolence

As Pagans, we honor all life. When that life is a friend, a flower, or a dolphin, we find honoring their spirit easy.

But when it's an angry right-winger, an impatient cop, or a frustrated teacher, it can be a lot harder.

When we take part in nonviolent civil disobedience actions, groups often reach consensus ahead of time on some basic understandings around nonviolence. This helps build trust, knowing that others in the streets with us – including folks we've never met – have agreed to the same guidelines.

These guidelines and the accompanying discussions come from 1980s anti-nuclear activists, who learned from Quaker organizers, themselves educated by the U.S. civil rights movement of the 1950s and 60s....

These tactics have continued to be used to the present day, including major actions at the 1999 WTO protests in Seattle and the Foreclose the Banks blockades during the 2011 Occupy movement.

What Does Nonviolence Mean?

Nonviolence is an alternative way to initiate change. Nonviolence minimizes bitterness and isolation in people affected by our actions, and tries to break the cycle of violence breeding more violence.

Read more about nonviolent direct action and its connections to consensus and feminism in the Direct Action handbook and other activist handbooks – available at DirectAction.org.

Guidelines for Nonviolent Action

These guidelines are understood as basic agreements, rather than philosophical/political requirements.

The guidelines are meant to act as a basis of trust among participants who often have met only for a specific action. The guidelines are under constant discussion and are seen as our current working understanding, not as statements etched in stone.

1. Our attitude will be one of openness, friendliness, and respect toward all people we encounter.
2. We will use no violence, verbal or physical, toward any person.
3. We will not damage any property.
4. We will not bring or use drugs or alcohol other than for medical purposes.
5. We will not run.
6. We will carry no weapons.

The use of nonviolence in campaigns has led to many successes, such as ending racial segregation on buses in Montgomery, Alabama, as a result of the 1956 boycott.

A large part of the direct action movement has decided to incorporate nonviolence into the heart of our strategy.

The following assumptions and goals help us understand the rationale for practicing nonviolence:

- Respect all life.
- Transform opposition rather than destroy it.
- The means must be consistent with the ends.
- Use creativity, humor, and love.
- Aim for fundamental change.
- Nonviolence is active.
- We can withhold cooperation from those who abuse power.

continued on next page

MAGICAL ACTIVISM

Our Commitment to Nonviolence (pg 2)

Dynamics of Nonviolence

The conventional view of politics sees government and corporations as having power over society, with the rest of us dependent on the good will and caprice of "power-holding" institutions such as military, police, courts, and bureaucracy.

The theory of nonviolence proposes a different analysis: that government depends on people, and that political power depends on the cooperation of groups and individuals. The withdrawal of that cooperation restricts and can even dissolve power.

Power depends on continued obedience. When we refuse to obey our "rulers," their power begins to crumble.

Practicing Nonviolence

When we interfere with the smooth operation of the machine, even if we are nonviolent, we may be met with aggression and violence. How do we remain nonviolent in the face of violence from the police and others?

The first thing is maintaining human contact with your perceived "opponent." Body language is important – especially making eye contact. Listening rather than talking may also help prevent conflicts from escalating.

When we act nonviolently, we demonstrate another model of human nature for all who witness us – people taking a humane and principled stand for the world and for all life.

Planning Ahead

It is crucial that affinity groups meet ahead of time to discuss and role play responses to potentially violent situations. For instance, an affinity group can physically surround someone being assaulted, while continuing to distract or calm the attacker.

Responses such as this demonstrate the full power of nonviolent direct action. We intervene so that corporations and governments can't do more harm and abuse, even as we model the world we vision.

Photos: Nonviolence In Action

Blockade and support action at the entrance to the main offices of Wells Fargo in San Francisco. Foreclose the Banks protest, 2011.

Many more photos from actions from the early 2000s at ReclaimingQuarterly.org.

Direct Action: An Historical Novel – dozens of action stories and photos (see page 154).

MAGICAL ACTIVISM

Finding Your Own Activism

Activism means many things within Reclaiming, from changing our daily lives to Pagan Cluster street protests. What unifies us is our belief that we can create a better world for humans and all beings.

Reclaiming's Principles of Unity state, "All living beings are worthy of respect. All are supported by the sacred elements of Air, Fire, Water, and Earth. We work to create and sustain communities and cultures that embody our values, that can help to heal the wounds of the Earth and her peoples, and that can sustain us and nurture future generations."

On the next page, you'll find a ritual that helps focus and express your concerns about the world.

✪ **Book of Shadows** – here's a chance to reflect on what activism means to you and how it might be part of your life.

EXERCISE: Activism Questionnaire

If I could change one thing in the wider world, it would be:

If I could change one thing about my own life that would make the world a better place, it might be:

Something I do well that does or could make a difference in the world is:

One type of activism I've seen or imagined is:

Something that gets in the way of going to an activist event or meeting is:

One magical act I could do toward changing the world (and myself) is:

If I did one "activist" thing that involved leaving my own house, it might be:

If one thing in my life needed to change for me to be more "active," it might be:

True or false: To get involved in an issue, I'd need to see others working on it first. If true, what difference would it make?

True or false: If I were to "get active," I would have to be more flexible. If true, in what way?

True or false: Going to meetings or events would be easier if I knew someone else who was going. If true, what's one thing you could do to improve your odds of finding someone?

Reflect: Are you a hopeful person? What are you especially hopeful about (or not)? When is it hard to be hopeful?

MAGICAL ACTIVISM

Salt & Apple
A Ritual to Share Our Concerns About the World

INTENT

Speaking and sharing our concerns and dreams about the world is part of activism. When a group gets held in jail for even a few hours, we do a check-in circle where we share what brought each of us to the action that day. Even in the most focused action, like the Foreclose the Banks protests that were part of Occupy San Francisco, every person had their own reasons for taking part – their own intention.

As we engage in any sort of organizing (rituals, activism, dance or theater, youth work...), we learn the importance of finding time to share our thoughts and feelings – in a circle, with a friend, and/or with our journal.

Here's a simple ritual to share concerns and commitments.

SPACE/TIME/SIZE

Any number, alone or in groups of two to eight. Room for groups to spread out. 20-45 minutes depending on number of people.

PREP

Decide on a way to create sacred space. See Ritual Skills: Sacred Space: Quick Ways for ideas.

Need a small bowl of salt water for each group, plus a bowl of apple slices and one whole apple per group.

It helps if there is a priestess in each group who knows the plan – or you can write out these simple instructions and give a sheet to someone in each group – this person can go first to model the working.

WORKING - Sharing Our Concerns

Gather folks around the apples and bowl of water. Share names. Close your eyes and breathe together. Then tell people we will do two rounds. People can speak or hold silence when it is their time. Listeners maintain attentive silence – no cross-talk.

First round – pass the salt water. Each person holds the bowl for 30-60 seconds and shares (aloud or silently) something that deeply concerns them about the world. At the end of the go-round, silently look around the circle and breathe together.

Repeat go-round, passing the whole apple and sharing one thing you already do or feel called to do. When all have gone, look around and take a breath together. Then pass out the apple slices. Together say: "So mote it be!" – and eat a slice.

Re-circle and charge the magic with a song: We Are the Power in Everyone; We Are the Rising Sun; She Changes Everything.

SOLO WORKING

Prep – need bowl of salt water, apple, journal. Create a simple (or elaborate) altar that you can sit beside for this working. Place the salt water and apple on it. You may want background music such as Labyrinth Meditation Music (see page 113).

Get comfortable near the altar. Close your eyes and think for a couple of minutes about something in the wider world that concerns you – not just your own life, but something that affects other people or living beings. Then dip your fingers into the salt water, take up your pen, and write about your thoughts. At the end, dip your fingers in the salt water again.

Now close your eyes and consider things you might do – from the grandest to the smallest – to help make the world better.

✪ **Book of Shadows** – write about (1) something you already do to make the world better; and (2) one further thing you feel called to do. When you finish #2, add a sentence saying one simple step you could take toward that goal.

When you finish – take a bite of the apple. Close your eyes as you chew, affirming your commitment to action.

Charge your intention with a song – see ideas above. Finish eating the apple and compost any remains.

MAGICAL ACTIVISM

Preparing for Action

Group Process

Group decision-making – Reclaiming groups work by "feminist process" – a catch-all term for things such as small-group process, non-hierarchy and/or rotating leadership, consensus decision-making, listening skills, and more.

The ways we work together – rotating leadership, equalizing talk-time, valuing the different ways that people contribute – these may be as important in creating a new world as the issues we are working on.

These skills and outlooks come to us from the feminist and gay rights movements, which have challenged not just male oppression and hetero-normatism, but all kinds of hierarchy and domination.

Activist Skills: Read up!

At DirectAction.org you'll find links to various activist handbooks, including a 16-page Direct Action handbook – partly written and influenced by Reclaiming affinity groups which helped create the anti-nuclear and anti-war movements.

This handbook has short sections on consensus, nonviolence, feminism, and masculine oppression. You'll also find writings on racism and homophobia – ways that people are brought into conflict one another.

Before you "take it to the streets" with some of the actions below (or ones you cook up), look through this handbook. Ask others to read and discuss it as well.

Is Reading Enough?

In 2011, Dress and Starhawk, two "nonviolence preppers" from the Bay Area, anchored a weekend activism workshop for teens from TEM and Witchlets, teaching skills for civil disobedience. You'll see pictures from that prep in this book, as well as from Solstice in the Streets, a day of street theater that TEM teens helped organize that Summer.

Although we wish this chapter could offer a direct action training, protesting is one of those practices that is best passed along in-person and experientially.

Why? How is it different from rituals, which we don't seem shy about writing up?

When civil disobedience and other protests go wrong, people can be physically injured or sent to prison. If you're feeling called to this kind of activism – and we hope some of you are! – look for local trainings with experienced people. Visit page 154 for Pagan Cluster links, or check with Unitarian or Quaker congregations or Food Not Bombs for nonviolent organizing.

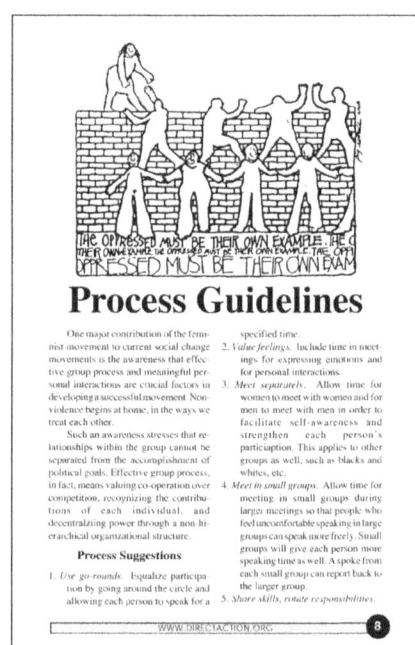

Learn more about activist skills from the Direct Action handbook– available at DirectAction.org/handbook/.

Taking Art to the Streets

Art actions are creative, inspiring – and generally safe – ways to do street activism. See the end of this chapter for several ideas. With banners, chalk actions, street theater, or mystery posters, any of us can step out and bring our message to the wider public – and the planning is half the fun! Gather some friends and spend an afternoon creating your props. Take time for scrub-jay lines – see next page. These are a fun way to prepare for interactions you might have.

✪ **Book of Shadows** – how can you include magic in your planning and actions? Can you see some advantages to grounding and casting a circle together before you start? What allies might you invite (and remember to thank/devoke at the end)?

continued on next page

MAGICAL ACTIVISM

Preparing for Action (pg 2)

Scrub-Jay Lines: Preparing for the Streets

Scrub-jay lines (also known as hassle lines) are a fast, fun way to explore energy around personal and political issues. This is good practice before doing a public action – we can role-play conflicts that might arise. (See also Workings: Boundaries: Scrub-Jay Lines.)

Here's an example using the question, "Is protesting worthwhile or a waste of time?" Form two equal lines, each person facing another person. Each round lasts 30-60 seconds. To change partners, one line shifts one space to left.

(A) Decide which line will be pro- or anti-protesting for this round. On a signal, argue strongly for your view without listening to the other person – interrupt, talk over them, ignore what they say – just keep arguing for your view. Facilitator, egg people on!

(B) Change partners. Decide who is Yes and who is No. The question is, "Is protesting a waste of time?" On a signal, just start repeating your word: "Yes! Yes! Yes!" or "No! No! No!" Do your best to out-talk the other person. Even if you start laughing, try to keep going.

(C) Change partners once more. Decide who is "Yes" and who is "No." On the same question, have a calm discussion and really try to listen to one another. Go a little longer on this round, or let people change roles.

Come together as a circle. Facilitator asks:

"How did it feel to be so invested in a view? How did it feel to have someone else try to persuade you? Talk over you? Ignore you?"

"How did the Yes/No round feel? Did people laugh? If so, what was up? Do you often get to simply say 'No' without explaining?"

"In the final round, did anything you said or did especially reach the other person? What made someone laugh? What misfired or got nowhere? Of all the rounds, what behavior was most satisfying to you, personally? What might you try another time?"

More ideas – here are some more ways to use scrub-jay lines to prepare for activism – make up your own for your issue and/or city.

- One side are interested passersby, the other are protesters trying to explain, "Why I am here today." (Trade roles so each person does both sides.)
- Cops vs protesters, yelling and/or trying to dialog.
- Pretend you are talking to a friend about what you are doing – what might inspire them to join?
- One side is chalking sidewalks, other side is a local resident who doesn't want you doing it.

Photos: A Scrub-Jay Line

Teens at an activism prep do a scrub-jay exercise.

Scrub-jay lines, or hassles lines, let us role-play possible interactions and conflicts – and also practice talking to people about our beliefs and passions – before we go out into public.

Sometimes the lines explode into group dancing!

MAGICAL ACTIVISM

Magical Skills for the Street

Street Magic – Remembering How to Stay Grounded

One of our challenges when doing street activism is staying centered and grounded amid tension and pressure. Remaining calm while the person next to you is screaming at a riot cop can be a challenge to the most experienced priestess!

When we do activism with magical friends – a Pagan affinity group or Pagan Cluster, we say – we (ideally) take time before we march into the streets to do a short ritual, tapping our magical skills to strengthen our focus and groundedness.

Grounding – alone or in a group, we take a breath and remember our deep connection to the Earth. In the streets (or any intense situation), it's good to practice grounding with eyes open. "As I ground, I visualize a deeply-rooted tree, and I anchor that image in my center. Whenever I touch my center, I can call back the image and renew my sense of groundedness."

Circle casting – in an affinity group, we can cast a flexible circle around all of us, helping us feel our connection to the group as well as the boundary between us and the wider world. "I cast a personal circle of protection and awareness – I invoke the directions and elements and ask them to alert and protect me whenever I encounter discordant energy."

Invoking elements – maybe this is part of our circle casting, as above. If we have time, we invoke the elements with a song.

Invoking allies – here's a key piece of activist magic! We can invoke magical heroes and protectors (maybe Hermes for quick movement and clear communication), political models such as Martin Luther King Jr, ancestors such as the Diggers or Suffragettes, artistic activists such as ACT UP, etc. Who would you want walking by your side as you step out? Invite them!

Anchoring the magic – we can anchor the magic by picturing a symbol such as a crystal or a tree which we place in our own center, touching the spot to fix the symbol. Any time we need to remember our grounding and allies, we can touch this spot.

Dream Actions: Stirring the Activist Cauldron

Goal: A visioning brainstorm where we let our imaginations run free. In our ideal activist group – what would we like to do?

Space/Time/Size: Alone or in a small group (form circles of five or six if it's a larger group). Space to gather comfortably.

Materials: A cauldron (a metal or glass bowl will do, or you can simply use an altar cloth); flowers, crystals, and other small, earthy objects of beauty – place in and around the cauldron or on a cloth in the center; a small bowl of salt water.

Working: Ground and cast a circle. Invoke elements and an ally or two. Gather comfortably around the cauldron or altar. Lie on your back if you wish. If you're a group, lie with your heads toward the center.

Practicing affinity group maneuvers – TEM activism prep.

Brainstorm your dream direct actions. Extravagant theater, huge encampments and blockades, a roving spiral of chanting Pagans, giant puppets shutting down the financial district of a major city.... Don't worry about being realistic here – there'll be time for that later. Share inspirations, visions, and laughter.

As the energy wraps up, invite people to share any last thoughts – especially if someone has been quiet.

Sit up and gather around the cauldron. Each person speak one word. Begin stirring clockwise, singing Weave and Spin or She Changes Everything She Touches (see pages 112-113). Sing until the energy seems complete, and let the song wind down.

Using your hands as a scoop, dip into the cauldron and draw up some of the energy, as much as you need. Drink in the energy like cool water. End by saying: "Blessed be!"

Devoke allies and elements you invoked and open circle.

MAGICAL ACTIVISM

Climbing Skills: a Special TEM Workshop!

Reclaiming: An Activist Tradition

Reclaiming has several decades of activist experience and engagement, from the anti-nuclear protests of the 1980s, through the forest protests of the 1990s, on to the anti-globalization and Occupy movements of more recent years.

Teen Earth Magic teachers and campers have been involved in some of these movements, and we also reach out to folks in the wider grassroots network to create trainings for young people in our community.

At Teen Earth Magic 2014 and 2015, Earth First! activist Fly set up a climbing rig. Several teens did a prep that covered techniques and safety – then, one at a time, they scaled the tree to a platform 50 feet up.

Climbing Trees – and Oil Derricks!

Climbing skills are part of forest defense actions. Tree-sits are a nonviolent way to slow down loggers and road-builders.

Activists also climb oil derricks and construction equipment, scaling rigs to hang banners and shut down machinery.

And San Francisco's Billboard Liberation Front has used climbing skills to create radical public artworks.

MAGICAL ACTIVISM

Climbing Skills: a TEM workshop (pg 2)

First – the Prep

Activism begins with planning and training. Just as civil disobedience participants take part in a street activism prep, climbers spend time learning about their safety equipment and climbing skills.

The Figure-Eight Knot

"Make friends with this knot – your life will depend on it!" – *Earth First! climbing activist Fly.*

Teens spent the first part of the workshop on the ground getting acquainted with knots, harnesses, and climbing gear.

MAGICAL ACTIVISM

Climbing Skills: a TEM workshop (pg 3)

Into the Trees

The first ten feet took a while, as the climbers grappled with their gear. Once they understood the knots and movements, all quickly scaled the rest of the way to the makeshift platform.

Earth First!

Earth First! has a long history of front-line eco-activism. Some Reclaiming activists have joined and supported their actions and organizing.

Keep up with environmental and solidarity actions in your area and around the world by visiting the website of Earth First! Journal:

EarthFirstJournal.org

MAGICAL ACTIVISM

Activist Workings

Introduction – Legal Street Actions

Direct action often means "taking it to the streets" – but it doesn't always have to mean risking arrest. Sometimes our goal is to get our message out to people, not to disrupt anything.

Even when some people plan to risk arrest in a civil disobedience action, a larger group can find other ways to reach a wider audience – street theater, banners, music, giant puppets....

Here are several ways for a small group of friends (a circle or affinity group, we say) to do street activism with minimal risk of arrest – although that doesn't mean everyone you meet will agree with your action (see Sidewalk Chalking on next page).

Street Theater

Street theater is a way we can have fun, tap deeply into our creativity – and help create world change

A few people doing a three-minute performance with simple costumes and props can engage and educate the public. And if you do it as part of a larger action, you'll raise everyone's spirits!

With street theater, as with banner hangings, rallies, sidewalk chalking, chanting, drumming, etc, we directly intervene in public space and challenge popular consciousness. Seeing people taking public action sometimes touches bystanders as much as the particular message we're trying to deliver. People remember what they saw, not what they heard – a good argument for colorful props and minimal dialog.

Materials – posterboard, scissors, and markers for signs, masks, etc. Masks and costumes as needed (think thrift shops!)

Solstice in the Streets – *TEM teens created props and street theater for 2011's Solstice in the Streets. After an opening circle, we did a procession around downtown San Francisco, stopping to do performances and music at banks, oil companies, and nuclear energy corporations – but also at sites like public fountains and plazas, where we celebrated our vision of Summer in the City. Photo by George Franklin.*

Choose your issue or focus – brainstorm an issue. If you already have the issue, what will be your specific focus? This is a good chance to use some of the group process skills we talked about above – see Preparing for Action. Take your time and give everyone a chance to share ideas, concerns, and hesitations. Look for an issue and action that unites your group.

Creating the theater – will you do the "writing" together, or do one or two people have an idea that others will support? Either way, leave plenty of room for individual inspirations. Let people create their own parts where possible.

- Skits – keep it short. Repeat the same one-minute piece over and over. Keep dialog to a minimum and go for colorful, larger-than-life images. Masks draw attention – and help you stay anonymous if you wish.

- Signs – think of sign-boards, like in silent movies – an easy way to convey a simple message.

- Silence – using masks and props, silently "occupy" a visible public space. After ten minutes, march silently to a new location.

Start and end with magic – as with any of these actions, you can start and end by grounding, casting a

continued on next page

MAGICAL ACTIVISM

Activist Workings (pg 2)

circle, and invoking allies. Whether you're two people or a thousand, a short opening circle will help unite your group.

At the end, do a circle where each person shares about their experience (in a larger group, use small groups of six to eight). Devoke and open the circle – and if there are new people, pass around a sign-up sheet – a key part of magical activism!

Sidewalk Chalking – a Legal Direct Action

Goal – Again we directly intervene in public space and challenge popular consciousness, this time with that simplest of magical activist tools – a stick of chalk. We'll work not with slogans, but with questions and simple phrases, aiming to spur people to think about an issue for themselves.

Sidewalk Chalking – chalking on public sidewalks is an accepted form of free speech in San Francisco, Berkeley, Oakland, and hopefully your town as well!

Chalking is part of many other actions – wherever people gather, out comes the chalk!

Materials – multicolored sidewalk chalk; cloth or plastic bags; rags.

Space/Time/Size – if the group is more than 10 people, form sub-groups of a half-dozen which will make their own decisions within the broader action. Allow a half hour for the action and at least that long for debriefing.

Choose a site – one that's good for chalking, with wide sidewalks and plenty of foot-traffic. Make sure your site is a public sidewalk, not a private area such as a mall.

Brainstorm your issue – choose an issue you want to work on, then brainstorm a list of points you would like to raise. Once you have a half-dozen points, see if you can turn some of them into short questions, or find ways to make the points in one to three words. Can you say things in a way that would make *you* stop and think?

Other roles – are there artists in your group who can add a quick drawing? Do you want lookouts? Will you talk with people who approach you? How will you decide when the action is complete?

A note about conflict – despite being legal, sidewalk-chalking may bring us into conflict with people who have limited ideas of how public space ought to be used.

Brainstorm nonviolent responses to several possible occurrences – shop-owners threaten to call the police; the media shows up and wants to interview you; a bystander scuffs out your message; other bystanders want to join the chalking; the police order you to stop. Do scrub-jay lines around a couple of these possibilities (see page 161).

Decide how to respond – after a few scrub-jay rounds, decide what you'll do in situations that may arise. Maybe you want to designate one or two people to talk to anyone who approaches? If asked to stop or move, will you? Do you have a back-up site in mind? If Oprah invites you live on-air, what will you say? Use more scrub-jay exercises to role-play possible scenarios.

Action! – at the site, take a minute and circle up. Ground by breathing together. Cast a circle. Laugh out your jitters. Review your plans. On a clear signal, start chalking, all together. Everyone get their hands on the chalk, unless other roles such as

continued on next page

MAGICAL ACTIVISM

Activist Workings (pg 3)

lookouts have been assigned. Keep going until the agreed ending time, or someone interrupts you. If interrupted, circle up and decide what to do.

Debrief – do a go-round, one minute each, where you share a highlight. Leave "critiquing" for another time, after you've slept on it. If there's extra time, brainstorm more actions rather than critiquing this one.

Mystery Posters

Goal – postering, like bannering, is direct action aimed at educating our community. By taking our message outside the "approved" channels (media, newspapers, books, pulpits, classrooms), we claim public space for political dialog and take our message directly to other people. Postering is an intimate medium that people experience close-up. It invites us to share images, concerns, poetry, philosophical questions….

Materials – plenty of paper, including colored construction paper; thick and thin colored markers; brushes; glue-sticks or paper-glue; scissors; simple collage materials (optional); duct tape; thumb tacks; snacks while you create posters and/or afterward.

Space/Time/Size – any number, in groups of 3-6. Allow an hour or more. Scout out the postering possibilities – you need enough sites so you can divide into small groups. This may mean a list of campus buildings, phone poles on busy pedestrian streets, etc. This sort of logistical planning can be done ahead of time by a small group.

Prep – most of this action is prep. Hanging the posters may only take a few minutes – although you can make a magical ritual out of it, remembering to ground and cast a protective circle before you go out. What allies would help with this work?

These aren't exactly "mystery" posters, since we included contact information – hand-colored posters for Solstice in the Streets, 2011.

At TEM 2011, people colored posters in their spare time. Poster design by K. Mogg. Coloring by TEM campers.

Video of 30 hand-colored posters: WeaveAndSpin.org/tem-chants

After creating your circle in a quick, fun way, talk for a little while about things and issues on your minds and about ways you might awaken the curiosity of others. Might you use slogans? Questions? Cartoons and drawings? Collages? Poetry? What kinds of designs will catch attention?

Share ideas and inspirations. Then take 20 minutes or so and create hand-made posters. Don't worry about details or perfection – aim for what will grab attention. The more obviously hand-made the posters are, the better. When complete, do a quick show-and-tell where you admire one another's creations.

continued on next page

MAGICAL ACTIVISM

Activist Workings (pg 4)

Action – ground and cast a protective circle, then hang the posters as secretly as possible. Unless you choose otherwise, the origin of the posters will be a mystery.

Afterward – return to the place you created the posters. Circle up and take a few breaths together. Go around and let each person say a little about how the action felt, a highlight, etc. Remember to open your circle and say goodbye to each participant.

Bannering – a Legal Direct Action

Goal – create a banner and hang it in a public space. Bannering is direct action – by taking our message outside the "approved" channels (media, newspapers, books, pulpits, classrooms), we claim public space for political dialog and take our message directly to other people.

Materials – heavy paper (several sheets at least 3 x 6 feet); pencils; a few colors of poster-paint; half-dozen brushes; duct tape.

Prep – discuss and reach consensus on: (A) what goes on the banner (words and images), and (B) where to hang it (a hallway, a balcony, the side of a panel-van, the front door of city hall...).

Action – if folks in your group are willing, ground (or take some breaths) together. Cast a circle. Invoke elements and an ally or two.

Involve everyone in the group in drawing and painting the banner. For purposes of this action, no one is an expert. Use pencil-sketches, ruler lines, etc to make painting easier. Once you've agreed on the message, don't worry if the artwork isn't perfect – it will magically be exactly how it needs to be.

Document the action – photos are fun, but be sure to get permission before you photograph people at a direct action. If the banner connects to local issues, you might want to let local media know about it. Provide local media with an "unposed" photo of your group putting the banner up and they may put it on their website!

Afterward – return to the place you created the banner. Circle up and take a few breaths together. Go around and let each person say a little about how the action felt, a highlight, etc. Remember to open your circle and say goodbye to each participant.

More Ideas for Actions & Exercises

- **Bubbles** – move through town or around a mall blowing bubbles.
- **Puppets** – puppets (hand-held or wearable) liven up any occasion. You can find directions for building big wearable puppets and other props on youtube and elsewhere.

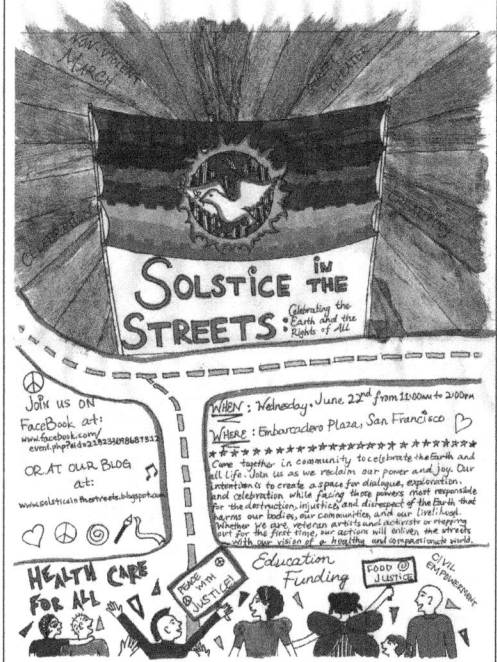

Hand-colored poster for Solstice in the Streets – see preceding page.

- **Masks** – make or buy masks and wear them to do simple street theatre. Masks can quickly identify a character or an emotion for onlookers – and wearing a mask can help free us from stage shyness.
- **Workings: Shadow: Composting Oppressions and Composting Headlines** (see Workings chapter, pages 262-265).
- **Workings: Spectrums** – spectrum exercises help us articulate hopes, doubts, beliefs, and commitments. Try some spectrums around what people believe, how willing they are to do certain kinds of activism – and why (see Workings chapter, page 268).
- **Solstice caroling** – find a few friends, learn some songs, and busk on the street for Solstice, Equinox, etc. Since your audience will keep changing, you only need to know a few songs! For ideas, see our chants lists on page 112-113, and hear our Resistance Chants mix at WeaveAndSpin.org/playlists.

MAGICAL ACTIVISM

Activist Allies & Kindred Spirits

Spirit-based activists, and especially young folks, can bring a lot of magic and energy to the streets, from music circles to giant puppets to spiral dances and much more.

Luckily, we don't have to organize every event we're part of. In any city you can find street artists, soup kitchens, and local festivals. In rural areas you can look for Earth First! and other nature defenders.

Groups such as Unitarians, Quakers, and Jewish Renewal often host activist circles.

Here are some allies we've found over the years – with many more to come!

Photos: Food Not Bombs groups gather donated surplus food from local markets and restaurants and collectively prepare free meals. That's Reclaiming co-founder and Berkeley-Oakland FNB activist Judy Foster at top right and middle left.

Right: Bay Area activist groups including Reclaiming march in solidarity with Indigenous resistance at Standing Rock, 2018.

Solidarity events happen in many cities and for many causes – young people are always especially welcome!

Solidarity photo by George Franklin.

FNB photos by Lydia Gans, courtesy of Reclaiming Quarterly.

MAGICAL ACTIVISM

Activist Allies & Kindred Spirits (pg 2)

Right: The Brass Liberation Orchestra, along with Sista Boom and other street music ensembles that often include Reclaiming folks, have long enlivened peace and solidarity marches.

Maybe it's time to dust off that old sousaphone or piccolo in your closet!

Check with music stores for local bands – or post a note and start a group yourself.

Above: Local artists and residents gather in a Mission District park to create outdoor altars to the beloved dead for the annual Dia de los Muertos (Day of the Dead) commemoration in San Francisco.

Below: Earth First! forest defenders take to the tripods to defend the Cove Mallard wilderness in Idaho, c. 1995. Tripods can slow or prevent logging. Photo courtesy GroundWork magazine.

WORKINGS

Workings & Exercises

Intro & Teacherly Techniques 173	Magical Writing 239
• Transitions, Small Groups, Milling 176	Mirror Affirmations / Boundaries / Goddess 241
Affirmations 180	Nature Sit / Night Sit 244
Allies Circle / My Own Best Ally 181	Non-Judgmental Listening 246
Altars / Scavenger Altars 184	Overflowing Cup / Ace of Cups Spell 248
Auras / Aura Carwash 190	Pentacles Magic: Intro / Pearl / Great Turning 249
Automatic Writing 196	Purification: Bridge Challenge / Star Purification ... 255
Bead Ceremony 197	Ritual Skills Day... 257
Blessings & Star Goddess 199	Shadow Work 259
Book of Shadows 202	• Shadow: Tarot & Mirrors / Shadow Party 260
Boundaries: Collages / Scrub-Jay Lines 203	• Composting Headlines & Oppressions 262
Campfire Activities 206	• Costume Shadows 266
Circle Workings 208	Spectrums of Belief & Choice 268
Collages 211	Spellcrafting 271
Costume Magic 213	• Spell: Breaking a Commitment 274
Divination: Nature Readings / Oracles / Scrying 214	• Spell: Burning or Composting Putdowns.......... 275
Flaming Cauldron 219	• Spell Candles 276
Games - Cooperative / Quick & Active 221	• Spell: Charging with Fire & Flour 278
Grounding: Red Cord Spell 225	• Spell: Temperance Pouring 279
Harvest Stations... 227	• Spell: Waters of the World 280
Intuitive Practices 229	• Spell: The Wicker One 281
Labyrinth Workings.. 230	• Spell: Yarn Binding 283
Letter to Myself 233	Tarot: A Key Magical Practice 285
Liberation Circle 234	• Tarot Reading: Quick Intro (one page) 288
Lifting Each Other Up 236	• Tarot: Intuitive Reading 289
	• Tarot: Reversals & Difficult Cards 293
	• Tarot: Living Tableaux 295
	• Tarot: Speed Readings 296
	• Tarot: Tarot Stories 298
	• Tarot: Journey of the Spirit................................. 299
	Tools of Magic / Magical Correspondences 303
	• Tools Cakewalk 307
	Trance: Place of Power (Online) 309
	Transformational Tableaux 310
	Trust Walk, Trust Run, Trust Fall................................ 312
	Voice Magic 317
	Wand-Crafting 322
	Younger Groups – Some Ideas 323
	Zap 324

172   TeenEarthMagic.org

WORKINGS

Workings: Intro

A Magical Compendium of Workings from Teen Earth Magic

At Camp, Alone – or at a Party?

The workings in this chapter are the core of our rituals and pathwork at Teen Earth Magic, Witchlets' Ravens Path, Redwood Magic Family Camp's Ursa Path – and many are used at other WitchCamps and local classes.

This is a "greatest hits" from 12 years of our camp!

We've described the workings just as we do them in camps and classes, gathering in groups of a half-dozen to 20 or so.

At the end of most pages you'll find a paragraph called "Solo Working" that suggests ways to adapt the practices for one or a few people.

Many of our exercises work as well for one person as for a group. Others can be done with a few friends.

And they're not all "Pagan." Some of these make perfect birthday-party activities – what could build group spirit better than lifting one another overhead?

We hope you use these workings in many ways to add power, awareness, and energy to different parts of your life.

Sacred Space

When we use these exercises in a morning path at Teen Earth Magic, we weave the workings into a ritual by finding a simple way to create sacred space at the beginning. We gather again for a few minutes to open the circle at the end of path.

For evening rituals, we often do more extended invocations, calling the elements one at a time, invoking a few allies, and singing a song or two.

There's a reason we do these exercises within sacred space. This work involves our focused attention and intuition. Before we jump into a working, we take a few minutes (or longer) to clear our attention and to awaken our intuition.

It doesn't always have to be an elaborate process, but it's generally a good idea to take a few minutes to bring ourselves fully present by grounding, casting a circle, and invoking a few allies. For ideas, see Ritual Skills: Sacred Space: Quick Ways.

At the end of a working, remember to devoke your allies and open the circle – this can be done as simply or elaborately as you wish. Devoking elements or allies can be as easy as saying their name, taking a breath, and offering, "Thank you!"

Adapting These Workings

We're glad to see these exercises used by other groups and traditions. Truth be told, we've borrowed more than we can remember.

You can continue the tradition. If you pick and choose and reshape and adapt to create a ritual for your group, you're doing just what we do every Summer.

Some workings are quiet and reflective, such as this collage workshop at TEM 2014.

continued on next page

WORKINGS

Workings: Intro (pg 2)

A Magical Compendium of Workings from Teen Earth Magic

Teaching This Material?

If you want to borrow workings from this book – welcome to the lineage!

We're glad to have you use the book for your camp or classes. Please keep passing them along.

If you use or adapt this material, we ask that you not present yourself as a Reclaiming or Teen Earth Magic teacher.

Reclaiming is a formal tradition with trained teachers. Teen Earth Magic and Reclaiming youth camps also have processes for training new teachers.

If you want to participate and study in the Reclaiming Tradition, a great place to begin is at a WitchCamp – find camps in many regions at WitchCamp.org.

If you feel called to teach young people outside of accredited schools, we strongly urge you to base your work in family organizing. See the final section of this book – Organizing a Family Camp.

No Grooming or Recruiting – this book is not to be used to recruit youth for circles or classes apart from knowing and communicating with their families.

No Reclaiming material is ever to be used to groom young people.

If you have questions about anyone teaching this material, you can contact Quarterly@Reclaiming.org or TeenEarthMagic@gmail.com.

No Teachers Needed

Anyone can use the workings in this book to create your own unique rituals and classes – no teachers needed.

You don't even need to be a teen. Adults have been known to get a lot out of some of these workings as well!

If you're using this book on your own or with a self-directed group, take a look at the agreements we make at our camps – they'll help lay a basis of trust. Read Intro: Agreements.

Some workings have everyone up and moving, such as this cooperative game at TEM 2009.

Let the Magic Begin!

Whether you begin by choosing one of these workings, jumping into the Rituals chapter, or reading more of the book first – trust your intuition.

Are there others you might circle with? What workings might appeal to others you know?

When in doubt, we recommend the ancient divination tool known as bibliomancy – skim through the book and let something jump out!

April's Book of Games

The Teen Earth Magic workbook – a compendium of our exercises and workings – was inspired by a booklet of games and exercises for younger and middle-school kids created by the late April Cotte, our co-teacher some years at Witchlets and Redwood Magic Family Camp.

You can download a PDF of April's Book at our organizing resources page: WeaveAndSpin.org/resources.

Our thanks to April – what is remembered lives!

WORKINGS

Workings: Tips for Teachers

TEM Teachers' Top 13 Tips (in no particular order)

Here's a bunch of handy tips that we've learned (and re-learned) along the way – we wrote them down so we don't forget next Summer!

For our teaching teams, we look for a mixture of skills, personalities, ages, genders, etc. No one person has every skill.

Ring the changes – a chiming bowl and/or gong marks mood changes, gathering times, etc – without you speaking a word.

Sing the changes – similarly, when you complete a working and move to the next, mark the transition with a song that pertains to one or both – you'll find lots of ideas at Ritual Skills: Chants (pages 112-113).

Don't dumb it down – 'nuff said.

Right-to-pass – everyone is present and tuned in – but no one has to do or say anything, and people can also move to the sideline and take a break.

Active exercises – eg, spectrums vs sitting in a circle and posing questions.

Increase participation by using go-rounds, small groups, dyads and triads, etc. Invite small groups to take on ritual roles, camp tasks, etc – this way, quieter folks might be drawn into participation.

Mix it up – this is true for adult classes too. Have a mix of active and quieter exercises. Use "stations" rituals (see Rituals: Stations Format) as a way to give people choices and variety.

Quick games and songs are important when you need to fill ten minutes.

Make agreements, not rules – where strict rules are needed (for instance, no one goes off-site), explain why, and ask if people will "agree" even though it's not really a choice – ask campers' buy-in on as much as possible.

Create opportunities for youth leadership – young people are more cooperative if they also get to lead. As organizers, our longterm goal is: "To teach ourselves out of a job!"

Simple drumming focuses energy. Play a heartbeat while someone speaks or leads a trance or song.

Invite young people to be involved in planning – everything from helping plan an evening ritual at camp to being part of our year-round Weavers organizing group. Match younger / newer people with older / experienced folks to pass along skills. Use small groups to help quieter folks join in.

Invite games and songs – some teens will have games, songs, and activities they want to lead. Create time for camper offerings (we like to schedule afternoon workshops that anyone can offer) and provide good support (ie, teachers and mentors show up and take part).

Involve parents and families – create ways for teachers and parents to meet and talk. Ask parents (including caregivers whose kids are not at camp) to help with cooking and other at-camp work – TEM was originally hosted on land owned by a Reclaiming family.

Teacherly Toolkit

- timer
- bell / chime / bowl
- fire starters (non-toxic)
- tea lights & lighters
- altar cloth
- knife & scissors
- rope (several sizes)
- tape (several kinds)
- paper, pens
- markers (different sizes)
- pad of large paper
- planning notebook
- magical tools:
  - athame
  - chalice
  - mirror(s)
  - tarot deck(s)
  - drum(s)

WORKINGS

Intro - Some Handy Techniques

Here are various ways of working with group energy that we've found handy with the workings and rituals in this book – mix them as needed to keep the energy moving.

Some of these are techniques for people sharing about themselves within larger groups – sharing tends to be easier when we are speaking to one or a few people rather than the whole circle.

Use milling or wagon wheels to get people moving and interacting – movement often helps loosen up sharing.

Use Chants as Transitions

Chants can draw us out of our thinking brains and into a trancey space. We like to use simple, familiar chants to gather our circle – instead of yelling, "Hey everybody, shut up and form a circle," we start singing, "Air I Am" and get the same effect.

Chants are a good way to wrap up the energy from one working and clear the deck for the next. Many of the workings in this section include suggestions for chants. In the Ritual Skills: Chants pages you'll find more suggestions and online resources.

Teach chants at the beginning of a class or ritual, so when the time comes everyone knows them and can jump right in. Priestesses or a ritual wrangler keeps track of when to start chants. When the time comes, don't announce the song, just start singing.

If you're using a chant as a transition, let the singing or toning fade and pause a moment. Then ring a bell or simply begin the next section of the ritual or class.

Bells, Chimes, & Gongs

Transitions can be marked by chimes or bells – a nice chime or ringing bowl will save much yelling and trying to get people's attention. A chime or bowl can be heard even in a big group of talking people. When the chime rings, people tend to tune in.

Use chimes to let people know when to switch partners in a working, and also as pleasant punctuation between workings. When one section is complete, don't say anything more – just strike the bell and let it ring till it fades. Then begin the next section.

Gongs are just plain fun! Strike a gong unexpectedly and watch people light up. We have a 15-inch gong that travels from camp to camp – it's great for calling the group together, announcing meals, and waking up late sleepers. However, it might be distracting to use a gong to ring every transition within a ritual.

Small groups allow for more intimate communication than a big circle.

Small Groups

Small group process was pioneered by the feminist and gay rights movements, as a way to support human-scale interactions within large groups of people. Six or ten people can sit in a circle and truly see and hear one another in a way that thirty or a hundred cannot.

Small groups make good support groups – sometimes we call them affinity groups at WitchCamps or direct actions. These small groups meet daily and give people a chance to check in and share in a circle where everyone can be seen and heard.

Sometimes a class or circle is already a small group. If your group is 10 or more, try breaking into groups of five or six. Everyone will get more time to share, and more chance to see and be seen by the others.

Small groups work well for planning, invocations, etc.

continued on next page

WORKINGS

Intro - Some Handy Techniques (pg 2)

Ask a group of three to five people to invoke an element. Some of the funniest invocations of all time have been done by small groups at Teen Earth Magic!

Five is the ideal number for ritual planning – if a planning group is bigger, we brainstorm together, then send a smaller group off to do the detailed planning.

Dyads/Triads

Dyads (pairs) and Triads (groups of three) carry the small-group ideal further, and open up a lot of time and space for people to share.

Checking in or debriefing in pairs or triads allows each person a lot more time and more intimate attention – sometimes it's easier to talk to one or two people than 20. Each person can talk for a couple of minutes, and the process can be finished in 10 minutes total.

Some years at the annual Spiral Dance ritual in San Francisco, hundreds of people break into triads in the middle of the ritual to share with a couple of other people about loved ones who have died in the past year. This level of sharing would be impossible even in a group of 10 or 12, let alone 1000 – but a triad is perfect.

Why triads? Compared to dyads, two listeners double our chances of someone really paying good attention – but it only takes 50 percent longer. It's good magical algebra!

It helps to have a chime to ring the transitions. Invite people to get into triads and decide who is going first. The other two just listen and appreciate the speaker. After a couple of minutes, ring the chime and ask people to switch.

After each person has a turn, give the groups a few more minutes just to chat before calling people back.

Sometimes after doing dyad / triad check-ins, we come back to the circle and do a "one word" go-round, as below.

Go-Rounds

Sometimes the whole group needs to come together and hear one another. But if 20 people talk for one minute each, plus some transition time, there goes a half hour. You can save time by having each person say just one word or phrase.

At the Brigid ritual each Winter in San Francisco, over 100 people will step up to the Goddess's cauldron and make a pledge for the coming year. If everyone talked for a minute, half of us would miss the train home. So we ask people to pledge in "nine words or fewer." Mostly it works, and often fewer words become richer and more poetic.

In a circle of 25 people, a good way to come back from an exercise is to go around and invite everyone to say, "one word about how you're feeling right now." If people pass, come around a second time and see if any of them want to speak now. The whole group can be heard in a minute or two.

The time to do longer go-rounds is when something upsetting or controversial has happened. Then each person needs time to speak and be heard by the whole group. Sometimes there's no substitute for spending an hour hearing each person one by one.

If this happens – what magical tools do you have to move stuck energy afterward?

Moving Stuck Energy

Even the best circle gets stuck sometimes. Maybe you've done a long go-round and everyone has been heard, but there is no resolution. Maybe you've done a long, slow magical working that left everyone sluggish.

continued on next page

WORKINGS

Intro - Some Handy Techniques (pg 3)

Shaking our bodies, getting fresh air – these are quick ways to move energy. Sometimes what is needed is to debrief in dyads or triads (see above) – give people a chance to open up and talk with one or two people before moving on.

What about something wordless like an Aura Carwash (see Workings: Aura Carwash)? How about reinforcing our circle with some high-impact rounds of Pass the Knot (see Workings: Circle: Pass the Knot)?

Or maybe you need an upbeat song like Rise with the Fire of Freedom or We Are the Power in Everyone.

Wagon Wheels

A wagon wheel allows people to share in ever-shifting pairs, with minimal transition time. This is a good way to weave together a group of new people. Allow 15 minutes or so. Use a bell or chime to ring changes.

Choose your questions to suit the working you are doing. This is a chance for people to share deeply and from the heart – so it's more about feelings and experiences, and less about what people think about a topic. (See also Workings: Tarot: Speed Readings for a way to use this with tarot readings).

Wagon wheels need ten or more people (up to about 50). Break into two exactly equal groups. One becomes the inside circle, the second group outside – each person faces one in the other circle.

The priestess leads and invites one of the circles to share something, for instance: "Inside circle, share for a minute with your partner about a time when you felt strong and in your power. Outside circle, listen to your partner silently and with full support."

After a minute of sharing: "Inside circle, thank your partner. Now, outside circle rotate one person to your left. Outside people, share a time when you felt strong and in your power. Inner circle, listen with full support."

Thus, each person has a chance to share (although with a different partner), and it is always clear who is next to speak.

After a minute or so, either or both circles rotate to the left again, and a new question is posed, for instance: "Inside circle, share a time when you doubted your power. Outside circle, listen with full support."

And so on – four to five questions are good. Afterward, do a song or something that reunites the whole group.

continued on next page

WORKINGS

Intro - Some Handy Techniques (pg 4)

Milling

Milling is a way to mix people's energy, and can also be a deep working. It is often done in silence (or can be modified to include verbal sharing.)

Prep – any number – you'll need light to see one another's eyes, so if it's a night ritual, build up the fire. Enough room for people to "mill about" without feeling cramped. Allow 15 minutes or so. A chime is helpful for transitions.

Working – begin in a loose circle. Priestess invites people, in sacred silence, to start milling around, passing one another and briefly meeting eyes. When the chime rings, come to a stop facing one other person.

When people are facing partners, priestess speaks: "Continuing to hold silence, gaze into your partner's eyes and see another person who, like you, _____." (Fill in the blank to suit your working – see below for samples.)

Let people eye-gaze for up to a minute – a bit longer than is comfortable. Then ring chime and invite people silently to thank their partner and resume milling.

People stop and gaze about a half-dozen times, each time beginning with, "Gaze into your partner's eyes and see another person who, like you, etc." (See next column.)

At the end, bring the whole group back together with a song and/or a spiral dance – something that reunites the circle.

Song – Harvest Chant (Our Hands will Work for Peace and Justice); Weave and Spin; Sweet Water; We Are the Rising Sun.

SOLO WORKING – Mirror Magic

This milling exercise could be done as a mirror working – within a sacred circle, hold a hand-mirror. Read each line, beginning with "See" – "See a person who worries about the state of the world," etc.

After reading each statement, gaze at yourself for a long moment – at least 30 seconds. Let go of any judgment and just see yourself as if the words you read are true. Look away from the mirror and take a breath before reading the next line.

✪ **Book of Shadows** – which of these lines were difficult? Which felt most true of you?

Sample Milling Statements with Silent Gazing

Here are some "milling statements" we used at a Fall Equinox ritual, where we were balancing fears and hopes (balancing for Equinox – get it?).

We used alternating voices, so the "worries" were in a different voice than the "dreams and realities."

(1) Continuing to hold silence, gaze into your partner's eyes and see another person who, like you, came here today to be part of a magical community.

(2) Gaze into your partner's eyes and see another person who, like you, worries about the state of the world.

(3) … who, like you, has dreams of a better world.

(4) … who, like you, worries that they are not doing enough.

(5) … who, like you, is perfect just the way they are.

(6) … who, like you, worries that all their efforts will come to nothing.

(7) … who, like you, is harvesting the fruits of their gifts and wisdom.

(8) … who, like you, believes in the power of community.

Can you create more "like you" statements that will inspire you and your circle?

Milling exercises help stir up the energy, and can be adapted to your theme.

WORKINGS

Affirmations: Words of Power

INTENT

A humorous, active way to get in touch with our own brilliance, beauty, wisdom, etc. Can be awkward and challenging for some people, but hopefully ends on a positive note for all.

People are asked to interact a lot. Can be difficult for a brand new group, but a good opening exercise on day two or three.

TIME/SPACE/SIZE

Up to 20 — if more, break into smaller groups. 15 minutes including transitions and debrief. Enough space to mill around.

PREP

Need note cards with affirmative words written on them, one large word per card – see below for a list of ideas. Words should be ordinary ones that are easy for people to guess. Need as many cards as participants. Don't let people see them ahead of time.

- Set of 16 words below, and add your own.
- Tape to affix the cards on people's backs – people cannot see their own, yet it is easy to see each others' words.

WORKING

Gather people in a circle and affix one word to each person's back, so the person doesn't see their own word.

When all are ready – people walk around speaking to one another as if their affirmation was true of that person. For instance – if Sally Ann's word is "Brilliant," people might catch her attention and say, "You are so smart! You shine like a diamond!"

The goal is to guess your word. Some will get theirs right away, others will be stumped. Priestesses help the last few people.

When complete, gather in a circle. Go around and each person speaks their word, allowing a pause after each to let it sink in. At end, priestess says: "Each of these words is true of every one of us. These are our birthright, our true being. Breathe them in."

Song for wrapping up: My Soul; Opening Up in Sweet Surrender; Let the Beauty We Love.

SOLO WORKING

Need – Book of Shadows; note cards or slips of paper; pen or marker. Write one affirmative word at the top of each note card or slip of paper.

Scramble them, then draw the words like divination cards – for each card, write at least three more positive words.

After you've drawn five or more cards and written for each, go back and underline a half-dozen words. Make a short poem that includes these words – read it aloud three times, breathing between each reading and reminding yourself that every word you read is true about you.

Affirmation Words

Intuitive	Skillful	Lovable	Brilliant
Insightful	Fantastic	Radiant	Powerful
Amazing	Wonderful	Strong	Beautiful
Gorgeous	Incredible	Passionate	Talented

WORKINGS

Allies Circle

INTENT

This is a powerful working which illustrates our connections with others and the deep support available from our community.

This working could follow a shadow working or meditation – one that touches places where we feel alone or powerless.

We've used Allies Circles as the final ritual working at several camps – a culmination of our time together. Doing the working around a campfire adds an extra touch of magic.

It could also be done as the first working in the final morning path, followed by Lifting Each Other Up.

SPACE/TIME/SIZE

Each person will speak, and many will want to go more than once.... In a circle of about 12-25 people, this working can take an hour or more. Any more people than this and it will get long, so consider limiting people to speaking once each.

You'll need room for a loose circle. A fire or altar in the center helps focus the energy. Circle should be 8-10 feet back from center.

PREP

Ritual fire in center, or create a central altar.

If you are not already in ritual space, cast a circle and invoke elements and allies for this working as a strong magical container. Remember to devoke afterward.

Need one or two priestesses to do a short meditation and facilitate the working – a good chance to pair a veteran and a newer teacher.

Ask a couple of mentors or teachers who have done this working before to go first and second, to model how it works (and to offer examples of the sorts of things people might share – some people will know right away, and others will have to think about it).

Examples might be:

"I can't concentrate at school and it's hurting my grades."

"I have chosen my own name."

"I don't fit into the gender role that was assigned to me at birth."

"Sometimes I've done things to hurt myself."

Priestesses also prepare one or two final statements that will close the working on a solid, inclusive note. For example: "I feel stronger when I am surrounded by friends and allies."

continued on next page

WORKINGS

Allies Circle (pg 2)

WORKING

Gather in a circle. Priestess explains working: "We will be doing an Allies Circle. One by one, we will have a chance to step into the circle and say something true about ourselves where we want to know that we are not alone, and feel the support from our allies. A couple of mentors will go first, and then people can go whenever they are ready. Let's allow everyone to have a chance to speak once before we go a second time. As with all of our workings, you have the right to pass."

Priestess leads a short meditation about where in your life you might want allies, where you might feel alone or unsupported. What would it be like to ask for and receive support from this circle? Give people a few moments to think about this.

First person (a mentor chosen ahead of time) takes a couple of steps into circle, and makes a statement such as: "I can't concentrate at school and it's hurting my grades."

Priestess: "Anyone who wants to claim this statement as true for themselves, take a couple of steps forward. (Usually at least a few people step up, sometimes most of the circle.)

"Take a look at those who have stepped in with you. (They look around.)

"Now turn and look at the outer circle – your allies. (Any teachers and mentors in outer circle model support – good attention, perhaps holding your palms open toward center.)

"Inner circle, acknowledge your allies, and return to the circle." (Inner folks nod, touch their hearts, etc, then rejoin outer circle.)

Second person steps in, perhaps saying something more challenging such as, "Sometimes when I'm depressed I feel like hurting myself."

Priestess repeats guiding steps above ("those who claim this statement step in," etc). After a few rounds, priestess won't need to say so much, but it often helps to give simple directions for each round.

Continue until all have had a chance. When everyone has gone once, invite people to stop and take a breath.

If time permits and people seem focused, people can go a second time.

At some point, you'll want to close the working.

Closing the working – this exercise can go on and on, as people think of more ways they can ask for support. The challenge is to feel when the energy is starting to slacken, and have a strong closing ready.

When time is short, you could say, "We have time for a few more..."

Priestess or someone else has pre-planned the last round or two – statements that are likely to include most or all people in the group. Example: "I feel stronger when I know that I have allies."

Song – I Would Know Myself In All My Parts; Let the Beauty We Love; We Are Alive As the Earth Is Alive; My Soul.

SOLO WORKING

This is a hard one to do alone, or even with a few people. A good solo working for this material is Allies: My Own Best Ally.

WORKINGS

Allies: My Own Best Ally

INTENT
Recognizing that we have the skills and tools to be great allies to ourselves.

SPACE/TIME/SIZE
Any number. 15 minutes including transitions. Room for people to sit and write – close enough to hear priestess.

PREP
Sheets of paper or Books of Shadows, pens or markers (markers are easier on uneven surfaces).

WORKING
Each person gets a pen and several sheets of paper (or blank journal pages). Priestess guides:

(1) Write at top of page: "If I were embarking on a magical quest, my ideal companion / ally / guide would be like this" – then free-write for a couple of minutes. Write as fast and continuously as you can, without editing or over-thinking. Just keep writing.

(2) Take a breath, then go back and underline some key words in your writing that describe your ally. Here is an example:

"They would be strong and dedicated, unwavering in their support. They would be good-humored and able to laugh at mistakes, wrong turns, etc. And they would be intelligent enough to figure out when they are doing something useful and when they are wasting their time."

(3) Below this, write: "As an ally, some secret magical tools I possess are:" – and make a list of the underlined words:
- strong
- unwavering
- intelligent
- good humor
- support
- doing something useful

(4) On a fresh page, write: "When I think about doing something amazing in the world, what I worry about is" – free-write for a minute or two. Here's an example:

"That I will not be able to maintain a focus, that I will get distracted and try to do too many things, that I will misestimate my talents and waste my time pursuing dead ends."

(5) Underline a few key worries, and make a list of them:
- get distracted
- misestimate my talents
- waste my time

(6) Now look back at your list of ally-skills. Next to each worry, match a "secret magical tool" from the first list. Here's an example:
- get distracted / unwavering
- misestimate my talents / use my intelligence
- waste my time / doing something useful

(7) Write in your journal: "To apply these skills, what would I need to change in my life? What would I need to do differently? Is this something I am willing to do? What is one step I can take toward this goal?" (Maybe also do Workings: Letter To Myself.)

(8) Talk in dyads or triads – "What would it mean to be my own best ally? How would I need to grow? What's one step I can take?"

(8) Re-circle. Go around – each person says one word from their "secret magical tools" list. Hear the words as a poem.

SOLO WORKING
Same as above.

WORKINGS

Altars

INTENT

An altar is any dedicated space set apart from the mundane world. Setting up a magical altar can represent "making space" for magic – and making time and space for yourself.

It might be a dresser-top, a table in a corner, or a favorite spot in a garden or woods. It might live inside a suitcase or box and be brought out only for special occasions. It could be on the nightstand – a place you visit daily. But you might consider a more versatile space that supports more varied types of workings.

If you like making art, an altar can be like an installation and can include other artworks you create. Altars at public rituals like the Spiral Dance are sometimes interactive installations created by local artists.

Altars can also be very simple – a carved glass pitcher on a blue cloth could be an elegant West altar. A stack of rocks in a grassy field can anchor North.

At this participatory Spiral Dance altar from 2008, people could write a name or place a pebble for a beloved ancestor. Photo by Michael Rauner.

Place or remove items from an altar with intention. Pause, breathe, and be aware of your actions.

TIME/SPACE/SIZE

Any flat space that won't be disturbed. A dresser-top, a nightstand, a window sill. Time – however much you want to devote to setting the altar up, then later adding to and tending it.

Altars are a great solo working – and see the following pages for some group-altar ideas.

PREP

Prepare your altar by visioning and gathering magical items and accoutrements. The prep never ends!

Altar Health & Safety

Food – unless you are intentionally creating an altar to honor ants and flies, remove food offerings at the end of the day. Compost leftovers to send them back into the cycle of life.

Fire – magic can be distracting. Whether you're in your bedroom or a forest, take extra precautions. Indoors, use glass jar candles, not open flames. Keep wall-hangings away from your altar. Tie back curtains. Have a smoke detector and extinguisher handy.

WORKINGS

Elemental Altar(s)

A dresser-top might offer enough space to create mini-altars to each element (Air in the East, Fire in the South, Water in West, Earth in North). Perhaps Spirit/Mystery in the center can be a different tarot card every day.

Limited space? How about an elemental altar that changes daily (or weekly or when you get around to it). Begin with "Air" items, changing to Fire, Water, Earth, and finally Center/Mystery. Tarot cards can be part of this elemental altar too – see the correspondences under Workings: Tools of Magic.

continued on next page

WORKINGS

Altars (pg 2)

Ancestor Altar

At Samhain (Halloween, a season for ancestors in many traditions) we build altars to honor ancestors of our families, our spiritual and cultural traditions, and also the First People of the land we are on. Photos, books, musical instruments, old tools or artifacts.... What speaks to you of your own past?

Prepare a meal for the cultural heritage of one of your ancestors. If you're making a new dish, go online and find out how and when this food was traditionally served.

Before eating, prepare a dish of food for your ancestor and place it on your altar with words of remembrance and offering. Afterward, compost leftovers so they'll go back to the cycle of life, death, and rebirth (and not the cycle of ants).

As you eat, listen to music, read poetry – whatever that connects you to that culture.

✪ **Book of Shadows** – before you clean up, sit quietly, and write in your journal.

Interactive Altar

Add this working to any altar – cut small strips of paper large enough for a word or phrase. Place them on your altar next to a nice bowl. Each time you pass your altar, stop for a moment and write a word inspired by your altar. Place the writing in the bowl. Later, stop at your altar, take a breath, pull a strip of paper, and read it.

✪ **Book of Shadows** – want a quick inspiration for your writing? Contemplate your altar, then pull a tarot card, set it on your altar, and write the first thoughts that pop into your head.

Altar to Your Dreams

Sketch (on paper or in your mind) an altar that celebrates and honors your dreams, your vision for your life.

What is the centerpiece? What colors are the altar cloths? Does it include "natural elements" such as water or fire?

How might it be interactive (ie, what is something that you or someone else might *do* at your altar)?

A Spiral Dance altar, created by people attending the 2014 ritual. Photo by Michael Rauner.

Words of Inspiration

Copy favorite quotes, questions, challenges, etc. Place them intentionally on your altar.

What other objects do you see on this altar?

How will you know when to remove the writings?

Magical Workbench

Altars are ideal spaces for magical work – a place to ground, cast a circle, do divination, charge magical tools (see Workings: Tools).

Like any craftsperson or artist, we want our tools handy and uncluttered. For some of us, that means

continued on next page

WORKINGS

Altars (pg 3)

placing items neatly on shelves. For others, it might mean storing them in a drawer.

Ideally, do you want your magical tools laid out like a workbench? Or do you want them out of sight after a working?

What belongs on your magical workbench? Is it elemental tools like a chalice and blade? Is it a deck of divination cards, face down and ready to draw?

Is it your latest tarot reading or throw of the runes, lingering partly as inspiration and partly as decoration?

SOLO WORKINGS

A personal altar can be a magical workstation. It's a place to ground, cast your circle, read tarot or runes or do other divination, charge magical tools (from athames to guitar picks), bless your art or writing...

A simple, powerful altar to the Fey – Spiral Dance 2009. Photo by Michael Rauner.

It can also be a work-in-perpetual-progress – an ongoing magical experiment made up of your workings and readings.

GROUP WORKINGS

Labyrinth Challenge Ritual (see Rituals: Labyrinth Challenges) – as their first challenge, invite each person to use whatever objects they find (if indoors, bring a variety of objects), and create an altar that honors their work with the group. Perhaps a second challenge is to return to the altar and do nature divination (See Workings: Divination: Nature Readings).

Living Altars – in a small group of about six people – take a moment and each envision an ideal altar (perhaps to honor a decision or commitment they have made). Each person quickly describes their altar – and the others join to make a human sculpture of it.

Giant Altar – a favorite with younger groups – build a giant elemental altar using found objects, some as big as anyone can haul back. Set a few guidelines ("Don't bring back a living tree, no poison oak, no small creatures, etc.") – and go for it!

A sparkly floor altar greets people arriving at the 2015 Spiral Dance. Photo by Michael Rauner.

186   TeenEarthMagic.org

WORKINGS

Altar: Scavenger Altars

INTENT

Elemental Altars Scavenger Hunt – a fun way to engage with the elements in the outdoors. Especially good for younger groups, and for folks who want to be active.

Can include all five elements, or focus on just one.

SPACE/TIME/SIZE

Any number, in groups of three to five. Allow a half hour or more. If outdoors, set some general boundaries. With a young group, include a mentor or teacher in each group.

PREP

Make scavenger lists in advance – include some items people are likely to find for each of the elements (see next page for sample list). Invite people to add other magical items they find for each element.

Set boundaries and figure out where people can make altars. Tell people how long they will have, and ring a bell as a five-minute warning.

WORKING

In groups of three to five – hand out scavenger-hunt lists. Depending on time, groups could each take one element, or each do all five.

Challenge people to find items, then construct a simple altar to the elements. Bonus points for finding cool objects not on list.

Ring a bell when five minutes remain and suggest people stop searching for items and focus on "sculpting" their altars.

When altars are finished (or time runs out), do a Tour des Altars. Each group shows off a few special items, and says why they feel those items belong with this element.

End with an elements song (see Ritual Skills: Chants – page 112).

SOLO WORKING

Using the list on the next page (or your own list), go outdoors and find as many items as you can. Make an altar in your yard or in an outdoor spot. Sing or listen to an elements song.

continued on next page

An impromptu scavenger altar at California WitchCamp.

Photo by Otter.

Altar: Scavenger Altars (pg 2)

All items to be found in nature – no human-made objects. Add more objects to suit your habitat. For each element, try to find at least three items on the list – plus at least one additional object that signifies the element to you.

AIR
- A feather
- Something fluffy / airy from nature
- A white flower
- Decayed wood that is mostly air
- One additional object that says "Air" to you

FIRE
- Bit of burnt wood or charcoal
- Red rock
- Red flower or red leaf
- Something fiery from nature
- One additional object that says "Fire" to you

WATER
- A stone worn smooth by water
- Something muddy
- Something that looks like a bowl or cup
- Something other than wood that will float
- One additional object that says "Water" to you

EARTH
- A seed of some sort
- An unusual piece of wood
- A rock exactly the size of your fist (or thumb for small altars)
- Three kinds of fallen leaves
- One additional object that says "Earth" to you

CENTER
- A natural spiral
- Something round
- Something with a hole in it
- Something mysterious
- One additional object that says "Center" to you

WORKINGS

Altar: Youth Visions

INTENT

At the annual San Francisco Spiral Dance ritual, organizers have asked teens from TEM and our family camps to anchor one of the major altars. Some years teens do Air, other times a theme altar like Youth Visions or Endangered Species. Over the years the teens altar has tended to be in the Air corner of the venue, creating a familiar gathering space as young people arrive.

This is an example of encouraging youth involvement by creating "teens space." The area around their altar becomes an informal teens corner – teens gather there throughout the evening, knowing they'll find friends and peers.

Organizers for the San Francisco Spiral Dance and also the Faerie Ball have been strong supporters of youth involvement. This includes creating teens space and giving free tickets when needed – teens can get into the ritual as volunteers by arriving early and working on invocations or altars. A few even stay late and help with cleanup!

Here's ideas for creating an altar or display for a community event. Our example is for a Samhain ritual – adapt as needed.

SPACE/TIME/SIZE

From a few people to 20 or so. If more, divide into sub-groups of 10-15. Allow an hour or more – the more people, the longer it will take. Space as available – the key is to create a distinct area which feels like "teens space."

PREP

You'll need a solid surface and a backdrop – maybe a table pushed up against a wall?

Supplies needed (ideally) – white cloth; twinkly white lights; extension cord; power strip; three-prong adapter; duct tape; drafting tape; twine; scissors; colorful markers; finger paints; white poster board; rags; a half-dozen pomegranates and several bowls.

Altar items – invite teens to bring items that say "youth" or "expression" or "vision." At the Spiral Dance, people bring things like musical instruments and sheet music, books, ribbons, photos of activism, a disco ball, etc.

Select a couple of altar priestesses to keep the project on track even as people wander around and socialize. A teacher or two can help with quiet support.

Priestesses let people know the gathering time, and arrange for teens doing altars and invocations to get free tickets if possible – their spirit will more than compensate!

WORKING

Gather early arrivals. Ground and cast a flexible circle. Call in energies such as inspiration and creativity.

Altar priestesses do a quick talk-through of available materials and possible design ideas. Quick discussion produces a rough design. People break into smaller groups – a few work on the backdrop and lighting, some work on signs and painted decorations, and others start thinking about how to lay out items.

As the altar takes shape, a couple of people start to loosen and remove seeds from the pomegranates. New arrivals and stray people can join in – this quickly becomes a lively chat-circle, and will keep folks busy for a while. Seeds are gathered in bowls and placed on the altar with a sign inviting people to eat a few (recalling young Persephone's first visit to the underworld).

When the altar is complete, gather everyone in a circle. Go around and everyone share a word of inspiration or blessing for the group. End with toning or a song.

SOLO WORKING

You can create a youth visions altar in your own space. Maybe you want to get some fingerpaint and pomegranate seeds to link to our Spiral Dance altar. Or maybe you have other inspirations. What will say "youth visions" to you?

WORKINGS

Auras

INTENT

Our aura is the life-energy that fills and surrounds our physical body. One's aura can change size or texture depending on our mood, physical health, etc. When we say someone has "big energy," we're talking about their aura taking up a lot of space.

The size of our aura varies, depending on mood and physical energy – typically it extends about 4 to 12 inches from our bodies.

Our aura is the way we experience the world. When we are in a peaceful, life-filled place like a forest or a room full of friends, we feel love and inspiration filling our aura, our entire being.

When we are surrounded by pressure, unhappiness, anger – our auras can't help but be affected. Soon our own energy feels more stressed and anxious.

Sensing Auras

Some people sense auras by moving their hands a few inches from the physical body (rubbing your hands together first may help). You may notice warmth or cold, various textures, or tingling. You might sense areas of tension or pain.

Some people see auras as colors, or as a kind of radiant energy (a plain white background might help). Some sit silently facing a person and "read" their aura (gently touching your third eye may help).

By experimenting, each of us finds our own ways.

When we become aware of our own and others' auras and personal energy, we can take steps to strengthen or change how we are in the world and how we experience other people.

Here are some ways to work with auras, including becoming aware of our own and others' energy, finding ways to shift our aura, and learning to shield ourselves from others' energy.

SPACE/TIME/SIZE

These exercises can be done alone or in a group. With more than 20, break into sub-groups. When it's time to share, form triads if you're over a half-dozen. You can do one or two of these workings in 20-30 minutes, or build a longer sequence. Try alternating quiet and active workings.

PREP

Read through the exercises so you have some ideas ahead of time (especially for the Aura Fills). If you're a group, choose a priestess to lead each working.

SENSING AURAS

Begin by becoming aware of your own energy. Rub your palms together, then hold them about six inches apart. Close your eyes and slowly move your palms closer. You may start to feel pressure, as if you are compressing a balloon, or a springiness like a rubber band. Maybe you feel radiant warmth. Play with this until you find your own ways of sensing this energy.

Practicing with a Partner

Practice sensing others' energy by working in a group or with a trusted friend. Sit facing one another but not touching – touch will distract you during this exercise.

One person (whose energy will be read) sits quietly, closing your eyes and breathing steadily. Let your mind wander without trying to figure anything out.

continued on next page

WORKINGS

Auras (pg 2)

Second person (reader), using your various senses but without touching or talking to the person, see if you can sense your partner's aura. Move around as needed. Try doing this for a specific amount of time – say three to five minutes.

- Hold your open palms three to six inches from the person's head, neck, belly, or hands – hold your hands steady, then slowly move them closer and further – can you feel a difference?
- Sit facing the person – if possible with a plain background. Soften your gaze and notice the colors around the person. Of course you'll see actual colors of the person and surroundings – let these be, and notice whether other colors glow around the edges of the person. You may see ripples or waves of energy. Don't worry about figuring it out – just spend a minute or two noticing.
- Sit facing, soften your gaze, and notice the person's energy-body – using your intuition, where is the person holding energy? Where is it flowing freely? Where do you sense strength? Where are worry or fear?

When time is up, both people stand and stretch, then sit down and each take a turn sharing what the experience was like. Use "I" statements and speak gently – "I felt this or that, I sensed this or that." Try saying, "I sensed cautious energy around your heart," not, "You have bleak, hideous energy stuck in your heart!"

Stand and stretch again, and change roles.

When both are complete, do something to shift the energy – put on music, dance, read tarot cards, pet the cat...

AURA MAGIC / AURA SHIFTING

British occultist and author Dion Fortune described magic as the art of "changing consciousness at will." We can change how we are in the world by consciously shifting the energy of our aura.

In real life, this can be difficult! If you feel insecure, you can't just snap your fingers and be confident. But you can practice ahead of time and learn ways to shift your energy. Here are some aura games that you can do alone or with a group.

Ground first – eg, close your eyes and breathe for 60 seconds – then touch the Earth and breathe three times.

Cast a circle around the space. Then each person take a minute and cast a personal circle (actually a sphere) around yourself. You can do this by closing your eyes and on a series of easy breaths be aware of the space around you, as if you are inside a bubble. Breathe into this sphere to inflate it – then bring it in about six inches away from your body. Sense its boundaries. This is roughly your aura.

Noticing Our Aura

Pay attention to the boundaries of your own aura. You might rub your hands together and then use the palm of one hand to feel the edge of your energy-body.

When you can sense the edge of your aura, close your eyes and notice what is going on inside. How is your physical body doing? Are you nervous? Relaxed? Afraid you're doing it all wrong? Just notice, let go, and notice again.

Moving Within Our Energy Bubble

Imagine yourself inside a big soap bubble. Use your breath and hands to push the bubble out from your body. Feel its edges. Patch up any leaky spots.

Without speaking, and with soft eyes, move around the space, letting yourself feel what it's like to move within your own personal energy bubble. (We do this all the time – but now we're really paying attention!)

continued on next page

WORKINGS

Auras (pg 3)

Can you move around the room and still feel a solid circle around you? If it wavers, can you stop and restore it with a silent breath? What helps you stay focused on your own present experience?

Boundaries – Inflated & Deflated Aura

Create an energy bubble as above. Take a few breaths and see if you can bring it about six inches from your physical body. When you have it, move slowly around the space, noticing how it feels to move past other people.

Inflated Aura – take some easy breaths and inflate your bubble. Pump your energy larger – use your hands and arms if it helps. Feel yourself inside an inflated bubble. Now move around the space. Notice that your energy probably overlaps with other people or objects. Notice what this is like.

If you're a small group, stop and do a bit of sharing (larger group break into triads – if alone, write in your journal):

What was this "inflated aura" like? What colors and/or emotions does it make you think of? What situations does it remind you of? Would you be inclined to inflate your aura at a party? At a mall or in a cafeteria? Around your friends or family? If you are leading a magical working or making a presentation? If you are scared?

Deflated Aura – take some easy breaths and deflate your bubble. Let extra energy flow down into the Earth, and draw your aura in very close – use your hands and arms if it helps. Feel yourself inside a very tight bubble. Now move around the space, keeping some distance from other people or objects. Notice what this is like.

Do some sharing or write in your journal: What was this "deflated aura" like?

What colors and/or emotions does it make you think of? What situations does it remind you of? Would you be inclined to deflate your aura at a party? At a mall or in a cafeteria? Around your friends or family? If you are leading a magical working or making a presentation? If you are scared?

Boundaries – Aura Fills

Now that we've become aware of the difference that a shift in our aura can make, let's take it a step further. What if we consciously filled our aura with a specific energy? What if we could fill our auras with positive energy when we feel uncomfortable, with calming energy when we feel nervous, or with sparkly energy when we need to shine?

Here's a game that lets us practice shifting our aura – "changing consciousness at will." Create an energy-bubble surrounding you, as above. Notice the overall energy inside your bubble... What color is it?... Do you have a name for this type of energy?

Now let this energy fall down into the Earth, and call into your aura the energy of cold steel.... Let cold steel fill your aura.... With each breath, feel yourself encased in cold steel.... Now soften your eyes and move slowly around the space, noticing what it feels like to move as cold steel.

After a minute, stop. Let that energy slide down into the Earth. Take a breath and let it go. Now with a breath, fill your aura with lime jello.... Let green lime jello fill your energy-body.... Breathe deep, and feel yourself immersed in lime jello.... Now soften your eyes and move slowly around the space, noticing what it feels like.

Continue with a few more – if you're a small group, invite others to call out ideas. In a bigger group, have a priestess or two to do this. Here are a few more ideas:

• Fluffy pillows; cactus; smiles; peanut butter.

• Moods: seriousness; gloom; confidence...

• M&M auras (one flavor on the inside, one outside): fuzzy kitten inside / cactus outside; guard-dog inside / smiley-face outside.

continued on next page

WORKINGS

Auras (pg 4)

At the end, come together and do a bit of sharing or write in your journal: What were the different energies like? Did any feel more "natural" to you than others? Did any feel uncomfortable? Can you see ways you might use this to change energy in your daily life (maybe not the lime jello...)?

To close, do a quick purification – take five breaths – on each exhale, let go of any stray or unneeded energy. Then stand straight and tall and take three deep star-breaths – calling bright star energy to purify your aura from head to toes (see Workings: Purification: Star Purification for a full version of this working).

Earth Auras

Our aura radiates from the core of life at our center. Other living beings have auras too. Cats, trees, bees, flowers....

Find a natural setting such as a park or garden (or a redwood forest if one is handy). Take a short walk through the area. Then stop and ground, cast a personal circle, and invoke energy such as openness and awareness.

Find a plant that calls to you – a tree, a fern, a flower, a weed. Sit down next to it. Say hello. Close your eyes. Tune in to the energy of the plant. Try using your hands to sense its aura (without touching it). Use your heart to sense its life rhythm. Notice without attachment – notice and let go.

✪ **Book of Shadows** – what did you notice about the plant? How is its aura similar / different from humans? What feelings came up for you? What did you notice about yourself?

At the end – thank the plant for sharing, and appreciate yourself for noticing it.

SOLO WORKINGS

Many of the workings above can be done solo. Maybe you can find a friend who will try aura sensing with you?

WORKINGS

Aura Carwash

INTENT

Our aura – the energy that fills and surrounds our physical body – is how we experience the world. When we are in a peaceful, life-filled place like a forest or a green meadow, we feel peace and inspiration filling our aura, our entire being.

Our aura varies in size depending on our mood and physical energy – for many of us it typically extends about four to eight inches from our bodies.

When we are surrounded by pressure, by unhappiness, by anger – our auras can't help but be affected. Soon our own energy is more stressed and anxious.

The aura carwash is a fun way to clear out scattered, unhelpful energy as a preparation for magical work. In others words – it's a great purification.

At Redwood Magic Family Camp, we've done this at our opening circle as a way to wash away the stress of getting ourselves to camp. We've also used it as a purification prior to TEM rituals – we start at the end of the field and use the carwash to work our way down to the fire circle.

It can also be used as a transition between two workings with very different energies. In morning path we might do a pair of workings that are not directly related, such as a Permaculture working followed by a trust walk. An aura carwash is a playful way to shift the energy.

Body Respect

In the aura carwash we are cleansing and reviving auras – ours and others' energies. Our hands scrub and fluff the energy around their body without touching them.

SPACE/TIME/SIZE

You'll need at least a dozen people – if you have fewer, do the "aura scrubdown" in pairs (see next page).

The space needs to be open and flat. This is a moving exercise – people line up in two lines facing one another. The length of the starting lines is half of the length needed (ie, if the facing lines stretch 15 feet, the total space needed is 30 feet). If necessary, curve the lines to fit the space.

For 20-100 people this takes 5-15 minutes including transitions.

PREP

Get people in two facing lines about three feet apart (lines don't have to be evenly matched). Figure out if you'll have enough room or if the line needs to curve.

Determine who will priestess the working – one or two people explain and keep it moving.

WORKING

With people already in line, priestess explains and helps people get the motions and sound-effects going:

"One by one, people have a chance to go through the aura carwash. The first few people on each side will be hosers – they will hose down your aura without touching you and without water. (Priestess demonstrates with exaggerated motions.)

"The next few on either side will be scrapers – scraping gunk off your aura. Sound effects are encouraged!

"After that come polishers, and finally aura fluffers – all working without touching you.

continued on next page

WORKINGS

Aura Carwash (pg 2)

"When I complete the process, I join the end of the line. Meanwhile, the next person has already started down the line, about ten feet behind me."

Pause and make sure people get it. Then add:

"Now there's one more thing. As people start down the line, we lose our hosers. So the scrapers have to start hosing, and the scrubbers start scraping, and so on. As I join the end of the line, I'm automatically a fluffer for the next few people. As we move up the line we'll eventually take all the roles."

PAIR WORKING – AURA SCRUBDOWN

If you're a smaller circle, try an aura scrubdown. Decide who will be the scrubber and who will be the scrubbee. Scrubbee, stand tall and relaxed, eyes closed. Scrubber, go through the steps of the aura carwash, doing each one in succession. As above, no touching the person's body – hose, scrape, scrub, polish, and fluff their aura with lots of sound effects!

SOLO WORKING – AURA SHOWER

If you're alone, do an aura shower – go through the steps of the aura carwash, doing each one in succession. Do this without your hands actually touching your body and with full sound effects. (Why not try it in the shower?)

WORKINGS

Automatic Writing

INTENT

Here's a good exercise to loosen up creativity and expression. Legend says that author Ernest Hemingway began his workday with automatic writing – typing a page as fast as he could, ripping it from the typewriter, and hurling it into the trash can. Only then he was ready to write for keeps.

This exercise also works as a discernment and self-divination technique (see below).

SPACE/TIME/SIZE

A quiet, comfortable space for writing. Any number of people. Allow at least 10 minutes.

PREP

Pens and paper for each person (or laptop, etc if you prefer). Create a circle.

WORKING (basic and as divination)

Get a clean sheet of paper and a pen (or set up a fresh computer document). Get comfortable. Set a timer for five minutes. Or write for the length of a favorite pop song or dance jam.

Start writing, and don't lift your pen from the paper (or fingers from the keyboard). Keep writing no matter what comes out.

If you get stuck – write about getting stuck. Write about having nothing to write about. Write about how much you hate writing!

Assume that no one else will ever see what you write. Let strange voices come through. Let weird comments and half-finished sentences spill out. Change gears as often as you feel the inspiration. Just keep the pen (or your typing fingers) moving.

Afterward – go back and underline promising bits that you might want to follow up.

Self Divination

Before beginning, frame a question and write it at the top of the page. Breathe into this question. Now do a page or more of automatic writing, letting it go where it will.

Go back and underline a few key points, re-read your initial question, and do some more writing starting from those points.

Read it back and ask yourself – what have I just told myself about my question?

Wrap-Up – in a group – go around and read a single sentence that has power for you.

Thank yourselves and open the circle (or go on to another working).

SOLO WORKING

This makes a great personal writing exercise (ask Hemingway!).

Journaling at Teen Earth Magic 2011.

WORKINGS

Bead Ceremony

INTENT

The bead ceremony has been part of Witchlets and Redwood Magic Teens Paths for many years. It's a tangible way to show group identity and belonging – a ceremony in which each person receives a unique bead as a symbol of their being part of Teens Path (also known as Ravens Path and Ursa Path).

Sometimes we've done the bead ceremony early in the week so people can wear the beads during camp.

Other times we've done it as a culminating piece, such as at the end of the Labyrinth Challenge ritual on the final day of path. The bead is then the "reward" for completing both the labyrinth and the path (see Rituals: Labyrinth Challenges).

SPACE/TIME/SIZE

Any number – if more than 20 people, it may get long. Space for a comfortable circle, with or without a campfire.

This can work either at a night ritual or a during daytime. A good end-of-session working. Allow half-hour for up to 25 people.

PREP

Ahead of time – buy enough fancy and unique beads for the whole group, plus a few extras. For Witchlets, we like using locally-blown glass beads, each one guaranteed to be unique. Cost about $2-3 per bead. You can get fancy store-bought beads for $1 or so.

A pouch that is easy to reach into to draw a bead.

A big spool of waxed necklace string (ask a bead store for what you need) – test that it will fit through the beads you get (yes, we've made that mistake). Precut string into two-foot lengths, and have scissors and extra string handy.

A center altar with a basin or large bowl, a pitcher, and some jugs of water.

Decide who is priestessing which parts.

WORKING

In a prior working, each person comes up with a magical commitment to themselves – something they pledge to do or change.

Gather in a circle. Priestess has pouch of beads, with pre-cut string handy. Don't give out string until the end – it's distracting.

Priestess invites people to recall their magical commitment to themselves, and to find a way to express it in five words or fewer.

One by one, people are invited to step into the circle and state their pledge aloud (or in silence).

The rest of the group responds, not in unison but each in their own way: "We hear you, we believe in you, we support you..."

Priestess asks: "Have you heard the support of this circle? Breathe into the support. Then reach into this pouch with your non-writing hand and draw out a bead that symbolizes your pledge and the support of this circle."

One by one people step in. If someone doesn't want to participate, play it by ear – perhaps their bead can symbolize the group's support for the person doing things their own way.

When everyone who wants a bead has one – hold them over the bowl, everyone reaching out into center. Tone together.

The priestess then pours water lightly over everyone's hands and beads as people tone. After 20 seconds or so, a second priestess who is part of the bead circle begins slowly raising their voice and lifting their bead. All join in slowly lifting their

continued on next page

WORKINGS

Bead Ceremony (pg 2)

beads toward the sky, voices rising into shouts of release as the toning reaches its peak.

Gently bring the beads and energy back down. Priestess invites people to touch their bead to their own center and state their commitment to themselves.

Priestess brings in the pre-cut string and distributes it. People string their beads and put them on.

Song – something that consolidates the energy without raising it further. Examples: We All Come from the Goddess; The River She Is Flowing; Water and Stone (Solid as a Rock); Let the Beauty We Love.

Someone may ask – can we trade beads? You may want to suggest that part of the magic may be which bead you "randomly" draw – or which bead drew you. If you still decide to trade, rinse the beads with water and find some way to re-charge them after the exchange.

SOLO WORKING

The bead ceremony symbolizes "belonging to this group at this time." Perhaps you and some friends want to make such a commitment to each other? Could you ask for this at your birthday?

Alone – here's a way to make a commitment to yourself.

Using meditation, a tarot reading, etc – come up with a simple statement of commitment to yourself. It could be something specific: "I pledge to practice music every day this Summer," or general: "I pledge to love myself more."

After you have your commitment or pledge – visit a bead store and find a tray of assorted beads. Close your eyes, breathe to your pledge, and with your non-writing hand draw one of the beads. Pay for the bead with coins if possible.

Back home, set a bowl of cold water on your altar. Rinse the bead. Then state your commitment to yourself. Blow on the bead three times to fill it with your energy and resolve. Fasten the bead onto a necklace or string.

Say your pledge aloud again. Put the bead around your neck. State your pledge a third time. Give yourself a hug.

Song – end with a song that wraps up the working without raising energy: We All Come from the Goddess; The River She Is Flowing; Water and Stone (Solid as a Rock); Let the Beauty We Love.

WORKINGS

Blessing: Elemental Blessing

INTENT

A participatory way to share the blessing of an element (or a forest, a season, etc – substitute what works for your group).

We created this working for an Air ritual, where we were thinking about communication and language, but it can work for any element, deity, or energy.

SPACE/TIME/SIZE

Any size group. Works with large groups. Enough space for people to mill around. Allow 10-15 minutes including transitions.

PREP

Supplies – colored markers, small notecards or pieces of paper.

Choose and learn closing song – see below. Teach this song at the beginning of the ritual or right before this working.

WORKING

Everyone chooses a colored marker and small notecard.

Priestess invites people to hold the colored marker over their hearts and invoke their power of expression and communication (give people a moment to do this).... Then priestess calls upon Air's powers of inspiration, hope, new beginnings, freshness, etc – whatever energies of Air you want to call.

Now invite each person to write on their card, in one to five words – a blessing of Air. Invite people to use their intuition and write whatever sincere blessing comes to them. Give people a minute or so – if someone seems stumped, say, "Try saying 'Air,' take a breath, and write the first word or phrase that comes to you."

When ready – invite people to turn to someone, exchange cards, and each say: "Blessings of Air to you." Each person silently reads the card they've been given, then together they take a breath and nod their thanks.

Turn to another person and exchange cards with them, saying: "Blessings of Air to you." Continue for several rounds.

Song: After a few rounds, priestess starts singing and gradually gathers all voices – here's a few ideas: My Soul (good for call-and-response if one person knows it well); Let the Beauty We Love; Never Lose Our Way to the Well (See Ritual Skills: Chants).

Fade song. Priestess calls out (and others echo): "Welcome Air!"

SOLO WORKING

To do this working alone, you'll need to write a half-dozen Air-cards (one to five words each).

Where will you get your ideas from? You could start by taking a breath and writing whatever comes to your mind.

When you have written a half-dozen cards, mix them face-down. Close your eyes and take a few breaths. Draw a card and say to yourself: "I welcome the blessings of Air." Then read the card aloud. Repeat for as many cards as you wish. Or leave them on your altar and draw one now and then.

✪ **Book of Shadows** – what are your blessings of Air? Which do you need, and which can you offer?

Finish with a song – see above for ideas.

WORKINGS

Blessing Line

INTENT

A chance for each person to receive the blessings and encouragement of the entire group – and for each of us to participate in blessing and supporting one another.

This is a good exercise for near the end of a class of camp – after people have worked together for a while.

Note that this is similar to the Aura Carwash – which works well at the beginning of a camp or class. With the Aura Carwash, we're washing away unwanted energy. Here we are offering energies the person might want to receive.

It can also work at a birthday or coming-of-age party.

This working could be preceded by some sort of divination – tarot, meditation, etc – where each person comes up with a commitment or affirmation that they want the group to support.

SPACE/TIME/SIZE

Need a long flat space – 20 feet or more. If less space, you'll need to adjust your lines from time to time.

PREP

Nothing needed – although this working may follow a divination working (meditation, tarot) where each person comes up with a commitment or a "next step" that they want the group to support.

WORKING

Two lines facing each other – doesn't matter if lines are exactly even. Decide which direction the line is moving.

Priestess invites people to close their eyes and imagine what sorts of blessings, affirmations, words of encouragement, etc you would like to offer to people you really care about. Invite folks to hone their blessings to one or a few words that they can repeat, perhaps accompanied by a simple gesture.

Beginning at the head of the double line, one person steps out, takes a breath, and moves down between the two lines. As the person slowly walks between the lines, the others shower them with blessings, affirmation, words of love and support, etc.

When you reach the end, join one of the lines and help bless the following people. Keep going until everyone has had a chance. In a small space, adjust the lines as needed.

Optional – before the person begins their walk, they can state a decision or commitment, something that they are working on, or the sorts of blessings they want. For instance, one might say: "I commit to writing every day." As they walk between the lines, in addition to words of love and general support, some people might also call out, "We believe in you! You're such a powerful writer! The world wants to read your writing! Etc!"

End with a song – I Would Know Myself in All My Parts; Let the Beauty We Love; Let It Begin Now.

WORKINGS

Blessing: Star Goddess

INTENT
A simple pentacle blessing – blessing us with deep healing energy from within our own heart. This working was developed for the Love point of the Pearl Pentacle (see Workings: Pentacle: Pearl Pentacle).

SPACE/TIME/SIZE
Any number, working in pairs (or as a solo working). Enough space for pairs to be arms' length apart. Allow 10 minutes.

PREP
Teach song ahead of time.

WORKING
Priestess – explain the working first, then verbally guide people through it. Remind people this is a no-touch exercise.

In pairs, decide who will be Goddess and who will be Star first. Goddess will do a blessing for the Star.

Star – facing Goddess, cup your hands in front of your heart. With gentle breaths, pour your own healing, self-loving energy into your cupped hands. When your hands feel full, pour the energy into the non-writing hand of the Goddess in front of you.

Goddess – receive the energy into your non-writing hand as if you are holding a jar of paint. Imagine your writing hand is a paint brush. Dip it into the healing self-love and paint a pentacle onto the aura of the person in front of you, starting with their head.

Paint broad strokes onto the Star's aura in this order: head - right foot - left hand - right hand - left foot - head. Paint several cycles, layering on their self-love. As you paint, notice the person's aura field. Are there blockages? Spots of bright or fiery energy?

End by painting a clockwise circle around the pentacle-person's aura, then come to rest. Thank one another and debrief.

Star – what did you notice about your own energy? Could you feel your own self-love being painted, or was it hard to tell?

Goddess – what did you notice about your energy as you painted? Speaking gently – what did you notice about the Star's aura?

Switch roles and repeat.

End with a song: Body of the Earth; I Would Know Myself; Let the Beauty We Love.

SOLO WORKING
To do this blessing alone, you'll work both roles.

First, cup your non-writing hand in front of your heart. With gentle breaths, pour your own healing, self-loving energy into your hand. When it feels full, take one more breath to seal the energy.

Dip your writing hand into the energy. Close your eyes and begin painting a star onto your aura with your own healing self-love.

Paint broad, rich strokes, in this order: head - right foot - left hand - right hand - left foot - head. Paint several cycles, layering on your self-love. Finish by painting a clockwise circle around your aura. As you paint, notice your aura field. Are there blockages? Spots of bright or fiery energy? Murky places?

✪ **Book of Shadows** – when you finish, get your journal. What did you notice about your own energy? Could you feel your self-love being painted, or was it hard to tell? What did you notice about your aura? Were there any stuck spots? What is your thought about those places? When you finish writing, place your hands over your heart and thank yourself for your work.

End with a song: Body of the Earth; I Would Know Myself; Let the Beauty We Love.

WORKINGS

Book of Shadows

INTENT

Create a Book of Shadows (also called a magical journal) that can accompany you on your magical journey.

Is it a grimoire? Sort of. In ye olden tymes, grimoires were collections of spells and invocations. Herbal lore, healing practices, and practical astronomy were mingled with random invocations, assorted superstitions, biblical numerology, and sometimes-misguided advice.

Did anyone practice these spells and rituals, or were they concocted to defraud gullible aristocrats? Some famous grimoires such as the Key of Solomon and The Book of Abramelin the Magician can be found online – enjoy them with a grain of salt.

Many people today use the phrase "Book of Shadows" to signify one's personal magical compendium. You can collect spells, wise words, exercises, dried flowers, chants, recipes, jokes – as well as keeping a running record of your magical evolution.

The book you are reading right now is Teen Earth Magic's Book of Shadows – and it's changing all the time!

Your Book will grow and change – and the cover may as well. In this working, we will create the first version.

SPACE/TIME/NUMBER

Any number, given space and supplies. Allow an hour including set-up and transitions. Enough room to spread out and work.

PREP

Each person needs a fresh, undecorated journal with lots of pages – bound or looseleaf.

Collage supplies (see Workings: Collage) – invite people to find other images too, and/or to leave room for adding images.

Large envelopes to put unglued images in. Pen or marker(s). Music – try Labyrinth Meditation Music (see page 113).

WORKING

Priestess leads a short meditation: "Hold your undecorated book in both hands and close your eyes. Feel its solidity, its weight. Feel the angles of its corners. Open it and feel the smoothness of the paper.

"Take a breath and begin to picture your own Book of Shadows. What colors do you see? What images?

"Look over the collage supplies. Without too much thought, select some images to begin with. You can add more later.

"Try them out on the cover of your book. If something feels right, lightly glue or tape it down. If you're not sure, keep experimenting. Maybe the cover will never really be finished – a magical work in progress!"

When time is up, gather the images. Go around and let each person have a chance to share one image from their Book.

Charging the Book

When time is up, bring the newly-forming books to the center. Priestess invites each person to think about the power, beauty, and wisdom that will fill their book. Ask the universe to provide the words and images that are right for your work.

Song: holding your Book, sing a song to charge the magic: Weave and Spin; My Soul; Let the Beauty We Love.

As the song fades, kiss your Book of Shadows and welcome it to your magical journey.

SOLO WORKING

Same as above. Set a timer for 30 or 45 minutes. At the end of that time, stop and collect your images and ideas. Sift through them without attachment and let them speak to you. Say one word for each image that you believe you will use on the Book.

✪ **Book of Shadows** – throughout this book you'll find suggestions to develop in your Book – let the magical writing begin!

WORKINGS

Boundaries: Collage Shields

INTENT

A tangible way to strengthen our sense of identity and personal boundaries. Each person creates and collages a coat of arms that (A) shows who they are, and (B) sets a boundary to their personal space. This is a good first-day exercise – as class goes on, people may reveal more of themselves.

This is a variant of collaging – see Workings: Collages for details.

SPACE/TIME/SIZE

See Workings: Collages, which has lists of materials and space / time needed. This exercise will take up to an hour.

PREP

See Workings: Collages.

Plus, each person needs a piece of cardboard or posterboard about two feet square – these can be pre-cut into shield shapes.

You'll also need: duct tape to make arm-loops; paper and pencils for sketching.

WORKING

Each person gets a piece of cardboard for shield, blank paper and markers. Collage materials, glue, scissors, etc are ready.

Priestess leads short meditation encouraging people to think about parts of ourselves we want the world to see, and parts that we don't. The shields we create have two sides – one side that shows ourself to the world, and one that only we see.

On paper, take a few minutes and sketch some ideas for emblems, signs, or words that would represent what you want the world to see – your "coat of arms." Think how they might fit on your shield. You might divide the shield into sections, or interweave different aspects of yourself into one figure. Add words if that helps.

Once you have your sketch, look over the collage materials. Choose images that belong on your shield – and also images that you might want to put on the back side – images that show parts of yourself that you do not want to share at this time, but which you accept or claim as your own.

Use collage materials to decorate your shield. You can also draw or write on the shield.

If there's time, fasten a duct-tape handle on the back. Then gather in a circle with shields facing outward.

Priestess: Invite people to hold shields over their hearts and move silently around the space looking at one another's shields.

After a couple of minutes, circle up. One by one, people take about 30 seconds and share a few highlights of their shield – whatever they would like to show or name.

Priestess: "Look at your shield – both sides – and breathe into all of these parts of yourself. Consider the possibility that during this class/camp you might decide to add other parts of yourself to your shield. Look around the circle and recognize that each person here is considering the same thing – that we might share more of ourselves this week."

Song – one that calls us to our deepest selves: My Soul; I Would Know Myself In All My Parts; We Are the Power in Everyone.

Afterward, find a way to display the shields in a way that the back sides don't show.

SOLO WORKING

Same as above. If alone, name the parts of your shield aloud. Set the shield facing you and write about it in your journal.

WORKINGS

Boundaries: Scrub-Jay Lines

INTENT

Scrub-jay lines (also sometimes called hassle lines) are named in honor of the feisty little blue-feathered birds that taught us this exercise (Western Scrub-Jay, Aphelocoma californica). This is a fun, powerful way to practice boundaries.

This can raise a lot of chaotic, unfocused energy – follow it with something that strengthens our ability to establish and hold boundaries. Try Workings: Aura Fills.

See also the Activism chapter (page 161) for ways we use this to prepare for street theater and other direct actions.

SPACE/TIME/SIZE

Any number, in pairs. Enough space to stand in two equal facing lines – adapt to the available space. Allow about 15 minutes including transitions.

PREP

Ground first, then cast or strengthen the group circle. Consider what will follow this chaotic exercise.

WORKING

Line up in two rows with each person facing a partner. Name one line A and the other line B.

Each side is given a "position" to argue – often just a single line or even one word – and then given one minute to talk as loud and fast as they can, with absolutely no attempt to listen to or understand the other. Be as loud and obnoxious as you want – but no touching the other person.

Here are some lines to give to the sides:

A = Yes! / B = No!

A = I am blockading a military building / B = I need to get to work

A = Pizza! / B = Burritos! (or cake vs ice cream)

A = Police breaking up a crowd, "everyone must leave!" / B = Protester refusing to leave

A = Shut up! / B = No, you shut up!

A = Such-and-such needs to change immediately! / B = Change is a gradual process and requires patience

Make up your own – make them as polarizing as possible.

After a minute, ring a bell – it will take people a moment to settle down. Then ask: "What was that like? Did you have any impact on the other person? How did it feel not to be listened to? If you had it to do over again, would you say or do anything differently?"

Now ask people to take a breath, change partners and repeat a couple more scrub-jay lines. Ask: "What was different about how you approached it? Did anything change for you in later rounds?"

Next – do something that strengthens our ability to establish and hold boundaries. Try Workings: Aura Fills.

SOLO WORKING

Try this at a party – simple games such as "Yes / No" or "cake vs ice cream" can raise a lot of fun energy.

WORKINGS

Breathing

INTENT

Breathwork includes a range of exercises and practices that help us get in touch with deep, intuitive parts of ourselves.

Breathwork is done in some other spiritual traditions, and in non-spiritual psychology and personal-growth groups. Some Reclaiming teachers also offer workshops in different kinds of breathwork.

In this working, we look at "breathwork" in its simplest form – breathing.

Breathing is at the core of grounding, centering ourselves, personal healing, and many other magical practices. Powerful breathing underlies singing and public speaking (including invoking).

Breathing steadily can be part of a trance or meditation – but this working is not a trance. Here we go back to the basics and simply focus on our breath. This is a good opening exercise in a class or workshop.

SPACE/TIME/SIZE

You'll need a quiet, private space. Any number of people. If you're a group, give yourself room to spread out and be comfortable. Allow 20 minutes.

PREP

Need – journal and pen; drinking water; warm, comfortable clothes. Consider light drumming or instrumental music such as Reclaiming's Labyrinth Meditation Music (see Ritual Skills: Chants).

For a group, choose a priestess to quietly remind people to follow their breath.

Think about what will follow this working – something a bit more active and interactive, but not jarring.

WORKING

Priestess guides in a plain, non-trancey voice (for solo working, read this section first, then close your eyes).

"Make yourself comfortable in a way that you (probably) will not fall asleep. Sleeping during a trance is fine, but try to stay awake for this breathing exercise.

"Close your eyes and breathe as deeply as is comfortable without effort. Watch your breath as you inhale and exhale, inhale and exhale. Each time your mind wanders, gently call yourself back to your breath."

Priestess pauses for a minute or two, then periodically reminds people: "If your mind wanders, gently bring it back to your breath."

After 10 minutes, priestess gently calls people back: "With your awareness on your breath, pick up your journal and write for a few minutes – whatever comes to you."

Finish by going around the circle and sharing one word each.

Next – what follows this breathing exercise? How about something more active and cooperative, but not jarring?

SOLO WORKING

Taking time to intentionally breathe is a good way to start any magical working – or any day. Consider setting a timer that will play music after five or ten minutes. Read the Working section above, then close your eyes and breathe. When your mind wanders – take a breath and pay attention as you inhale and exhale.

TeenEarthMagic.org

WORKINGS

Campfire Activities

INTENT

Hanging out around a campfire is one of the great memories people take home from camps. But it doesn't happen in its own.

Left on their own, teens seem to gravitate to the dining hall, where they can listen to music, play card games, get snacks, etc.

But if singing or a game happen quickly after the ritual (and if snacks magically materialize!), folks may stay at the fire. It's nice to have a choice of indoor and outdoor spaces, if possible located close enough that people can move back and forth.

In the early years of Older Kids Path at Witchlets, the "night campfire" became a key part of weaving group identity. A nightly routine evolved of circling up at the teens fire in the mid-evening. Sometimes we did rituals or some other activity. Most nights ended with snacks and campfire games.

Telephone was an early favorite game with a younger teen group. As people got older we experimented with Circle Stories, Two Truths and a Lie, and other ways that people can share parts of themselves.

As some of the group grew into their later teens, guitars and ukuleles starting popping up, and singalongs (everything from Woody Guthrie to the Beatles to Tracy Chapman to Kimya Dawson) became a regular part of our campfires.

SPACE/TIME/SIZE

WitchCamp rituals sometimes include over a hundred people. For folks to connect at a personal level, 20 might be the maximum, and smaller is always nice.

As it gets later in the evening, be aware that others might be trying to sleep nearby.

PREP

Think ahead about several activities – be ready to drop one and start a new one fast.

If you'll be singing, make a songlist specially for the occasion – which songs might people already know? Which songs are super-easy to learn? Can you photocopy some lyrics ahead of time?

See if there are others in the group who have guitars, drums, ukes, etc – people may be shy about stepping out. Ask if there are teens who have ideas for games, songs, etc – help make space for teen leadership around the fire.

Snacks – having snacks ready right after a ritual helps the transition to campfire activities. If there's dessert at the dining hall, send an expedition to bring some back if possible.

Don't forget the fire! Who will collect extra wood while it's still daylight? Who can tend the fire? Who will stay and make sure it is safely extinguished? (See Ritual Skills: Firetending.)

SPECIFIC CAMPFIRE IDEAS

Note – it's a plus if whatever you do at night is not "compulsory." Leave space for people to sit and talk or just stare at the fire. We've been lucky at some sites to have two or three locations for teens to gather at night that are near each other (such as a fire circle, soccer field, and dining hall), so people have a choice, and can move back and forth if they want.

Singing – a great way to start

If we want to keep the circle going after a ritual, quick music helps. Have guitars, ukuleles, drums and percussion instruments, etc on hand. A few folding chairs are nice too – it's hard to play guitar sitting on the ground or in a floppy camp chair.

Singalongs engage people – the more songs that people can join in, the better. Save performances for the talent show. Look

continued on next page

Campfire Activities (pg 2)

for songs that people might already know the chorus to. If you start a song and no one sings – keep it short and shift to something else.

Let different people offer songs. An informal priestessing role is to occasionally ask if anyone new wants to offer a song – sometimes it takes new or quiet folks a while to speak up. If one person plays a few in a row, see if someone else wants a turn.

Here's some winners – Beatles, youtube hits, songs from current movies, old folk songs, chants, Broadway favorites, etc.

Story-Telling Circles

This is not one person telling a story – save that for the talent show. This is a group story-telling game.

A dozen people is ideal – up to 25 will work if each speaks only one phrase or word. The story moves clockwise around the circle, as quickly as possible – keep it moving!

Story Go-Round – each person says one phrase or sentence, attempting to move an increasingly complex story along. Someone with a funny idea begins, and it goes from there. The story will inevitably pull in odds and ends from camp – a favorite meal, something that happened during a ritual, a mouse that ran through the dining hall. Aliens and zombies might appear. Magic often plays a role. The story ends when it ends – 20-30 minutes is common.

One-Word Version (try this with a larger group, or for an interesting challenge). Each person adds a single word. Punctuation words like "period" or "quote-unquote" can also be used, and count as a turn.

Lazy Version – someone starts a story, and whenever they run out of steam, someone else picks it up. When anyone has an inspiration, they can try to interrupt. With a small group, this sometimes works.

Two Truths & a Lie – a non-competitive game

It might seem odd to play a game that involves deception at a camp where we are working to open our hearts to one another. The trick is that the "lie" is intended to be unmasked, and then becomes a self-chosen vehicle for revealing something about yourself.

First player thinks of three "facts" about themselves – two are true and one is false (but sounds true). These can be about anything the player wants to disclose.

Player can "disqualify" friends or siblings who would already know the answer.

Player states their three "facts." Then others discuss among themselves which they think is false. Finally the group takes a vote – it's fun to see if people generally agree or not. Then the player reveals the answer, usually with some explanation of why they chose it (the "lie" often masks some interesting truth about the person).

Telephone – fun for younger folks

This game was very popular with a young group (mainly ages 11-14). The ability of almost any phrase to morph into something obscenely silly is uncanny – unlike Truth or Dare, though, it doesn't get personal.

Truth or Dare – not advised for mixed age-groups

For several reasons, this is not a great game for a mixed-age group. Bantering with teens about drugs, sex, and illicit activities can put those over 18 in a difficult personal and legal position.

Also, in Truth or Dare, people can feel pressured to reveal things about themselves rather than getting to choose what and when they reveal. Refusal to divulge a "truth" can result in humiliation. And if something difficult does get spoken, is this game really the place to bring it up?

We strive to create space for challenging topics at camp – but we do it in path and ritual, not as a game.

WORKINGS

Circle Blessings

INTENT

A simple, musical way to bless each person individually. Can be used to charge their commitment, put power behind a word or phrase they have created in a prior working, or bless each other as we head back to the mundane world.

This working can also be done by singing people's names to them.

Helps create an intimate feel. Works well toward end of a ritual or class, as a final working before devoking.

SPACE/TIME/SIZE

Need an open circle with no fire or altar in the center. Enough room for a tight but comfortable circle.

Each person will step in for about a minute, plus a few minutes for transitions. Over 25 people may run too long.

PREP

This working is a good wrap-up to a class or workshop – so prep includes determining which working this will follow.

A good working before this is one where people come away with a word or short phrase that is both a powerful affirmation and an ongoing challenge to them. For instance: "I am an incredible singer!" or "I love myself more every day!"

WORKING

Form a tight circle, shoulder to shoulder. Priestess invites people, one by one, to step into the circle and speak aloud the power-phrase they developed in a prior exercise (or to state their name).

The rest of the circle sings / tones the phrase (or name): "You are an amazing singer," "Incredible voice," etc. Person closes their eyes and just listens.

What if someone chooses to step into the circle but remains silent? Others could still tone or sing their name to them.

SOLO WORKING

In a safe, quiet space, speak your affirmation aloud. Breathe into it. Now try singing that affirmation to yourself. No one is listening – sing to yourself.

End by placing your hands over your center – wherever that is for you – and breathing again. State your affirmation aloud. Breathe into it again.

Consider combining this with Workings: Mirror Affirmations.

WORKINGS

Circle: Pass the Knot

INTENT

Great teamwork game – teens like doing this over and over and "racing against the clock."

But it's more than a game. Do this the first day of class to cast the circle, and repeat daily as a fun way to reinforce it.

This is especially helpful with a younger group that doesn't want to keep holding hands – they can hold the rope and still be in the circle.

When we're not using it, the rope can be left on the ground and picked up whenever we want to emphasize the circle – for instance, during a go-round after an exercise, we pick the circle up and each say one word. If we "pass the knot" as we speak, it seems easier for people to stay focused and participate.

TIME/SPACE/SIZE

Space to form a circle – okay if a fire or an altar are in the center.

As a clock-racing game – each round lasts 30-60 seconds including analysis and strategizing – allow a total of five minutes for several rounds.

Any number can participate, but above 25-30 will start to get unwieldy.

PREP

Set up open space.

Need a smooth rope – quarter-inch is good, but any size works so long as it doesn't lead to rope-burn (ie, too small or too coarse) and can be knotted. Cut the rope so it is the size of your circle, with a little space between people. Tie a good solid square knot.

A timer or stopwatch will add to the drama of the race against the clock!

WORKING

The idea is to pass the knot around the circle, the whole group cooperating to get maximum speed and minimum rope-burn.

Teens have fun racing against the clock, and in some camps we've done this every day, trying to set a new speed record.

You can also pass it slowly as a way to share in a circle. Each person as they receive the knot can speak their name, or some magical intent or invocation (eg: each person call in some quality of energy they want in the circle that day, or speak one word about a working we just did). This works well with a younger or less-focused group.

When complete, set the rope on the ground. Pick it up later to re-establish the circle.

SOLO WORKING

This probably doesn't work alone – but you could get friends to play this game without saying that it is "Pagan." Do it at the beginning of a party and use it to build a circle of energy.

WORKINGS

Circle: Yarn Web

INTENT

A fun way to weave the circle together – a good early exercise in a camp or class.

Use this also to "charge" group intent – each person speaks one word of what they are invoking as they toss the yarn.

SPACE/TIME/SIZE

Need an open space to make a circle with no altar or fire in the center. Any number, but over 25 will slow things down. Time: about 20-30 seconds per person plus a few minutes for transitions.

PREP

A large ball of strong, colorful, all-natural yarn.

WORKING

Explain that we are "invoking" qualities that we want for our circle during camp or class. It helps to have a teacher or older teen go first, and they can toss the yarn to another experienced person to get things rolling.

Stand in a circle. First person has the ball of yarn. They hold onto the loose end, speak one or a few words about what they are calling in ("in-voking") for the group, then toss the ball across the circle to someone else.

Second person wraps the yarn loosely around their wrist, speaks their invocation for the group, and tosses the ball to another.

When all are woven together – feel the connections. Tug a little. Trace the yarn to see who you are connected with.

Try moving or rotating as a web – can you keep all the connections taut?

With a small group at Redwood Magic, we passed the nodes – each person passed the point they held to the person on their left, then we'd look to see the new ways we were connected to people.

Song – before ending, charge the web with a song: "We are the flow, we are the ebb / We are the weavers, we are the web." (See Ritual Skills: Chants– page 112-113.)

At an early Witchlets path, the teens wanted to preserve the web, so we carefully moved it to the side of the circle and laid it on the ground. Otherwise, gather the yarn up when you're done and consider burning it at the end of the ritual or camp.

SOLO WORKING

Like many of these exercises, you can do this with friends without calling it Pagan or magic. Try a yarn web at a party, especially when people don't know one another well. Invite people to speak their name aloud and call in qualities they want for the party and for each other.

Alone – on a big sheet of paper, write the names of yourself, friends and family, pets, allies, goddesses, etc in a big circle. Using a marker, connect the points using some random method. You could roll dice and count around the circle to that number, or drop something onto the paper and whoever it lands closest to gets the thread next.

When you're finished, see what patterns emerge. Soften your gaze and look at the web that connects you to all of these beings.

✪ **Book of Shadows** – write about the personal connections you have, and those you can envision – maybe with people you haven't even met yet. What do you want and expect from your friends? What do you offer?

WORKINGS

Collages

INTENT

Collages are a chance to work with visual and tactile media and express ourselves in non-verbal ways.

For some folks, collaging is a great means of tapping deeper wisdom. Others will rush through the project. Start collages in class or path, then let people work on them more during free time, or take them home to finish.

Collages can help focus issues in our lives. Will you collage about "the state of my life," "what I want for the world," "endangered species," or what?

We also use collage in other workings – see Workings: Boundaries: Collage Shields and Workings: Book of Shadows.

SPACE/TIME/SIZE

You'll need plenty of table / floor space, plus room for supplies to be available and completed collages set aside to dry.

Any number of people, depending on supplies. Allow 45 minutes with optional time later.

PREP

Collage supplies – pictures, magazines, etc. Pay attention to what you bring – fashion and exercise magazines promote dubious images of young people's bodies and lives.

Posterboard for each person. Scissors and glue-sticks. Manila envelopes are handy for saving unpasted images.

Would ambient music help? How about Labyrinth Music? (See page 113.)

WORKING

Invite people to ground and center. Recall prior workings or rituals that you hope might influence the collaging. Invite people to look over the collage materials and let images come to them.

Some teens like the quiet, reflective space of the collage table.

Work on collages. Let people know when 15 and five minutes remain. Pass out envelopes to hold unpasted images.

At the end, display or present the collages. Each person can make a one-minute presentation of their art. Even if the cuttings are not yet glued down, people can share images and say why they chose them. Use a timer or people might go on forever!

If it makes sense – put all the images in the center and raise some energy over them with a song.

Songs: Weave and Spin; Let the Beauty We Love; We Are the Power in Everyone.

SOLO WORKING

Choose a theme. Spend a week or more gathering images. Lay them out in various ways without gluing them down.

Step back and look. What images are you missing? What needs to move? When you're ready, glue things down.

How will you honor and charge your work when it's complete? Is there someone you can share it with?

WORKINGS

Costume Magic

INTENT

Are you the sort of witch or magician who doesn't feel like you can cast a spell or invoke a goddess unless you are properly attired? You will feel right at home at Reclaiming WitchCamps!

Some years at California WitchCamp an entire cabin is dedicated to magical costumery – a place anyone can stop en route to the ritual circle and find the perfect gown, corset, top hat, or feather boa. Priestessing the costume cabin is a camp volunteer chore.

On the other hand, if you are one of those people for whom "dressing up" means wearing a colorful T-shirt, for whom comfort is the first law of fashion – you too will feel at home. Reclaiming's dress code is one place we are in complete agreement with ceremonial magician Aleister Crowley: "Do what thou wilt shall be the whole of the law."

Witchy garb can be a fun way to "dress the part" – and also to challenge our "shadow" sides. We can use clothes to discover and encourage different parts of ourselves. For some of us, wearing colorful costumes is a major magical challenge!

If costumes are your calling – whether always or as a special working – read on!

SPACE/TIME/SIZE

Allow a couple of hours, or an afternoon. This is a good working for a small group, where each person can really be seen by the others. Space will vary – and may include a visit to a local thrift shop.

PREP

Look through the workings below – most need a bit of wardrobe prep.

Decide whether you'll take photos – people might feel more free to experiment without cameras.

WORKING

This is your working. You can create sacred space as simply or as elaborately as you wish. Here's a simple way:

DIY witchy fashion – TEM style!

Ground using your breath – can you take five consecutive breaths, focusing on your breath, without your mind wandering? (Start over when you find it wandering.)

Casting the circle – how will you cast a strong circle to hold your experiments? Would wearing a costume help?

Invoking elements – sing a song that invokes all the elements; invoke each element with a few words that come to mind; change the color of your scarf for each invocation; or even change costumes – what color or mood will help you invoke Air? Fire?

Deciding What To Wear

If you need this book to help decide your costumes, you are indeed in need of wardrobe magic! But don't despair – help may be closer than you think. Here are a few possibilities:

continued on next page

WORKINGS

Costume Magic (pg 2)

(1) Trust your intuition – if your heart calls out for you to wear a pointy hat and curly-toed boots (or maybe punk or goth or hippie or hip-hop styles) – try it out. Close the door, ground and cast a circle, invoke allies – and let the alchemy begin!

(2) Get wardrobe consultants – go thrift store shopping with friends. Get some help with a make-up experiment. Ask someone whose wardrobe you like, even if it's not "your usual style." Ask them to help you find your own style – they might be delighted at the opportunity! And while you're at it – maybe this is someone interested in mixing in a bit of magic?

(3) Try some shadow magic. If your heart says "yikes!" – go with it. After you dress in some shadow-costumes, everything else will seem more comfortable! See Workings: Shadow: Costume Shadows.

Fashion Laboratory

For some people, WitchCamp is a week-long fashion laboratory. Costumery abounds, and a special space may be dedicated to costumes. Some stop by the costume cabin, tent, tarp, or duffel bag every evening on their way to the ritual. For others, it takes a special magical challenge to get them to experiment.

Teens have done costume workshops (pre-planned and impromptu) at some of our camps, providing a safe space for costume-shadow work – dressing (and cross-dressing) in the most challenging ways we are willing.

Prep – gather clothes, scarves, wraps, ribbons, shoes, gloves, cloaks... Can you find some sparkly clothes or fabric? What about kids' toys that spin, flash, etc? Gather fancy clothes, simple clothes, strange clothes... Do you have siblings, cousins, or friends who can help? Do you have a budget for a trip or two to the thrift shop?

You may also want to use make-up and face paint – make sure no one is sensitive to products before you get started.

Glitter – we avoid sparkle-glitter. Most glitter isn't biodegradable, and it's hard to sweep up from carpet or forest floors!

Fashion Designer

What is your ideal magical outfit? How about your wackiest? Or maybe the way you would *least* like to be seen?

Take some time, ground yourself and cast a circle, then daydream for a while about how you will be attired. Do you stand and move differently in certain garb? Where do you see yourself? Indoors or out? Alone or with others?

✪ **Book of Shadows** – when you have an image, draw or write a description in your Book of Shadows. Find some clothing magazines that you can clip details from, and collage together your costume(s).

Make a short list of costumery you would like – the essentials, not every accessory. Choose one item and do a quick brainstorm on what it would take to obtain it – is it money? A trip to a special store or festival? A sewing lesson? More clarity on exactly what you are looking for?

Write down one step you will take toward your envisioned costume and a rough timeline. Close your journal, and put a scarf or a favorite item of clothing on top of the book. Take a breath and say: "So mote it be!"

Costume Shadows

All of us have costume shadows – edgy clothes that would make us cringe to be seen in! This is a fun and challenging shadow working that can be done with friends without calling it "Pagan." Consider turning off cameras to encourage experimenting.

See Workings: Shadow: Costume Shadows.

SOLO WORKING

You can do this working alone – but maybe there are others you know who might enjoy it? Maybe a Fashion Lab Party?

WORKINGS

Divination: Nature Readings

INTENT

Here's a chance to do free-form divination, not from a tarot deck or horoscope, but from nature. A multi-colored rock, a gnarled branch, the flow of water over a creek bed – what do these have to teach us?

This is a solo working that can be done in any sized group. Use this working to gain clarity around a question or issue.

Divination from nature, candle flames, etc is sometimes called "scrying" – see page 218.

SPACE/TIME/SIZE

Any number, working alone (or in dyads). Allow 30-40 minutes – 5-10 for intro, 10-15 for divination, and 10 for debrief.

Outdoors or inside, you'll need room to wander and come across rocks, trees, water, etc.

PREP

You'll want a bell or drum to call people back.

Outdoors – space for people to spread out and do personal divination.

I can stop for a moment to scry into a puddle. Photo Max Pixel.

Indoors – ahead of time, collect more items than there will be people – interesting rocks, driftwood, moss, sprigs of ivy, etc. Lay them out on an altar or cloth, or around the edges of your room.

What will follow this? Perhaps it will lead to a decision or commitment followed by a charging working such as the Overflowing Cup Spell or Charging with Fire & Flour?

Redwood bark may contain mysterious messages for us! Photo WikiCommons.

WORKING

Priestess – invite people to take a breath and consider a question or issue that is up for them. If several, choose one. If nothing specific comes to you, just open your mind to a message from nature. Priestess says:

"In a moment, you'll have a chance to find a natural object that calls to you (we'll call it a rock here). Remembering your question (or clearing your mind), soften your gaze and look at your rock and ask: 'Who or what are you?' Listen, then say or write the first things that come into your mind.

"Next, turn the rock or move yourself to a different angle. Ask: 'What is you story?' Listen, then say or write your first thoughts.

continued on next page

WORKINGS

Divination: Nature Readings (pg 2)

"Once more, either turn the rock, or move to a different angle. Ask: 'What is your lesson for me?' Listen, then say or write your first thoughts.

"Take a breath and look at the object, recalling the things you've heard. When the bell rings, return to the circle."

Outdoors – wander silently, letting your gaze fall on pieces of wood, rocks, tree stumps, flows of water, etc. Find one that speaks to you. View it from different angles, and question it three times: "Who or what are you? What is your story? What is your lesson for me?"

Indoors – establish a simple order – perhaps youngest to eldest, or going around the circle. Each person, without further reflection, pick the first object that calls to you. Find a place to sit alone, turn the object around to different angles, and question it three times, as above. Ask and listen with all your senses.

What do rocks have to teach us about ourselves? Let's ask! Photo WikiCommons.

Priestess – ring bell to call people back after 10 minutes. Invite people to find a partner and decide who will go first. Give each person two minutes to share what they experienced in their divination, and what it might say about their personal question. Partner listens non-judgmentally.

Closing – go around the circle and each person share one word about their divination.

Song for transition – My Soul; Let the Beauty We Love; I Would Know Myself.

SOLO WORKING

Same as above – bring your journal. You may want to come up with your question or issue before going outside to find an object. Or you may want to go out with an open mind and invite the wisdom of nature to come to you.

Find an interesting object.

Ask: "Who or what are you? Listen with your senses. Just listen for a couple of minutes. Then write.

Ask: "What is your story?" Listen, then write your first thoughts.

Ask: "What is your lesson for me?" Listen, then write your first thoughts.

When you finish the questions, free-write for a few minutes about what you have experienced, and what it might mean for your question. Don't worry about making sense – just write.

End by going back to your nature-responses and underlining three key words. For each word, take a breath and speak it aloud three times.

Finally say: "So mote it be!"

"I see a lobster and a porcupine dancing a tango! I wonder what the clouds are telling me about my life?" Photo Max Pixel.

TeenEarthMagic.org

WORKINGS

Divination: Oracles

INTENT

A multi-layered working in which some people will act as oracles and some will receive readings.

Work with tarot decks or other oracle cards – or try it with a pendulum or nature scrying. We'll describe it here as tarot.

In Reclaiming Tradition, we say, "Each person is their own spiritual authority." This means that no oracle, however extraordinary, can gift-wrap the truth for you. The most an oracle can do is to make a provocative insight, or ask the perfect question that will help *you* discover the answer you are seeking.

This is doubly true if you are using a tarot booklet or other resource as an oracle. No matter how fancy or expensive the book or how famous the author – the most they can do is inspire you to make your own discoveries and insights.

Use this working to come up with a commitment or insight, and follow it with a working that will "charge" your commitment – some ideas are: Lifting Each Other Up; a spiral dance, or charging with the Overflowing Cup Spell.

This working is described as a pair-share. It can also be done as part of a stations ritual (see Rituals: Stations Format) – oracles could be one of the stations that people visit. This is a good role for older teens and student teachers.

SPACE/TIME/SIZE

Two people could do this working, or any number of pairs. You'll need enough room for folks to spread out a bit. Allow at least 10 minutes per person (so each pair needs minimum 20 minutes) – more if you do multi-card oracles.

As a stations ritual, have a few older teens or student teachers act as oracles that the others will visit as part of their stations work. In this case, the oracles probably will not get to do a reading. After the working is over, an experienced priestess should "brush down the auras" of the oracles and help them re-ground.

One year at Witchlets we did a tarot exercise with the teens – then in the afternoon some of the teens offered a tarot salon and acted as oracles for the adults in camp.

PREP

Each pair will need a tarot or other divination deck or tool. Each person should also have their journal handy.

Lead priestess gets people in pairs. Decide who will be the oracle (divination priestess) and who the querent (questioner) first.

WORKING

Oracle – ask querent to relax and clear their mind – take a few breaths and let go of whatever you don't need to be present.

Invite querent to take a moment and think of a question or an issue for the reading. This question might come from an earlier working or station. If querent does not have a question or issue, suggest that they simply open their intuition and see what messages come through.

Invite querent to draw a card face down, take a breath to open to its messages, and then look at it. Oracle can then ask a series of questions (pause between each one to allow person to reflect):

- What objects and beings do you see in the card?
- Which object is "you"?
- What is going on in the card?
- Is there something you would change or add to the card?
- Finally: What does this card tell you about your question? Trust your first thoughts and intuitions.

continued on next page

Workings

Divination: Oracles pg 2

When the reading is complete (or time is up) – querent takes a few minutes and writes in their journal. Person who has been oracle can also write in their journal, or use the time to think about a question or issue for their own reading.

After a few minutes, lead priestess invites people to stand, shake themselves off, and move around a bit without talking. Then switch roles and repeat the oracle working.

After both people have had turns, you may have gained some insights and perhaps a new commitment or inspiration. Next, do a working to charge this insight or commitment – some ideas are: Lifting Each Other Up; the Overflowing Cup Spell; a spiral dance; or charging with fire (see Workings: Spell: Charging with Fire & Flour).

Good songs for charging an oracle reading – My Soul; Weave and Spin; Let It Begin Now; She Changes Everything She Touches (Kore Chant).

SOLO WORKING

You'll need – a tarot or other divination deck or tool; your Book of Shadows.

Can you act as an oracle for yourself? Maybe that's why somebody invented tarot! (For more about tarot, see Workings: Tarot.)

Ground yourself and take some breaths to open your spirit to the oracle. Let go of expectations or anxiety and just allow the oracle to speak.

If you have a specific question, write it at the top of a clean page, along with the date. Or you may simply want to do a "how's it going" reading.

Draw a card, face down – or maybe draw three – see Workings: Tarot for ideas on simple three-card spreads such as past-present-future. Hold the card(s) face down and take a breath to open yourself to the inspiration.

Turn the (first) card over, and say the first things that enter your mind. You might want to write in your journal – what are the first thoughts and feelings you have when you see the card? What is going on in the card? Try making up a simple story.

Take another breath or two. Now ask: "For my question – what does the card tell me?" Write your first thoughts and feelings.

For a three-card reading, repeat these steps for each card – then look at all three cards together.

When you're finished, how will you charge the working? Perhaps by laying your cards on an altar and reading aloud your oracle notes? Conclude by clapping your hands three times and declaring, "So mote it be!"

End with a song – try My Soul; Weave and Spin; Let It Begin Now; She Changes Everything She Touches (Kore Chant).

Lots more divination –
Workings: Tarot

WORKINGS

Divination: Scrying

INTENT

Gaze into a hazy surface and see with the mind's eye. Scrying is a form of personal divination, a way of tapping into our subconscious and into the magical energies around us.

The classic scrying tool is a crystal ball. Cloud-gazing is a playful way of scrying, as is staring into the embers of a fire. You can also use elemental tools, such as a large bowl of water (perhaps with a few drops of oil), a candle flame, an unusual rock, or the bark of a tree. Any of these can help tap our inner seeing, intuitive sight, and clairvoyance.

We can scry in search of a specific answer, or we can simply open ourselves to whatever comes through. Scrying can also be a prelude to another exercise which develops or deepens the scrying information. For instance, I may come out of scrying with a sense of a next step or a commitment. A working like the Overflowing Cup Spell could then charge the commitment.

SPACE/TIME/SIZE

Any number, with one candle, bowl of water, etc for every few people. Space to cast personal circles and be comfortable. Allow 30 minutes including prep and journaling. Fire safety note – see page 31.

PREP

Decide what your scrying medium will be and then prepare it. Here, we'll speak of a candle flame or bowl of water, but you can adapt as needed. At a camp, try nature scrying – each person finds a tree (or fern, etc) to sit and scry into.

Need – candle or bowl of water; journal and pen; optional Labyrinth Meditation Music (see page 113).

Decide how long to scry – 10 minutes is good to start. Don't stop early. You may want to set a timer, or in a group choose a priestess to watch the clock and ring a bell.

Set your bowl or candle on a low altar or surface so you can easily see it from where you will be sitting.

WORKING (group or solitary)

In a group, the scrying priestess speaks this part as needed. Solitaries can do the working as they read along.

Ground and center yourself. Invoke elements or any allies you wish – perhaps with a song.

If you want to work with a specific question, take a moment to frame it. Write it at the top of a journal page and set it aside.

Make yourself comfortable. Close your eyes and take a breath. Now open your eyes and gaze softly at the flame or water.

Don't try to see anything. You may feel insecure: "It's not working," or "I'm not doing it right." Acknowledge the fears, then let them drop into the Earth. Don't worry about what you see, whether it makes sense, etc. Later when you write in your journal, you may be surprised about what comes into your mind.

After a while, the flame or surface of the water may seem to speak or "mime" to you. Its dancing may seem to tell a story. You may see or be aware of images. Notice them, and let them float past. If your mind wanders, close your eyes, take a breath, and gaze again. Scrying may take practice. It might help to put on meditative (instrumental) music, or to close your eyes and gaze at your eyelids. With experience, you'll find ways that work for you.

At the end of the allotted time, stop scrying. Stretch, then write in your journal. At the end, underline three powerful words.

If you're a group, go around and each person shares their three words (maybe in three rounds, to build energy). If solitary, stand and face the altar again and speak your three words, breathing between each. At the end, touch your own center and breathe.

Song – a gentle song is good: Let the Beauty We Love; The River She Is Flowing; My Soul; The Welcome Flame; Born of Water.

Devoke and open your circle.

WORKINGS

Flaming Cauldron

INTENT

This working evolved as a part of the annual Brigid ritual (aka Imbolc or Candlemas) in the San Francisco Bay Area – pledges for the coming year are made to the Goddess before a flaming cauldron.

This is a simple yet dramatic working. This might be used as a commitment ritual toward the end of a camp, ritual, or class – "What is my work as I go back into the world?"

Do this outdoors or in a large, well-ventilated hall. Don't light a cauldron in closed spaces.

PREP (lots of prep for this working)

Central altar – card table or low table that can hold a hot cauldron – eg, with a heat-proof brick or wet towels under it.

• large basin of water (in which the flaming cauldron will be set).

• greenery and flowers to decorate the basin.

• the iron cauldron itself is placed into the basin (see below for cauldron prep).

Anvil & hammer – ideally a real anvil or a piece of railroad track – needs to be heavy. Use a short-handled sledge hammer.

• could also use a deep-sounding bell or bowl – a high-pitched bell or a gong is the wrong tone for this working.

Priestesses – lead the opening meditation and explain the working; lead spiral dance; anvil priestess.

Songs – Holy Well and Sacred Flame; Never Lose Our Way to the Well (visit WeaveAndSpin.org/tem-chants for our Brigid chants playlist).

Prepare cauldron *(practice the cauldron ahead of time – it's fun – but see cautions below!)*

• standard sized cast-iron Dutch oven with lid (not an heirloom – it may get slightly damaged during cleanup).

• epsom salts — about an inch layer in the bottom of Dutch oven.

• isopropyl alcohol 91 percent (get several bottles – you don't want to run out).

• don't add alcohol until you're ready to light the cauldron – then add to about a quarter-inch above the salt.

• wet towels.

• fire extinguisher.

• altar table that can stand heat (or use concrete, brick, ceramic tile, etc).

• for a lot of people (60+), have a second cauldron with epsom salts ready, swap after about 20-30 minutes.

Cauldron Cautions!

• as flame begins to sputter out, use the cauldron lid to completely extinguish the flame.

• *never* add alcohol to a cauldron with even the tiniest flame! The tiniest flame can instantly ignite fresh alcohol.

• once flame is completely out, pour in more alcohol and relight.

• don't try to burn slips of paper in a cauldron fire – it just makes a soggy mess.

• cleanup is a challenge. The longer the cauldron burns, the more the salt hardens. A chisel or screwdriver is often needed.

continued on next page

WORKINGS

Flaming Cauldron (pg 2)

WORKING

Create sacred space. You might want to invoke Brigid, Vulcan, or the Sacred Well to join you.

Once sacred space is established, priestess leads a short meditation to help people come up with a pledge or commitment. One way is to have folks walk counter-clockwise around the central altar as the priestess guides them to think about the coming year and a change or commitment they might want to make. When a person knows their commitment, they turn and walk clockwise, until everyone is walking that way. Priestess then invites people to take a breath into that commitment and find a seat around the altar.

When the cauldron working is ready to begin, the cauldron is lit (priestesses have quietly poured 91 percent alcohol into cauldron at the last minute).

Sing – "Holy Well and Sacred Flame" (this simple chant can recur whenever the flame goes out and cauldron needs refilling).

People are invited to take seats around the center altar, leaving room for others to step forward.

The anvil is struck three times to signal the start of the working. If no anvil, use a deep-sounding bell or bowl.

One at a time, people approach the cauldron and state their commitment. Remind people to keep their pledge brief. Pledging in silence is always an option. Have one or two experienced people step up first and model brevity.

After each person states their pledge, the anvil priestess strikes the anvil or rings the bell once.

When most have gone, priestess invites remaining people to step up and pledge.

When pledges are complete, priestess strikes the anvil in three sets of three (nine total) to complete the working.

A good way to empower the pledges is a spiral dance. Begin slowly to give people time to shift their energy (see Ritual Skills: How to Lead a Spiral Dance).

A good song for this working is Never Lose Our Way to the Well.

SOLO WORKING

You can do a pledge ritual using a glass jar candle.

WORKINGS

Games: Cooperative Games

INTENT

An active game can be a fun way to start a class, even before casting the circle. Or it can be a good change-of-pace after a meditation or a quiet working.

These games are fun when you're waiting for something (such as the last few people to show up before you start a working). Have a couple of these in the back of your mind for those stray moments.

They're also great party games! Play some of these games early to loosen folks up.

SPACE/TIME/SIZE

These games work for five to twenty people. For more, break into smaller groups. Allow ten minutes or so for each of these games. They're fun outside – some such as the Human Pyramid don't work so well on a hard surface.

Access – if some people in your group are differently abled, use a wheel-chair, etc – find ways for them to be involved.

PREP

The only prep needed is to arrange a suitable space (see below for details). For Amoeba, you'll need some rope.

Afterward – when these games end, the energy may be rather chaotic. Bring the circle back together by going around and inviting each person to say one word about what they are feeling. Close with a song.

WORKINGS: Cooperative Games

Amoeba

This is a good game mid-week, when people already know one another. It allows physical contact in a safe, fun way.

Prep – you'll need a long rope (about a foot for each person). Ahead of time, scout the area and make a simple "obstacle course" – some places where people have to squeeze through, step over, etc. Remind people about agreements regarding respectful touch.

Working – gather people into a tight circle, facing out. Wrap a rope around the circle and pull people in a bit tighter. Ask each person to have two hands on the rope, facing whichever way they need. Tighten a little more so they are really crowded. Tie a knot.

Now instruct the group to follow the obstacle course, moving as a group – as an amoeba.

Standing Up Back to Back

No prep needed – this one is quick, and can be a fun way to end pair check-ins.

Invite people to pair with someone roughly their same height.

Seated back to back, loop your elbows together. Now stand up together, without releasing your arms. Teachers watch that no one gets hurt trying to lift someone else on their back.

Human Knot

This is a good game mid-week, when people already know one another. It allows physical contact in a safe, fun way. Any

continued on next page

WORKINGS

Games: Cooperative Games (pg 2)

number, but the more people, the more likely to form double loops or impossible knots. If you have more than 20 people, do two groups and have a race. Differently-abled folks or those who opt out are coaches.

Form a circle, with any movement-limited folks seated in the center. Everyone reaches into the center and grasps the hands of two people across from you. Congratulations! You are a human knot.

Now – can you untangle without letting go? It's not always possible, but it's fun to try. It's okay to loosen grips to avoid getting hurt, but otherwise, try to keep hold. If you get completely stumped, see if there is a single change you can allow that will make unraveling possible.

Counting Games

Here's a quick "gathering" game to help a group merge its awareness and really pay attention to one another. Starting at one, the group begins to count as high as it can go. Anyone can say the next number – but if two people speak at once, start over at one. It's surprisingly hard even to reach 10 – hence the need for folks to tune into group energy.

Circle of Chairs

This game draws everyone into equal participation and allows physical connection in a safe, structured way. The outcome – whether or not it finally works – is fun.

Needs enough space for the group to make a circle. This has worked with as many as 30 people – is there an upper limit? It may actually be easier with more people, since the curve is more gradual. Lasts 10 minutes, can be ended when needed.

Have people stand in a circle shoulder to shoulder, then all turn and face clockwise. The goal is for everyone to end up seated on the knees of the person behind them. People can move around to whatever position they think will work. It can usually be done – see if you can figure out the easiest way.

Access note – having one or more people using wheelchairs might make this easier!

Nature Twister / Carpet Twister

Remember Twister, played on a plastic cloth? Well, it's more fun on a carpet or the ground. Like original Twister, this game encourages contact – ask agreement beforehand that people be aware and respectful around physical contact.

This is a fun game for two to four people at a time. We've played Carpet Twister for a long time, with players coming and going. Although it is "competitive," it's silly enough to be fun regardless of who wins.

Prep – a multi-colored or patterned carpet, or an open clearing where you have laid out things like pieces of bark, large leaves, etc. Make the boundaries of the space pretty small, since the idea is to get people knotted up.

Like Twister, the leader calls out something like, "Right hand red" – everyone finds a patch of red carpet and puts their right hand on it. Outside, we might say, "Left foot bark," or "Right hand fern leaf."

When someone falls over, they drop out – last one standing wins the round, and new challengers step up.

Pass the Knot

A fun group challenge that also reinforces the circle – see Workings: Circle: Pass the Knot.

April's Book of Games - an online resource!

The Teen Earth Magic Workbook was inspired by a booklet of games and exercises for younger and middle-school kids created by the late April Cotte, our co-teacher some years at Witchlets and Redwood Magic Family Camp.

Download a PDF of April's Book and much more on our website:

WeaveAndSpin.org/resources

WORKINGS

Games: Quick, Active Games

INTENT

A fun, energetic ways to start a class or morning path. These quick, active games show how the slightest movement of one of us can set off a whole chain of consequences. The outcome is often a big blob with lots of laughing.

These are good games to have in your pocket when a group finds itself having to wait around for 10 minutes.

TIME/SPACE

Need a large room or open space with clear boundaries. If you're outside, people will want to go beyond game boundaries, so beware of poison oak, breakable objects, hidden pools of quicksand, etc.

Each round lasts a couple of minutes – allow 7-10 minutes for several rounds.

PREP

Set up open space and boundaries. Clear stuff out of the way. Check for poison oak or hazards nearby.

If someone has mobility limits, they can remain seated or stationary while others move around them.

A bell is handy to get people's attention.

Conclusion – after several rounds, come back into a circle with a song that reconnects the group: We Are a Circle; We All Come from the Goddess; We Are the Power in Everyone.

GAME – Danger & Shield

Instruct each participant to silently choose one person who is a "danger" to them, and one different person who will be their shield. Don't let those two – or anyone else – know who you have chosen.

If A chooses B as shield and C as danger – then A's aim is to move around so that B is always between A and C.

Of course, B and C have chosen different people, and are moving themselves.

The outcome is often a slowly revolving clump and lots of laughter.

GAME – Triangle Crystals

Ask if someone can explain what an isosceles triangle is. For fun – invoke Euclid of Alexandria, the famous (Pagan) geometer.

Each participant silently chooses two other people with whom they will attempt to form a perfect isosceles triangle (three equal sides and angles). Don't let those two – or anyone else – know whom you have chosen.

If A chooses B and C, then A's aim is to move so that wherever B and C wind up, the three of them form a perfect triangle.

Meanwhile, B and C have no idea what A is doing. They have each chosen different people and are moving around themselves.

Occasionally the triangles will seem to come together ("crystallize") – then one person will move and all will be chaos again. After a round or two, point this out – one person's slight movement can throw the entire field into motion.

But finally, if all goes well and the spirits of geometry are with us, everyone will wind up standing still – the whole grid has crystallized.

SOLO WORKING

This working will be difficult alone – but it could be a fun party game.

WORKINGS

Game: Wink Murder

INTENT

A fun game for post-ritual hangout time.

This game worked well at Loreley WitchCamp in Western Europe, where teens spoke different languages – it's pretty much wordless. (For more on Loreley WitchCamp, see page 332.)

SPACE/TIME/SIZE

Room to sit in a circle. Up to about 15 people, after that it will get clumsy. Each round takes about five minutes.

PREP

If you're around a campfire, have enough light that people can see each other's eyes.

WORKING

Everyone sits in a circle. One person volunteers to be the detective first. Detective leaves the circle for a minute.

While the detective is gone, the circle secretly chooses one person to be the murderer, who will "kill" by winking at people. The murderer remains in the circle with the others.

Detective returns and stands in the center, turning and watching people. Murderer takes any opportunity to secretly wink at people. When someone is winked at, they can die quietly or very dramatically – but they should make it clear within about 10 seconds that they have been killed (while not giving away the murderer).

Detective gets three guesses, whenever they want. Murderer's goal is to avoid getting caught, or at least to kill as many people as possible before getting caught.

You can help the game work for everyone by ensuring that different people get to be the detective or the murderer.

SOLO WORKING

This will be difficult to do alone unless you have a homicidally split personality. However, it makes a fun party game.

WORKINGS

Grounding: Red Cord Spell

INTENT

A simple spell that reinforces grounding – great for a new group that is just learning about grounding. We sometimes do this on the first night of Elements of Magic classes, and it's a good camp working as well.

This is a spell working, not a grounding per se. It assumes the group has already done a strong grounding as part of creating sacred space – this working will build off of the earlier grounding.

People often end by tying the cord onto their wrist, ankle, or waist. Some people choose to wear their grounding thread "until it falls off," which can sometimes be quite a while.

SPACE/TIME/SIZE

Any number. Enough room for people to spread out. Allow 20 minutes including transitions.

Music if you wish: Labyrinth Meditation Music (see page 113) or a simple heartbeat played on a frame drum.

PREP

Need red embroidery floss – enough for everyone to have a three-foot length. Have some extra embroidery floss along with scissors. Pre-cut three-foot sections and lay them aside where they won't get tangled.

WORKING

When we do this spell, the group has already done a full grounding such as the Tree of Life at the beginning of class – so this exercise can simply call back people's groundedness from earlier (see Ritual Skills: Grounding).

Explain a bit about spellwork. Here's a recap – see more at Workings: Spellcrafting:

- a spell is a combination of your intention plus a physical working, charged with magical energy.
- when doing a spell, strike a balance between (A) being clear and specific, and (B) leaving the Goddess / universe room for creativity.
- be careful what you ask for (you just might get it).
- beware doing spells that affect another person – these can misfire and/or return on you three-fold, according to a magical law (see Introduction: Curses).
- put an end-term on a spell.
- treat and dispose of spell materials carefully and with clear intention – "I am now discarding these old spell materials."

Red Cord Spell

Priestess hands out threads. Invite people to play with the string and feel it in their fingers as they meditate.

Start music or drumming (optional).

Priestess leads short meditation, touching on these points (leave silent pauses after each phrase):

"What is your foundation? Start with your body. Where is your own physical center? Where is your body strong? Feel your body and your senses as your unique connection to the material world. Tie a knot into your cord for that connection.

"Feel your connection to the Earth. Feel the pull of gravity. Breathe into your connection to the Earth. Feel the energy move up and down between you and the Earth. Anchor this experience by knotting it into your cord.

continued on next page

WORKINGS

Grounding: Red Cord Spell (pg 2)

"Think about what gives you a sense of stability, belonging, and connectedness in your life. Is it your home? Your family and friends? Cooking a good meal? Your work? Tie a knot for this sense of stability.

"Do you have a connection to the Goddess or to spirit? Do you have a daily practice of magic? Meditation? Prayer? Exercise? Gardening? Walking? Think about things that connect you to the divine, and tie a knot in your cord for each.

"For everything that helps you feel connected, that calls you back to your groundedness, that strengthens your foundation, make a knot in your red cord."

Allow people a minute or two to complete the work. Then invite them to hold the cord in their hands and breathe up Earth energy into it. "Feel the physical substance of the cord and the knots that signify your groundedness."

Begin a low toning. Others join in. All tone until it fades. Keep it low – you are not raising energy here.

Completing the Spell

The priestess says something like:

"Breathe in the strength of this circle and state to yourself a simple affirmation of your own groundedness. (Pause.)

"You may want to fasten the cord somewhere on your body. If so, fasten it with a final knot while holding in mind your intention to strengthen your grounding.

"If you wear the thread – decide how long you will do so. Will it be for the length of this camp or class, for a moon cycle, until you go to bed tonight, until it falls off? State this aloud to yourself.

"If you do not intend to wear the cord, tie a final knot to create a circle. Decide what to do with it – place it on an altar, bury it in your garden, carry it in your pocket. Decide for how long."

Binding the Spell

The priestess leads the group in a call-and-response spell-binding:

> By all the power of three times three
> This spell bound round shall be
> To cause no harm nor return on me
> As I do will, so mote it be!

Priestess reminds people: "When the spell is complete – whenever you have decided – dispose of the string magically. Thank it for its work, declare it once again just a piece of string, and bury or burn it. If you decide you need to remove the string before the time declared – do the same as above – do it magically and intentionally."

SOLO WORKING

You can do this spell alone, reading the meditation as you go. You may also want to review Ritual Skills: Grounding.

Weave this working into a simple ritual. Ground, cast a circle, and call in the elements. Invite an ally or two who will help you feel more grounded (deity, energy, animal ally, etc). Remember to thank and devoke in reverse order at the end.

Remember to set an end-time for the spell, and to dispose of the materials magically when the spell is complete.

WORKINGS

Harvest Stations
for Fall Equinox or Anytime

INTENT

To contemplate our relationship to abundance and scarcity – the ways we harvest abundance and satisfaction, the places we are disappointed – and those magical moments when we harvest something completely unexpected.

This can be the core working of a short ritual. It could also be a pre-dinner ritual that ends in a feast!

This working was created for a Fall Equinox ritual in San Francisco (comments in parentheses below refer to that ritual).

SPACE/TIME/SIZE

Any number of people. 20-30 minutes. Space to "journey" around perimeter of room with a large central table / altar.

PREP

Ask people to bring food to share. Create a central food altar with two tables – one is abundant and beautiful, the other has some pieces of stale bread and a nearly-empty pitcher of water.

Bring loaves of good bread for the food blessing. Bell or ringing bowl for transitions.

At the edges of your circle, place three simple stations around the space – each has a cloth for the ground with a bucket or basket on it. (We had hand-lettered signs that said Abundance, Scarcity, and Possibility.)

(1) Scarcity – a bucket of small, plain pebbles – enough for everyone to get a small handful.

(2) Abundance – a basket filled with colored glass beads – ten or more per person.

(3) Possibility – a basket with "fortunes" on slips of paper – see next page.

Priestesses – one for each station, plus a guide who facilitates the movements.

Teach song beforehand: Harvest Chant (Our Hands Will Work for Peace and Justice).

WORKING

After sacred space is created, guide gathers people around central altar and introduces working with a harvest meditation about ways that we reap abundance or scarcity in various parts of our lives – material, emotional, political, creative...

(1) Guide leads people to Scarcity station. Priestess picks up bucket and hesitantly invites people to take a small handful of pebbles, saying in a worried voice: "Just a few – there may not be enough!" Short meditation on ways that we don't harvest what we dreamed, that our hopes and plans are not coming to fruition. After two minutes, ring bell.

(2) Guide leads to Abundance station. Priestess holds basket of beads and invites people to take some. "There are plenty!" Short meditation on places of abundance in our lives – places we notice and those we look past. After two minutes, ring bell.

(3) Guide leads to Possibility station. Priestess holds basket of "fortunes" (see next page) and invites folks to take one. Short meditation on possibility that sometimes we may harvest the unexpected, and that we can make room for magic to work. Invite people to meditate for a moment on the words on their slip of paper – then turn to someone and share for a couple of minutes how "possibility" might work in their life. Let sharing go on for a few minutes if people are connecting.

(4) Guide leads people to central altars and notes the two harvest tables – Abundance and Scarcity. Invite people to feel the balance of the rocks and the glass beads in their hands – to feel the possibilities of our own harvest. Then use the pebbles and beads to create an artwork on the barren table (at Equinox, people made meandering patterns around the table).

(5) Circle around altars – go clockwise and each person say one word of possibility.

continued on next page

WORKINGS

Harvest Stations (pg 2)

Song as, or after, we create the artwork: Harvest Chants (Our Hands Will Work for Peace and Justice).

Bring song to cone of power, or let it fade. As people ground the energy, the guide can bless the abundant harvest.

Pass around bread, berries, etc – each person offers some to the next, saying: "May you never hunger!"

Devoke, then open the circle, feast, and socialize.

SOLO WORKING

You could do this ritual alone or with a few friends. Gather the station supplies above, and bring substantial food that you'll look forward to eating. Bring your journal and write afterward.

Fortunes for the Possibility Station

Copy these onto strips of paper, or create your own:

- What are your hidden blessings?
- What have you harvested that you are not aware of?
- What are you grateful for this year?
- What if this harvest is a stepping stone for next year?
- What is your abundance?
- What might you harvest that you didn't plant?
- What harvest is possible?
- What is the abundance around you?
- What kind of scarcity would you welcome?
- What kind of abundance scares you?
- What can you share?
- What if your harvest is barren?
- What if you already have your harvest?
- What if the barren harvest disguises a blessing?

Altar –
Spiral Dance 2009.

Photo by Michael Rauner.

WORKINGS

Intuitive Practices

INTENT

Intuitive practice is a good description of many magical workings. This page shines a special light on this part of our magic.

We're working intuitively when we sense and work with energy, when we read tarot without an instructional book, when we do a spell that we created or modified – and also when we learn to pay attention to our gut feelings and first impressions.

Is every gut feeling or first impression correct? Hardly! Sometimes people whom we instantly love turn out to be less than perfect allies. And likewise, people we initially hold at a distance wind up being our closest friends.

Yet how many times do we say, "If only I'd paid attention to my gut feeling," or "If I'd just have listened to my doubts…."

Our goal is not to follow our intuition blindly – but to learn to listen to it and pay heed to its signals. Intuition is a flashing light saying, "Pay attention! Something might be happening here!"

Intuition is like any other skill – we're born with a certain amount of aptitude, and after that it's up to us to learn to use it. Our intuition – our ability to see, hear, feel, sense, and understand inner messages – grows stronger the more we exercise it.

Luckily, intuitive workings are often simple and fun – tarot, pendulums, dreamwork, scrying…

SPACE/TIME/SIZE

Intuitive practices are great solitary work. You'll want a quiet, private space. In a circle, have plenty of room for people to spread out and get comfortable. Allow plenty of time – a half hour is good for a working.

PREP

See each working below for materials needed. You'll need your Book of Shadows, a pen, and drinking water.

Before doing any of these workings, do a short grounding and cast a circle (see Ritual Skills: Sacred Space: Quick Ways). Invoke an ally or two to support your work. Remember to devoke / thank the allies and open your circle at the end.

WORKINGS

Intuitive workings are scattered through this book. Here are a few key exercises for strengthening your intuitive skills.

Intuitive Tarot

The images of a tarot deck are an invitation to open our intuition. Set aside the deck's booklet and see what comes to you. Not an experienced reader? Perfect – intuitive reading is a great introduction to tarot. See Workings: Tarot: Intuitive Tarot.

Nature Divination

Opening awareness to nature can bring us in touch with our deep selves. See Workings: Divination: Nature Readings.

Scrying

Scrying means gazing into a hazy surface and seeing with the mind's eye. Scrying helps us tap into our subconscious and into magical energies around us. We can scry into a flame, tree bark, the surface of water… See Workings: Divination: Scrying.

Auras

Learning to read others' auras, and to modify our own, is a magical skill that's useful in day-to-day life. See Workings: Auras.

WORKINGS

Labyrinth Workings

INTENT

A labyrinth is a great tool for focusing a meditation. Following the twists and turns of a labyrinth carries us into a magical realm. This page offers several ways you can use labyrinths in rituals and classes.

If a labyrinth is not available at your site, you can create one in an hour, following directions on page 232. Once you've blessed a labyrinth, people can walk it on their own, especially if you give them some ideas.

There are three typical labyrinth layouts: three, seven, and eleven.

Eleven circuits is a traditional form that appears in European churches such as France's Chartres Cathedral and has been replicated in some North American churches. These have very elaborate layouts with many twists and turns.

Seven circuits appear in ancient Mediterranean sites and elsewhere. The layout is simpler, yet resembles eleven circuits in that one does not move steadily from the outside to the center.

Three circuits is a simplified arrangement that we use for TEM workings such as the Labyrinth Challenges ritual (see page 125).

Solo – you can also create a handy finger labyrinth for personal use and portability – see next page.

SPACE/TIME/SIZE

A limited number of people can move through a labyrinth at once. If the group is too large for your labyrinth, try using it as part of a "stations ritual," where you work as smaller subgroups (see Rituals: Stations Format, page 130).

It's difficult to do any labyrinth working, including transitions, in under 30 minutes. If time is short, share some ways to work with labyrinths, and let people do it in their free time.

If you're making a labyrinth, you'll need at least 10 feet square for a three-circuit, and 15 feet for a seven-circuit. Outdoor labyrinths can be bigger. We made a seven-circuit at Witchlets from fallen tree branches that was 40 feet across.

PREP

If no labyrinth is available, make one (see page 232), or create a finger labyrinth (see next page).

WORKINGS

Walk & Meditate – 7 or 11 Circuits

Walk a labyrinth with magical intent. Approach the entrance with a question or issue in your heart. At the entrance, kneel and touch the Earth, grounding yourself at the portal. Walk slowly, doing your best to keep your question or issue foremost in your mind. As you follow the turns, let go of linear thought and allow images to float past.

Each time the circuit turns, stop for a breath and recall your question or issue before starting off in a new direction (with 11 circuits, you'll be stopping a lot!). When you reach the center, kneel and re-ground and be receptive to insights and intuition. Do this again when you exit the labyrinth. Journal afterward.

Chakra Meditation – 7 Circuits

In some Eastern traditions, chakras are energy centers running up the spine. You can match the seven circuits to the seven chakras, with the outermost circuit corresponding to the root chakra. As we make our way through the circuits, we can meditate in turn on each chakra, applying its insights and tools to our question. (You can find chakra meditation tools online.)

continued on next page

WORKINGS

Labyrinth Workings (pg 2)

Labyrinth Challenges Ritual – 3 Circuits
See Rituals: Labyrinth Challenges (page 125). This is a stations-type ritual using a three-circuit labyrinth.

Mirrors at the Center – a Shadow Working
Set up a small table in the center as an altar. A veiled priestess stands at the center of the labyrinth. Place some hand-mirrors face down on the table. Having several mirrors lets several people do the working at once.

This takes a cue from the ancient Greek story of Ariadne, Theseus, and the Minotaur, and could be part of a larger ritual arc based on that story. What if the creature at the center of the labyrinth is your own reflection?

This working needs enough light for people to see themselves in a mirror. Also – unless you're a small group, everyone won't be able to do this at once, so you'll need something for folks to do as they wait their turn – fire or water scrying, tarot, drumming....

A second priestess begins with a short meditation about walking the labyrinth and opening up to the parts of ourselves that we do not usually see and acknowledge. Priestess asks: "What if the creature at the center of the labyrinth is parts of myself that I don't want to look at?"

As people arrive at the center, they are invited to gaze into a mirror and get acquainted with the "creature at the center of the labyrinth."

As they walk back out, they are invited to meditate on what they just saw.

Song: Let the Beauty We Love; Opening Up In Sweet Surrender.

Finger Labyrinths
Draw a seven-circuit labyrinth on a sheet of paper (see next page for directions). When it's complete, ground yourself, then slowly trace the circuits with your finger. Try doing a chakra meditation this way – see page 230.

One Reclaiming teacher drew a large seven-circuit outline, then went back and carefully drew in hundreds of "stones" along the lines that separate the circuits, meditating on each one as if she were laying the stones in a real labyrinth.

SOLO WORKING

Labyrinths are a great tool for personal meditation and workings. You can draw a labyrinth with chalk on concrete, or make yourself a finger labyrinth.

Try any of the above workings on your own. You can even do the Labyrinth Challenges working (see Rituals: Labyrinth Challenges). Journal afterward.

If you can return to a local or regional labyrinth, keep an ongoing journal about your experiences. What thoughts and images recur for you? What distractions keep popping up? What changes over time?

LABYRINTH MYTH: Ariadne, Theseus, & the Minotaur

The ancient Greek myth of Ariadne, Theseus, and the Minotaur is built around a magical journey into (and back out of!) a labyrinth. We've used this myth as the core of a one-day workshop, and at Witchlets in 2012.

See Ritual Skills: Theme & Arc for details about how we used this myth in ways that challenged older gender assumptions.

Labyrinth directions on next page

WORKINGS

Labyrinth Workings (pg 3)

How to Draw a 7-Circuit Labyrinth in One Easy Lesson!

Here's how to draw a seven-circuit labyrinth. It's easy after you practice a few times.

The distance between the tips of the lines is the width of the paths.

Note that the cross is not the center of the labyrinth – the cross is below and to the left of the center.

The first loop you draw is the actual center – you might want to make this more of a bubble so there's extra space.

Where To Make Your Labyrinth?

If you have a driveway or patio, sketch one in chalk.

You can draw a 15-foot diameter version on dirt with about 30 pounds of corn meal (plus extra just in case).

Or scratch the design into the ground and place rocks along the lines.

At the 1996 California WitchCamp at Mendocino Woodlands, the Earth Path made a daily practice of gathering and laying rocks for a 7-circuit labyrinth.

The Woodlands staff liked it, and years later the labyrinth is still there, the rocks long since embedded in the ground.

Drawing a 3-Circuit

This is not a common layout, but we've found it a perfect design for our Labyrinth Challenges (see Rituals: Labyrinth Challenges – page 125).

If possible, make the paths two to three feet wide for this working.

Start the labyrinth from this diagram, and follow the same procedure as above.

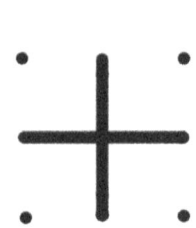
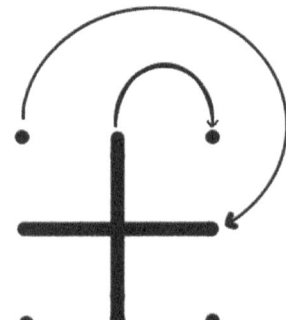

TeenEarthMagic.org

WORKINGS

Letter to Myself

INTENT

Here's a way to send our magical intent into the future – our own future. Each person mails a unique magical message to themselves. It's a good working toward the end of a camp or class. It never gets old, and we've done it at various camps.

This working can build off a prior exercise that develops a commitment to take the power of camp or class back into our daily lives – consider preceding the letter writing with a tarot reading, meditation, silent sit, etc.

SPACE/TIME/SIZE

Any number. Room for people to sit and write. Allow 20 minutes including transitions.

PREP

Sheets of fancy paper for everyone, plus a bunch of small slips of colored paper (three to four per person). Fine-point magic markers (they're colorful plus they write well on uneven surfaces).

Blank letter-sized envelopes and enough first-class stamps for everyone. A basket or colorful bag to put the letters in. A priestess to collect and later mail the letters, plus a list of people's names and addresses (perhaps from registration forms).

WORKING

Prior working establishes a commitment we want to take back into the world, or perhaps a sense of our own power and resolve.

Priestess hands out paper and pens, and invites people to write a letter to themselves "back home" – but don't sign it yet.

This letter is only for you. Capture the power and spirit of camp / class, and write a letter to inspire you when you read it later.

Write things from camp / class that you want to remember. Write thoughts you have had during the class / camp about how powerful and creative you can be, and about what you want your life to be like. Write specific commitments.

Don't worry about elegance. Write your first thoughts (priestess ring a bell for three-minute warning).

When finished, read it over and add an affirmation – something like, "I believe in you!" Then if you're ready – sign it.

Priestess passes out envelopes, and invites people to address one to themselves. (Some teens won't know their full address – have them write their name, and get the address later from their registration form.)

Each person places their letter in an envelope – but *don't* seal it.

Power boost – here's an idea inspired by Jamba Juice. Each person takes a few slips of paper. On each slip, write a word or phrase of power, encouragement, support – things like Go, You can do it, We believe in you, Keep trying, Strength, Love, Beauty...

Fold the slips and put them into the basket or bag. Tone over the basket to charge the words.

Each person now draws a few out. Without reading them, drop them into your envelope. Then seal it.

Collect all the letters in a basket or colorful bag in the center.

Song to raise energy over letters: My Soul, We Are the Power in Everyone; Let It Begin Now,

Then tell people – we will mail these to you a few days after camp / class ends.

SOLO WORKING

Do the working above and write a letter to yourself. Seal it in an envelope and address it. Let it sit for a few days. Then mail it. When it arrives, cast a circle and read it.

WORKINGS

Liberation Circle

INTENT

This is a general working that you can shape to suit your group's specific needs. Decide ahead of time what the theme will be.

A liberation circle can follow a tarot reading or meditation that involves people choosing an act of liberation for themselves. Perhaps they want to enact taking a risk, hear words of support, hear their name sung to them, etc.

Taking chances / circle of support – each person is invited to take chances doing things that they are usually scared to do in a group. For instance: singing alone; dancing; silently looking into people's eyes.

Circle of affirmation – each person steps in and states an affirmation that they would like to hear spoken to them (a tarot reading or meditation beforehand can help people come up with their affirmation).

Singing with support – each of us sings with the support of the group, then alone, and again with support – so we can hear our own voice ring out alone, then be supported again (this is scary for many people!). See Workings: Voice Magic (page 318).

SPACE/TIME/SIZE

Groups of about six to twelve people – if more people, work in smaller sub-groups. Have enough room for sub-groups to spread out a bit. You'll need about two minutes for each person in the circle, and about 10 minutes for transitions.

PREP

Choose focus of working.

Teach songs ahead of time so you're ready to sing when it's time (see ideas below).

WORKING

Here are several workings that you could do within a liberation circle. You can also adapt them to your work.

Taking chances / circle of support – priestess invites people – one at a time as they are ready – to step into the circle and do something risky such as sing, dance, or simply be seen. People can ask for the types of support they want, such as silent attention, smiles, words of support and encouragement, etc.

Note – how do we fully support each other while remaining honest? If someone is taking a chance and singing in a shy, awkward voice, we don't want to tell them, "You have a beautiful voice" (they may not believe that) – but we can say, "It's wonderful to hear you sing!" (which they may be delighted to learn).

Between people, everyone sings the song: Inanna (Deep Calls to Deep); My Soul chorus; Perfect Offering.

Circle of affirmation – do a short meditation or tarot working ahead of this, so each person comes up with one word or a short phrase they would like to hear.

Priestess invites people – one by one when they are ready – to step into the circle and tell the rest of the group what affirmation they would like to hear. They close their eyes, and the group says and sings the words to them – some boldly, some in whispery voices. Go for about 60 seconds, then come to silence.

Between each person, everyone sings a simple song: Inanna (Deep Calls to Deep); My Soul chorus; Perfect Offering.

Singing with support – each person will have a chance to sing with the support of the group. Easiest way is to go around clockwise, letting people pass and go later if they wish. Note – allow extra time for this working – the debrief might take a while. (See also Workings: Voice Magic.)

continued on next page

WORKINGS

Liberation Circle (pg 2)

Decide who will go first. Let that person laugh and shake out any nervousness before you start.

Group (including that person) sings a tone together. After 30 seconds or so, priestess signals with hands for everyone except the one person to fade out – the one person who continues is encouraged to keep toning boldly, and if possible look around at people – the rest of the group silently supports with their eyes. After 20 seconds, priestess signals rest of group to fade back in, then everyone fades down together.

All take a deep breath before the next person's turn. If someone is having feelings, encourage them to stay with it as the next person begins.

Afterward – leave plenty of time for debriefing. Do a go-round and let each person say how they felt while singing alone. Priestess can speak gently if it makes sense: "What would it be like to sing boldly all the time?" "I'm sorry that anyone ever told you not to sing loudly," etc. Be ready for some emotions to flow.

Finish these workings by singing a gentle song together.

Song Ideas – Let the Beauty We Love; My Soul; Let It Begin Now.

SOLO WORKING

Try the Singing with Support exercise above with recorded music. Look online for some trance music or some other simple, continuous sound (dance music, Sufi music – anything that has a fairly consistent sound that you can tone to). You'll also need a recording of a song you really like to sing for the end.

Create sacred space quickly – use a song for the elements to loosen your voice up (see Ritual Skills: Chants).

Put the music on, take a smooth, deep breath, and begin to tone with it – find a comfortable tone that seems to fit the music, and relax into it. See how strong and bold you can make your voice (this is scary for some of us – even those who like to sing!).

Once you are toning steadily, fade the music out. Keep toning for a few seconds, as steadily and boldly as you can. Notice the feelings of insecurity or fear that come up, and let them pass. Just keep going. After 10-15 seconds, fade the music back up as you continue toning.

Pause and take a deep breath. Laugh if you want to. Shake your body out. Try it again.

✪ **Book of Shadows** – after three to four times, stop and write in your journal. Did it get any easier as you repeated it? Did you notice anything else that made it easier?

Repeat if you want.

Song – end by singing a favorite song along with a recording. Choose any song you want – if in doubt, visit our Ritual Skills: Chants pages and try My Soul or Let the Beauty We Love.

WORKINGS

Lifting Each Other Up

INTENT

This is a good final working for a class or camp – each person is lifted and held by the circle. Do it toward the end of a class or ritual, and then close with a spiral dance.

This works well after a working where people have made a commitment to themselves (via meditation, tarot, labyrinth, etc) – now each gets to feel the support of the whole group for their commitment.

We often accompany this lifting-up with the song "Humble Yourself," a contemporary Christian song with a few strategic Pagan changes (see below for search info).

> Humble yourself in the arms of the wild
>   you gotta lay down low and
> Humble yourself in the arms of the wild
>   you gotta ask Her what She knows and
> We will lift each other up, higher and higher (2x)

Pagan version by Beverly Frederick on youtube. Original lyrics: "Humble thyself in the sight of the Lord," by Robert Byron Hudson – available on youtube, spotify, etc.

SPACE/TIME/SIZE

You'll need at least eight people, and no more than about 12. If you have more than 15, find a magical way to separate into smaller groups to do this working, then come back together for a final spiral dance.

A space of natural beauty is ideal, with enough room for a circle of 10-12 people and a little extra room.

Allow about two minutes per person plus a few minutes of transition.

PREP

This follows a working where people make a self-commitment – perhaps in a meditation, a tarot reading, or walking a labyrinth.

Teach the song Humble Yourself (ideally at the beginning of class or ritual). If you don't know it or don't want to use the song, you can tone as you lift. Practice toning together at the beginning of the class or ritual.

Talk for a few minutes about respectful touch and ask people to agree to pay attention to this.

continued on next page

WORKINGS

Lifting Each Other Up (pg 2)

WORKING

In groups of eight to twelve, gather attention and priestess explains:

"One at a time, people will have chance to step into the circle and be lifted and held by the group.

"When it's your turn, step into the circle and (if you wish) state your pledge / intention from the earlier working. Then close your eyes and hold silence. Cross your arms so your hands are on opposite shoulders. When the circle is ready, gently lay back.

"Lifters circle person to support all points. Join wrists with the person across from you. Someone prepares to cradle head and neck. Strong people at shoulders and hips.

"Lifters sing Humble Yourself – or tone – as person lays back. Catch body and lift legs until the person is held at your waist level. You can cradle the person there, or gently lift them overhead.

"Continue singing or toning for a minute or so. Then lower the feet back down and gently lift the person to standing. Bring the song to a close or fade the toning as the person comes back to their feet."

The person rejoins the circle, and the next person goes. People go when they are ready. If there is a lull, priestess gently asks, "Are there others who are ready to go?" and leaves some space before wrapping up – usually everyone will take a turn.

SOLO WORKING

This is a good working for a birthday party – lift the birthday person first, then invite others to take a turn. Maybe there's a non-Pagany way to create a circle to help stay focused and let go of silly energy (save it for later in the party).

WORKINGS

Luscious Eating

INTENT

A fun, sensuous way to get in touch with the earthiness of our bodies via eating delicious fruit – a great way to end any ritual or class!

Works well after a trance or after another intense working - a nice way to re-ground into our bodies.

The advanced "feed one another" version (see below) can be a sweet working in a group that is ready for this. Try this is a later class or path, maybe after an especially intense working that leaves people very open.

SPACE/TIME/SIZE

A quiet, private space where people can gather in a circle. Number of people – however many can share food. If more than a dozen or so, break into sub-groups.

PREP

Fruit – especially juicy berries. Ripe raspberries or blackberries are ideal, as are melons cut into small pieces. Try banana slices, tangerine sections, peach quarters, etc.

Toothpicks are great, especially if people will be feeding one another.

A nice serving tray heightens the magic.

WORKING

Explain that many fruits grow from five-petaled flowers and have five seed pods. Slice an apple crossways and hold it up: "Behold the mystery of the pentacle!"

Then bring out trays of fruit and invite people to eat intentionally, one piece at a time, savoring the luscious earthiness.

Advanced work – feed one another. This is edgy for some people – be prepared for this to take over the energy if you do it. Toothpicks help for this work.

Song – end with a gentle song that celebrates being together: Air Moves Us; Barge of Heaven (Pour It Out for Me); Let the Beauty We Love; The River She Is Flowing.

SOLO WORKING

This can be a solo working. Try doing it after some other intense magical or personal work (or after finishing difficult homework). The key is intentionality. As you prepare and then eat the fruit, focus on the earthiness of your body and the food you are eating.

Journal afterward.

WORKINGS

Magical Writing

INTENT

What does writing mean to you? Something you do at school? A dream job? A nuisance? A glimmer of an idea for a story you want to tell?

Writing, like rituals, spellwork, and other aspects of magic, involves working with and shaping flows of energy.

Whatever our writing ambitions, we can benefit from a magical practice. If you have a daily magical practice, you'll find ways to weave support for your writing.

If you don't have a regular practice – here's a chance to develop one!

The Magical Writer is a Reclaiming-style writing class created by author Luke Hauser that applies the tools of magic and ritual to our creative practices. It is occasionally taught in the Bay Area and has been offered as an online class. You can also do the work alone or with friends.

The Magical Writer course can help you build a steady writing and magical practice. You'll develop skills such as:

- Creating magical writing space
- Invoking allies and characters
- Shadow work: integrating our inner critic
- Plot, story, and myth
- The alchemy of editing

SPACE/TIME/NUMBER

For one person or a small group. A writing group reminds us that we are not alone with our work. We can learn from one another's experiences and find ways to share inspiration and practical lessons.

PREP

Download the free Magical Writer course booklet – visit WeaveAndSpin.org/freebies.

Think about where you want / need to create a writing space that works for you. Is it your room? Your back yard? A local café or library? On the bus or train? Where will you start?

Will you work best alone, or will finding a friend or three help you stay focused?

Do you need a computer? Blank paper? A new journal with a hand-decorated cover? Will a special pen or marker(s) help?

WORKING (Solo or Small Group)

The Magical Writer booklet includes about a dozen sessions. Cumulatively they offer a survey of basic writing skills. Each

continued on next page

TeenEarthMagic.org

WORKINGS

Magical Writing (pg 2)

lesson features a short introductory essay plus a page of tips and exercises.

Workings include tarot readings, creating a writing altar, outlining a favorite movie, rant-writing, talking back to our inner critic, telling vs showing, taking our writing into the world, and more.

You can work the Magical Writer course on your own or with a writing group by downloading the class booklet, which features a seven-unit class plus several bonus sessions. You can work the sessions in sequence, or pick and choose among those that call to you.

Skim the booklet, choose a working – and let the magic begin!

Free Magical Writer course booklet – visit the website, WeaveAndSpin.org/freebies.

More Reclaiming Classes

You can study Reclaiming magic online, by joining a local class, or on your own.

BayAreaReclaiming.org lists local offerings.

WorldTreeLyceum.org offers classes online – including Reclaiming's core magic classes.

The Magical Writer, created by Luke Hauser, is a seven-week course plus advanced lessons – each session featuring magical and practical exercises and workings.

Download the complete Magical Writer booklet – visit WeaveAndSpin.org/freebies.

240   TeenEarthMagic.org

WORKINGS

Mirror Affirmations

INTENT

An affirmation is a simple statement of how we want to be (and be seen) in the world. Examples: "I will speak boldly. I am a really smart person. I will treat other people with respect."

We can use a mirror to strengthen this sense of who we are and who we want to be.

Combine this with a prior exercise that develops a few personal affirmations – a tarot reading, a meditation, etc.

SPACE/TIME/SIZE

Any number – each person needs a mirror. Enough room to spread out a little. Allow about 15 minutes including journaling and transitions.

PREP

Ask students to bring a hand mirror to class. Each person should also have a journal and pen handy.

Each person will need two or three personal affirmation statements. You may want to use a prior exercise to develop these affirmations – a tarot working, a meditation, etc. Or they can be developed as a meditation at the top of this working.

WORKING

Find a space. Ground and cast a circle around yourself.

If you already have affirmations from a prior working, call them forth now. If not, take a couple of minutes and come up with two or three simple statements that say how you want to be in the world. Write them down.

Now make yourself comfortable. Take a few deep breaths and on each exhale let go of any judgments.

Gaze into the mirror and meet your own eyes. Welcome yourself. Exhale any judgments.

Now state one of your affirmations, gazing into your own eyes. As quickly as judgments and opinions come up, take a breath and let them go. Then repeat the affirmation. As often as other thoughts pop up, just keep repeating the affirmation and gazing into the mirror.

After a minute or so, put the mirror face down. Exhale. Shake yourself out. Get a drink of water. Breathe.

Try it again with a different affirmation.

✪ **Book of Shadows** – after a few rounds, get our your journal and write a bit. Ask yourself – where did it get difficult? What affirmation was the easiest and/or hardest to accept? What is so difficult about looking into my own eyes?

Group sharing – go around and share one word or phrase. Close with a song such as Let the Beauty We Love or We Are Alive.

Daily practice – consider repeating one of the mirror-affirmations each day for a month, or for a year and a day. Keep a journal about how your experience changes over the period.

SOLO WORKING

Same working.

WORKINGS

Mirror Goddess

INTENT
A simple way to remind ourselves that we are the Goddess. Can be used as a Goddess invocation in a small group, or as a pair-working with multiple mirrors.

SPACE/TIME/SIZE
Either a circle of up to about 30 people, or enough space to spread out in dyads if you prefer. You'll need a mirror for each group.

As a circle, this will go quickly – 20-30 people in few minutes. Any larger and it's hard to keep the focus.

As dyads, allow three minutes..

PREP
Need a hand mirror for group invocation, or one mirror for every pair in larger group. If this is a class, ask people to bring small mirrors. You may want to combine this with other mirror workings in the same class or ritual.

WORKING
Group invocation – first person holds mirror up to person on their left and says: "Behold the Goddess." Hold mirror for several seconds as they gaze at their reflection – longer in a small group.

Pass mirror to that person, and they do it for the next person. When circle is complete, say: "Welcome Goddess!"

Devoke by going in opposite direction, or simply have people look around at one another and see the Goddess prior to thanking Her (ourselves) and bidding Her (ie, our Goddess-selves) farewell from this circle.

Pair-working – same idea, but do it in pairs, with each pair having their own mirror. Go back and forth three times.

SOLO WORKING
Choose a short song or chant that you like. Let the Beauty We Love is great for this working (see Ritual Skills: Chants).

Start the song about a minute from the end (or however long you want to gaze).

Gaze into a mirror and say aloud: "Behold the Goddess." Gaze into your own eyes and see the Goddess until the song ends.

WORKINGS

Mirror Shielding

INTENT

A simple, physical way of establishing our boundaries and personal energy as a strong shield. Useful in stressful situations such as protests, arguments, or life in general.

For more on working with personal energy and boundaries, see Workings: Auras.

SPACE/TIME/SIZE

Any number, with enough room to spread out at arm's length from one another. Five to ten minutes depending on how much people get to practice.

PREP

A hand-mirror is helpful but not necessary.

WORKING

First, breathe deeply and re-establish your own grounding and center. Now breathe in energies you want – groundedness, peace, calm, clarity, etc. With deep, gentle breaths, fill yourself with these energies.

Using either a hand-mirror facing out, or the palm of your hand facing outward (like a cop saying, "Halt!") – circle it around your head, keeping the mirror-face or palm facing out, and say:

> For all other energy sent toward me
> May it harmlessly reflected be

As you speak this rhyme (chosen because it's so simple that it takes no concentration), keep your attention entirely on the positive qualities you called in – on your own center. Let the mirror do the outer work.

Repeat around your heart, and again around your pelvis. The whole time, keep your attention on your own center. Speak the rhyme (or something simple that requires no particular thought) and move the mirror (or your palm), keeping your attention on the positive qualities you are invoking.

Finally, pass the mirror (or your palm), still facing out, up and down in front of your entire body, saying: "So mote it be!"

Place the mirror aside, face down. Touch the Earth or your own center to ground any extra energy. Breathe again to your own center to complete the working.

SOLO WORKING

Same working.

WORKINGS

Nature Sit / Night Sit

INTENT

A challenging personal meditation – sitting alone in a field or forest, we open to mystery (doubly so if it's night-time!).

This working draws on each person's own inner resources and responses to their environment. As one TEM teacher put it – "We'll take people out into the woods and let the trees do the teaching."

This is a good working for near the beginning of a ritual – create sacred space, then go on a hike and silent-sit. Come back to the circle and do a working that pulls people back together – an allies circle is a good contrast to the solo work of silently sitting. Or use Workings: Overflowing Cup to empower insights that came to you as you sat alone.

SPACE/TIME/SIZE

This is planned as an outdoor working – you'll want a patch of field or woods, away from people, dogs, and traffic – and a space in which people can safely sit alone. It could also be done in a large building such as an old church, where you could hike through darkened hallways.

For night sit, priestesses need to be familiar with the space so you can lead a hike in the dark – then go back and find everyone!

Any number, but the more people, the more space you need to spread out. Allow about 20 minutes for the sitting, plus about 20-30 more minutes for prep, hiking, and wrap-up – the more people, the longer it will take.

PREP

This working requires a fair bit of prep, especially if you plan a night hike. You'll need to know the route well, and be sure there isn't poison oak, swampy ground, loose dogs, etc.

You'll need a long circular trail that begins and ends at your ritual space.

You'll need at least five priestesses. Walk the trail together ahead of time and get comfortable leading a hike around the space. For a night sit, do it the night before, walking in the dark.

Find a bunch of spots along the way where someone can comfortably sit for 20 minutes. Return in daylight to check for poison oak, bee-hives, swampy ground, trip hazards, etc.

Dogs – before the ritual begins, check about dogs on the land. Some people will not want to sit alone if they are worried about roaming dogs. Can dogs be leashed or inside during this working?

Cars – if there are vehicles on the site, can you negotiate a 30-minute no-drive period, or choose a trail away from roads?

Tell folks to wear warm, comfortable clothes.

Ahead of time – let people know what you will be doing. If someone really resists, find a way to work with them – perhaps their sit-spot can be near the main fire circle, or they could bring a camp chair with them.

Priestesses – you'll need a lead priestess for the hike, another to follow at the end of the line – and a couple of roving priestesses who tap people out of line and sit them in the dark. A fifth priestess stays and anchors the ritual space – a bonfire, or an altar with candles and a bowl of water, etc.

Beforehand, count the number of sitters. If you don't know every person, make a list of names.

WORKING

This description is for a night sit. For a nature sit, look for the most beautiful area you can find. Place people far enough apart that they can't see one another.

continued on next page

WORKINGS

Nature Sit / Night Sit (pg 2)

Sacred space is already created, and a fire or altar established for people to return to afterward.

Priestess gathers people, explains the working (do it now, not earlier, so people aren't fretting over details). Invite people to leave behind flashlights, phones, water bottles, etc – take only warm clothing.

Ask that once the walk starts, people remain silent until all return to the ritual circle.

Priestess speaks: "We are going on a silent hike and night sit. This is an opportunity for you to encounter the mystery deep in your own center – what insights rise within you when you are alone in the dark? What questions, doubts, or fears arise? What new possibilities shine before you?"

Invite people simply to be open and let thoughts and feelings flow through them.

Gather in a single line and commence sacred silence. Check that all priestesses are ready. Lead priestesses begin the hike. Go slowly – this creates a spooky mood, and allows the roving priestesses time to seat people in the dark and catch up again.

Once everyone is seated, priestesses wait until 20-25 minutes have passed from the start of the hike, then slowly go back around to gather people. Be as quiet as possible so folks further along don't hear you coming until you are close.

When you have retrieved the last person, count everyone and make sure you didn't miss anyone. If you did, start singing and send a priestess back around the circuit.

When the hike is complete and all are back together – do a quiet song to unify the group: The River She Is Flowing; My Soul; Let the Beauty We Love.

SOLO WORKING

You can do a nature sit by yourself, as part of a longer personal ritual or as its own working. You could follow the nature sit with a tarot reading (see Workings: Tarot: Intuitive Reading), and/or charge the working with Spell: Overflowing Cup.

Find a safe, quiet spot where you won't be disturbed, and a second spot nearby where you will begin and end.

Bring a timer, your journal, and some solid, grounding snacks for afterward (nuts, berries, bread, apples). Dark sunglasses might help you create your own private space.

Create sacred space for yourself at the beginning spot. You can do this quickly and quietly – try "invisible casting" (see Ritual Skills: Circle Casting). Call in an ally or two to support you.

Then say to yourself: "I am going on a silent hike and sit. This is an opportunity for me to encounter the mystery deep in my own center – what truth comes to me when all is silent and dark? What questions, doubts, or fears arise? What new possibilities shine before me?"

Take a breath, then slowly and silently walk to your sit-spot. Make yourself comfortable. Set your timer for 20 minutes. Close your eyes and relax.

After 20 minutes, stand and stretch. Silently walk back to your starting point. When you get there, sit down and write in your journal for a few minutes.

✪ **Book of Shadows** – consider answering these questions in your journal: What surprised me? How bored or irritated did I get? What thoughts kept popping into my head? How did I feel about my daily life?

After you finish writing, how will you bring this working to completion?

For a short wrap-up, try a song: The River She Is Flowing; My Soul; Let the Beauty We Love.

If you want to do a longer ritual, follow the sitting with an intuitive tarot reading (see Workings: Tarot), then charge your reading with Workings: Overflowing Cup Spell.

Remember to devoke any allies you called and open the circle.

WORKINGS

Non-Judgmental Listening

INTENT

The intent is to truly listen to another person with no judgment, advice, or attempts to fix anything. This working reminds us that each of us is an amazing magical being – and that we are okay just as we are.

The good news is – we are! Humans are okay, even when we make mistakes and hurt one another. Our task is to do better in the present and future, not to feel lousy about the past.

Non-judgmental listening can be a good way to check in at the start of a class – but you'll want to do some teaching before you turn people loose with it. It can be hard for some people to just listen (or be listened to)!

We have used this exercise as part of a "listening stations" ritual on the first day of Teen Earth Magic – small groups rotate among three stations – listening to nature, listening to myself, and listening to one another (where we practice non-judgmental listening). See Rituals: Stations Format.

This sort of listening is not a replacement for the ways we usually talk with family or friends – it's another way of being together. Try setting aside 10 minutes and doing this with a friend(s) the next time you're together.

This practice is based on techniques from co-counseling (aka reciprocal peer counseling).

PREP

Get people into dyads or triads, preferably with someone they do not know very well (sometimes it's easier to be open with someone whom we don't have a lot of other connections with).

Groups of three take a little longer, and are not quite as intimate – but they increase our odds of having someone really listen to us.

Use a timer and give people three to five minutes apiece. A bell to ring changes is handy.

Let people know how long they will have to talk, and that you will signal when it's time to switch, so they don't have to worry about the timing. Remind people about agreements around confidentiality – this is doubly important if we are to feel safe and "non-judged."

SPACE/TIME/SIZE

Any number, in dyads or triads. Enough space to spread out a bit. Allow about five minutes per person (10 minutes total for a dyad, 15 for a triad), and a few minutes for transition. You may want a few minutes at the end for the entire circle to de-brief if this is the first time your group has done this.

WORKING

Get people into dyads / triads, then ask for their attention. Priestess speaks: "We are going to practice listening to one another with no judgment, no advice, and no attempt to fix or take care of one another. This can be harder than we think!

"Each of you will have a three-minute turn. Listeners, give the speaker your full, silent attention – show them with your eyes that you are fully present. Let go of judgments, advice, or helpful support. Try thinking things like, 'What an amazing human being! I bet they can handle anything life throws at them! Wow, what a wonderful person!'

"There is no need to speak, nod, smile, affirm, or actively support the speaker – just be fully present. At the end, everyone simply say, "Thank you."

"Speaker – when it is your turn, take a breath. Three minutes is a long time! Go slowly. You can talk or be silent as you wish,

continued on next page

WORKINGS

Non-Judgmental Listening (pg 2)

but use your entire time. Look your listeners in the eye when you can. Talk about what you wish. If feelings come up, let them flow. This is your time. Feel what it is like to have other people fully present with you – people who are not judging you or trying to fix you. They are simply listening to you."

Let people talk, ringing the bell for changes. At the end, call people back.

If time permits, ask folks to share a bit about how this felt. Some might say things such as, "That was hard – I really wanted to say something supportive." Others might say, "Wow, I'm not used to being listened to that way!"

At the end, especially if this has been difficult for some participants, re-affirm that we have just done powerful magical work – we have been fully present with one another!

Song: Let the Beauty We Love; I See Myself In You.

SOLO WORKING

We can actually listen to ourselves non-judgmentally. Take your Book of Shadows and find a quiet, solitary space. You may also want to bring a hand mirror and combine this with the mirror affirmations working (page 241).

Close your eyes and breathe a few times. On each breath, say this simple affirmation: "I am okay just as I am."

After a few breaths, stop and write a bit. Try writing: "I am completely okay – and that means..." – and free-write from there.

When self-judgments come up, breathe and let them go. Repeat aloud: "I'm completely okay just as I am."

Repeat this several times – breathe and say the affirmation a few times, then write.

✪ **Book of Shadows** – what do you notice? Does the writing change? What feelings come up?

Try it again – take a breath and say, "I am okay just as I am." Write some more.

At the end, close your journal. Take a breath and remember the affirmation you have spoken. Say: "So mote it be!"

Song: Let the Beauty We Love; I See Myself In You.

WORKINGS

Overflowing Cup (Ace of Cups Spell)

INTENT

Picturing the overflowing Ace of Cups tarot card (see the Rider-Waite-Smith deck), we weave a gentle, watery spell for charging an intention or commitment, or for calling abundance into your life.

This is a good climactic working for a class or ritual, for instance after a trance or tarot reading where people arrive at a "next step" commitment. It can also fit well after workings where people are challenged to welcome abundance into their lives (often naming the abundance they desire).

TIME/SPACE/SIZE

Takes a minute per person, plus a few minutes of set-up and a song at the end. More than 25 people will risk losing focus.

A quiet space with an open center where an altar with a large bowl can be set up, or place altar next to a low fire.

PREP

Need:
- a large bowl.
- pitchers of drinkable water (or one pitcher and some jugs of water) – at least two full cups of water for each person.
- cups for all – if a class, invite people to bring a chalice or favorite cup.
- a few towels.
- small table to elevate bowl if available – greenery or cloth to decorate central altar around bowl.

Teach songs: Born of Water; Let the Beauty We Love (or My Soul).

WORKING

This spell builds on a prior working such as a tarot reading or a meditation where people make a commitment, or decide what energy they want to invoke in abundance. Sacred space is already cast.

Place bowl and pitchers in center. Have cups handy – people may already be holding and charging them from a prior working.

Song – gather around the bowl and sing: Born of Water.

One by one, people step up and say: "I call into this cup _____ (such and such commitment or energy – eg, "I call into this cup awareness of the abundance of love around me," or "I call into this cup my commitment to sing daily").

Hold cup over the bowl. Priestess begins slowly pouring. As cup fills, let it overflow into the bowl until person says, "now."

Focusing on their intention, the person drinks the water. When they finish, all call out: "So mote it be!"

Song – when all have gone, bind the spell with a song: Let the Beauty We Love (or My Soul).

Afterward – open the circle. Offer surplus water to the Earth.

SOLO IDEAS

You can pour an overflowing cup for yourself. Set up a bowl and pitcher, and do each step slowly and with intention.

Begin with a meditation or tarot reading where you think about your life and what energy you would especially like to call in.

Once you know what you want to call in, do the Overflowing Cup Spell above. After it overflows, drink slowly from the cup, focusing on your intention.

End with a song.

WORKINGS

Pentacles: Intro & Running Energy

INTENT

Learning to run pentacle energy through the body and aura can be used as a meditation, for grounding and purification, and as a daily (or occasional) personal practice. For some, the Iron or Pearl Pentacle becomes a core part of their magical practice.

The work is simple: we name each of the five points as a quality, then run energy through those qualities.

Pentacles can be the basis of a class or WitchCamp path, working with one of the points each session. We did a teens' Pearl Pentacle workshop in 2013, squeezing all five points into one very busy weekend.

Reclaiming inherited two pentacles from the Feri tradition, in which some early Reclaiming teachers were trained: Iron and Pearl. You'll find an intro to Pearl below, and you can read more about the Iron Pentacle in Starhawk's book The Spiral Dance and T. Thorn Coyle's Evolutionary Witchcraft.

Various other pentacles have been created and taught. In the mid-2000s, Free Cascadia WitchCamp developed the Pentacle of the Great Turning based on Joanna Macy's work. Teen Earth Magic used this as our camp theme in 2010 and again in 2017. You'll find more on the Pentacle of the Great Turning in this chapter (page 252).

SPACE/TIME/SIZE

Any number, with room to spread out at more than arm's length. Allow 10 minutes including transitions.

PREP

Whatever pentacle you are doing, run it over a period of time until you can do it in your sleep. Doing (and especially leading) a pentacle working requires steady concentration. Struggling to remember the points of a given pentacle is a distraction.

WORKING – Running Pentacle Energy (Pearl Pentacle)

This working uses Pearl Pentacle as an example – substitute other pentacle points as desired.

Many Feri initiates run the pentacle only around the outer ring, as described by Starhawk in The Spiral Dance. However, others do it across the body, and it is often taught this way in Reclaiming. This working runs energy across the body and then around the circle. You can do it while standing or laying down.

Priestess invites people to spread out and be comfortable, then make a star with your arms, legs, and head. (Think of Leonardo Da Vinci's image of "Vitruvian Man" standing inside a circle.)

Begin by renewing your grounding and finding your center. Breathe to your center and gather your attention there.

Now on a gentle breath, lift that energy until it comes to rest slightly above your head. Some people see / feel this as a colored ball, others as a vague wave of energy. Some just pretend they feel something. It's all good.

Love (Head) – Name the energy point above your head Love. Breathe to Love, to the love you feel in your life, to the love you have for friends, for community, for all the Earth.

continued on next page

WORKINGS

Pentacles: Intro & Running Energy (pg 2)

On a breath, drop the energy down to a point just above your right foot. Again, feel this energy however you can – each of us does it differently. Just notice the energy above your right foot.

Law (RF) – Name this right foot energy point Law. Breathe to the many forms of "law" in your life – gravity, alarm clocks, government, rules of grammar, your daily schedule.... Let go of judgments and feel the many roles Law plays in your life.

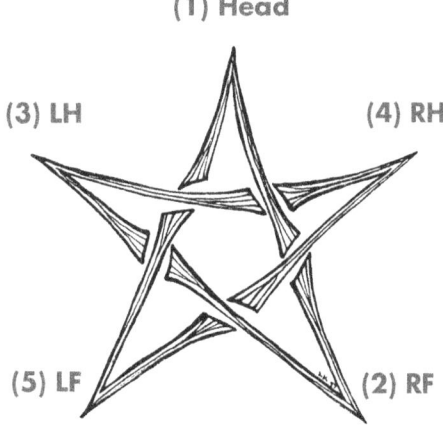

Running The Pentacle
Pearl, Iron, & Other Pentacles

(1) Head
(3) LH   (4) RH
(5) LF   (2) RF

Stand as a relaxed star. Take a breath to your center. Let that energy rise gently to a point just above your head.

Begin at the top. Draw the pentacle on your body three times as shown (1-2-3-4-5-1), pausing for one or more breaths as you contemplate the meaning of each point (see this page for Pearl points).

Finally, trace a circle around the star (1-3-5-2-4-1), taking a breath at each point, and finishing at the top.

Let the energy rest there for a moment, then drop gently back to your center for completion of the cycle.

*   *   *   *

Note – compare this to the invoking pentacle on page 72. Why is the "invoking" pentacle a mirror image of the "running" pentacle? Possibly a coincidence?

Some say that with the invoking pentacle, we are inscribing it onto the air in front of us. Whereas when we "run" a pentacle, it's as if the Goddess is facing us and inscribing it onto our body – hence it creates a mirrored image.

On a breath, let the energy rise and cross your body to a point just above your left hand. Feel this energy however you can.

Wisdom (LH) – Name this left hand energy point Wisdom. Breathe to your own innate wisdom – the many ways that you understand life and love and art and beauty. Breathe to that part of yourself that has always had this wisdom, waiting only for it to be awakened.

On a breath, let the energy cross your body to a point just above your right hand. Feel this energy above your hand.

Liberty (RH) – Name this right hand energy point Liberty. Breathe to liberty and freedom in your own life – political freedom, freedom to think your own thoughts, freedom to change and grow, free time, etc. No need to judge – just breathe to Liberty's many forms.

On a breath, drop your energy across your body to a point just above your left foot. Feel this energy hovering above your foot.

Knowledge (LF) – Name this left foot energy point Knowledge. Breathe to the many forms of knowledge and "know-how" you have acquired, that your community and society share – breathe to your own desire for more knowledge, more skill and expertise.

Finally, on a breath, let the energy rise again to the point above your head and say again, Love.

Running the pentacle – now that you know the five Pearl points, let's run them in order. Review as needed: Love - Law - Wisdom - Liberty - Knowledge.

Take a breath to your center. Then, beginning just above your head, see if you can pass the ball of energy steadily through the five points, pausing to say the corresponding word and feel the presence of each point.

Run this pentacle three to five times, ending back at Love.

Then, beginning at Love, run the energy *around* the circle, moving to your left: Love - Wisdom - Knowledge - Law - Liberty. Do this one or more times, ending again at Love.

Finally, on a gentle breath, let the energy drop back to your center. Anchor the Pentacle of Pearl in your center. Feel the rays run from your center out to the five points. Breathe to this connection.

You are the Pentacle of Pearl!

continued on next page

WORKINGS

Pentacles: Intro & Running Energy (pg 3)

WORKINGS: Shadow & Imbalances

Can you feel the "shadow" sides of the pentacle? What would the opposites or contradictories of these points be? What if a point is too strong or too weak? The shadow side of the Knowledge point might be acting like a know-it-all – or getting brain-freeze at test time. What are your personal Pearl Pentacle shadows?

You can work with shadow energy, or with points that feel weak or out of balance.

Slowly run the Pearl (or any) Pentacle. As the energy alights at each point, notice which points feel out of balance with the others. Are any points heavy? Wobbly? Weak? Overpowering?

Use your breath to reshape the energy. Add or release power around that point. Use slow, deep breaths to steady and strengthen a point. Continue until the five points feel more in balance.

For shadow work, run the pentacle in full, then come back and reshape the energy of a specific point. If I am a victim of brain-freeze at test-time, I might picture the Knowledge point (left foot of Pearl) so warm that my frozen knowledge thaws at the slightest touch. Picture the facts unfreezing and becoming as soft and malleable as warm clay. Repeat this for a few days until you can easily call up the thawing images.

At the end of each session, run the entire pentacle again, and try to feel the Knowledge point more in balance with the others.

SOLO WORKING

Same as above. Running pentacle energy is a great personal practice. Run it quickly sometimes, and other times stop and meditate on each point.

Do a weeklong Pearl Pentacle working. Cast a circle which you will quickly renew each day.

On the first day, after creating sacred space, take some time to run the full Pearl Pentacle and meditate a little on each point. For the next five days, after running the full pentacle, spend five minutes meditating on one of the five points, in order.

On the seventh day, focus on the full pentacle again. Feel the balance (or not) of the five points. What has changed over the past week? Where is the pentacle still unbalanced?

✪ **Book of Shadows** – what changed over the course of the week? Which points need strengthening or healing? Is this a daily practice that you want to continue?

Remember to devoke and open your weeklong circle at the end.

More Pentacle Readings

- Pearl Pentacle interviews – WeaveAndSpin.org/pearl-pentacle
- Starhawk – The Spiral Dance
- T. Thorn Coyle – Evolutionary Witchcraft
- Jane Meredith & Gede Parma – Magic of the Iron Pentacle

Magic, activism, and much more – in our back issues!
Download all 101 issues of Reclaiming Newsletter and Reclaiming Quarterly
Free – at WeaveAndSpin.org/back-issues
Image – RQ #77, Winter 1999 – Magical activism at the WTO protests in Seattle

WORKINGS

Pentacle of The Great Turning

Based on the work of Joanna Macy

Desire
Surrender
Transformation
Solidarity
Manifestation

You can use the pentacle-working ideas in the preceding pages, as well as advanced workings from T. Thorn Coyle's book Evolutionary Witchcraft, with this activist pentacle. We've used the Pentacle of the Great Turning twice as our TEM theme – and we'll probably revisit it again in a few years!

Here's an introductory article by TEM teacher Riyana, plus thoughts on living during the Great Turning by Joanna Macy on the third page.

By Riyana Moon

Around the world, different ancient cultures have prophesied a time of great change: the sensation of time speeding up, Mother Earth becoming less and less able to support life, species going extinct by the thousands, the whole world being torn asunder by greed, ignorance, and lethargy. And in the midst of this, a great awakening – a turning, a rite of passage into a new, greater consciousness.

Ecospiritualist Thomas Berry calls this evolution of consciousness the "Great Work" of our era.

Joanna Macy, an elder of the Buddhist tradition and an anti-nuclear activist for over thirty years, calls it the Great Turning: "It's the essential adventure of our time: the shift from the industrial growth society to a life-sustaining civilization."

Healing the Earth

For witches and other people who practice daily to send roots down and connect deeply with the Earth, we sometimes feel our own hearts and spirits torn apart by the devastation of our Mother. Some of us feel the confusion of the many creatures whose homes and families are dying, like a daze we can never quite shake off. Still others are haunted by the sorrowful songs of the dammed rivers and the Salmon who cannot find their way back to their ancestral homes.

Healing the Earth and learning to live harmoniously with Her ways may be the Great Work of our time, but it is hard work. Activists get burned out, Earth healers become encumbered by their own wounds, and dreamers close their eyes to the visions they see, because it's simply too much at times.

The Pentacle of The Great Turning is a tool that was created through a community visioning process by Free Activist WitchCamp in 2007 to honor, inspire, and give birth to this Great Work. The points of the Pentacle were harvested from dreamings on Brigid Eve, visioning under the full moon, and, of course a series of seemingly endless consensus meetings, from which we emerged with a true witches' tool: one that paradoxically works inwardly and outwardly at the same time – which is precisely the magic needed to bring about the awakening we dream of.

Desire – the work begins in Desire. This is Desire in its multi-faceted, bright and shadowy sense: our deep, loving connection to the Mother, our irresistible attraction to life, our hunger for ecstasy, our yearning to know Her in our bodies, our hearts, our souls. It is through deepening our connection with Her and with our love for life that we can viscerally understand the extent of the destruction facing our planet, and the intensity of the coming storms if we do not find another way of living.

continued on next page

WORKINGS

Pentacle of The Great Turning (pg 2)

The sheer enormity of what we have done and what we must learn to do in order to survive and ensure the survival of other living beings is overwhelming to think about – nuclear waste with a half-life thousands of years long, 50 percent of all species disappearing, an island of plastic waste twice the size of Texas floating in the Pacific Ocean. It's tempting to turn away, to return to the much smaller and more manageable details of our private lives, but that's not how the Great Turning is woven.

Surrender – all we can do is Surrender to the fears that threaten to close our hearts like a stone, the sorrow that makes us feel brittle like dried leaves, the rage that thunders against the hollows of our stomachs like sticks, the apathy that feels like empty death. We Surrender into faith. We may not know if there's anything we can do to stop the destruction, but we choose to try to do something rather than let our worry of personal failure hold us back. We open to the luminous, bright light of adventure.

Transformation – in that opening, an amazing Transformation blossoms. Some traditions call this blossoming the inklings of enlightenment; some call it becoming indigenous, rewilding, or finding the primal self; some call it coming through the dark night of the soul into knowing the love of the divine. In the many names and forms of this Transformation, there is a common thread: we open up to the great web of life as our selves, we see how this web holds us, is within us, and that we are of it. We are nature, we are the land. We are nature and the land healing herself.

Solidarity – from this knowing, we can move into true Solidarity with all of our relations. Lila Watson, Aboriginal activist, once famously said, "If you have come to help me you are wasting my time. But if you have come because your liberation is bound up with mine, then let us struggle together."

In the Great Turning, we extend Watson's insight beyond the boundary of species lines to include the Salmon and the hazel trees, the orcas and the wild bunch grasses, the stray cats in our neighborhoods and the scrub-jays that drive us crazy at dawn with their scratchy cawing. We reach out with our hearts and prayers to listen to the wisdom of all beings, knowing that we need the voices of all of them in order to create truly meaningful, culture-altering, save-the-world solutions.

Manifestation – the last point on the Pentacle is Manifestation: not only the communal manifestation we are creating – The Great Turning – but also the unique callings of our individual lives that make up our own personal part of it. This brings us back to Desire – what we want to do with our lives to help the healing of the Earth, the work that we are yearning to do, the visions we long to bring to fruition.

For some of us, a big part of the work of the Great Turning is our activism, whether in the streets or in community centers. For others, our work is as healers and artists and ritualists working to change the consciousness beneath the actions that are so detrimental to the planet. Still others are crafting new initiatives and new systems for our culture, finding visionary ways to manifest the Great Turning in the here and now.

Most of us dance between many different spheres of the work, following our hearts and minds and the wise words of our guides to find the right road for us.

In all of these places, the points of the Pentacle of the Great Turning can help keep us grounded, inspired, and connected in the wider context of our work. May it be so.

Riyana adores the magic of song, women's blood mysteries, herbs, and incorporating writing and poetry into her witchy work. She has taught at WitchCamps and intensives across the U.S. and abroad, and often crafts ritual and facilitates classes in her local community in the San Francisco Bay Area.

This article first appeared in Reclaiming Quarterly.

Running the Pentacle

As per the preceding pages, ground yourself. Draw your personal energy to a small ball in your center. Let this energy rise to a point just above your head.

With gentle breaths, move the energy to each point and let it rest for a moment. Run this cycle three times, ending at the head. Finally, bring your energy back to center.

Head: Desire

Right Foot: Surrender

Left Hand: Transformation

Right Hand: Solidarity

Left Foot: Manifestation

Pentacle of The Great Turning (pg 3)

by Joanna Macy

The Great Turning is a name for the essential adventure of our time: the shift from the industrial growth society to a life-sustaining civilization.

The ecological and social crises we face are inflamed by an economic system dependent on accelerating growth. This self-destructing political economy sets its goals and measures its performance in terms of ever-increasing corporate profits – in other words by how fast materials can be extracted from Earth and turned into consumer products, weapons, and waste.

A revolution is underway because people are realizing that our needs can be met without destroying our world. We have the technical knowledge, the communication tools, and material resources to grow enough food, ensure clean air and water, and meet rational energy needs.

Future generations, if there is a livable world for them, will look back at the epochal transition we are making to a life-sustaining society. And they may call this the time of the Great Turning. It is happening now.

Whether or not it is recognized by corporate-controlled media, the Great Turning is a reality. Although we cannot know yet if it will take hold in time for humans and other complex life forms to survive, we can know that it is under way.

And it is gaining momentum, through the actions of countless individuals and groups around the world. To see this as the larger context of our lives clears our vision and summons our courage.

Personal Guidelines for the Great Turning

Come from Gratitude

To be alive in this beautiful, self-organizing universe – to participate in the dance of life with senses to perceive it, lungs that breathe it, organs that draw nourishment from it – is a wonder beyond words. Gratitude for the gift of life is the primary wellspring of all religions, the hallmark of the mystic, the source of all true art.

Furthermore, it is a privilege to be alive in a time when we can choose to take part in the self-healing of our world.

Don't Be Afraid of the Pain

This is a painful time, filled with suffering and uncertainty. Like living cells in a larger body, it is natural that we feel the trauma of our world. So don't be afraid of the anguish you feel, or the anger or fear, for these responses arise from the depth of your caring and the truth of your interconnectedness with all beings. To "suffer with" is the literal meaning of compassion.

Dare to Vision

Out of this suffering a new world can arise, not to be constructed by our minds so much as to emerge from our dreams. Even though we cannot see clearly how it's going to turn out, we are still called to let the future into our imagination. We will never be able to build what we have not first cherished in our hearts.

Roll Up Your Sleeves

Many people don't get involved in the Great Turning because there are so many different issues which seem to compete with each other. Shall I save the whales or help battered children? The truth is that all aspects of the current crisis reflect the same mistake, setting ourselves apart and using others for our gain. So to heal one aspect helps the others to heal as well. Just find what you love to work on and take joy in that. Don't try to do it alone. Link up with others – you'll spark each others' ideas and sustain each others' energy.

Act Your Age

Since every particle in your body goes back to the first flaring forth of space and time, you're really as old as the universe. So when you are lobbying at your congressperson's office, or visiting your local utility, or testifying at a hearing on nuclear waste, or standing up to protect an old grove of redwoods, you are doing that not out of some personal whim, but in the full authority of your 13 billions years.

JoannaMacy.net

Learn more about Joanna Macy's work at JoannaMacy.net.

TEM cooks the Great Turning – see page 341!

WORKINGS

Purification: Bridge Challenge

INTENT

A simple but powerful purification for a class or ritual. Sometimes we've done this on the opening night of Witchlets, as a way to transition from our mundane lives to the magic of camp. People think they're just walking across the bridge to the fire circle, and suddenly they are stopped and challenged.

A robed and veiled priestess stops people as they approach the ritual space and challenges them with a question. The question relates to the ritual or path we're about to do.

This can be done in any space. Because we cross a wooden bridge to get to the teens fire circle at Witchlets, this has become known as the "bridge challenge."

In recent years we've let the Witchlets' Newts Path (age four to seven) do a campfire at the teen circle one evening after dinner. A couple of teens meet the kids and their parents at the bridge and challenge the young ones with some vintage Monty Python magic: "What is your name? What is your quest? What is your favorite color?"

SPACE/TIME/SIZE

Any number – the challenge is quick and can be done for more than one person at a time if needed. No extra time is needed, since this happens as we gather.

PREP

Need robe and veil or sheer fabric for bridge priestess(es).

Need a "wrangler" for each priestess – someone who will accompany the priestess and help them ground afterward (wearing a veil and playing a role like this can leave people very spacey).

Wrangler can also act as a grace (ie, magical usher) to steer people toward the priestess if there is more than one way to approach the space, or to facilitate if a line starts to back up.

Prepare question / challenge in connection with ritual plans. Keep it short and simple – the Newts' challenge above is too long if there are 30 people. Consider whether you want people to answer, or merely to contemplate the question and keep moving.

Sample questions: Are you ready to begin this working? What matters more to you than anything in the world? What dreams are you afraid to admit even to yourself?

WORKING

As people approach, the priestess(es) – in robe and veil – stand blocking the bridge. If you don't have a bridge handy, find some place that anyone approaching the ritual space must pass (have graces direct people if necessary). Indoors, meet people at the door as they arrive. Put a cloth over the doorway and stand just inside to make it more mysterious.

When a person steps up, priestess gazes silently for a moment. Then in a slow voice they speak the question or challenge.

Depending on the challenge, priestess may wait for an answer, or simply state the question and gesture the person forward.

When all have passed, wrangler helps priestess re-ground. Brush down their aura. Ask them to name some random things that they see – bring them back into this world.

SOLO WORKING

The idea is that when you enter ritual space, make it a magical transition. You could write down some challenge-questions on note cards and draw one. Or stop, place your hand on your center, and think about your personal intention for the magic you are about to do. When you are ready to enter, do it with clear intention.

Purification: Star Purification

INTENT

A simple, physical way of clearing dissonant energy and filling your aura with fresh star energy.

Remember – our bodies are of the Earth – and the Earth is of the stars. When we call down star energy, we're tapping into our own ancient source.

Balance star and Earth energy. After you have filled your aura with star energy, draw up Earth energy and mingle them in your center. Let yourself be the connection between stars and Earth.

SPACE/TIME/SIZE

Any number, with room to spread out at arm's length. Allow 10 minutes so people have time to practice.

PREP

Priestess demonstrates this working, then each person practices on their own.

WORKING

Priestess describes and demonstrates:

Ground yourself and find your center. Breathe to your center.

Now, using your hands as gentle guides, draw up Earth energy. Tease it up through your aura with your breath – let a column of energy rise effortlessly through you, entering your feet or the base of your spine and flowing out the top of your head.

Imagine all the various energies inside you as multi-colored clouds filling your aura, swirling inside you.

Now, hold your two hands in front of the top of your head, palms down, elbows out to the side.

On an out-breath, smoothly push the multi-colored Earth energy down through your body and aura, all the way down and out of your roots.

As you push the colors down, let your breath draw silver star-energy from above to take its place. As your hands push the colors downward, let yourself fill with silvery energy from above. Focus your attention on this silvery star energy entering your body and your aura.

When your hands go below your knees, shake them off. Breathe to the silvery energy filling you.

Repeat several times – use your hands to gently draw multi-colored Earth energy up, then use your palms to push the swirling colors down and out, breathing in silvery star energy from above.

After a few times, breathe and feel the silvery star energy filling you.

Now, from below, call up clean, pure Earth energy and let it mingle with the star energy in your center. Let this energy drop and re-ground you to the Earth.

Song: Body of the Earth ("We are of the body of the Earth / the Earth is of the body of the stars").

SOLO WORKING

Same working.

WORKINGS

Ritual Skills Day: A Stations Ritual

INTENT

To teach and develop our ritual skills, we create an interactive, experiential skills day – a festival of ritual practices.

This is an example of a "stations ritual" (see Rituals: Stations Format – page 130).

One year at Witchlets we had a big group that was about half older teens who'd been part of our circle for a while, and half newer and younger folks. We decided to take one of our morning paths and do a skills day.

Small groups of teens rotated among several stations – grounding, circle casting, and invoking – practicing skills and coming up with fun and creative ways to do these ritual roles.

Each station was a mini-workshop, and taken together they taught the most common ritual skills. Teachers aimed to keep the work fun, embodied, and fast-paced.

For that evening's ritual, the younger teens took the main roles and tried out their newly-honed skills.

This format worked so well that in recent years the first morning path at Teen Earth Magic has often been some sort of stations working that helps people get their magical skills percolating. For some stations options, see page 131.

SPACE/TIME/SIZE

This working will fill most of a morning path or afternoon workshop – 90 minutes to two hours including set-up and closing. Enough room for several stations to spread out.

From a few to 30 people or so. If fewer than 15, consider doing the stations one at a time, everyone together.

PREP

Decide what stations will be offered and by whom, and how long they will be (perhaps 20-30 minutes each).

Each sub-group of priestesses gathers whatever materials they will need and plans their working – not much is needed for this process, but you may want some props for circle casting or invoking.

Decide where stations will be, and how rotation will work. Sub-divide the group if needed (see above).

Choose and teach a simple transition song and a final song. See Ritual Skills: Chants. Here are some ideas:

Song for transitions: We Are the Flow.

Final Song: Rise with the Fire; She Changes Everything She Touches; Weave and Spin.

WORKING

Gather and explain the format of the day. If a larger circle, find a way to form sub-groups. Teach songs.

Create sacred space in a quick, simple way. Invite everyone to invoke energies that will be helpful – things like creativity, focus, spontaneity, etc. You may also want to invite magical ancestors (known and unknown).

Priestesses move to stations. Sub-groups move to their first station and begin workshop.

Example – Invoking Station

At this station, we might start by talking a little about "what is invoking?" Everyone can share ideas. Then talk a little about different ways of invoking – again all can share, with priestesses filling in gaps and adding commentary.

Then the group tries out some of the ideas. Priestesses can suggest and reinforce ways that might involve and energize the

continued on next page

Ritual Skills Day (pg 2)

whole group. Experiment with "instant invocations" – ways of invoking an element in five seconds or less. Try invoking silently, with movement, or with song. See if the group can do multi-media – some sing, some dance, some might wave scarves or greenery – and still remain focused. (See Ritual Skills: Invoking for lots more ideas.)

After the allotted time, sing a song as people rotate to the next station: We Are the Flow.

Rotate and repeat for each station.

After the whole group completes all stations, form into groups of three. Each person take a couple of minutes to talk about their experiences, what they learned, and what roles they would feel comfortable doing in a ritual (if anything).

Come back together and sing a song.

Song: My Soul; She Changes Everything She Touches; Weave and Spin.

Devoke, remembering to thank the energies that everyone called in – people can just call out the energies they invoked, then a priestess say thanks to all of them.

Planning the Ritual

If the skills day is a prelude to a later ritual (at a camp, or as the climax of a workshop), take a few minutes now to decide who will priestess which parts of the upcoming ritual, and who will do the overall planning. At TEM or Witchlets, the planning group will find a time to meet before the ritual – sometimes during dinner.

Planners will look for ways to put the group's new skills to work, and to involve people in creative and magical ways.

SOLO WORKING

Can you create your own skills day? How about a personal ritual where you spend 15-20 minutes practicing each skill – grounding, casting the circle, and invoking. Use this book to create your own exercises.

Challenge yourself to find at least one new way of doing each ritual role.

Then use the new skills to craft your own ritual. Take as long or as short as you wish.

✪ **Book of Shadows** – before devoking, write in your journal about these magical skills and what you have learned.

WORKINGS

Shadow Work

INTENT

Shadow work is at the core of Reclaiming magic – knowing yourself in all your parts. There is great strength in fully knowing yourself – and with it come opportunities for change.

What is one's shadow? Shadow is those parts of ourselves that we repress, ignore, or pretend don't exist.

Shadow is sometimes negative – shame, fear, doubt. Your shadow may include greed and selfishness. It may include feelings that are too scary to let yourself know. Sometimes we refer to screwed-up politicians or pop stars as embodying society's shadow – they act out our worst patterns.

Other times our shadow can be our big, colorful, flamboyant parts. Some people's shadow includes speaking up in groups, singing out loud, or being silly. Others' might include sleeping late or taking a day off.

Shadow is those parts of ourselves that we don't want anyone to see – sometimes not even ourselves!

Shadow can be very uncomfortable – we don't always get to choose when these issues come up and demand our attention. Parts of ourselves that disturb or scare us might come leaping forward at the worst possible moments.

Why do we do magical shadow work? Perhaps if we create a safe container to allow our shadows out, we can defuse some of their energy and make them less likely to pop up unexpectedly. Also, our shadows often hold a lot of old pain, shame, or guilt. These old feelings hold us back from being our best and brightest selves.

Our goal in this work is to provide a safe circle where our shadows can come forward. Maybe we'll discover things we want to work more on – for instance, expressing ourselves more boldly, or wearing more colorful clothes.

Confidentiality – in much magical work, and shadow work in particular, it is important that we be able to trust those with whom we are open – trust them to hold us in a strong circle, and trust that our experience will not be turned into gossip. See Introduction: Agreements.

What Balances Shadow Work?

Shadow work can be intense, and calls for balance.

The intent of shadow work is to spend time with unfamiliar and uncomfortable energies. In a class or ritual, we'll want to balance the energy before we end.

With a shadow party, the working provides its own balance. In that case, try coming into a close circle with arms around shoulders and singing one of the songs below.

If you have more time and/or more is needed to bring the group out of shadow-space, try one of these workings:

- Post-Shadow Mirror Milling (see end of this section)
- Workings: Blessing Line (takes one minute per person)
- Workings: Luscious Eating (takes 10-15 minutes)
- Workings: Allies Circle (takes longer – major working)
- Workings: Lifting Each Other Up (major working)

Shadow work at the center of the labyrinth.

If the shadow work leaves people quiet or contemplative, consider doing a low-key spiral dance with deep eye-gazing.

Songs: Opening Up In Sweet Surrender; Let the Beauty We Love; My Soul.

continued on next page

WORKINGS

Shadow Work (pg 2)

SPACE/TIME/SIZE

Any number of people, with enough space to move comfortably – the space should be private enough for folks to feel safe showing themselves and being vulnerable.

PREP

Scarves and costumes can help some people step into their shadows. Hand mirrors and tarot decks are also helpful for some workings. Journal or Book of Shadows. See below for specific prep for each working.

WORKINGS: GENERAL SET-UP

For any of these workings – ground and cast a circle. Invoke allies – each person might call an ancestor / ally to support them in this work (this can be done all at once – priestess simply invites people to each call their own ally – perhaps by people calling their names into the center). Remember to devoke and open your circle at the end.

In a group, priestess can propose or remind people of agreements about confidentiality and respect. We want to create a safe circle to share our full selves – and we may not want the rest of the world to know about it quite yet!

Shadow workings can be preceded by a short meditation. Priestess invites people to look inward and see what parts of themselves lie hidden… dormant… what parts might feel safe coming out today…. What parts of myself might enjoy a chance to wear different clothes and move in different ways…. With a breath, welcome those parts of yourself, both known and yet-to-be known… welcome them to the safety of our circle.

WORKINGS: Discovering My Shadow

Writing My Shadow

In your magical journal or on a blank sheet of paper, list one or more answers to each of these questions:
- something my family does not do / is not good at is _____ (list a few)
- something about my family background that I don't like is _____
- an adventure I would never undertake is _____
- something that really embarrasses me is _____

Go back and underline any strong words and any words that appear more than once. Now ask yourself – what do these words tell me about the parts of myself that I don't usually like to acknowledge? What is one part of my shadow that I could work with today? Write that at the bottom of the page.

Tarot Shadow Discovery

You'll need your journal and a deck for each person (or people can share a card if they both select it). Lay out the cards face up. Each person sift through them and find three to five cards that you do *not* like – trust your gut.

In a pair-share and/or in your journal, speak and write the card's title and a couple of sentences about what you don't like. After a few cards, go back and underline any strong words along with words that appear more than once. Now ask yourself – what do these cards and words tell me about the parts of myself that I don't like? What is one part of my shadow that I could work with today? Write that at the bottom of the page.

continued on next page

WORKINGS

Shadow Work (pg 3)

Mirror Shadow Discovery

Looking in a mirror can bring up shadow material – fears that I am not good looking, that my skin isn't clear enough, that I'm clumsy and scared and can't even look into a mirror right! Set a timer for a few minutes and stay with steady eye contact until the timer rings. Afterward, debrief in pairs and/or write in your journal about what feelings came up.

The final working of this section, Post-Shadow Mirror Milling, is a nice balance to this discovery working.

WORKINGS: Working With My Shadow

Shadow Party

Here's a playful yet intense way to draw out our shadows. All of us have costume shadows – clothes that would make us cringe!

For the well-dressed, it might be baggy jeans or an old button sweater. For the casual crowd, our costume shadow might be a fancy dress, tight pants, or a gaudy feather boa. It's different for each of us.

How about gathering a variety of clothes, some mirrors, and see what shadows show up?

For more on this working, see below, Workings: Shadow: Costume Shadows (page 266).

Stepping Out As My Shadow

This working is best for groups of 12 or fewer – if more, try smaller sub-groups. Each person takes a minute and steps into the middle of the circle and embodies their shadow – step in and act like the parts of yourself that usually get held back.

Maybe you dance and sing a song. Maybe you look people in the eyes and say, "I love you." Maybe you let yourself be sad in front of others. Some people may simply step into the circle and let themselves be seen. And some may take the right to pass.

Having a mentor or older teen go first may help break the ice.

A good way to follow this is Workings: Circle Blessings or Workings: Blessing Line.

Letting the Shadow Speak

Automatic Writing is a way to let our inner shadow voices speak. By writing so fast that we don't have time to censor ourselves, we may hear some of those buried voices. See Workings: Automatic Writing.

Labyrinth Shadow Work: the Monster at the Center

What if the monster at the center of the labyrinth turns out to be a mirror? See Workings: Labyrinth Workings.

Composting Headlines and Composting Oppressions: Activist Shadow Workings

On the following pages you'll find two shadow workings for when we feel weighed down by negative headlines or the heaviness of other people's attitudes and behavior – see Shadow: Composting Headlines and Shadow: Composting Oppressions.

CONCLUSION: Post-Shadow Mirror Milling

This is a nice balance to the Mirror Shadow Discovery working above, or to any shadow work. Use this to wrap up an intense round of shadow work.

You'll need half as many mirrors and veils as people in the group. Half of the group wears veils and hold up mirrors, milling around saying things like, "Look at this amazing person! What a beautiful person! Behold the Goddess! You can do anything!"

The other half mills about silently, gazes at themselves in the mirrors, and listens to the truth.

WORKINGS

Shadow: Composting Headlines

INTENT

We did this exercise at the very first Teen Earth Magic camp, as a way to deal with oppressive and disempowering news headlines by transforming them into compost.

This is a good mid-week working – and a hard place to begin or end. You'll want to follow this with something upbeat.

SPACE/TIME/SIZE

Enough room for a group to gather. Outside is best – dig a hole if you can.

Since each person will read and bury their headline, more than 20 people will get clumsy. Allow a few minutes per person plus about 15 minutes for group work and transitions.

PREP

Presumes people are already grounded and a circle has been cast. This is not a good first or last working in a class – do something lighter before, and uplifting afterward.

In the class or ritual where you do this working, invoke some powerful world-changers as allies.

Dig a small but deep hole – set the dirt aside to refill it. If no hole is available – get a washtub half-filled with dirt, plus a bucket of extra dirt – the dirt will end up in a compost bin, so it's fine if it has twigs or other organic debris mixed in. You'll want a dropcloth or towel for the floor. Make a plan to compost or recycle the dirt afterward.

Prepare a bunch of news headlines – gather some ahead of time if you can, but also make some of your own – print them out ahead of time if you can (samples on next page). Fold them.

WORKING

Gather in a circle. The priestess leads a short meditation about the state of the world and the way our society bombards us with bad news – an alarming amount of which is true – and most of which seems calculated to make us feel hopeless and powerless. We are going to begin to change this at a magical level.

Bring out folded headlines and invite each person to select one. (Priestesses might pre-select a few they want to include.)

Go around the circle and slowly read the headlines aloud. Hear them. Feel their weight. When the circle is complete, take a couple of minutes to groan and shout and shake it off.

Priestess comments: "This is the version of reality that is fed to us every day. But we can challenge this version." Go around again and read one headline at a time. People hiss and boo while the reader rips the headline into tiny bits and drops them into the hole or basin. Reader picks up a scoop or handful of dirt and tosses it over the fragments.

Repeat until all headlines have been read and buried. Toss in more dirt to cover all of the paper.

Balancing the Shadow With Positive Headlines

Priestess leads a short meditation to help people come up with positive news headlines for the world we are building. Then everyone calls out ideas. Dream big!

Song: She Changes Everything She Touches (Kore Chant).

Afterward – fill the hole and transplant a few hardy weeds over it. If you used a basin, dispose of the dirt in a compost bin.

continued on next page

WORKINGS

Shadow: Composting Headlines (pg 2)

SOLO WORKING

Gather / make seven news headlines, and/or use some below. Dig a hole or get a basin of dirt as above. Bring your journal.

Ground and cast your circle and invoke some world-changing allies.

Read the headlines slowly, pausing for a breath after each. Let yourself feel their weight. This is the "reality" that you hear about every day.

Now read them again, one at a time. Take a breath, and state a simple contradiction: "This is wrong," "This has to change," etc.

Rip the headline apart and drop it in the dirt, tossing dirt after each one. At the end, toss three more handfuls of dirt.

✪ **Book of Shadows** – turn away from the composted headlines. Close your eyes, breathe deeply, and let some positive headlines come to you. Picture the world the way you want it to be and write about it in your journal. When you have several ideas you like, read them aloud, followed by saying, "So mote it be!"

When you are finished, raise your spirits by singing She Changes Everything She Touches (officially known as Kore Chant).

Open your circle (ie, devoke). Put the dirt you used into the compost.

NEGATIVE HEADLINES – Some Examples

- **Polar Life Nears Extinction**
- **30,000 Die Annually in Car Accidents**
- **Government Denies Climate Change**
- **Logging Increases in National Parks**
- **Education Budget Cut To Fund Military**
- **Prescription Drugs Kill Thousands**
- **Gridlock Ties Up Government**
- **Student Loan Burden Rises**
- **Gun Limits Rejected**
- **War Enters Another Year**
- **Banks Tighten Credit Policies**
- **Transit Fares Rise - Service Cut**
- **Only 2% of Old Growth Forests Remain**
- **Budget Cuts Hit Poorest Citizens**

WORKINGS

Shadow: Composting Oppressions

INTENT

Here's a variation of the Composting Headlines working, this time from Teen Earth Magic 2018. We were looking for an energetic way to transform oppressive and disempowering ideas and words, from personal to political to ecological.

Since our camp theme that year was Mushrooms & Fungi, we hit on the idea of collectively breaking down and composting a tree of oppressions.

Just as it can take generations and even centuries for fungi to break down a fallen redwood tree, the changes we envision may take a long time to manifest. So we invoked time magic to travel far into the future, to an age when the oppressions had been broken down and transformed into justice, ecology, etc.

This is a good mid-week working, or midway through a workshop.

SPACE/TIME/SIZE

Enough room for a group to gather. Outside is best – dig a hole if you can (if not, see prep below).

Good working for 10-25 people. For more, form sub-groups. Allow about 20 minutes for group work and transitions.

PREP

Need:

- Small but deep hole – set the dirt aside to refill it. If no hole is available – get a washbasin half-filled with dirt, plus a bucket of extra dirt – the dirt will end up in a compost bin, so it's fine if it has twigs or other organic debris mixed in.
- Pile of garden debris – leaves, dirt, twigs, etc (no thorns). Some buckets of water.
- Lay out the "tree" – a long strip of light newsprint or butcher paper (about three feet wide x 12 feet long). Use light-weight paper so it can easily be torn and trampled.
- Thick-point colored markers, plus two to three people to scribe (ie, write down words as people call them out).
- If inside, you'll want a dropcloth or towel for the floor and a plan to compost or recycle the dirt afterward.
- One priestess leads a short meditation about oppressions, and another leads the debris-throwing part, starts song, then facilitates transition to composting the scraps of torn-up paper. A third priestess can help by doing simple drumming.

This presumes people are already grounded and a circle cast. This is not a good first working in a class, and not easy to follow – do something lighter beforehand. After – either make this the final working for a class, or try something meditative like tarot.

In the class or ritual where you do this working, invoke some powerful world-changers as allies.

Teach songs at start of class / ritual if possible – we used Weave and Spin (See Ritual Skills: Chants), plus this new "prequel" verse. When teaching the prequel verse, consider invoking the history of anarchism – in the past, it often meant "smashing" the state, capitalism, etc. Whereas today it often means working cooperatively and nonhierarchically, building alternatives, etc.

Weave & Spin (on Campfire Chants album)
Weave and spin, weave and spin
This is how the work begins
Mend and heal, mend and heal
Take the dream and make it real

Tear & Shred – TEM Prequel Verse
Agitate! Demonstrate!
Organize to smash the state!
Tear and shred, tear and shred
Rip it up until it's dead!

continued on next page

WORKINGS

Shadow: Composting Oppressions (pg 2)

WORKING

Gather in a circle around the "tree." Priestess leads short meditation about oppressions – personal, societal, economic, etc – all the ways we're made to feel that we do not belong or that the world does not support our dreams and visions.

Drumbeat begins. Priestess invites people to begin calling out or writing words and short phrases, from the biggest and most global to the most intimate and personal. Scribes write words as fast as people call them out, or people can write their own.

When this slacks off, and/or paper is getting covered with words, priestess invites people to add last words or phrases. Drum fades. Then all step back and take a breath.

Priestess says wise words about how these oppressions can seem overwhelming – but by working together, and by taking small, steady actions, we can transform this tree of oppression into new life.

Invite people to pick up handfuls of debris and start throwing them onto the paper tree. Start song: "Agitate! Demonstrate!" Others get water and splash it onto tree. People dance and jump on the tree – finally getting down and tearing apart the soggy paper until it's a big mess.

As energy winds down, let song fade. Step back, take a breath, and look at the mess. Then quietly begin to pull the bits and scraps of paper out of the pile and start throwing them into the compost hole (or bucket).

During this part, priestess can talk about how, when fungi break up a dead tree, there are some mushrooms which sprout first and break up the big chunks, then others come along later and break down the smaller pieces. Some people will do the same. Keep going until every scrap and bit of paper is in the compost hole.

Circle round the compost hole. One by one, each person takes a handful of dirt and throws it into the hole, calling out a word of power: "Justice! Peace! Happiness!"

Song – shovel in the rest of the dirt and take turns dancing on it as you sing the original lyrics to Weave and Spin.

SOLO WORKING

It will be hard to raise this sort of energy alone – try the previous working, "Shadow: Composting Headlines" – and add some "words of oppression" as well.

WORKINGS

Shadow: Costume Shadows

INTENT

This is a fun and challenging shadow working that can be done with friends without calling it "Pagan."

All of us have costume shadows – the clothes that would make us cringe to be seen in!

For the well-dressed, it might be baggy jeans or an old button sweater. For the casual crowd, our costume shadow might be a fancy dress, tight pants, or a gaudy feather boa. It's different for each of us.

Sometimes folks at TEM and other camps have planned costume workshops where people try on clothes – and personas – they ordinarily would never let themselves be seen in.

Other times the "work" emerges spontaneously during break time. Since one person's daily garb is someone else's shadow, the "costumes" are already on hand.

SPACE/TIME/SIZE

This can be done alone, but you'll feel more support if you do it with a friend(s). You'll need private space with room to move around. Allow an hour or more.

PREP

Need – journal; mirrors (full length if possible); and lots of clothing!

Music – favorite pop songs. Or how about playing Labyrinth Meditation Music on loop? (See Ritual Skills: Chants – page 113.)

Gather a variety of clothes, especially extremes – very flashy or very plain. You can find "shadow clothes" at a thrift shop – for some people, wearing a dress of any sort is major shadow work. For others, cheap jeans do the trick.

Spread the clothing out on a costume altar (perhaps a table or your bed) so you can see what you've got.

Confidentiality – you'll want to do this work with trusted friends. See Introduction: Agreements for trust agreements we use at TEM. You may also want to agree "no photos." If you do this as a "working," decide who will priestess the meditation below.

WORKING

Gathering & Meditation (start here for ritual-friendly groups)

If it works for your group, create sacred space – ground together and cast a circle. If your friends are not Pagan, maybe you can take a minute and breathe together? If it's a ritual-friendly group, you might want to invoke energies like "safe space" and "openness."

Ask if people will agree to confidentiality and to supporting one another through the working. Talk about this a little if needed, and see if you can reach some basic agreements.

Then invite people to get comfortable. Priestess leads a short meditation:

"Close your eyes and breathe easily…. Imagine yourself walking down a garden path… a beautiful garden path…. What colors do you see?…. What smells come to you?….

"Imagine this garden is your special garden, created just for you by your own imagination…. Let it come to life around you…. What do you see?…. What sounds come to you?….

"As you walk, you come to a small glade with a circle of plants and trees…. Around the edges of the glade are big mirrors, and

continued on next page

Shadow: Costume Shadows (pg 2)

as you walk you catch glimpses of yourself.... Glimpses of your smile... of your glowing aura....

"Gradually you stop in front of a mirror and gaze at yourself... You see that you are dressed in a most unusual fashion!... in fact, you are dressed in a way you would ordinarily *never* dress... but here in the safety of your garden, you are fascinated....

"Gaze gently and lovingly at yourself in the mirror.... Let that reflection know that it is welcome and accepted here in this garden.... Ask that shadow-reflection to come along to a costume party...."

Shadow Party (start here with "non-Pagan" groups)

The leader puts on music and invites people to gather around the clothing. At first just gaze and imagine. Then slowly begin to try on items that might appeal to your shadow. Go for extremes – if you usually dress carefully, go for the sloppiest look possible. If you always wear pants or shorts, try a dress. Don't forget to accessorize!

As you experiment, give one another support and encouragement, without pushing things on one another. Let each person discover and adorn their own shadow.

After a while, settle on a shadow costume and finish up. Then gather in a circle. Take a couple of breaths together, silently looking around. Then begin silently milling around. Move as your shadow – if your shadow is flashy, move that way. If your shadow is grungy, move that way.

Meet one another's eyes and give smiles of welcome to all the shadows. If you're two people, you can do this less formally – just take a few minutes to silently appreciate one another.

After a few minutes, get into groups of three and talk. How does it feel to dress and move in the world in such a different way? What does it show you about how you usually are? Anything new that you'd like to carry back to your daily life?

✪ **Book of Shadows** – take a few minutes and write in your journal.

Completion & Commitment

When you are ready to complete the working, gather again. Go around the circle and each person say one to three words about the experience. Then say thank you to your shadows – you might close your eyes, touch your heart, and quietly say thank you (knowing your shadow is always with you).

Take a few minutes and get back into your usual garb. Set the costumery carefully back on the altar.

Come back together and do a quick aura brushdown – without touching the other person, brush all the stray energy out of their aura, from head to foot. Especially brush the heart, belly, and voice. Remember to brush the back side as well. When you're done brushing, shake your hands off so the energy falls back to the Earth. Then use your hands to fluff the person's aura – starting low, fluff the energy up like a billowy cloud (for more on this, see Workings: Aura Carwash).

If you created sacred space, remember to devoke any energies you called in and open your circle.

SOLO WORKING

You can do this working alone – where will you get clothing really different from what you usually wear? Is there one other person you know who might enjoy this working?

Solo – you'll want a variety of clothes, a mirror, a timer, music, and your journal.

Create sacred space. Set a timer for 20 minutes, Put on music. Read the meditation above. Start experimenting. Look often in the mirror, and each time say to yourself: "Is this a part of me?"

✪ **Book of Shadows** – when the timer sounds, settle on a shadow outfit – the stranger the better! Then take some time and write in your journal.

Complete the working as above (Completion & Commitment), taking time to thank your shadow.

WORKINGS

Spectrums of Belief

INTENT

A spectrum breaks down binary oppositions into a range of responses. Instead of yes or no, black or white, we have gradations. This exercise tends to get teens talking more than if we raised the same issues while seated in a circle.

At Redwood Magic Teens Path we do this some years on opening day. Immediately, people can see that they're not alone in their beliefs and skepticism, and that all of us (including teachers) move around on the spectrums of beliefs and practices.

Later in the week we did Cross Spectrums, a way to carry this working into our daily lives (see next working).

SPACE/TIME/SIZE

Room to spread out in a line without crowding. If you're in an open space, set boundaries – some people will go past the space's limits, and will probably want to explain why. Check for poison oak, swampy ground, etc.

Ten rounds will take at least 20 minutes. Allow more time if people want to go on.

PREP

Clear the space. Have some statements ready. Choose a couple of priestesses to explain the working and get things going.

WORKING

Designate one end of the line as Strongly Agree and the other as Strongly Disagree. Priestess reads a statement. For each statement, people move around and choose their own place on the line – toward one end, or perhaps near the middle.

Once folks settle into their positions, priestess asks people in various places on the line to explain why they chose that position. Some people will really want to talk — priestess calls on several people each time and equalizes participation.

After a few rounds, open it up to others to call out a statement. Be ready with a few if needed, and a good one to close with.

Song – a favorite song to pull energy back together: Let the Beauty We Love; Sweet Water.

SOLO WORK

Draw a line on a piece of paper. Left end is Strongly Agree, right end is Strongly Disagree.

Read first statement below. Write the number "1" above the line where you would fall. Below, write the number and then a sentence or two about why you chose that position. Repeat for a half-dozen or more statements.

Look back at what you've written. What patterns do you see? Underline a few words or phrases and read it aloud as a poem.

STATEMENTS (or create your own)

(1) I consider myself a spiritual person.

(2) I have an altar.

(3) I believe the Earth is alive.

(4) Sometimes I have trouble fitting in.

(5) My family is religious / spiritual.

(6) Sometimes I feel hopeless about the world.

(7) I believe in or have some connection with The Goddess / God / Higher Power (change wording to suit yourself).

(8) Schoolwork comes easily to me.

(9) I enjoy new situations and groups of people.

(10) I am "out" as a Pagan with friends / family / work.

(11) Sometimes I find Paganism / magic sort of silly.

(12) Popular music (or _____) is important to me.

WORKINGS

Spectrums: Cross-Spectrums

INTENT

A chance for teens to think about and articulate their responses to various real-life situations, and see how others respond. This was created for the "Law" point at a Teens Pearl Pentacle workshop, but it also works as a stand-alone exercise.

This working seems to get everyone talking, much more than if we just sat in a circle and talked about the same things. It's a good "mixer," as people move on every round.

It's a good working for early in a class or ritual, as it will stir up the group's energy.

SPACE/TIME/SIZE

A dozen maximum, so everyone gets a chance to speak on each round. For more, break into smaller groups. Need about 10 x 10 feet for about a dozen people. Minimum 20 minutes, and allow more if teens want to keep going.

PREP

Signs for the four directions (see diagram) will save having to repeat them each time, but folks will catch on after a few rounds.

```
              WHINE &
              GRIPE
                         1
    REBEL         4        COMPLY
             3
                      2
              CREATIVE
              SOLUTION
```

Examples
1 - whine and gripe but comply
2 - creative way of complying
3 - rebel and look for creative way out
4 - a little of each!

WORKING

Explain the way the exercise works. Explain what each of the four directions means, and that people can position themselves anywhere within or just outside the circle – at one station, or between two or more.

Main axis = rebel vs comply / Cross axis = whine-and-gripe vs creative solution

Priestess poses a question such as those below, and people array themselves among the various options – usually placing themselves between two or three of the stations (eg, "I whine and gripe, but eventually I comply").

Once arrayed, ask people in various positions if they want to explain why they are there. Remind folks to listen, but a bit of cross-chatter doesn't hurt as long as the speaker gets heard.

If someone is not speaking much, quietly ask, "Sally Ann, is there anything you want to share?"

After a few rounds, open it up to teens to pose situations. Have a few more ideas in reserve, including a good "final question."

To close, come back into a circle. Go around and say one word about how you are feeling at the moment.

QUESTIONS/SITUATIONS

A mix of personal / mundane situations and more charged political situations (numbers are for Solo working below):

(1) Alarm rings and you don't want to get up.

(2) Friends invite you to do something that doesn't feel right to you.

(3) You hear that they are clear-cutting half of the Mendocino Woodlands (or another location).

(4) Parent tells you to do homework before going on the internet.

continued on next page

WORKINGS

Spectrums: Cross-Spectrums (pg 2)

(5) You see cops harassing someone, and when you try to film it they order you to stop.

(6) A friend tells you something potentially dangerous and makes you promise not to tell anyone.

(7) You promised to do something with your family, and now friends want you to do something else.

(8) Create more questions and situations for you and/or your group.

SOLO WORKING

Need – Book of Shadow sand the chart of page 265.

Write – draw a box at the top of a fresh page, with room underneath for writing. Label the four sides as in the drawing on page 265.

Read one of the situations above, or create some of your own. Think about where you would stand among the options of complying, whining, etc, and write the number in the box (see diagram above). Underneath, write the number and a sentence or two about why you chose that position.

Read or make up several more situations, each time putting the number where you would stand on the grid.

After you've done a few rounds, look back at the grid. What patterns do you see? Do you often wind up in one part of the box?

Underneath the square, write about what you notice. Do you feel okay about where you stand, or do you want to find different ways of addressing situations?

✪ **Book of Shadows** – what is one concrete thing you would like to do differently in your life? Write about it, then sum it up in a few words.

Speak those words three times, pausing for a deep breath after each time. At the end, say: "So mote it be!"

WORKINGS

Spellcrafting: Intro

INTENT

What is a spell? Some people say that a spell combines a clear intention, a physical act, and a charge of energy. This means that a spell is more than just wishful thinking – we will actually do something in the world to get results. Likewise, a spell is more than simply taking action – we also need to craft a clear and focused intention.

Spells aim to change something. We don't usually do a spell to keep everything exactly the same.

Sometimes a spell helps us do work we plan to do anyway – such as creating a Book of Shadows, practicing the sousaphone, writing a poem, etc. Making it a spell instead of a chore helps focus our energy and creativity.

If we want to practice music or work on our art each day, we could make it more magical by quickly grounding and casting a circle. Maybe we want to dedicate the time to the Muses and ask their assistance in bettering our craft.

Anything we want to accomplish or help bring about in the world can be woven into a spell.

Simple vs Complicated

Spells can be as simple as taking three breaths and lighting a candle, or as elaborate as an entire multi-day WitchCamp. Spells can be performed in a few minutes, or spread over a period of days or months. We could dedicate a corner of our garden to a living spell, tending it as part of a magical practice. We could charge a stone or piece of wood with our dreams and visions, then travel to the ocean or river and cast it into the waves to carry it into the wider world.

In the following pages we'll share some of TEM's favorite spells. First, though, we'll give you a basic outline so you can create your own, explain Threefold Return, and talk about how to reverse a spell.

SPACE/TIME/SIZE

Spellcrafting can be done alone or with any number of people. Sometimes a circle might work together to do a group spell – for instance, a healing spell for a friend or a spell for world peace.

Other times people may work in a group, but each does their own specific spell. When we teach spellcrafting in a class and make spell candles, each person comes up with their own magical intention and creates their own unique candle (see Workings: Spell Candle).

You'll need a quiet space, and enough room to spread out. Allow plenty of time – spellcrafting is a good "open-ended" working, where you take as much time as is needed. You'll know intuitively when your work is complete.

PREP

Gather materials you need – see the following pages for ideas. Collage materials and glass jar candles are always handy.

Have your Book of Shadows with you for working on your intention and writing about your experiences.

WORKING: Crafting a Spell

Including creating and opening sacred space, spellcrafting has six steps:

(1) Create sacred space.
(2) Craft your intention – what is the purpose of your spell?
(3) Create and perform your working – what physical actions will you do to bring your intention about?

continued on next page

WORKINGS

Spellcrafting: Intro (pg 2)

(4) Declare how long the spell-working will last (until the candle burns down, until next year's WitchCamp, a year and a day, etc).

(5) Charge and bind your spell – bring the creation of the spell to a close.

(6) Open sacred space.

Sacred Space

Begin by creating sacred space – ground, cast a circle, and invoke elements and allies so you'll have a strong energetic container for your magical work. See Ritual Skills: Sacred Space for more info.

Creating an Intention

Your intention will express what you are trying to bring about, and how.

Maybe you already know exactly why you want to do a spell – to get better grades, to find a job, to fall in love.... Or maybe you just have a sense that you want things to be different.

✪ **Book of Shadows** – take some time and think about what you want to accomplish with your spell. Why are you doing it now? Write down words and ideas as they come to you. After a while, go back and underline words you like.

Now try writing a fresh sentence that uses some of the underlined words. Include (A) what you are trying to change or accomplish, and (B) what you will do. Make it as specific as you can. Here are a few examples:

- In order to get into college, I will do a spell to help me study harder.
- Seeing a world filled with war and hate, we work a spell for peace and justice.
- When I feel alone, lighting this spell candle will remind me that my life is full of love.
- Knowing I am overcommitted, I perform this unbinding spell to break my pledge to help plan the Spring Bazaar.

Write your intention a few times in different ways, until you get a sentence that really captures your intention. Then re-copy it on a fresh page of your Book of Shadows.

Crafting the Physical Working

How will you enact your spell? What physical actions will you perform? How will the action relate to your intention?

- If your intention is to break an old habit or pattern of behavior, you could physically break something – a stick, perhaps.
- If your intention is to attract love, you might want to create and burn a pink or red spell candle.
- If your intention is to call for peace in a time of war, you might want to do a spell working outside a military base or government building, perhaps dancing in the street or even risking arrest as part of the ritual. This is actually how Reclaiming was formed around 1980, as part of anti-nuclear protests (see page 148).
- Candles can be decorated with images that show our spell coming to fruition. A yarn bracelet can remind us of our intention.
- Your spell working might also require accomplishing a real-world task, not just a magical one. If you do a spell for "better grades," you might have to include a commitment to study more!

Setting a Time Limit

Decide how long the physical working will take. We might want the effect of the spell to continue, but we put an end-date on the spell itself. This might be when a spell candle has completely burned, or when a yarn bracelet falls off. Or it could be a definite amount of time, like a semester or a week and a day.

When the time limit has ended, dispose of the leftover materials with solid focus – even if you're dropping stuff in the recycling bin, stop, take a breath, and remember that you are completing a magical task.

continued on next page

WORKINGS

Spellcrafting: Intro (pg 3)

Charging & Binding a Spell

When the preparation of a spell is complete – when all that remains is letting it do its work – we raise some magical energy and "charge" the spell. This can be done with a song (She Changes Everything She Touches is perfect), by singing a tone over the working, by dancing around it, by blowing our breath across it....

Then we'll put a seal on the working as a way of showing that the "crafting" part is complete. This is called "binding" a spell (not to be confused with "binding spells," which aim to control someone or something).

Before you bind the spell, state the time-limit for the spell aloud: "This spell will be complete in one month," or "This spell will be complete when the spell-candle is fully burned," etc.

You can bind the spell any way that works for you. With a candle, you might literally tie a bow around it. You can also use the power of your voice to state that the spell is bound. Here's a rhyme we sometimes use:

> By all the power of three times three
> This spell bound round shall be
> To cause no harm nor return on me
> As I do will – so mote it be!

Open Sacred Space

When you've completed the spellcrafting, remember to devoke any allies and elements and open your circle.

CURSES & SECOND THOUGHTS

Negative Magic & the Law of Threefold Return

What about spells directed at other people? Can we compel the object of our desire to love us? Can we bind and constrain another person who is competing with us? Can we bend someone's will to our own by the force of our spells?

As with any manipulative practice, we run the risk of harming ourselves more than impacting anyone else. The Law of Threefold Return is clear – whatever intentions or actions we direct at others are likely to return on us three times. These are poor odds, and tend to discourage most witches from doing spells against other people.

With Reclaiming magic, our goal is to make changes in our lives and in the world, not to manipulate others.

See Introduction: Curses and Negative Magic.

Releasing or Breaking a Spell

Once in a while, we have to un-do a spell. For example, when we did the working, our intention seemed clear. But later we can see that our spell and commitment are just digging us deeper into a lousy situation.

Luckily, magic is reversible – by using more magic. See page 274 for a spell for breaking a commitment.

SOLO WORKING

Spell working is often a solo working – Spell Candles and the spells for Breaking a Commitment, Temperance Pouring, and Waters of the World are perfect for solo working.

The Yarn Binding Spell is a favorite for symbolizing the bonds in a group – can you adapt this to a group of friends for a birthday party?

WORKINGS

Spell: Breaking a Commitment

INTENT

Sometimes we make promises or commitments that at the time make sense – but later we realize that the commitment is not good for us or others. "I'll help organize this event," "I'll always be here for you," "I'll do such-and-such for a year and a day"....

We strive to honor our word, to be people of integrity. Our word is our bond.

But situations change. There are times when carrying through on a commitment is not in anyone's best interest. What if, after giving the situation careful thought, we realize we need to break our word?

Here's a magical, intentional way to break a commitment while still honoring our word and our integrity.

We used this exercise with The Twelve Wild Swans story at Witchlets one year – at the plot-point in the story where the twelve brothers are forced to reconsider a vow they have made, we were invited to look at our own lives and consider whether there was a past commitment we needed to break. If we felt so, we broke a stick and cast it into the fire.

SPACE/TIME/SIZE

Any number. Room to wander about a bit if possible. Takes about 15 minutes including transitions.

PREP

Need a small, pencil-sized stick (or popsicle stick) for each person – if you're in the woods, tell people to find a stick ahead of time. If indoors or urban, find or buy enough. Make sure they can easily be broken in half.

You'll need something to do with sticks afterward – a fire to burn them, a compost bucket with dirt to bury them, etc.

WORKING

Ask people to find and bring a small, breakable stick (or pass them out at the beginning).

People begin walking clockwise. Priestess invites people to feel the solidity and inflexibility of their stick.

"We make commitments and give our word to do things, yet there are times we need to break a commitment for our own good and that of the world.

"Consider commitments you have made which are still open-ended. Is there one that you want to reconsider? Is there a commitment which may have once served you, but no longer does?" (Give people time to think about this.)

"When you think of a commitment that you need to break, turn and walk widdershins (counter-clockwise)."

When all have turned and are moving widdershins, ring a bell and ask people to find a partner and decide who will go first.

Priestess: "First person, take the stick in both hands. Take a breath and balance yourself. State that you are about to break a commitment that no longer serves you or the world. There's no need to give details unless you want to. Partner silently witness.

"When you are ready, snap the stick in half and place both pieces _____ (in the fire, in a compost bucket, etc.)."

Switch roles.

When everyone has gone (or passed on their turn), charge the work with a song.

Song: Letting Go; Let It Begin; My Soul; She Changes Everything She Touches (Kore Chant).

SOLO WORKING

Same as above. Even if alone, state your intention aloud. Before and after breaking the stick, write in your journal.

WORKINGS

Spell: Burning (or Composting) Putdowns

INTENT

All of us have heard harsh putdowns such as, "You can't do that," "You don't look right," or "You don't belong" – and dozens of variants.

Sometimes even people who love us will say hurtful things that are meant to be helpful, such as: "That talent doesn't run in our family," or "Don't try that, you'll just end up getting disappointed."

Here's a simple, high-impact way to let go of past negativity in a safe, supportive group. Although each of us contributes a putdown, they are read anonymously, so it feels as if they could have been said to any of us.

Together we consign them to the fire (or compost bin).

Balancing the energy – follow this working with a balancing exercise that calls in positive energy – see Workings: Spell: Charging with Fire & Flour or Workings: Overflowing Cup Spell.

We have used this exercise at the opening night ritual at Witchlets for many years – see Rituals: Opening Night At Witchlets.

SPACE/TIME/SIZE

Any number of people – but over 25 will get long. Allow one minute per person plus five minutes for transitions.

PREP

Need strips of paper pre-cut, plus fine-point magic markers (easy to write on any surface). A basket to hold paper and markers.

Fire – find someone to gather firewood and build / tend the fire. You'll need a lighter and some paper or fire-starters. Check on fire safety gear, nearby water, etc. Firetender also stays to put the fire out at the end. See Ritual Skills: Firetending.

Compost – no fire available? Change this working to "Composting Putdowns" – you'll need a bucket of dirt. After reading a put-down, tear it up and use a hand-trowel to bury it. Afterward, dump the whole thing into a compost or green waste bin.

Choose and teach a song to complete the working – see below for ideas, or visit our chants playlists – links on pages 112-113.

Working

Each person gets a slip of paper and a marker.

Priestess: "Think of a time when you were in a group and you did not feel safe or welcome. Think of something someone did or said that hurt you or made you feel less welcome or safe. Write it down in one or a few words – print clearly so another person can read it. Don't include your own or anyone else's name or anything that would identify you. Fold paper up."

When finished, gather markers and folded papers. Circle around the fire. Pass the basket and invite everyone to draw one piece of paper – it doesn't matter if you get your own, just don't say so.

One by one, someone reads a "put-down" aloud, then wads it up and throws it into the fire (or compost). Whole group chants "Burn! Burn!" or hisses, boos, etc. Do this quickly, one after the other, so you build momentum.

Song: seal the working with a song: Step Into the Flow; Let It Begin; She Changes Everything She Touches (Kore Chant).

SOLO WORKING

You can do this alone or with friends. Unless fire is available, use a compost bucket. What if you did this at the beginning of a party?

WORKINGS

Spell Candles

INTENT

This working weaves a personal intention into a magical candle.

Each time the candle is lit, the spell is strengthened. For instance: "As this candle burns, I will become more and more aware of the love that fills my life," or, "As this candle burns, it will release my creativity!"

When the candle is completely burned, the spell is fully activated.

SPACE/TIME/SIZE

Quiet indoor space with room to spread out. Any number of people, given enough space and supplies. Allow up to an hour with prep and transitions. If people are taking candles home, leave time for glue and paint to dry sufficiently to travel.

PREP

Enough tall glass jar candles for each person. Plain candles with white wax allow people to decorate with colors they choose.

Collage materials. Color xeroxes of tarot, goddess, or animal divination cards work well for this spell, as well as a variety of positive images and words from magazines.

Mod Podge glue works best (get Mod Podge Washout for Kids), but half Elmers glue / half water will work if you press the images down for a few minutes. Have cheap brushes handy to apply the glue.

Colored package-ribbon, little beads and shells, etc (to decorate candles). Markers or paints that work on glass.

How will people carry their candles away? Wrapped in tissue paper and tape?

For more details, see Workings: Collage.

Music: Labyrinth Meditation Music is perfect for this working. See page 113.

Magical Candle Safety

Tall glass jar candles are safer than open flames. But no candle is fire-proof.

- Dedicate a flat, fireproof altar to candles.
- Extinguish candles any time you leave the room and relight them when you return.
- Keep candles away from curtains, wall-hangings, magazines and papers, and cans of gasoline.
- If you have long hair, tie it back when working with fire.

Please take extra precautions when mixing fire and magic.

WORKING

Finding My Intention

For this working – and for most Reclaiming magic – we like to say: "Do spells for yourself, not for (or against) others."

Magical energy sent toward others without their consent can misfire badly, even if it's intended as "positive" – and whatever energy we send out or call forth can return on us threefold (see page 28).

Priestess leads a short meditation, asking: "What is one part of my life that I would like to strengthen? Where could I use some magical support?" Invite people to come up with a single, clearly stated answer to use for this working (you can always create more candles for additional intentions).

When you have a short, clear answer, state it in positive terms. Try saying, "I invoke confidence when I perform," rather than, "I want to get rid of stage fright."

State your short, clear intention three times so you won't forget it. Write it down in your Book of Shadows. The spell is underway.

continued on next page

WORKINGS

Spell Candles (pg 2)

Crafting & Charging the Spell Candle

Start music. With your intention clearly in mind, find some collage images that will reinforce your spell. Get ribbon, paints, and anything else you need. Take 20 minutes or so and create your candle.

Give people a five minute warning. Then come back into a circle.

Each person holds their candle in front of them. Priestess says: "Take a minute and look around and see the candles. Know that each one of us has crafted a spell to bring magical support to some part of your life. Together we are going to charge those spells."

Holding candles, go around and each person say one word or phrase. Then tone together for a couple of minutes – weave dissonance and harmonies to create a pool of energy that finally ends in harmonies. Let the tones subside to silence.

Priestess: "Feel your candle in your hands…. Speak your intention softly into the candle and anchor it as a spell…. Breathe the power of this circle into your candle."

To bind our intention into the candle, repeat after Priestess:

> By all the power of three times three
> This spell bound round shall be
> To cause no harm nor return on me
> As I do will – so mote it be!

The spell is now anchored in the candle. It will be activated when the candle is lit. Unless you declare otherwise, the working will be complete when the candle is completely burned.

Burning the Candle to Activate the Spell

To activate the spell, light your candle at home, within a sacred circle.

Place the candle on your altar.

Ground and cast a circle. You can do this quickly – just be clear about what you are doing. See Ritual Skills: Sacred Space: Quick Ways.

Welcome the spirits of Fire who will help with this spell.

Before you first light your candle (and every time you re-light it), re-state the intention of the spell aloud. Some say that stating it three times strengthens the spell.

Light the candle with the clear intention that the spell will come to fruition. When the flame is lit, take a breath and say: "So mote it be!"

Extinguish your candle and relight it as often as you leave the room – for safety and to reinforce the spell. Each time you light it, state your intention and say: "So mote it be." This simple act reinforces the power of the spell.

When the candle is completely burned down, the spell is complete. State your intention three more times. Thank the candle and Fire for their work.

Dispose of the candle intentionally – even if you put it in the trash or recycling, do it with care and one last farewell.

SOLO WORKING

A spell candle is a uniquely personal working. A solo spell is the same as above. Hold your candle and tone to charge the working. If it helps to put on music and sing along, try that. For ideas, see Ritual Skills: Chants.

WORKINGS

Spell: Charging with Fire & Flour

INTENT

A dramatic way to charge an intention or commitment.

We have used this exercise for the Teens Path opening night ritual at Witchlets and more recently at Redwood Magic as a way to call in the qualities and experiences we want at camp. See Rituals: Opening Night At Witchlets.

SPACE/TIME/SIZE

Any number of people – but more than 25 may run long. Allow one minute per person plus five minutes for transitions.

PREP

Need a five-pound bag of flour for every 15 people.

If there's not already going to be a fire, find someone to gather firewood and build / tend the fire – don't wait until after dark to start! You'll need a lighter and some paper or fire-starters. Check on fire safety gear, nearby water, etc. Have someone who agrees to stay until the end and put the fire out. See Ritual Skills: Firetending.

WORKING

Firetenders have a steady fire burning – plenty of flames, not just coals.

Priestess invites people to close their eyes and envision a quality or experience they want to invoke for their time at camp – something they want to see happen, to be part of – and find a way to say it in a few words. (Typical things people say are: "Make new friends; Learn about myself; Have fun with my friends; Do some new magic.")

One by one, people are invited to step forward and take a handful of flour. They state their "invocation" aloud (or silently) – then hurl the handful of flour into the center of the fire. The fire will flare brightly but harmlessly.

After everyone has a turn, some may want to do a second intention – if there's time and more flour, why not?

As the energy winds down or the flour runs out, gather the circle again and sing a song to seal the working.

Song – a simple, upbeat song to charge the working: Weave and Spin ("this is how the work begins"); Let It Begin (teach at the top of the ritual – not easy for new people to pick up); My Soul ("I am stepping out into the unknown" – this chant works as a call-and-response on the verses, then all sing the chorus together).

SOLO WORKING

You need a steady fire for this working, so this will be difficult unless you have an outdoor fire pit. If so, try doing the above working to charge a commitment.

You might even want to make a short list of commitments and do several at once!

Create a circle for yourself and do some journaling. Then step up to the fire, state your commitment clearly, and throw the flour into the flames.

How will you complete the working? A song? Gazing into the fire? Reading a poem aloud? Remember to devoke and open your circle afterward.

WORKINGS

Spell: Temperance Pouring

INTENT

Temperance – we take the name of this working from the Temperance card of the Rider-Waite-Smith tarot deck, where an angelic figure pours a blue liquid from one chalice to another. Temperance here means the process of bringing conflicting energies into a healthy balance.

This spell draws balance into our lives and helps us develop our ability to work with discordant energies.

This working might follow a meditation or exercise where we become aware of some opposing tendencies within ourselves – eg, the desire to achieve great things versus the desire for a relaxed, peaceful life, or the desire to please my family versus the desire to live my own life.

This is a nice end-of-class working – after an earlier exercise that brings up the conflicts, use this spell to bring yourself back into balance.

SPACE/TIME/SIZE

Up to 25, although 10-20 is optimal for intimacy. Room to gather around an altar. About 30 minutes including transitions.

PREP

Simple yet beautiful Center altar with pitchers, jugs of water, and two drinking cups per person. If a class, ask people to bring two cups about the same size for themselves.

WORKING

From a prior working or meditation, each person has an idea of two energies within ourselves that we want to learn to balance. Here we'll use the example above about achieving great things versus relaxing.

In a circle, each person picks up their two cups. Priestess leads a short meditation in which we reconnect with the two energies we want to balance.

Go around the circle, and one at a time each person names their drinking cups (aloud or silently), thus:

"By art I name thee (first cup) 'achieving great things,' and by art I name thee (other cup), 'a relaxing, peaceful life.'" (We're using the word "art" here in the sense of "the magical arts.")

Priestess pours each cup half full. Go around the circle and each person names their cups. Priestess fills all halfway.

Priestess invites people to begin gently pouring the water back and forth from one cup to the other, being aware and silently naming each one, back and forth. Do this for about three minutes.

Then come to rest with each cup again half full. Name the first cup to yourself – drink it. Name the second cup to yourself. Drink it. Feel their blended energy within you. Slosh around a little to really mix them. Finally, take a deep breath and relax.

Song: Step Into the Flow; My Soul; Let the Beauty We Love.

When all are done – devoke the cups: "By art wert thou named, and by art unnamed. You are now just a ceramic drinking cup (or mug or whatever)." Repeat for your second cup.

Take a drink of water from one of the cups and enjoy it simply as water. Offer any leftover water to the Earth.

SOLO WORKING

Same as above – a good solo working. Remember to un-name the cups at the end.

WORKINGS

Spell: Waters of the World

INTENT

Join an international, decades-old spell for pure water! This is an ongoing collective working to cleanse and revive all waters on our planet. Each person is invited to bring a small sample of water from a place significant to them and add it to the mix.

This spell was initiated in the 1980s. Gradually, waters from every continent including Antarctica have been added. At the end of the ritual, people are invited to take a small sample home and pass it on.

This spell is part of many WitchCamps and the annual Bay Area Brigid rituals. It can be done as a Water invocation, or as a separate working. It is sometimes done by the Pagan Cluster at direct actions.

Some people carry small vials of Waters of the World in their pocket at all times, just in case Waters might be needed!

Caution: Do not ever drink Waters of the World – the spell is still in process, and we can't yet guarantee the purity of all water on Earth. Also, don't leave Waters standing – keep mixing them with other water and/or offer them to your garden or a local park.

SPACE/TIME/SIZE

Any number, although people might not go one-by-one if there are 50 people waiting to participate. Space enough to circle with an altar in the middle. Allow about 10 minutes including transitions.

PREP

Ahead of time – invite people to bring small samples of water from a place significant to them (eg, the ocean, rainwater, a stream, a home faucet....)

Need a large bowl with some water in it, some spare water, and a magical spoon for stirring. If you have Waters of the World from a prior ritual, add a few drops at the beginning.

Glass vials for folks to take home samples are optional.

WORKING

Gather in a circle that has already been cast. Priestess says a few words about Waters of the World being a spell for healing and reviving all waters on the planet, a spell that has been going for several decades, in which each of us can take part.

Invite people to step forward and pour a small amount of the water they brought into the bowl, stating aloud where it comes from. In a larger group, several people can pour at once, rather than coming forward one by one.

When all are finished, priestess pours in a bit of the spare water, stirs it a few times, and declares: "May all the waters of Earth run free and clean!"

After the ritual ends – invite people to come forward and take a small amount of the Waters home. Sometimes planners bring along a bunch of small vials for people. Remind folks not to consume Waters of the World.

Finally, offer a few drops to the place you have circled as a farewell blessing.

SOLO WORKING

Prepare your own Waters of the World. Begin with a half-dozen sources near your home. Each time you visit a new site – around your town, and however far you travel – bring along a small bottle and gather samples. Keep a list of the sources and read it each time you add a new one.

Add some rain water – even a few drops will instantly connect your water to all waters everywhere on Earth!

Charge your Waters by singing a song: Born of Water.

WORKINGS

Spell: The Wicker One

INTENT

The Wicker One (formerly known as the Wicker Man) is an adaptation of ancient Celtic practice. In San Francisco, people have been known to ritually create and burn a Wicker One on Ocean Beach at Summer Solstice. This Celtic tradition also inspired the Burning Man festival.

No bonfire handy? The ancient Celts probably dealt with this emergency by composting the Wicker One, which is just as effective, if slightly less dramatic. How can you heighten the drama? Maybe bury the Wicker One and dance on its grave?

You can find lots of different ideas about the history and meaning of this practice online (some credible, some fanciful). As always in Reclaiming – use your own judgment. Our practices (and our understanding of our history) are always evolving.

As part of a ritual (often Summer Solstice, but you can do this at other times), we create a Wicker One out of wood, wicker baskets, twine, and other burnable material. We attach to it symbols of things we are letting go of or want to change and transform. At the peak of the ritual, amid much singing and dancing, we throw the Wicker One into the bonfire.

You can use this working to mark a transition in your life – a way to let go of the old and call in the new.

Make this the main or final working in a ritual – it's difficult to follow. You might precede this spell with some sort of discernment working such as tarot or a meditation – ask what changes are ripe in your life, then write them on slips of paper, attach them to the Wicker One, and burn (or compost) it.

SPACE/TIME/SIZE

Any number, although it may eventually get cumbersome to gather everyone around a fire and have each person attach something to the Wicker One. We've had up to 200 people participate at San Francisco beach rituals.

What if you don't have a fire? We've done several things. Composting is always a substitute. One year we built a Wicker One at Ocean Beach, did a ritual, then sent the charged doll off to California WitchCamp to be burned.

PREP

Create a Wicker One from branches, wicker baskets, etc – make sure everything you use is safely burnable. The Wicker One can be life-sized or larger, but needs to fit into the fire you'll have. If you're using a fireplace or BBQ, make a miniature Wicker One.

Bring along a bunch of paper slips and crayons (they're biodegradable, so if they get dropped on the beach, no big deal). People can write on them and tuck slips of paper into the wicker baskets, etc.

One year we cut a bunch of red construction-paper circles and attached brown twine to each one so it looked like an apple and stem. People wrote on the apple and tied it to the Wicker One. (See below for Apple Pruning Meditation.)

Fire – you'll need a safe place to have a bonfire (or make a miniature Wicker One and use your fireplace or BBQ) – if people bring wood, remind them to bring only clean wood – no construction scraps, plywood, painted wood, etc (may release toxic fumes and/or leave nails and metal scraps behind). Bring fire-starters, paper, and a lighter, and a bucket for dousing it later.

WORKING

In sacred space, Priestess invites people to meditate on how their life is going (see sample Apple Pruning Meditation below), and to focus on one thing that they would like to change. In order for this change to happen, what would you need to give up, to let go of? Once you have that, write it on a slip of paper and attach it to the Wicker One.

Apple Pruning Meditation (sample meditation) – "Around Summer Solstice in many climates, apple trees are putting forth

continued on next page

WORKINGS

Spell: The Wicker One (pg 2)

their fruit. The apples are on the tree, but not yet ripe. In fact, there is too much fruit – in order for some apples to fully ripen, we need to prune away others. Perfectly good apples will need to be pruned so the remaining ones have room to come to full ripeness.

"Look at your own life – where do you have too much going on? Where are you stretched too thin? Where will you have to make choices and prune away some of your own fruit, in order to bring the remaining fruit to ripeness?

"When you know what needs to be pruned, write it on a paper apple (see Prep above) and tie it to the Wicker One."

Raising Energy – when everyone has attached what they want to the Wicker One, priestesses launch into singing and dancing. At San Francisco Ocean Beach rituals, people also go down to the water and "plunge" as part of the working – some all the way into the water, some just their fingers and toes – then re-gather at the fire as the singing picks up.

Song: She Changes Everything She Touches (Kore Chant); We Are the Rising Sun; We All Come from the Goddess.

As the chanting and dancing builds, a priestess takes the Wicker One, lifts it high, and dances around the fire. As the cacophonic music rises higher and higher, the priestess tosses the Wicker One onto the fire. The singing peaks, then shifts to toning as the Wicker One burns and transforms our intentions into a spell to change our lives.

As toning fades, we ground the energy again. A priestess speaks a few wise words, such as: "Breathe in the power of our voices and our magical work – anchor it in your own center – and return any extra to the Earth." People kneel and touch the Earth to reground themselves.

Transition – this is a good time for a food blessing, and then get on with devoking. It will be difficult to do another working after this.

SOLO WORKING

You can do this on a small scale – start by figuring out a safe space for your fire. A fireplace? A BBQ? Make your Wicker One the right size.

No fire at all? Compost is just as effective, if slightly less dramatic. What can you do to heighten the drama? Maybe bury the Wicker One and dance on its grave?

WORKINGS

Spell: Yarn Binding

INTENT

This is a good final working for a class or camp, a simple working that weaves our energy one last time before we separate – and places a binding on our intention to take the energy back to our individual lives.

We use this working each year in the final all-camp circle at Witchlets and Redwood Magic – one advantage is, once everyone is looped into the circle, they can't escape! It's the only all-camp circle where almost everyone participates (a few sit out – an example of the "right to pass" – see Intro: Agreements).

This working sends each person home with a yarn bracelet – some folks show up at camp still wearing the yarn from the previous year.

SPACE/TIME/SIZE

This can be an all-camp working – we do it with 100-plus people at Witchlets. The bigger the group, the longer it takes to pass the yarn around. Including the spiral dance, allow about 20 minutes for a group of 100, and 10-15 minutes for a group of 25-30.

With fewer people it will move faster, and you might want to add a go-round at the end where people state a commitment.

Gather in an open space that will work for the final spiral dance – aim for a non-dusty field without trip hazards and gopher holes (we're still looking!). See Ritual Skills: Spiral Dance.

PREP

You'll need a large ball of colorful yarn – what color(s) symbolize your camp or class theme? Wrap skeins into balls ahead of time for easy handling. Get about six feet of yarn per person to allow plenty of slack.

You can also add a mirror-working as below – if so, you'll need a hand-mirror. This doesn't add any time to the working.

A few small round-tipped scissors will come in handy at the end, along with a few graces to cut the threads apart.

Decide who will be the priestess for the spiral dance, and who will be the tail (see Ritual Skills: Spiral Dance).

Teach the spiral dance song ahead of time, so when the time comes, you can start right in. You can teach it while the yarn is being passed.

Song ideas for the spiral dance – see Ritual Skills: Chants for lots of ideas – pages 112-113.

WORKING

Gather people in a circle. While the yarn is being passed (which can take a while in a large circle), priestesses can make final camp or class announcements, teach the song for the spiral dance, practice their stand-up comedy routines, etc.

Yarn priestesses – go clockwise around the circle, loosely looping the yarn around people's wrists with some slack. Note – leave enough slack between people so they can move their arms independently.

Mirror-working (optional) – a priestess goes just ahead of the ball of yarn, holding a hand-mirror up to each person and asking without waiting for an answer: "What do you hold in your heart from this year's camp? What will you take away with you?"

When all are looped, everyone joins hands.

Spiral priestess (or someone else) begins the song. Sing the song a couple of times through before you begin moving – then priestess slowly begins spiraling to the left.

continued on next page

WORKINGS

Spell: Yarn Binding (pg 2)

When spiral is complete and cone of power has subsided, priestess allows a silent moment, then says something like: "Breathe in the magic of this circle, the miracle of this time and place. Breathe in that special power and connection to this magic that is yours alone, that you will take away with you.... Breathe it in and anchor it in your heart...."

Graces circulate with round-tipped scissors as people are ready to have the yarn cut.

Priestess concludes: "If you wish, tie your length of yarn to your body as a spell to charge your magic, and decide how long it will remain there – for a day, a month, or until it falls off, as you so choose. Blessed be."

Devoke and open the circle. At Witchlets, we finish the spiral, cut our threads apart – then devoke and open sacred space for the last time. This way, we aren't still tied to one another as we are devoking.

SOLO WORKING (& small groups)

This is a good final spell for a circle or class. You can also use it as a solo working to mark a passage, honor a commitment, etc.

You'll need one or more balls of colored yarn (what color suits your working?). For solo work, bring your journal too.

Small group – if you're a circle or class, loop yourselves together, then go around clockwise and each person say one thing they have gained or learned from the ritual or class. Sing a song to raise energy – see Ritual Skills: Chants.

When the energy grounds, go around counter-clockwise and each person say one thing they are taking away from the class. When all have spoken, cut or break the yarn. Fasten it to your body, and decide how long it will remain.

Devoke and open your circle.

Solo – use this spell to charge a commitment or to honor the completion of a ritual, class, or project. Like all spells, be clear about your intention, and also decide how long the yarn will stay attached to your body – until the end of the ritual, for a week, until it falls off – whatever makes sense to you.

✪ **Book of Shadows** – on a clean page, write in your journal for a few minutes about what the yarn will symbolize – does it represent completion of a class or project or ritual? Does it symbolize a commitment for the future? What color(s) of yarn symbolizes this?

Within sacred space, hold the ball of yarn and state what the yarn represents. Finish by saying, "With this yarn, I honor my commitment."

Wrap some of the yarn around your wrist (or ankle, etc). Place your hands over the yarn, take a breath, and sing a few verses of one of the songs (see above).

When you finish, ground the energy and say, "So mote it be!"

✪ **Book of Shadows** – tape a piece of the yarn in your journal and write any final thoughts.

Devoke and open the circle.

WORKINGS

Tarot: A Key Magical Practice

Tarot is one of the most Reclaiming-friendly of all magical tools. With roots dating back to the Italian Renaissance, tarot can be used for many types of workings, from games to decision-making to a journey of the spirit.

The key is intuition – awakening our deep inspiration and awareness about our own lives, our community, and the planet.

Some people say that when we do divination, it's not cards we're readings – it's our own soul. Tarot cards are simply an aid.

In the following pages we'll share ideas about intuitive tarot. But let's start with the cards!

Finding the Right Deck

The past 50 years have seen an explosion of tarot and divination decks. Hundreds of decks have been created, drawn, photographed, painted, collaged....

Intuitive reading works best with a deck which spurs our creative thinking in the broadest way. Some beautiful or striking decks catch a mood or outlook well – but every card triggers the same response. We're looking for decks that stir a broad range of feelings, thoughts, and gut responses.

As with all Reclaiming magic – you are your own best authority. You'll know when a deck inspires you.

Maybe you already have a deck you like. Maybe you have a deck or three, but none of them inspire you. Maybe you have no deck at all.

Not to worry! Tarot decks are available for $20 or less at new age stores or online. Or see the next page for an online card selector.

Three Good Decks for Intuitive Readings

Rider-Waite-Smith – if there's such a thing as "the" tarot deck, this is it, and for good reason – Arthur Waite's designs are rich but uncluttered, and Pamela Colman Smith's calm, introspective artwork mirrors the widest range of moods and emotions.

Motherpeace – created by Vicki Noble and Karen Vogel around 1991, Motherpeace features simple, uncluttered artwork, including people of many cultures, genders, ages, etc. Round cards allow nuanced readings (eg, what might it mean when a card is not quite straight up, or rotated a little past upright?).

Marseilles Tarot – reproduction of circa 1750 cards by unknown artists, with simple, vivid images. Some of the images go back to the original 1400s tarot decks. Many modern decks reflect the Marseilles imagery.

continued on next page

TeenEarthMagic.org

WORKINGS

Tarot: A Key Magical Practice (pg 2)

Tarot Card Drawings – Online!

You can find websites online that let you draw single tarot cards and/or multi-card spreads, including three-card (our favorite for intuitive work), Horseshoe, and Celtic Cross.

Here's a great site that's active as of 2019. The deck is Rider-Waite-Smith, one of our recommended decks (see previous page). The site displays the cards with no interpretations – perfect for intuitive divination!

Tarot Card Generator: serennu.com/tarot/pick.php

Reading with the Mind's Eye

Here are a few tips for reading intuitively – see the following pages for more:

- Put away booklets and "expertise" – look to your intuitive response to the cards.
- No one can read for you – all they can bring is questions and random insights.
- Look at the pictures and describe – let the images awaken your intuition.
- Pay attention to first thoughts and responses – there is no wrong response.

Everything You Need to "Know" to Get Started

(1) There are three types of cards in a standard 78-card tarot deck: court cards, minor arcana, and major arcana. See "Jargon" below for details.

(2) No card has a fixed meaning, and no one else can tell you the cards' meanings for you. The magic of tarot is within you – let the images awaken your intuition to meanings that are uniquely yours.

(3) Some people like to pull cards with their non-throwing hand – ie, their receptive hand. Pull cards and lay them face down, according to the spread you are doing (see "Jargon" below). As you read, turn them up one at a time. At the end, look at all of them together. Write in your journal.

Tarot Jargon

Court Cards – these 16 cards, called King, Queen, Knight, Page, and other titles, are similar to the face cards in playing-card decks.

Divination – using a magical tool such as tarot, pendulums, fire-scrying, rock-reading, etc, in order to discover our own true meanings, attitudes, and intentions. Divination gives voice to the divine within each of us.

Major Arcana – the 22 "special" cards not found in playing card decks. In many decks they are numbered 0-XXI (21) in Roman numerals, with names like Magician, Star, or Tower. In the Renaissance game of tarocchi (google for more info), these cards were trumps. For divination, they're intriguing, but not inherently

continued on next page

WORKINGS

Tarot: A Key Magical Practice (pg 3)

more powerful or meaningful than the minors or court cards. Sometimes it's fun and/or enlightening to do an all-majors reading.

Minor Arcana – the 40 cards numbered ace through 10, as in playing-card decks. In most modern (post-1900) decks, these cards have pictures corresponding to older divinatory meanings. These images tend to depict situations that we find ourselves in.

Querent – the one asking a question and receiving a reading – or doing a reading for themselves.

Reader – the one offering the reading, either professionally, as a gift, or for one's self.

Spread – the pattern in which cards are laid out, with each card in the pattern having a particular focus, such as Past-Present-Future, Mind-Body-Spirit, or complicated spreads such as the 10-card Celtic Cross. For intuitive readings we tend to use simple three or four card spreads (so we can hold the entire spread in our mind). You can read about other tarot spreads online.

Tarot Workings in the Following Pages

• Tarot Reading: Quick Intro

• Tarot: Intuitive Reading

• Tarot Games & Exercises

• Tarot: Living Tableaux

• Tarot: Speed Reading

• Tarot Stories

• Tarot: Journey of the Spirit

Tarot images from Motherpeace, Marseilles Tarot, and an imitation of the Rider-Waite-Smith deck. Reproduced as fair use with review of decks – page 285.

WORKINGS

Tarot Reading: Quick Intro

INTENT

In Reclaiming we say: "Every person is their own spiritual authority" – and their own best tarot reader as well!

There are no wrong answers. When you're not sure – go with your first feeling or thought.

In the following pages we'll share lots of background and workings. Here's a one-page overview.

PREP

Frame a question: What question or issue do you want to explore with this reading? Or are you simply opening yourself to what comes through? Write it in your journal.

Spread: Decide on your spread (layout). For this intro, we'll use a three-card "Past-Present-Future" spread.

Draw cards face down: When ready – draw three cards and lay them *face down* as past, present, and future. (You can do this online too – see page 286.)

INTUITIVE READING – Four Simple Steps

Take a breath and center yourself, then turn the "past" card up. Take about 15-30 seconds for each step below.

1. Look at the image on the card. Focus on the picture, not the number or suit. Name three things you see with your eyes. Let go of stories and interpretations. Describe what you see.

2. Find one object or being in the card that is "you." No need to know or say why. Just feel it.

3. Tell a simple story about what is happening in the card, including the object that is you.

4. Now say briefly – given your question and the fact that this card represents "past influences" – what is its meaning for you?

Repeat for present and future cards.

When finished, recall your question, then look at all three cards together, face up. Soften your eyes and see what overall patterns emerge.

Write in your journal.

Ready for more? Turn the page!

WORKINGS

Tarot: Intuitive Reading

INTENT

Intuitive reading is a good introduction to tarot for one person or a group – no prior experience needed.

With intuitive tarot readings, we are not asking tarot to predict our future – we're asking it to reveal our own hidden secrets. We're using the power of its magical images to unlock our own inner wisdom.

In fact, take whatever experience and knowledge you have about tarot cards, breathe into it – then set it aside. All that information will just get in the way of your intuition.

Wisdom vs Knowledge

One of the advanced classes in Reclaiming is called Pearl Pentacle (see page 249). Two of the five Pearl points are called Wisdom and Knowledge. We always end up discussing: "What's the difference?"

Tarot shows the difference – when we work with tarot, we develop both knowledge *and* wisdom.

Knowledge helps us learn facts about the history of tarot, about the occult (ie, secret or hidden – that's what the word "occult" means) meanings of the images and numbers of the cards. Knowledge is what we can learn from teachers and books.

Wisdom is what tarot awakens in each of us. Wisdom is our inner truth, unique to each of us. Wisdom is what we seek when we close the book and listen to our own intuition.

You can gain tarot knowledge online or in other books – see Tarot Resources on page 294. In this working we're going to focus on awakening your deep wisdom by directly encountering the tarot images.

Resisting the Book

Can you resist the temptation to "look in the book" that comes with your deck? Trust your intuition – set aside the book until you have your own relation with the deck.

If you want to read about tarot, try Cynthia Giles' The Tarot: History, Mystery, and Lore. She explains what a tarot deck is, where tarot comes from, what major and minor cards are, different ideas about divination, etc – all without telling you "what the cards mean." That part is for each of us to learn for ourselves.

What Exactly Is Intuitive Reading?

When we read intuitively, we are actually reading our own souls! The cards (or other divination methods) are simply tools to help us gain access to our own deep wisdom, and to the wisdom of our species, our planet, and the cosmos.

Reading intuitively means opening ourselves to the images on the cards – images that echo back through history and through our own being.

There are no wrong answers or mistakes. Whatever pops into our minds could be a clue to the cards' unique meaning for us. Stay with the thread – tools like automatic writing and non-judgmental listening can help us hold our focus as the magic slowly emerges.

We can help others read intuitively too – instead of showing off our knowledge, we ask questions that help our partner tap their own wisdom and intuition.

Note – in a class or ritual, these exercises can be used to frame a commitment that can be carried into a further working – use the tarot reading as a discernment tool to ask something like: "What is my next step regarding such-and-such issue?" Then do an empowerment working such as Overflowing Cup or Charging with Fire & Flour to charge and empower your commitment.

continued on next page

WORKINGS

Tarot: Intuitive Reading (pg 2)

SPACE/TIME/SIZE

Quiet space. For a group, space where people can sit in pairs and hear the priestess. No size limit. A bell helps mark changes. Allow half-hour or more.

PREP

In a group, decide who will priestess this working.

Choose a deck (or decks – one deck covers about 15-20 people). See preceding page for deck-ideas.

Decide on a type of spread – three-card Past-Present-Future (or Soul-Mind-Body) work well – it's easy to keep all three cards in your mind at once. The 10-card Celtic Cross is complicated for intuitive work.

You can print out steps 1-4 below, so you don't have to keep repeating it. Or write key words on an easel or erase-board.

WORKING – Basic Intuitive Reading

Background: Explain that we are reading intuitively, not by book-learning. Invite people to set aside anything they already know about tarot. With intuition, there are no right or wrong answers, only inspirations and insights.

Briefly introduce the spread – for this exercise, we'll use a three-card "Past-Present-Future" reading.

Invite readers to frame a question. You may do a short guided meditation to help people clear their minds and discover a question or issue, or simply open themselves to mystery.

When ready – each person draws three cards and lays them face down as past, present, and future.

Decide who is reading for themselves first, and who is witness. Reader turns their "past" card over, and quickly answers these questions. Witness can remind the reader of the questions as needed, but otherwise simply listens and encourages.

1. Look at the image on the card. Focus on the picture, not the number or suit. Describe three things you see with your eyes. Let go of stories and interpretations, and just describe what you see.

2. Find one object or being in the card that is you. No need to know or say why. Just feel it.

3. Make up a simple story about what is happening in the card, including the object that is you.

4. Now say briefly – given your question and the fact that this card represents "past influences" – what does it mean for you?

Witness encourages reader to think out loud and "go with your first glimmer of thought." There are no wrong answers.

Trade roles, and the second reader does the same steps for their past card. Repeat for present and future cards.

When finished, lay all three cards face up and each take a turn sharing the patterns you notice and any further thoughts.

Come back to the circle and do a go-round where each person shares one word about what they saw or learned.

Solo – Take some time to look at the entire spread. Soften your eyes and see what patterns emerge. Write in your journal.

WORKINGS: Intuitive Tools for Personal Work

Daily Card Altar

Create a tarot altar – simple or elaborate. Each day, choose a card (randomly, or perhaps work your way through the Majors of a favorite deck?). Journal about the card – write for a few minutes first thing in the day and again last thing in the day.

continued on next page

WORKINGS

Tarot: Intuitive Reading (pg 3)

What changes? How did the card "play out" through the day?

Maybe you want to dedicate a page per card in your journal, so that you can add later thoughts – or even create a special tarot Book of Shadows.

Invoking the Cards

After you cast your circle, try invoking the tarot cards themselves. Invite the spirit of tarot into your circle. Flip quickly through the images and welcome them to your circle. Ask them to speak to you – promise to be a good listener! Remember to devoke at the end of your working – you can devoke with a simple, "Thanks!"

Ten-Card First-Thought Challenge

Ground and cast a circle. Take a couple of moments and either come up with a divination question, or open yourself to mystery.

Choose 10 cards, face down. Turn over each card – say the first few feelings / ideas / thoughts that pop into your mind. If you are working in pairs, scribe for one another. Solitary, quickly jot down one or a few words for the card. Repeat for each card.

After 10 cards, go back and underline a half-dozen words – especially any words that you repeated. Write a short poem using all of these words. In a group, share your poems. Solo, take a breath and read it aloud.

✪ **Book of Shadows** – how did this seemingly random reading comment on your life and/or question?

Face Ups

Write a list of moods and emotions that you often feel – for instance, anger, laughter, frustration, boredom, excitement.

Lay the cards face up. Look through them, gradually finding a card that most closely matches each word on your list. Write its name, and a sentence or two about why this card is the best match.

When you finish your list – flip through the deck face-up and choose a couple more cards that you especially like. At the bottom of your list, write the names of these cards – next to each one, write a sentence saying what appeals to you. Ask: "How would my life be different if I more often felt like this card? What is one step I can take toward that?"

Automatic Writing

Choose a card, speak its name aloud, and gaze at it for a moment. Then begin writing without lifting your pen from the page. Write about anything you want, but don't stop until you have filled at least half a page. Quick glances at the card are okay, but keep the pen moving. For more, see Workings: Automatic Writing.

Non-Judgmental Listening

Turn up a card, take a breath – and just listen. Let thoughts and judgments drift through your mind without sticking. On each exhale, let them go. After a few minutes, turn the card face down and write in your journal. For more on this technique, see Workings: Non-Judgmental Listening.

Create a Unique Card

Invent a new tarot card. Name it, describe it – you can even draw or collage it. When it's complete, how will you charge it? Maybe with a special ritual? Or maybe a quick zap? See Workings: Zap.

Some Reclaiming folks have created their own divination decks. You can google Dory Midnight's Dirty Tarot, Gaiamore's Earth Deck, Seneca's Creative Liberation Now tarot cards, and Elka's Seeds of Wisdom deck.

continued on next page

WORKINGS

Tarot: Intuitive Reading (pg 4)

Workings in the Following Pages
- Tarot Games & Exercises
- Tarot: Living Tableaux
- Tarot: Speed Reading
- Tarot Stories
- Tarot: Journey of the Spirit

Tarot Games

- **Doom** – this is a quick, fun game. Everyone gives the worst possible reading of a card – especially the happy ones! What is the most horribly pessimistic interpretation you can give to the Star or the 10 of Cups?
- **Scrub-jay lines** – in pairs, each draw a card. Set timer for 90 seconds, and argue over whose is best. (See Workings: Boundaries: Scrub-Jay Lines).
- **Tell a story** – from a face-up deck, choose eight or ten cards and use them to illustrate the story of your life.
- **Draw ten cards** face down – study them for a moment, then make up a story using every one of them.
- **Group story** – each player draw five cards. Going clockwise, and as quickly as possible, each person plays a card that adds to the story. If you're stumped, you have to draw another card until you can continue the story.
- **Go Fish** – use Major Arcana as wild cards. If someone asks for your sixes and you have none, you can play a wild card (Major) instead, and give it whatever number you wish. Try this with a new deck – you'll get to know the cards quickly.

Crazy Majors Story Telling

Here's a short, fast-paced story-telling game. Try this when you have ten minutes of spare time at a camp. We used this to de-brief from the first Mysteries of Samhain camp, and wound up re-telling the whole story of camp, complete with all of the rituals, our favorite late-night snacks, and the giant bug discovered in someone's cabin.

The game is similar to Spades or Crazy Eights. Each player draws five or seven cards and holds them in their hand. The goal is to tell a fast-paced story about camp (or whatever) – and to be the first to run out of cards.

Player #1 lays down any card – for example, the Four of Pentacles – and begins a story that refers to the card (in this case, a person holding four pentacles). :

"We arrived at camp with all our stuff and got settled in."

Player #2 can then play a Four, a Pentacle, or a Major – if they have none, they draw cards until they get one. Let's say they have the Four of Cups (a person leaving four cups behind and walking away):

"Then we put our stuff aside and began the journey."

Player #3 might lack Fours or Cups, so they play a Major – let's say the Chariot: "We hitched up our magical chariot and plunged ahead!"

After a Major, the next player must play a Court Card – let's say they don't have any, so they draw until they turn up the Queen of Wands:

"Right away we came to a magical priestess, who ordered us to stop!"

Next player can play a Queen, Wand, or Major – and so on, until people run out of cards and the story is complete.

continued on next page

WORKINGS

Tarot: Intuitive Reading (pg 5)

Tarot Check-Ins

A fun, visual way to do personal check-ins. Try this in dyads or triads, so people really have some time to share. It will help to have more than one deck.

Lay all cards face-up. Invite people to choose three cards that will help them share in a check-in. If two people want the same card, see if they can share and each use it in their turn.

Get into groups of two or three. Decide who is going first. Others lay their cards face down and give full attention. In one or two minutes, the person shows the cards and shares why they chose them and what they mean.

Tarot Card Pantomimes

Priestess tapes a tarot Major on each person's back - others look at it and try to help the person guess by pantomiming clues.

Tarot Shadows

Frame a question, or decide that your reading is open-ended.

Lay cards face down, choose ten. Turn them face up and choose your favorite seven cards.

Set those aside, and read the other three cards as your Body / Mind / Spirit shadows (see Tarot Reading: Quick Intro above).

Reversals & Difficult Cards

Reversals and "negative" cards are different things – but they can work together.

No tarot card is really negative – but some are harder to like than others! If we read just the superficial meanings of Death or the Hanged One, the outlook won't be very cheery. But what if we look past the obvious symbols and read other parts of the card intuitively?

Try the four-step reading above – look at the smaller details of the image – what do you see? What if you deliberately made up a funny or happy story about the card?

We can also stretch meanings – the Death card can mean the end of mortal life – but it can also suggest changes in general; the end of a situation (maybe one that you *want* to end?); a time of rest and repose; and/or a prelude to rebirth. Does the caterpillar "die" so that the butterfly can be born? How is this a metaphor for situations in your life?

Reversals

A reversal is when we draw a card and it's upside down. We can ignore this and turn the card upright. Or we can read "reversed meanings" – we can ask what is the opposite of the obvious meaning? What blocks or obstructs the usual meaning?

If the Six of Pentacles shows someone being charitable, a reversed meaning might be greed or stinginess – or it might mean that I am the one who needs help.

Motherpeace Tarot, which uses round cards, carries this a step further – cards can be upside down, or rotated forward or backward – imagine the possibilities! No wonder this is such a popular deck.

Can you see how reversed meanings might be useful when drawing negative cards? And also for reminding us that those wonderfully positive cards like the Lovers or the Star have reversed meanings, too.

Tarot shadows – reversed meanings can be seen as the "shadows" of the usual meanings of cards, and they show us how complex our shadows can be. The shadow of Justice might be struggling against injustice. The shadow of the Devil card

continued on next page

Tarot: Intuitive Reading (pg 6)

might be liberation – a positive shadow! Learn more about this at Workings: Shadow.

Reading a Difficult Card – an Example

We did a tarot working once where everyone drew one card and did an intuitive reading. Afterward, a teen said, "I got the Devil card, and I'm a little freaked out."

Our group stopped and looked at the card (from the Motherpeace deck), showing a pharaoh atop a pyramid holding smaller humans in chains. We talked about what was happening in the card, and what thoughts and feelings it called up for us.

Someone said the card suggested the ways we feel trapped or bound in chains – external chains, or those we put on ourselves.

Someone noticed the hierarchy of the pyramid, with the pharaoh at the top holding others beneath him.

We turned the card upside down – what might a "reversed" meaning be? If the card is about feeling trapped or chained, then the reversal might mean breaking out. Or maybe it's about the ways that we hold ourselves in chains of our own making. Each person will see different meanings – each unique to their situation.

If this were your card, can you see ways it might apply in your life? Can you see how even a "negative" card can carry very powerful and ultimately positive meanings?

Tarot Salon – Readings for a Camp

What if teens did a tarot workshop, then later some people practice their skills by offering readings to the wider camp – a tarot salon!

One year we did tarot workings in Ravens (Teens) Path at Witchlets, and then teens offered readings to the rest of the camp. Teens who didn't want to do readings helped decorate the space and acted as gate-keepers.

Tarot Altar – Wisdom & Knowledge

How about creating a tarot altar where you can set out specific cards, such as all the Aces, or a particular card such as the Magician or Tower from several different decks, etc.

Maybe changing the cards can become a mini-ritual of its own.

Tarot Resources

- Mary Greer – Tarot Mirrors, Tarot for Yourself, and 21 Ways to Read a Tarot Card – you'll gain knowledge *and* wisdom!
- Cynthia Giles – The Tarot: History, Mystery, and Lore – where did tarot come from, and why there are so many decks?
- Online tarot card generator (for readings): serennu.com/tarot/pick.php

SOLO WORKING

Intuitive tarot reading is a deeply personal practice. Even in groups, each person usually receives their own reading.

A tarot altar is a way to become acquainted with a new deck, or to see cards in new ways. See ideas above.

As a solitary, or with a few friends, close your door and cast a circle. When you read, speak your answers and interpretations aloud. Consider the possibility that one of your magical ancestors might be listening.

Resisting the Book – Solo Workers Too!

Can you resist the temptation to "look in the book" that comes with your deck? Trust your intuition – set the book aside until you have your own relation with the deck. Want to read about tarot? See Tarot Resources just above.

WORKINGS

Tarot: Living Tableaux

INTENT

A living divination exercise, and a chance to interact with tarot cards in a deep, embodied way. This can be a major working in a ritual or class, and a rich way to weave tarot into a ceremony.

This could also be done as Nature Tableaux (eg, enact the stages of the life-cycle of a species) or as Mythic Tableaux (doing scenes from a myth or fairy tale that the group is working with).

SPACE/TIME/SIZE

Any number of people from four up – we've done this at public rituals of 60 or more. Enough space to move freely, yet a contained space without outside interference. Allow 45 minutes including transitions.

PREP

Groups of two to four people will enact a tarot card. The Rider-Waite-Smith deck features easily-enacted scenes. Ahead of time, choose some cards that will make challenging tableaux – cards where there are several characters and some drama or action. What card-images resonate with the intention of your ritual?

You'll need a bell to ring changes, and two priestesses as below. For small groups, you can self-priestess.

WORKING

Gather people into groups of two to four people. Lay the cards face down and have each group select one.

Half of the groups will offer tableaux first. One priestess takes these groups aside and invites them to create a "living tableau" of their card. They can act it out, or create something inspired by the card. They can make small movements and speak short, repetitive lines if that helps create the image. Give groups time to plan their tableau.

Half of the groups will be querents (questioners – see "Jargon," page 286-287). Second priestess takes these folks aside and guides a meditation to open ourselves to the wisdom of tarot. (In a camp or class, people may bring questions or issues from a prior working – if so, reawaken the questions.)

Tableaux groups set up their enactments, with room for people to move among them. Querents wander through the tableaux and "get a reading" from the living tarot, witnessing and asking questions (which tableaux people may or may not answer).

After five to ten minutes, ring a bell three times and call people back together.

Reverse roles and repeat.

At end – bring entire group back together. Invite people to breathe into the wisdom they have received / created, and to anchor the experience in their heart.

Then ask people to shake themselves off, pat their edges and welcome one another back to this world.

Song – sing a song here as a transition to the next working, or as a spiral dance. Good songs for spiral dance: Harvest Chant (Our Hands Will Work for Peace and Justice); Weave and Spin; Let It Begin.

SOLO WORKING

Try this at a party or gathering of friends. Choose a few cards that suit the mood (eg, Death and Tower for Halloween).

WORKINGS

Tarot: Speed Readings

INTENT

A fast, fun way for a group to do tarot readings. This can be a good introduction to tarot, as it invites people to use their intuition to directly encounter tarot images. It also gives people experience at offering readings to others.

For beginning and experienced readers, these quick readings help strengthen our sense that intuition is the surest guide to the magic of the cards.

This working lets people explore a personal question, perhaps as part of a larger ritual flow. For instance, if we are doing an Allies Circle as the main working, we might do a tarot speed reading first and reflect on what sort of support we need in our life.

The structure we're using here is called a wagon wheel – two concentric circles facing one another. By rotating the circles, it's easy for everyone to switch partners with minimal commotion. (See Workings: Intro: Some Handy Techniques).

SPACE/TIME/SIZE

This works best for 10-25 people – if larger, break into smaller groups. You'll need enough space to form a loose circle.

Allow 10 minutes for a one-card reading and 20 minutes for a three-card reading.

PREP

Choose a deck – one deck covers about 15-20 people. A visually rich deck such as the minor arcana of the Inner Child deck, which few people will have seen before, works well. Other good decks: Voyager; Motherpeace.

Rider-Waite-Smith is rich and multi-layered – but can be familiar, encouraging readers to default to previous knowledge instead of directly encountering the images. The Thoth deck is too schematic for this work. Avoid decks with words on the cards.

Decide on a type of spread. You may want to do a single card, but once you've done all the set-up, why not go for three? Past-Present-Future or Body-Mind-Spirit are easy for beginners. Celtic Cross is too complicated for this work.

A bell or rattle helps mark changes.

WORKING

Before you begin – explain that we are reading intuitively, not by book-learning. Invite people to set aside anything they already know about tarot. With intuition, there are no right or wrong answers, only inspirations.

Briefly explain the spread – for example, a three-card Past-Present-Future reading.

Invite people to frame a question. Perhaps the question relates to the overall theme of the ritual. Or it may be a personal question. If you're doing a solo working, take a minute and write this in your journal.

When ready – each person draws one card which will represent Past Influences. Keep it face down.

Now form two equal circles, one inside the other. Outside face in, inside circle face out, so each person is facing another person from the opposite circle. Explain that people will speak one at a time, with their partner silently witnessing.

(1) Priestess rings bell and says: "Outer circle, look at your card and immediately say a few objects or beings you see in the card – no stories, just what your eyes see. You'll have about 30 seconds."

Give outer circle time – then ring bell and repeat: "Now *inner* circle look at your card and quickly say a few objects or beings you see in the card."

continued on next page

WORKINGS

Tarot: Speed Readings (pg 2)

Give inner circle time to read, then ring bell. "Thank your partner. Then outer circle rotates one space to the left."

(2) Priestess rings bell and says: "Outer circle, take a minute and make up a simple one- or two-sentence story about what is happening in your card."

After a minute or so, ring bell and invite inner circle to do the same. Give them a minute to share about their card, then ring bell. "Thank your partner. Then inner circle rotates one space to your left."

(3) Priestess rings bell and says: "Outer circle – given your question and the fact that this card represents Past Influences – what is the meaning of this card for you? Go with your first glimmer of thought. There are no wrong answers."

After a minute or so, ring bell and invite inner circle to do the same. Give them a minute to share about what they see in their card, then ring bell. "Thank your partner."

If you're doing a 3-card reading, invite people to take a breath and remember their question, then draw a second card for Present Situation. Again form two circles, with a few people switching sides to mix up the pairings.

Repeat steps 1-3 above for "Present Situation."

Then do the same for a third card – in this example, "Future Possibilities."

After all cards are read, rotate once more, and then invite each pair of partners to find a place to sit down together. Decide who goes first. Take a few minutes and lay all three cards face up and see what patterns you notice, sharing your thoughts with your partner.

After a few minutes, priestess rings bell and asks partners to switch. Second person reflects on their three cards.

Finally, come back to the circle and do a go-round where each person shares one word about what they saw or learned.

Song – finish with a song such as She Changes Everything She Touches (aka Kore Chant); Let the Beauty We Love.

SOLO WORKING

Working solo, you'll need a deck and your Book of Shadows.

Choose the cards and lay them face down. Then turn them up one at a time and immediately write your first thoughts about each. When you've done all three, set them side-by-side, take a deep breath, and see what overall patterns arise.

Also see Tarot: Intuitive Readings, which has variations of this working.

Death – An Example of a Difficult Card

The Death card – oh no! Our dreams are doomed forever! Abandon all hope!

Or maybe not. How else might we interpret the challenging image on this card?

Notice the scythe-wielding figure is "clearing the ground." As light bursts behind, even crowned monarchs get swept aside to make room for what may come next.

Are there parts of your life that you may need to change in order to "clear the ground" for new dreams to come to fruition? What might need to be pruned away?

Does making changes require chopping off heads? Maybe the card is suggesting that we could be a bit more gentle than the Grim Reaper? Or maybe not....

WORKINGS

Tarot Stories

INTENT

A fun way to do extended personal check-ins. For some folks, using the tarot cards will make talking about their lives easier.

Try this on a middle day of path or class (first and last days will be too busy) – allow time for long check-ins.

Tarot tip – this is a non-divinatory way to explore tarot and engage with the cards without the pressure of "doing a reading" – a chance to simply look at the images and think about how they might relate to your life.

SPACE/TIME/SIZE

Room to spread out in triads. Especially in a group where quality of attention varies, triads offer two listeners instead of one.

Any number – need a tarot deck for every half-dozen people at least. Having several different decks is fun.

Allow five minutes for explanation and gathering cards, and 10 minutes for story-telling in triads.

PREP

Need multiple tarot decks – at least one for every five to six people so folks have a choice of images (after all, everyone might want the Lovers or the Fool!). Invite people to bring their own decks if they want.

Any decks are fine, since people will select cards face-up. The familiar Rider-Waite-Smith is great for this work, since people might already recognize and have associations for the images.

You'll need a simple way to form triads before drawing cards, along with a timer and a bell to ring changes.

WORKING

Priestess spreads multiple decks face up on the floor or table, mixing them all together. Invite people to gaze at cards and see their own stories reflected. Using your non-writing hand, choose three to five cards that you can use to tell a story about what is going on in your life.

When you have your cards, find your triad and a place to sit down. Decide who goes first. Each person will have two minutes to share their story, with others silently witnessing.

First person talks about what is going on in their life, using the cards as props if they are useful. You may want to lay the cards out in a pattern if this shows their meaning for you. Or you may wind up ignoring the cards and talking about whatever you wish – it's your time!

Check-ins might begin: "I chose these cards because..."

Give first person two minutes, then ring bell and suggest people change. Ring bell again two minutes later and suggest that third person should be starting.

As time runs out, there may be a lot of chatter in the room as people connect – let this continue for a few minutes.

Transition – ring bell three times to call group back together and move on.

SOLO WORKING

Alone or with a friend, draw face-up tarot cards to tell a story about what's going on in your life. Lay the cards out in a pattern that shows how these parts of your life connect (or how they don't). Afterward, write in your journal.

WORKINGS

Tarot: Journey of the Spirit

INTENT

Sacred myths often include a journey where the heroine learns skills, faces obstacles, discovers allies, and finally passes a challenge that demands all of their talent and perseverance.

Journeys make great magical workings. Labyrinth workings are one form of journey, where we travel in and out of the magical circuits. Stations rituals (see Rituals: Stations Format) involve a journey among several workings, culminating in a group working such as a spiral dance. And going to TEM or another WitchCamp is itself a magical journey!

Tarot cards are perfect for personal journey work. The Major Arcana from I to XXI are sometimes seen as the Journey of the Fool – the Fool (card zero) begins with the Magician (I) and progresses through the various cards, meeting challenges, allies, and gifts to emerge into the World at card 21 (XXI).

We can use the tarot cards to create a story of our own journey. We choose the beginning and end of our story with our eyes open – we know where we are, and we see where we want to go. Then we draw cards that give us magical information about obstacles, allies, and challenges.

Solo Working – this working was developed for a class called The Magical Writer (see page 239 for free course booklet). Although we've used it in groups and classes, it is actually a personal working, perfect for a solitary ritual. It explores our personal goals and dreams, the obstacles that get in our way, and how we might address them.

Journey of the Spirit
A personal ritual of transformation

- Question
- Self-Signifier
- Call or Challenge
- Obstacle
- Ally
- Testing / Initiation
- Climactic Struggle / Showdown
- Triumphant Conclusion / Return
- NOTES

SPACE/TIME/SIZE

Allow 60-90 minutes including creating sacred space. Any number, but everyone needs their own deck (or a way to share cards, or an online card generator). Room for people to spread out a bit.

PREP

Figure out how you'll create sacred space – for ideas, see Ritual Skills: Sacred Space: Quick Ways.

Create a tarot altar for the working – simple or elaborate. You might want to think about lighting – mysterious, but enough light to see the cards clearly.

Need – a tarot deck for each person (or a few people can share cards), or an online card generator (see page 286). Use a favorite deck for this working – whatever calls to you.

Also need – Book of Shadows and pen; drinking water; anything needed for invocations, etc.

You may also need to do some prep for the Charging the Outcome step – see near end of this working.

continued on next page

WORKINGS

Tarot: Journey of the Spirit (pg 2)

Preparing Your Book of Shadows

On a fresh page of your journal or Book of Shadows, write the date and this title: Journey of the Spirit. Under it, write "Question" and leave an inch or so blank.

Below that, copy this list, leaving about an inch under each one (use two pages if needed):
- Self-Signifier
- Call or Challenge
- Obstacle
- Ally
- Testing / Initiation
- Climactic Struggle / Showdown
- Triumphant Conclusion / Return

INTUITIVE READINGS: A Quick Review

See Workings: Tarot: Intuitive Reading for a full intro to this topic.

Here's a quick way to read a card for yourself. Try using it for your journey reading, taking a minute or two per card.

Intuitive readings are a way of encountering tarot as a personal magical tool. The point is to discover your own unique relation with tarot, rather than looking up other people's meanings in books.

In intuitive readings there are no wrong answers, only fresh inspirations – the point is to tune into what our inner voice is telling us. Our first thought is often the truest, least-censored response.

(0) state your question – write it down. Then turn over your card.
(1) name a few objects or beings in the card that catch your eye.
(2) name one object or being that is you.
(3) make up a simple story about what is happening in the card.
(4) say in one or two quick sentences what the card tells you about your question and your life.

✪ **Book of Shadows** – write the name of the card and your thoughts. If you feel stuck, write the first thing that pops into your head. Follow your own muse wherever it takes you, and don't worry about what other people (or tarot books) think or say.

WORKING – Journey of the Spirit

When your prep is ready, step out of the space. When you are ready to re-enter, take a breath and let go of any expectations about what is about to happen. Take a breath and dedicate yourself to the magical flow. Step back into the space.

Create sacred space as you have planned – acknowledge First People, ground, cast the circle, invoke elements and allies.

As a final invocation, take a moment and say a few words of welcome to all the storytellers of history – from mothers at the crib to our favorite novelists. Welcome the magic of stories!

Tarot Reading: Your Question

Take a breath and close your eyes. Take as much time as you need to come up with a question about where your life is going. It might be specific ("Should I quit playing piccolo and take up the tuba?"), or it might be broad and general ("What can this reading show me about my art and creativity?"). When you have a question, speak it aloud. If it feels right, write it down in your book next to the word Question. Speak it again.

continued on next page

WORKINGS

Tarot: Journey of the Spirit (pg 3)

Drawing Your Cards

First, lay the entire deck *face up* (if online, find a way to view all the cards from a deck). Choose one card that signifies you – whatever card speaks to you. Then choose a second card (face up) that signifies the "desired outcome" – a card that shows generally how you want your Question to work out. Lay these two face-up cards about a foot apart.

Shuffle the rest of the cards and lay them face down (or set tarot-card generator for random). Soften your gaze and let your non-writing hand hover over the cards. Gradually choose five cards, placing them *face down* in a row between the two face-up cards. Set the rest of the deck aside.

Online, you may need to draw cards one at a time. If you get a repeated card, you can draw again.

First Card: Self-Signifier

In your Book of Shadows, under the word Self-Signifier, write the name of the first face-up card you chose. Write a little about why you chose this card to represent yourself, or what images attracted you.

Second Card: Call or Challenge

The next card, face down, will represent our Call or Challenge. If our journey was an ancient myth, this is the moment where the main character hears about a monster that threatens their village – and realizes they must fight it.

What will your personal challenge be? Tarot can't tell you – but it can help you discover it for yourself.

Turn the card over and do a quick intuitive reading. Let the card inspire you, not limit you. You can follow your own practice, or follow the four-step process above. End by saying what the card tells you about your Question and your Call or Challenge. Write down your first thoughts, along with the name of the card.

Third Card: Obstacle (External and/or Internal)

The next card will give you information about an Obstacle that gets in the way. Sometimes the Obstacle is external – a person or situation is thwarting us. More often, the true Obstacle is internal – it's not another person who blocks me, but my own doubts and fears of standing up to that person or finding a creative solution.

Turn the card over and do a quick intuitive reading, as above. Think about the Question you asked, about your Call or Challenge – then say what Obstacle is getting in your way. Write down your first thoughts, along with the name of the card.

Fourth Card: Ally

Our path may be blocked – but luckily we aren't alone on our journey. One or more Allies are ready to help. It may be another person that we need to seek. Or it might be a spirit helper or an animal ally who can bring energies that we need.

We may know some of our Allies. But there may be others we never suspect. Tarot can help discover those hidden Allies.

Turn over the next card and read it as above. For this step, think about your Call of Challenge and the Obstacle you face. Then, along with the name of the card, spontaneously write what sort of Ally you want or need. Is it a companion? A teacher? A fierce guardian? A trickster? Don't worry about being realistic or following the card – ask for what you want and need.

Fifth Card: Testing / Initiation

A magical journey often includes some sort of instruction, followed by a Test or Initiation. If the heroine is going to face their challenge, they need to gain (and prove) some new skills.

What new skills or knowledge do you need to answer your challenge? Turn over the next card and do an intuitive reading, as

continued on next page

WORKINGS

Tarot: Journey of the Spirit (pg 4)

above. Think again about your Call of Challenge, your Obstacle, and your Ally. Then, along with the name of the card, write about what new skills or knowledge you might need to gain. Write whatever comes to mind.

Sixth Card: Climactic Struggle / Showdown

Nearly every great myth, legend, or fairy tale winds up with a Climactic Struggle. Sometimes it's a battle with demons, such as Beowulf. Other times it's a showdown with an authority figure, such as the stepmother in Cinderella.

In real life, our struggles are usually less epic. Maybe our "Showdown" is a difficult talk with a parent, a friend, or a boss. Sometimes it's a change in our life, such as a commitment to study for a big exam in a class we hate, or a decision to eat healthier food.

You have framed a Question, answered a Call, and traced the steps of a magical journey. What Showdown or change is needed to bring the journey to completion?

Turn over the next card and do an intuitive reading, as above. Consider what action needs to be taken – and especially what difficult decisions need to be made. Along with the name of the card, write your thoughts – and consider writing at least one concrete step that you can take.

Seventh Card: Triumphant Conclusion

You've reached the final card, which you drew face-up – it's your ideal outcome, chosen before you had any idea of the path you would travel. How does the card look now? Is it still your desired outcome?

Close your eyes and take a breath. Open your eyes and do a quick intuitive reading, as above. For the final step, say aloud what this card means as far as the outcome of your Question and your entire Journey.

Then, along with the name of the card, write your thoughts.

If you are satisfied, you're ready to empower the outcome. However, if your final card now seems less than ideal, flip through the deck face-up until you find a "desired outcome" card that you prefer. Write a bit about why you would prefer this conclusion to your journey, including possible problems and pitfalls.

Charging the Outcome

As part of your Journey, you may have written down a concrete step that you feel you need to take. Read it again. If it seems right, move ahead to the working below. If not, write some more about what action, if any, you feel you can commit to.

To charge the outcome, you can do a working such as the Overflowing Cup (allow about 20 extra minutes). If time is short, how about a Zap? (See Workings: Overflowing Cup, and Workings: Zap.) Or choose an upbeat chant – see pages 112-113.

Opening Sacred Space & Journaling

When you have completed the working, open sacred space, remembering to devoke whatever you have invoked.

✪ **Book of Shadows** – afterward, take some time to write in your journal (or you may want to do it before opening your circle). If you're a group, see if you can agree on some journaling time before you move on to snacks and socializing.

SOLO WORKING – Journey of the Spirit

Same as above – this is essentially a solo working.

For more tarot-based magic and exercises, see The Magical Writer course booklet – see Workings: Magical Writer.

WORKINGS

Tools of Magic

INTENT

Magical tools – from cauldrons to athames to labyrinths and many more – are part of the lore and practice of magic.

Tools can extend and sharpen our practices the way a hammer or a paintbrush can extend what our hand alone could do. Using an athame (a single-bladed magical knife – see below) can help strengthen and "sharpen" my circle casting.

Tools can also become a distraction. If we're more concerned with the beautiful new chalice we're holding than with the spell we're casting, we're tripping over our own feet.

✪ **Book of Shadows** – when you get a new tool, tarot deck, cape, etc – create a page in your Book of Shadows where you can keep notes about the tool, how and when you use it, what surprises you, etc.

Also – see below for more writing ideas about magical correspondences.

Tools Lab

Let's think of this as a tools laboratory – a time to experiment, to work magic, to play with magic, to pick up tools and set them aside as intuition and experience dictate.

✪ **Book of Shadows** – dedicate pages to tracking your experiments. What works the first time you try it? What takes a few tries? What's exciting at first but doesn't grow deeper?

You can buy athames, cauldrons, chalices, and other tools at new age stores or craft festivals, online, at WitchCamps, etc.

You can also make your own – a powerful way to engage with a tool that will be uniquely yours (see Workings: Wand Crafting).

Elemental Tools

Reclaiming has adopted correspondences between the sacred elements and certain tools from older magical traditions.

continued on next page

Magical Correspondences / Correspondences Magical

Reclaiming shares these magical correspondences with many (but not all) other traditions:

Direction	Element	Season	Tool	Body-Tool	Tarot Suit
East	Air	Spring	Blade / Athame	Edge of Hand	Swords
South	Fire	Summer	Wand	Pointing Finger	Wands / Batons
West	Water	Fall	Chalice	Cupped Hands	Cups
North	Earth	Winter	Pentacle	Body-Star	Pentacles / Discs
Center	Aether	–	Labyrinth / Cauldron	Personal Center	Major Arcana

✪ **Book of Shadows** – can you extend this table to include other categories for each direction / element? What colors might fit with each element? What sorts of natural items? What types and colors of stones? What emotions? What types of music? What foods? What animals? What books or movies? What magical skills?

TeenEarthMagic.org

WORKINGS

Tools of Magic (pg 2)

These tools also correspond to the traditional tarot suits as shown on Rider-Waite-Smith and many other decks. (Note – not all older traditions agree on these correspondences, and not all Reclaiming people use these tools.)

Air = the blade (tarot = swords). Also called an athame (ah-thah'-may) – a magical knife that cuts through clutter and confusion.

Fire = the wand (tarot = wands). Wands direct magical energy – in movies, this energy is often portrayed as fiery.

Water = the chalice (tarot = cups). Cups and chalices hold energy, contain it, overflow with it, etc.

Earth = the pentacle (tarot = pentacles or disks). The pentacle or disk holds and supports energy.

Center = mystery! (tarot = major arcana). Center is not one of the four classical elements (which come down to us from the ancient Greek tradition), but in Reclaiming it is often invoked and worked with either as a fifth element, or as the synthesis of the other four. What tools might symbolize center? A labyrinth? A cauldron? A ring? A spiral?

Other Tools

There are an endless number of other magical tools. For a writer, a pen might be the perfect tool for casting a circle. For a gardener, pruning sheers might symbolize cutting away what we don't need from our own lives.

Tarot is a powerful and multi-faceted tool. Labyrinths are tools in various spiritual traditions. Meditation and trance are tools. The list goes on and on.

The Workings chapter of this book introduces various tools. How will you make some of them uniquely your own?

Tools Etiquette 101

Many magical tools come with centuries or even millennia of lore, legends, and practical advice. You can read endlessly online. Here's a few ideas we can pass along:

- Obtain or make your own tools – even if you buy a tool or get one second-hand, find a way to make it your own (see below).
- Keep tools on an altar, in a magical pouch, displayed on your wall, etc – not tossed in your sock drawer (unless that's the working you're doing!).
- Don't use magical tools in a frivolous way unless (A) you have created a strong magical circle, and (B) you are prepared to deal with the consequences. Having fun with a tarot deck can be a great magical practice. Juggling flaming cauldrons is best left to the experts.
- When you're getting rid of a tool, cleanse and dispose of it in a magical way (see below re "releasing" tools).
- Don't handle other people's tools, or any tool on an altar, unless the owner invites you.

Sharing Tools

Tools are like clothes – some you share, some you don't. Assume the same for tools – it's always a good idea to ask before picking up someone else's tool, whether it's an athame, a tarot deck, a drum, or a cordless high-speed power drill.

If you bring a tool, deck, drum, etc to a class or circle, others may assume it's okay to handle. If you're doing the Tools Cakewalk working (see below), the point is to handle various tools. If you don't want something touched, be clear at the outset.

If a tool is placed on an altar, it's usually hands off unless you are told otherwise. A magical faux-pas at a 1990s Bay Area ritual

continued on next page

WORKINGS

Tools of Magic (pg 3)

involved an altar created by local Native Americans. Several ritual participants picked up and handled items on the altar, which was not the way to build good cross-cultural relations. We learned to explain this etiquette ahead of time.

SPACE/TIME/SIZE

Working with tools can be done in a circle, a class, solo – or all of the above. Read the ideas below and allow yourself plenty of time to explore different sorts of tools and ways of using them.

PREP

Read the ideas below and obtain the tools or materials needed.

WORKINGS

Tools Altar

You can use a general magical altar to charge tools – perhaps give them a special corner, oriented toward the appropriate direction (eg, an athame might rest in or point toward East).

If you have space, you can also create a special altar where tools can be charged and re-charged. Maybe it's divided into sections, one for each element and its corresponding tools, tarot cards, natural objects, stones, etc.

The Toolular Body

Our bodies consist of a multitude of magical and practical tools.

The "chopping" edge of our hand is a blade that can cut through a magical morass. Imagine the focused power of a karate chop.

Our pointing finger is one of the most powerful wands around. As a game, try pointing at a friend with different "tones" – point in excitement, blame, laughter, anger.... If you have a circle, try "zapping" magical objects with your pointing wand-fingers (see Workings: Zap).

Our cupped hands are a chalice. The Greek philosopher Diogenes is said to have drunk from a battered cup until one day he saw a girl drinking from her hands. He threw away his old cup, saying, "A child has taught me about simplicity."

If we stand and extend our arms and legs (like Leonardo's picture of a Renaissance person standing in a circle), we become a pentacle, or a star. This comes in handy when we do pentacle magic (see Workings: Pentacles).

And each of us has our own center – although no one else can tell us exactly where it is.

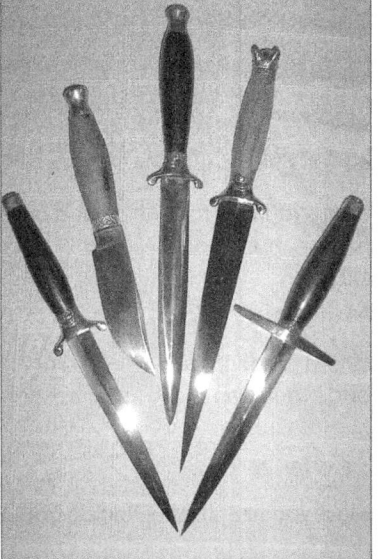

Athames – photo courtesy Glastonbury Witch Shop.

Charging, Blessing, Cleansing, & Releasing Tools

You can make a tool your own by cleansing, charging, blessing, holding and breathing, carrying, and sleeping with it under your pillow. You can also create a ritual to empower the tool.

Cleanse away old energy with water or fire, then immerse the tool in new energy. Create magical space (quickly or thoroughly, as you wish). Then hold a new blade or wand under running water or over a candle flame. Breathe deeply. As you exhale,

continued on next page

WORKINGS

Tools of Magic (pg 4)

picture any old energy held in the tool washing or burning away.

To call in fresh energy, fill a bowl with water. Place your hands on the bowl and breathe. Imagine the power you wish the tool to have. Picture yourself holding and using the tool along with specific ways you will use it. Breathe all of this into the water. Set the bowl down and touch your tool to the water. As you inhale, draw the magic from the water into the tool.

Finally, hold the tool in both hands and declare: "You are my _____ (chalice, athame, etc). So mote it be!"

Suppose that you have charged and used a tool, then decide it is not for you after all. Before donating it to your WitchCamp's silent auction, how will you release and cleanse your own energy so it doesn't cling to a tool someone else may be using?

You could create a short ceremony where you use it one last time – or do something as simple as laying it on the floor, walking three times counter-clockwise around it, then declaring: "You are no longer my _____. Hail and farewell!"

Tools Cakewalk

Here's a fun way for one person or a circle to experiment with various tools, share tools-lore and practical information, etc. See Workings: Tools Cakewalk.

Divination Tools

You can do divination using tarot and other kinds of decks, pendulums, crystals – or maybe the bark of a tree or a passing cloud? Tools can make introspection and discernment work richer (and more fun). See Workings: Divination.

Create a Tool

Even if you like discovering and buying beautiful or unusual magical tools, you'll learn by crafting one of your own.

Unless you have a home forge, you probably can't create a metal athame. But you could carve one. Let yourself see the blade you want. Then look around for a piece of wood that seems to "contain" the blade. To carve it, you'll use another blade – how will you magically charge this carving knife (and de-charge it when you're done)?

A spell candle lets you put your own creative energy into a simple magical tool – a flame. See Workings: Spell Candles.

Witches traditionally make their wands by hand, using a branch that calls especially to them. See Workings: Wand Crafting.

Tools, Tools Everywhere

Experiment with other magical tools such as tarot, labyrinths, meditation, etc. Which ones especially resonate for you? How will you make these traditional practices uniquely your own?

SOLO WORKING

Same as above. How will you make the tools your own?

WORKINGS

Tools Cakewalk (Divination)

INTENT

A quick, fun way to sample various magical tools, from wands and athames to tarot decks and runes, and also to get some magical input on an issue or challenge.

Players frame a question from their lives, then randomly visit several magical tools (or tarot decks, etc) to see if any might be useful for further work and exploration.

A traditional cakewalk moves around a large Monopoly-board type layout. Some of the squares have cakes, pies, etc. Some have funny things like onions or spinach. Music plays, and players move from square to square. When the music stops, you get whatever is on the square you're standing on. Charity money is raised by charging the players to participate.

Tools Cakewalk – some tools are magical (wand, crystal, athame, etc), some mundane (spatula, pliers, ballpoint pen, etc), some bookish (dictionary or cookbook).

Tarot Cakewalk – each square has a different tarot or other divination deck, or sub-sets such as court cards, majors, etc.

Divination Cakewalk – each square has a different divination tool – tarot, runes, astrology, animal spirit cards, oghams, herbal, coins to toss, etc.

SPACE/TIME/SIZE

Works best with about eight to twelve people. With more, use this in a "stations" ritual that has smaller groups coming to each working (see Rituals: Stations Format). This working needs an even number of people, so the guiding priestess can step out if the group has an odd number.

Takes 20-30 minutes including transitions. This can be a fun working, so leave time to extend it if people are engaged.

Need a quiet space with room for a floor-altar in the center (ie, no fire in the middle).

PREP

Need one tool (or deck, etc) for each player, plus two extra tools. For a class, you can ask people to bring a favorite tool, deck, etc – but make sure it's okay for others to handle it. Above are ideas for several kinds of cakewalks (see Intent above).

continued on next page

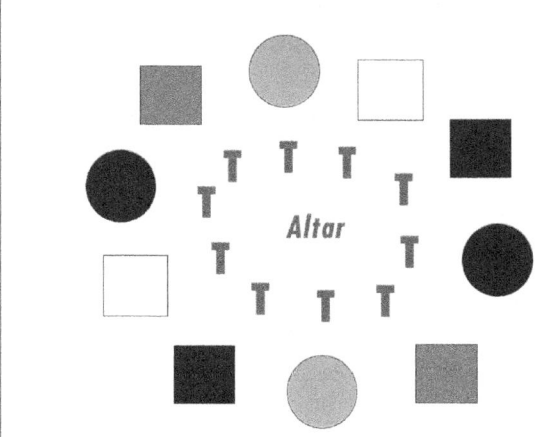

Tools Cakewalk Made Easy!

Layout for an eight-person cakewalk (with ten total spaces / tools). Tools or tarot cards (T) are arranged on a floor altar in the center, one per colored (or numbered) space.

Music plays or is sung, and people move clockwise. When the music stops, reach down and pick up the tool for your space.

Consider how this tool – or one it makes you think of – could help with your present challenge.

Colored spaces indicate which two people will do pair-share. Two unmatched colors (if any) form the final pair.

WORKINGS

Tools Cakewalk (pg 2)

Space-markers – one space for each player plus two extra spaces. Get multi-colored paper to mark the spaces (or use white paper and write numbers on them). Make two of each color or number – this facilitates pair-shares (see diagram above).

Lay out a circle of the colored (or numbered) squares, using two of each color or number mixed around the circle. Total exactly two more squares (and tools) than the number of players.

Lay tools around the edge of a central floor-altar so it is clear which square each tool connects to (but make sure they will not be stepped on).

Music – either sing a short song with a clear ending (such as Air Moves Us) or use recorded music that can be turned on and off easily.

WORKING

See diagram on preceding page.

Priestess invites participants to think about some issue or challenge in their lives for which a magical tool (or divination tool or tarot deck) might come in handy. Breathe to that challenge.

Start music (or begin singing a simple song with a clear ending). Players walk around the grid clockwise. When music stops, pick up the tool in your space. Priestess asks: How might this tool, or something else it makes you think of, be useful with your current challenge?

Turn to another player and share for a minute how you might magically use this tool (or something it makes you think of) to address your issue. With colored or numbered squares, find your match – if circle has two extra spaces, two colored squares may be unmatched – these two people should pair up.

Repeat three or four times.

Finally, ask each person to go and stand on the square of the tool that seems most useful, or which is most suggestive, regarding their question. More than one person can share a tool.

Go around and share briefly why that tool (or deck etc) called to you and how you might use it (it's always okay to pass).

SOLO WORKING

Gather a dozen "tools," ranging from magical (athame, chalice, divination deck) to ordinary (ballpoint pen, pliers, house keys). Lay them on the floor in a small circle.

Think about some issue or challenge in your life for which magical tools might come in handy. Breathe to that challenge.

Walk around the circle singing a short, simple song. When the song ends, stop and pick up the closest tool and ask yourself: How might this tool, or something else it makes me think of, be useful with my current challenge?

✪ **Book of Shadows** – after a few rounds, journal for a while. What tools seemed most useful? Which other tools do you wish you had landed on? What have you learned about your challenge?

WORKINGS

Trance: Place of Power
A Recorded Trance with Starhawk

INTENT

Here's a guided meditation for getting in touch with our personal power, led by Starhawk.

You'll find a recorded version on youtube – search <Starhawk Place Power>. It's also part of Starhawk's Way to the Well ritual, available on iTunes, youtube, spotify, etc.

A place of power is a personal magical space where you can go in your imagination when you need a quick reminder of your value and power as a living, breathing human.

This is a working you can return to time and again, renewing the strength of your place of power so it's there when you need it.

Here's how Starhawk describes the Place of Power in her book, The Spiral Dance:

"You will enter into a new space, a place in which you are completely safe and protected, where you are in complete control and in touch with your deepest sources of strength. It may seem to be indoors or outdoors – it may contain anything or anyone you like. It is completely yours. Wherever you may be, whatever state of consciousness you may be in, you can return to your place of power, simply by visualizing it."

You can weave this trance into your own working, as below.

SPACE/TIME/SIZE

Any number from one to a large group. Comfortable space for people to sit or lie down. Allow about a half-hour including transitions.

PREP

If you are doing this as part of a ritual, then you already have your plan for sacred space. If not, find a way to ground, cast a circle, and invoke – see Ritual Skills: Sacred Space: Quick Ways.

You'll want your journal and some drinking water. Wear loose, comfortable clothes.

Have your sound system ready and the track cued up.

WORKING

Once you have created sacred space, make yourself comfortable and begin the trance recording. Let your mind wander along with the trance. Trance is not a task or a chore – it's a relaxed journey.

The Place of Power Trance recording is about 12 minutes – you may want to play it through a second time and let yourself linger in the space.

When the recording is complete, let yourself relax for a few minutes. Write in your journal if you wish.

Remember to devoke and open the circle at the end.

SOLO WORKING

This is a perfect personal working. It's also part of the longer Way to the Well online ritual – page 115.

You can find more recorded works by Starhawk on amazon, iTunes, etc – Wiccan Meditations, Earth Magic – and her best-selling novel, The Fifth Sacred Thing.

WORKINGS

Transformational Tableaux

INTENT

Suppose we were in a difficult situation – one where we felt really stuck – and suddenly someone made a small movement and everything shifted?

One way of doing magic is to perform an action in a ritual that is intended to ripple out into our wider lives.

This exercise lets us create a tableau of a difficult situation with the help of several allies. Then we'll have a chance to make small changes in the tableau that – if the magic works! – can completely transform the meaning of the situation.

An example – suppose in your tableau you are speaking the truth to Sally Ann, who has her arm up like she is going to hit you – enacting a fear that speaking the truth is dangerous. After you and your group strike this pose, someone moves Sally Ann's arm so instead of threatening to hit you, she is reaching out to hug you.

This working might follow a meditation or exercise which brings you in touch with something that is blocking your growth.

After you do the transformative work, follow it with a spiral dance or other way of raising energy and charging the working.

SPACE/TIME/SIZE

Any number, working in groups of four to five. Each person needs about six to eight minutes, plus 10 minutes for set-up and another five to come back into the big circle – so allow an hour for a group of five.

Enough space for groups to spread out.

PREP

You'll need a simple way of getting into small groups of four to five people. It helps to have someone in each group who understands this working and can go first.

Priestess – if you have more than a couple of groups, have a priestess who is not in a group, but rather watches the overall energy, lets people know when there are 15 minutes remaining, etc.

Song – learn song for spiral dance, and decide who will lead the dance. Ideas:

- She Changes Everything She Touches
- We Are the Rising Sun
- Weave and Spin

WORKING

If possible, teach the song at the beginning of the ritual or class. If not, teach it at the beginning of this working.

Priestess invites people to close their eyes and picture a situation in which their energy is blocked

continued on next page

WORKINGS

Transformational Tableaux (pg 2)

or does not flow easily – perhaps a situation where you feel uncertain or where you hold yourself back. Picture yourself in the situation, and imagine a simple way for the group to help you enact it.

Get into small groups. One at a time, have the group enact someone's situation. When it's your turn, explain quickly what the situation is. Then others can help create a tableau where you enact the feeling of being blocked or stuck. Once the group has it, hold it for a minute so you can feel yourself in the situation. Feel what it's like to be stuck there.

Now ask others in your group to suggest very simple changes – maybe just one person moves – so that the meaning can change entirely. Try a few changes until you find one that really works for the person whose turn it is. Then hold that tableau for a minute. Feel what it's like for the energy to have shifted.

End by everyone shaking off the energy. Then the next person goes.

When all have taken a turn, return to the main circle. To bring the whole group back together, go around the circle and each person says a single word that captures their feeling at the moment. If there's time, go around three times – saying the same or a different word, as you wish.

Spiral dance – when the word-circle is complete, pause for a moment, then launch into the song and spiral.

SOLO WORKING

For a solo working, try this as a dance – start with your "stuck" pose. Make one small movement at a time and freeze, until you have shifted entirely to a "liberated" pose.

Once you have your movements, go back and see if you can make them into a simple, flowing dance.

TeenEarthMagic.org

WORKINGS

Trust Fall

INTENT

Stand on a ledge with your back toward two rows of your friends. Their arms are interwoven like a net. If you fall backward, you will fall into that net.

Do you trust your friends to catch you? Do you trust yourself to remain calm as you fall?

When we build bonds of trust at a WitchCamp or retreat, we realize our collective ability to work magic. As we prepare to catch one another, our group energy weaves a strong web. Each person lends their full attention and support. We realize that together we can catch the largest person in our group.

As each of us chooses to fall (or not), we face not just our fears, but also our desire to trust and believe in one another!

How far will you fall? With a younger group at Redwood Magic, we fell from 12 inches. At Vermont WitchCamp we raised a bench on top of a picnic table. At Witchlets, we dropped from a four-foot tree stump. For the given group, each height was powerful.

Right to pass – as always, each person has the right to pass on this exercise. We've encouraged reluctant teens to step up on the platform and consider doing the fall, then step down if they choose not to. When someone makes this choice, others spontaneously speak words of support and inclusion. (For more on the right to pass, see Introduction: Agreements.)

Differently-abled and -bodied people – folks with mobility limits and/or large-bodied people may not want to do this working. Your challenge is to find a way to include those who take the "right to pass." What support roles can they take? How will you weave the group again once the trust falls are complete?

Note to teachers – you are not exempt from this exercise! (See Organizing: Teaching Magic to Teens, page 328.)

Trust sequence – we've built a sequence of trust exercises: Trust Walks on Day 1, Runs on Day 2, and Falls on Day 3 or 4.

Safety note – before attempting to lead this exercise, find someone who has previously led it to demonstrate for you. This powerful working is not a good occasion for improvising. Unlike many of our workings, this is not a game or party exercise.

SPACE/TIME/SIZE

You'll need a solid, level surface at the chosen height (eg, a tree stump or picnic table). Three to four feet is a good height, although we've done it from lower (the catchers had to kneel down, but it worked). The "landing pad" where catchers line up also needs to be level, and preferably soft. If indoors, lay out pillows or sleeping bags.

Approximately 12-20 people. With more, some people will be standing around, so plan how you will maintain focused energy.

Allow several minutes per person plus 15 minutes of transition and explanation. With a group of 12, allow an hour.

It will be hard to refocus afterward, so make this the final working in a class or path. Follow with a song or spiral dance.

PREP

Arrange the platform. Decide which priestess will coach the person preparing to fall, and which will coach the catchers.

Teach song ahead of time. Here's a few ideas: We Are the Power in Everyone; We Are the Rising Sun; Weave and Spin.

continued on next page

WORKINGS

Trust Fall (pg 2)

WORKING

This explanation assumes that sacred space has already been created, and that you will open the ritual at the end. For ideas, see Ritual Skills: Sacred Space: Quick Ways.

Explanation

First, the priestess and catching coach describe in detail how the exercise works. Usually we don't explain a magical exercise before we do it, but with this working it helps relieve people's worries so they can focus on the task at hand.

Explain that people will fall one at a time and be caught by the others, and that although everyone is encouraged to take a turn, each person will have the right to pass. Describe the exercise below, step by step. This helps people visualize the working, and it will feel familiar when the time comes.

Then add this description of the Fallers and Catchers:

Faller – when it's your turn, you'll stand with your legs together, your back, neck, and legs straight. This will spread out your weight and make it easier to catch you. Put each hand on the opposite shoulder, like a mummy. Clasp your arms tight.

Just before you fall, the priestess will remind you to clench your buttocks to maintain your core focus, and to keep your back "stiff as a board."

When you fall, keep your legs and back straight and just drop backward. You do *not* want to flail your arms or make yourself into a human cannonball.

Catchers – your friends' health and well-being is literally in your hands! Your concentration and teamwork will provide the magic of this working. Not only will we catch each person – we'll feel more powerful each time we do it!

Catchers' tip – the greatest weight will be around the faller's hips – especially if they do a cannonball. So for bigger fallers, put your strongest catchers where the hips will land.

What if someone does get dropped? Don't worry – they won't crash to the floor like a bad stage dive. If everyone stays focused, the worst that happens is that the faller slowly slips through people's arms and gets laid onto the ground – with some catchers tumbling down as well.

The Fall: Trust Magic

The catching coach has about 10 catchers line up facing each other, with one person at the top to support the head. For bigger fallers, put stronger catchers around where the hips will land. Smaller catchers can be closest to the faller, so they are catching the legs.

Interweave arms without clasping – put strongest catchers where faller's hips will land.

Catchers – hold your arms out like you are carrying a big stack of laundry. Interweave your arms with the people opposite. Do *not* clasp hands or grip each others' arms – just alternate them to make a woven ladder of arms (this will protect the catchers as the weight shifts). The person furthest from the faller will catch the head and support the neck as the person lands.

Priestesses maintain group attention throughout the exercise, reminding people to focus as needed. If you doubt someone's attention, move them to a safer position or have them take a turn out.

Faller gets up on the platform. Priestess suggests they take their time, look down at the catchers, and let feelings arise. When

continued on next page

WORKINGS

Trust Fall (pg 3)

catchers are ready, priestess asks faller if they choose to do the working. If "No," ask them to look down and acknowledge the catchers again, then step down. Priestesses help raise words of encouragement and inclusion.

If faller is ready, priestess directs them to turn their back to the catchers. Priestess makes sure alignment is correct.

Priestess reminds faller – each hand holds the opposite shoulder, feet together, legs and back "stiff as a board." Clench your buttocks to maintain core focus.

Now priestess asks: "All ready?"

Faller and catchers, if ready, reply: "Ready."

But don't fall yet!

Priestess asks: "Falling?"

Only when the faller hears that question do they know everyone is ready. Now, when they are ready, they clutch their arms, make their back and legs stiff as a board, and declare: "Falling!"

They drop backward. For a long instant they fall – then are caught with a whoosh!

The immediate reaction is euphoria. Catchers lower the faller to the ground and gather round as the person laughs and shakes off the excitement. Catchers trade tips and shift positions, getting ready for the next faller.

Go-round – when everyone has had a turn, gather in a circle. Ask people to take a breath and look around at those who just caught them (or held them in the circle if they chose not to fall). Go around and let each person say one to three words about how they are feeling.

Transition – this is a "hard act to follow," so put it toward the end of a class or path. End with a spiral dance.

Spiral song: We Are the Power in Everyone; We Are the Rising Sun; Weave and Spin.

SOLO WORKING – nope, sorry...

Trust falls are not "do it yourself" magic, and aren't something to try for fun. Save this one for camp.

Please don't try this exercise without someone who has previously led it to demonstrate for you.

However – the trust workings on the following pages are great for a couple of people or a small group, and can be done on your own.

WORKINGS

Trust Run

INTENT

A challenging, fun way for people to test the limits of their trust in the group, and for the group to practice supporting someone even when that person has doubts. Trust Runs involve the entire group working together.

This is a good follow-up to Trust Walks – do Walks on Day 1, Runs on Day 2, and Falls on Day 3 or 4.

It will be hard to refocus the group afterward, so make this the final working in a class or path.

SPACE/TIME/SIZE

A flat road or field with no potholes or obstacles, about 30 feet long. This is the runway – literally.

Need at least 12 people. If more than 20 people, break into two groups and do a "stations" working (ie – have one group do the Trust Run, while another does some other working, then switch).

Allow 30 minutes including debrief and transitions.

PREP

A blindfold for the runner.

Scout the runway carefully and make sure there are no gopher holes, sprinkler heads, etc.

WORKING

All but first runner and coach-priestess line up along the runway. Three to four people are at the "goal line" to catch the runner. Others line up along sides, bunched toward the end of the runway, ready to catch someone who swerves.

Coach invites runner: "Look at the runway and the group lined up to catch you, and consider putting 'blind' trust in the group to catch you if you go astray."

Other priestesses help keep everyone's focus on runner.

Coach asks permission and blindfolds the runner, then settles them so they are facing straight ahead (no spinning around, etc). Rest of group calls out encouragement so runner can hear the direction they will be running.

At their own decision, runner takes off for the goal. Everyone else is ready to catch and re-steer them if they go astray.

Some people will run straight ahead or swerve into the sides and need to be caught. Others will take a few fast steps and then slow down, groping their way forward, walking and jogging. They are testing their trust – everyone keep calling out encouragement until they reach the end.

Afterward – debrief in pairs (give people a few minutes each to talk). Then re-circle and go around the circle, sharing one word about how we are feeling.

Song – Spiraling Into the Center; We Are the Power In Everyone; Step Into the Flow.

Transition – this is a "hard act to follow," so put it toward the end of a class or path. Transition to devoking and opening the circle.

SOLO WORKING

Get some friends and try this. Talk about it afterward. Later, journal about it.

WORKINGS

Trust Walk

INTENT

A fun, embodied way to build trust and awareness. Doing trust exercises with various partners helps weave bonds among a group.

Sequence of trust workings – trust exercises can build during the week. Trust walks are a starting place, progressing on later days to trust runs and falls.

SPACE/TIME/SIZE

Plenty of room to move around, and plenty of interesting obstacles. If indoors, see if you can use hallways and stairwells. If outside, set wide boundaries and let people go.

Any number, working in pairs – whatever the space will hold.

Allow 30 minutes including debrief and transitions

PREP

Enough blindfolds / scarves for half of the people in the group. Ask people to bring a blindfold to class. A bell or gong to call people back from some distance.

Prep the area so it's safe yet cluttered with obstacles – you may want to create a "journey" past various obstacles.

WORKING

Get people in pairs – try a quick game such as having teens line up by their birthdays, then go down the line and pair folks.

Invite people to stand near their partner and re-ground. Remind them: "You are about to do something in which another person will completely trust you. This is not the time for pranks or practical jokes. Trust is a sacred connection and responsibility. Look at your partner and ask, 'Can I trust you?'"

Invite pairs to decide who will be blindfolded and who will be the guide first. Take a moment to develop some nonverbal signals such as shoulder taps in order to communicate, and to agree to move slowly and carefully.

Once blindfold goes on, all talking ceases.

Give people 10 minutes or so to wander and explore. Guide can offer silent experiences such as touching moss on a tree, climbing over a fallen tree-trunk, putting fingers into creek-water, etc.

Priestesses walk around and keep an eye on the less-focused guides, walking along and coaching them as needed.

After 10 minutes, call people back and change roles.

Afterward – debrief by shaking off the energy, then go around the circle and share a few words about how we are feeling (in a larger group, share one word).

Transition – do something to re-establish the group – a group working such as a Blessing Circle or Lifting Each Other Up, or a song.

Song – Spiraling Into the Center; My Soul; Let the Beauty We Love; Step Into the Flow.

SOLO WORKING

Get a friend and try this. Can you find an intriguing place to explore while blindfolded?

The key is to establish and maintain trust throughout the walk. This is not the time for practical jokes!

WORKINGS

Voice Magic

INTENT

Our voices are a main way we put ourselves out into the world. They are a way we show the world, "I am here – I matter!"

Wouldn't it be magical if we awoke one day and had complete confidence in our singing and speaking voice? Unfortunately, it will take a little longer than one day. But we actually can improve both our voice and our confidence.

Strangely, we were all born believing we could sing. Watch little kids – you can't stop them from singing. They don't even wait to learn the words – they just jump in and sing along!

In our society, most people are not encouraged to use their voices except for plain, unadorned talking. Only the chosen few are encouraged to sing or speak in public. The rest are told that we don't have "good voices," and that things will go better for us if we don't risk singing.

What a loss! When we hold back, the world loses our unique voice.

Imagine a world where everyone who dared to sing sounded exactly the same – where every song sounded like a soft drink commercial. Is that a world you want to help create by your silence?

Some say that our voice is a divine gift – that our voices were given to us by the gods and goddesses so that we could call their names. When we "invoke" an element or a goddess, we are literally "in-voicing."

We can learn to raise and strengthen our voice – and our confidence in it.

SPACE/TIME/SIZE

See Workings below for size and time suggestions.

Safe space – you'll need a "safe" space for singing – a place where no one can hear you, or where those within earshot are going to be supportive. These workings will be less effective if we feel that others outside the circle are listening and judging.

PREP

Find / create a safe space for singing. This might be your room or basement, an ocean beach, or a solitary spot in the hills. Local schools might have practice rooms you can use free or cheap.

Before you begin this work – and every time you do voice magic – ask your voice to be your ally and to work with you. Place your hand on your throat and let your voice know you appreciate its courage.

WORKINGS

Sing A Lot / Sing Along

Half of the secret of a good voice is – sing a lot. The more we sing, the more relaxed our vocal chords become – and the better we'll know the secrets of our unique voice.

continued on next page

WORKINGS

Voice Magic (pg 2)

Sing along – dial up cheesy songs on youtube and join in! Peter, Paul, & Mary were made for singing along.

Sing with a mirror – see the first Solo Working below: How Could Anyone Ever Tell You.

Circle of Support

Up to about eight people – if more, do sub-groups. Allow an hour for eight people – strong emotions can come up around our voices, and you want time for them.

This is a simple, challenging, and powerful exercise that lets each of us hear our voice ring out strong and clear – and be supported by our circle. It's a good working for later in the week, when people know each other better. It's a "watery" working that can bring up strong feelings, and it can flow beyond time boundaries.

Priestess does a short intro – use the Intent section above for ideas. You might want to show people the hand-signals below (louder, softer, fade out).

Stand in a close circle. Decide who be the singer first – an older camper or student teacher might go first and model this exercise. Once you start, go clockwise around the circle. If someone passes, offer them another chance at the end.

Priestess invites the whole circle to sing a tone together. Take deep breaths, and sing the tone as long as you comfortably can, then breathe and come in again. Practice toning for a few minutes until it is smooth and easy for the group.

Now, priestess begins to "conduct" the group – when you lift your hands, people get louder – when hands go lower, get softer. When priestess makes a fade-out signal, everyone fades out – except the one singer whose turn it is. That person keeps toning steady and strong.

The first time, singer can close their eyes if they want – but keep toning steadily.

After 10 seconds or so (less at first, more later), priestess brings the rest of the circle back up around the singer.

Once people get the idea, you can go around the circle without stopping – each person getting 10 seconds or so of "solo" time, then the whole group fades up again and moves on to the next person.

After once around, stop and do some sharing. What did it feel like to sing alone? To have others come back in? Give people time to share their feelings.

Do another round, again about 10-15 seconds each. When this is complete, go around and each person take a moment, look around at the others, and say, with whatever strength you can give it: "I like my voice!"

Advanced working – the person who is toning looks around the circle meets others' eyes. The listeners simply mirror back love for the person – don't try to offer words of support, etc. Just listen and love the person.

At the end, do a circle of sharing. Give people a couple of minutes apiece, and more if emotions are coming up (see Workings: Non-Judgmental Listening).

Complete the working with a simple, beautiful song that everyone knows (teach it beforehand if needed). Song ideas: My Soul; Let the Beauty We Love; When We Are Gone.

Singing Our Intentions & Affirmations

Here's a way to use our voices to empower an intention or affirmation we have made. Up to about 15 people. Larger than that, make smaller sub-groups.

From a prior working, each person comes up with a word or phrase of power or affirmation. This could be tarot or another divination working, walking a labyrinth, etc – complete that working by coming up with one word (or phrase).

continued on next page

WORKINGS

Voice Magic (pg 3)

Gather in a close circle. One at a time, each person *sings* their word or phrase – and the rest of the circle sings it back, adding harmonies, descants, echoes, etc. Sing it a second and third time with more power, and hear it sung back.

When everyone has taken a turn, finish with a gentle song like Let the Beauty We Love or My Soul.

Stage Fright: A Mini Laboratory

Want to get rid of stage jitters? The secret is to feel them ahead of time. A couple of us invented this working one year before singing a new song at the talent show. The singer quickly experiences a whole range of audience responses, has nervous reactions to them – and moves on.

No prep needed – you just need a partner or two. Larger group, split into triads. Allow five minutes per person plus a few minutes for transition.

One person is the singer (or any performer – we'll say singer here). The others are listeners.

Singer – sit or stand comfortably, ready to perform. Use your actual performance, or choose a song or chant that you enjoy singing. Your task is to sing your song (or read you poem, do your dance, etc) for the listener – and fully experience whatever emotions come up. When you feel irritated, nervous, amused, upset, hopeless, etc – stop singing and stay with the emotion. The point is to feel the emotions, not to plow through the song. If you find yourself laughing, yawning, crying, sighing, groaning – you're doing great! Just let it flow.

Listeners – sit or stand face to face with the singer, a little closer than is comfortable. You will display all sorts of responses to the singer, about 10 seconds each. For example: (1) adoring attention, (2) boredom and yawning, (3) start asking the singer a question about the song, (4) start applauding joyously, (5) say in a flat voice, "That's really great, good job," (6) start singing along, but out of tune or the wrong words, (7) scoot in really close to the singer without touching them, and so on. Try different ways until you get a response from the singer. Then:

Listeners – whenever the singer stops singing, switch to supporting any emotions they are having. If they are laughing or crying, just sit with them. However, if they stop singing and start talking, encourage them to go back to singing. For more on this, see Workings: Non-Judgmental Listening.

After each person has a turn, take time to debrief. Talk for a minute apiece about what came up, and what you learned.

End with some affirmation – a hug (always good to ask first), or perhaps each person says one word of encouragement to the others. Take a moment and choose the word carefully – what will your gift of a single word be?

SOLO WORKINGS

Singing is one of those things that, like sleeping or dying, you have to do for yourself. Fortunately, practicing is fun. Dial up youtube, find your favorite old songs, and get to work!

Here are some magical voice workings you can do on your own:

How Could Anyone Ever Tell You?

You'll need a hand mirror, some privacy, and a connection to youtube or iTunes. Have your journal handy too.

Go online and find the song How Could Anyone Ever Tell You, sung by Elaine Silver. Listen until you can sing along (it's easy).

Ground and cast a simple circle. Invoke the mystery of your own voice. Touch your throat and gently ask your voice to work with you – promise to support it and believe in it.

Now look into your mirror and breathe. Just gaze for a moment. Then start the song and sing along. When it ends, start it over or put it on loop. If emotions come up, let them flow. There's no rush – this is your time. Most of us have old, deep messages

continued on next page

Workings

Voice Magic (pg 4)

that insist our voices are *not* beautiful, not whole, not a miracle.... It will take time to let go of these old, mistaken messages and get back in touch with our true voices.... How amazing when we stop and remember that every single voice is a miracle!

If this exercise works for you, stay with it as long as you can. Bookmark the song and return to it from time to time.

✪ **Book of Shadows** – finish by journaling for a while. Remember to devoke any allies and open the circle.

Mirror Singing

You'll need a hand mirror and some privacy. Have your journal handy too.

Ground and cast a circle. Call an ally or two – maybe a fearless animal? Finally, invoke your mirror – without looking into it, ask it to support your voice, and to work with you to unleash the magic of your voice.

Close your eyes and tone a bit, letting your voice wander freely. Go low, high, soft, loud – all with no strain. Try falsetto, try short bursts of notes. Try moments of silence in between the sounds.

Now pick up the mirror.

Amazing – gazing silently into the mirror, make a face that says, "You are so amazing!" Close your eyes, take a breath, and sing this line in your most operatic voice (make up an opera tune): "My voice is the most beautiful in the world!" Open your eyes and see if you can repeat it while giving your "amazing!" look (don't be surprised if it's hard). Try it a few times, then jot any thoughts in your journal.

Bored – now make a face that says, "This is so boring...." Close your eyes, take a breath, and sing a line from a song or chant you like. Open your eyes and repeat it using the bored expression. What thoughts come up? Jot them down in your journal.

Curious – make a curious face that says, "I wonder what my voice really sounds like?" Close your eyes, take a deep breath, and on the exhale let go of judgments about your voice. Do this a second time. Now take a breath and sing a simple, clear tone. Open your eyes and look into the mirror. What emotions do you see in your eyes? Try this a few times, then write in your journal.

Try a few other emotions if you wish. Then finish with this one:

Belief – make a face that says, "I think I can do this." Gaze into your eyes for a minute until you can really feel at least for a moment that it is possible – you can sing! Now, continuing to gaze into the mirror, sing a simple tone or song. See if you can hold this expression of belief – "I can do it." If your voice wavers, stop and let any emotions come up. Then close your eyes, take a breath, and begin this step again. Stay with this for a few minutes and see how long you can sing while believing in the possibility of your voice.

✪ **Book of Shadows** – after a few minutes, stop and write in your journal.

Finally, devoke what you invoked, including thanking the mirror for its support.

Singing with Support: Solo Version

Some of the beauty of this working is feeling each person take a risk and sing out (see page 318). Maybe you know a few friends who like singing and might want to try this exercise?

You can also work it as a solo exercise, as below.

Prep – you'll need private singing space; a music player and some trancey music; a hand mirror.

Choose music that is simple and "trancey" – music without words or virtuoso solos. Some ideas are new age meditation music, Sufi trance music (Qawwali), or electronic dance music. If you use your computer for music, cover the screen with a scarf to lessen distractions.

continued on next page

WORKINGS

Voice Magic (pg 5)

Alone or with One or Two Others:

As the music plays, try toning along with it – see if you can find one tone that you can just sing and hold, even as the rest of the music changes. Take your time until you have a tone that you can strongly hold as the music plays.

With the music still playing, practice getting softer and louder – then when you're ready, get a good breath, hold your note strong and steady, and turn the music down. Hold the tone for 10 seconds or so, then bring the music back up.

Try it a few times. Then stop and do a bit of sharing – with others or with your journal. What did it feel like to sing alone? To have the music come back in?

Now gaze into your mirror. Meet and hold your own eyes, letting go of judgment. When you can take a full breath without judgment, look at yourself and say with whatever strength you can give it: "I like my voice!" Continue gazing for a few seconds, and then say: "Thank you!"

Put the mirror down and try the exercise a few more times.

✪ **Book of Shadows** – write: "I like my voice" – then whatever you think next. Try automatic writing, keeping the pen moving no matter what comes out. Try filling a page with thoughts about your voice. What changes do you notice by the end of the page?

Close the working with a song that you enjoy. It could be a Pagan song (see end of Working above), or a favorite pop song – whatever makes you happy to sing along.

Singing in Tune: How to Practice

Singing in tune with other voices or instruments is a magical experience. Music consists of vibrations in the body and in the air. When our voice closely matches the pitch of another voice or instrument, the vibration is literally doubled. Instantly we feel a magical strengthening of our voice!

No one is born knowing how to sing "in tune" – ie, to sing exactly the same pitch as another tone. Some people seem to learn at a very young age. Others learn later.

Tone Deaf – no one (unless you have sustained a serious injury to the ears or brain) is "tone deaf." If you think you are, you simply haven't learned the magic of singing in tune. When you do, you will be amazed how powerful it feels.

However well we sing, we can benefit from practicing this skill – here's a fun way.

Need – an instrument that produces a clear, consistent pitch while you sing at the same time – a piano, guitar or ukulele is ideal.

Play a single note and listen. Just listen. Play the same note and listen again. Appreciate that note. Now play the note, then stop the sound and see if you can still clearly hear it in your head. Try this a few times – strike the note, then stop it and hear the pitch in your head.

Now, play the same single note, listen, and try to sing the same pitch you hear. Let your voice waver all it needs. Strike the note again as often as needed.

If you aren't sure, you probably do not quite have it – when you get it, you'll feel a strengthening. Take a break. Ask your voice to be your ally, and to work with you. Place your hand on your throat and let your voice know you appreciate its courage!

Try again – once you feel you are singing the same pitch, tone it steadily. Strike the note again and see if it still seems to match your voice. If so – repeat with a different pitch.

Sleep on it – if it doesn't feel like you're getting it, take a break for an hour or a day ("sleep on it") and try again.

If you're getting it, try the Singing with Support exercise above, which encourages you to hold tones longer. As you sing, listen for the strengthening feeling that comes when you are in tune.

Thank your voice – finish by thanking your voice. Take a drink of water and feel it slide past your voice box. Touch your throat and thank yourself for singing!

TeenEarthMagic.org

WORKINGS

Wand Crafting

INTENT

In Reclaiming and other magical traditions, the wand is the tool of Fire. The wand can direct and focus energy (think of the power of pointing at someone – and multiply that by the strength of your wand). It can be used to charge other workings (use your wand to zap things – see Workings: Zap).

It can be used to amplify energy for casting a circle or invoking Fire. The wand extends your hand and increases its energy as you draw a pentacle or make other magical gestures.

Wands are tools of transformation. The wand we're making will probably not turn people into newts. But try pointing it at your homework, then take a breath and demand that it be easier. Do this three times. It might work!

Any time we use a wand or any magical tool or working, remember the Law of Three-Fold Return – whatever energy we put into the world or toward other people has a way of returning on us three times (see Introduction: Curses).

SPACE/TIME/SIZE

Any number, depending on supplies (see Prep below). Space to spread out and do craft work. Allow at least 30 minutes, plus time and space afterward for glue or paint to dry.

PREP

Each person needs a wand-sized stick. Traditionally, people find their own stick (ask people to find and bring one to the class or ritual, and teachers bring extras). A wand is often the length from the inside of your elbow to the tip of your middle finger.

When you think you have found your stick or other object, take a breath, quiet your thoughts, and ask: "Are you my wand?" If you get a negative answer, keep looking. If you get no answer after a couple of tries, use your intuition – *is* this your wand?

Wands can be made of many objects – stones, seashells, metal rods, fountain pens.... You can do online research about the different magical qualities of various trees and materials. The important thing is to ask the material if it is your wand, as above.

Wand-decorating supplies might include: crystals; ribbon; beads and string; paint; fine-point pens for inscribing symbols; fine wire; glue.... Whittling knives and sandpaper are handy. Music might help cut down on chatter (try Reclaiming's Labyrinth Meditation Music – see Ritual Skills: Chants).

WORKING

People gather with their wand-sticks. Materials are laid out.

Priestess shares wand lore – what wands are good for, how they might be used, cautionary tales (see Intent section above).

Priestess leads short meditation on the power of wands and making a wand your own. People are holding their sticks as they meditate. Priestess invites people to envision their wand, to see what it looks and feels like.

Then, still in trance, people are invited to decorate their wands, mainly in silence.

When time is up, gather in a circle with wands. Hold them out for others to see. Go around and invite each person to say a word or phrase about their wand or the wand-making experience (remember the right to pass).

Song to charge wands: We Are the Power in Everyone; Rise with the Fire; Air Moves Us (includes all elements); Toning.

Finally, bring people fully out of trance by having them pat the edges of their body and say their name aloud three times.

SOLO WORKING

You can make a wand as above. How will you charge your wand? A song? Holding it over a candle or under running water?

WORKINGS

Younger Groups – Some Ideas

INTENT

In the early years of Teens Path at Witchlets, our campers were a younger bunch, ages 11-14. We had to grow our older teens a year at a time!

Our first challenge was bringing together a circle and engaging young people enough that they wanted to come back the following Summer. Here are some ideas we found helpful.

See also the essay, Teaching Magic to Teens, on pages 328-333 – the essay was written around the time we launched TEM, and reflects on working with younger groups.

PREP

Some of these workings have their own prep. Items in **Bold Caps** below have a page dedicated to it in the book (see index).

When possible, have a fire! Although it may be daytime and plenty warm, even a small fire gives your circle a center, and can be a part of many workings. If you're inside, how about a central altar with candles or twinkly lights?

WORKINGS & IDEAS

Keep things short and fast-paced. Don't spend too long on anything the first time you do it. If something catches on, bring it back, or create time outside of path / class – eg, **Collage** supplies or **Tarot** decks can remain available outside of path-time.

Negotiate about participation. We found that letting teens lead group games such as Two Truths and a Lie for the final 30 minutes worked as a trade for getting them to participate in the other 90 minutes of morning path. As a trade-off for teens taking part in evening rituals, we agreed that one of the evenings would be dedicated to teen-led games of Werewolf. Teachers can support youth leadership by taking part in these games. See Workings: Campfire Activities.

Make agreements about participation (showing up, respecting one another, right to pass, etc) – see **Intro: Agreements**.

Go with the flow. If everyone has wandered down by the creek as morning path gathers, join them and create sacred space there. If people are tossing pebbles in the creek, try weaving that into an invocation.

Be flexible. Let go of a cherished working or song if it isn't happening (maybe you can bring it back for a later path or ritual). Have backup activities planned in case there's extra time, or you have to scrap something that isn't working. Have a few simple **Cooperative Games** in mind.

Some Specific Ideas

Find simple, fun ways to create sacred space – eg, try **Pass the Knot** to cast the circle – have a stopwatch handy, as teens will want to break their own speed record! Also, see **Ritual Skills: Sacred Space: Quick Ways**.

Spectrums are great ways to get teens talking. Start light and work up to heavier questions.

Offer multiple choices of activities – some active, some more meditative. Try a **Stations Ritual** where several options are offered – participants go where they are called, not necessarily to all stations. How about an **Altar** made of the biggest branches, stones, etc that people can find and drag back?

Flashier, tangible magic works well (for bold items, see Workings) – **Charging with Fire & Flour,** reading **Tarot**, digging a hole and **Composting Headlines or Oppressions**, going on a night hike and **Night Sit**....

Rituals: Opening Night at Witchlets is a good example of a ritual developed for younger teens, with two simple but dramatic fire-workings.

The **Bead Ceremony** has proven a favorite year after year. Sometimes we do it early in the camp, so teens can wear their beads. Other years we do it on the last evening as a culmination of our work together.

WORKINGS

Zap – Charging Magical Objects

INTENT

Zapping is a fast, powerful way to charge magical objects, people, intentions, etc. The goal is for the entire group to make a big motion and a sharp sound at the same time.

We have zapped beads, writings, magical shields – and we've put people in the center who are making a commitment or a transition and zapped them. When two Witchlets teachers got married, we zapped their wedding rings during the ceremony.

SPACE/TIME/SIZE

Any number – the more people, the clumsier *and* more powerful this will get. We've done it with 25-30 people.

Room to circle – fire or altar in the center are fine. Takes one or two minutes – less after the group gets good at it!

PREP

No prep needed – but you'll want to practice this a bit if it's the first time a group does it.

WORKING

The sound is simple – "Zzzzaaaaap!" The timing is everything.

Gather in a circle and use your wand-fingers (or actual wands) to point at the object or person to be zapped. Already we'll feel power if we all point together.

Still pointing, rotate your arm down and all the way around (like a cricket pitcher), starting to make the "zzzzzz" sound.

As your arms and fingers come back around to point at the object again, everyone together finish the word: "Zzzzzzaaaaaap!"

With a little practice, you can hone your timing and get a sharp crack from the final sound – and you'll know that it worked!

SOLO WORKING

You can do this alone, although the fun is trying to get a bunch of people to do it exactly together.

ORGANIZING & RESOURCES

Resources, Organizing, & Miscellany

- Organizing a Family Camp
- Youth Organizing at Reclaiming Camps – History Notes
- Developing Young Adult Leadership
- Connecting with Teen Earth Magic & Other WitchCamps
- Reclaiming Musical, Activist, & Magical Resources
- Complete & Helpful Index To the Book
- Lots of Other Fun Stuff!

Want to organize a teens' magical retreat? TEM grew out of a Reclaiming family camp – the first TEM teachers and campers met at Teens Path at Witchlets in the Woods. Read on to learn more about organizing camps in the Reclaiming Tradition. Photo by Alla Irwin.

ORGANIZING & RESOURCES

Start with a Family Camp

Witchlets in the Woods was birthed by the desire to create a sacred space for Pagan families to come together and honor the gifts that witches of all ages bring to the world.

We create a place where families are surrounded by magic, where children and adults feel safe and free to step into their magical power. It is an opportunity for Pagan families of diverse kinds to build community resources and expand extended family.

This camp belongs to all of us – please step forward and volunteer!

– from Witchlets' mission statement

Want to Organize a Camp Like Teen Earth Magic?

Start with a family camp. Whether you're a teen, a community organizer, a parent, or an aspiring teen magic teacher, you'll find that getting families involved will be invaluable. Even if you're great at organizing camps, you'll need parents' support and trust. That won't come overnight. There's no better place to build that trust and support than at a family magic camp.

Teens may want their own camp – big surprise! – but first, draw families into creating a camp, and negotiate "teens space" within the camp. Within a family camp like Witchlets or Redwood Magic, teens tend to form a sub-community with their own morning path, evening campfire, dining hall tables, and late-night gatherings. (For more on this topic, see the section on Autonomous Teens Space in the essay Teaching Magic to Teens, below.)

While some parents have complained, "I come to a family camp and I barely see my teen," the flip side is the gradual development of a community of teens who are excited about attending a spiritual retreat.

Parents, teachers, and organizers can be allies to young people by supporting their desire for their own space within the camp and other community events. When we started looking for a site for our second family camp, Redwood Magic, one of our first questions was, "Is there a second fire circle for the teens?"

Next – A Teens Retreat?

When a family camp is thriving, teens and parents might want to try a weekend workshop. Things to consider: Will teens show up? Who will help with meals and rides? Can you find teachers to dedicate their time? Is an affordable site available?

Reclaiming teens take part in family camps such as Redwood Magic and Witchlets – which in turn serve as the larger container that holds Teen Earth Magic.

An alternative is weaving a teens retreat into a family camp. Maybe your Teens Path can hike away from the main encampment for a few days at a nearby site?

TEM Teachers For Your Camp?

Maybe you want to pool resources and bring TEM teachers to visit – a TEM workshop might spark ongoing teens organizing!

You're also welcome to use this handbook to create the event and program that's right for your community. (Please do not present the event as "Teen Earth Magic" unless TEM-trained folks are involved – thanks!)

Organizing Resources

On the following page you'll find resources for organizing a family camp. Or visit:

WeaveAndSpin.org/resources

ORGANIZING & RESOURCES

Family Camp Resources

Starting a Camp!

Want to start a camp for your own group or tradition? Best wishes! See the Witchlets Manual and other resources on our website – WeaveAndSpin.org/resources.

Want to start a **Reclaiming Tradition camp** in your area, or link your camp to our network? Start by attending one of our camps, where you'll meet teachers and organizers and get a feel for Reclaiming's ever-evolving culture – visit WitchCamp.org for camp info as well as contacts for the WitchCamp Council.

To be a Reclaiming camp, you'll need at least a couple of Reclaiming-trained teachers (who in turn can help train local teachers for your community). Maybe you already know them? Or contact us to find teachers in your area.

Visit WitchCamp.org, or email TeenEarthMagic@gmail.com.

Bring TEM Teachers to Your Event

Already doing a camp or other event? Whether it's a retreat, workshop, conference, or class, TEM teachers can anchor offerings for youth and/or adults and bring fresh inspiration and deep Earth magic to your event. Weave your community into the Teen Earth Magic web!

Email us at TeenEarthMagic@gmail.com.

Over the years, Witchlets teens have grown into young adults. Some have stayed part of camp, helping pass along the magic to a new generation!

Witchlets Organizing Manual & More Camp Resources

Starting a new camp or retreat doesn't have to mean reinventing the logistical wheel. We've learned our craft from others, and gladly pass along our lessons.

Visit our Organizing Resources page, where you'll find manuals, forms, and other stuff we've found useful, including:

Witchlets organizing manual – timeline, tasks and roles, waivers, camp culture guidelines, and more – a complete how-to manual.

Redwood Magic camper packet – the PDF we send to campers a few weeks before camp – bring-list, camp culture guidelines, info about schedule and kitchen, map and directions....

Promo cards and brochures – samples.

Waivers and forms – liability and medical waiver, photo release, ethics agreement.

Group process resources – consensus, feminism, nonhierarchy, dealing with sexism, racism, homophobia, and more.

Find these and more online at:

WeaveAndSpin.org/resources

ORGANIZING & RESOURCES

Teaching Magic to Teens

Early Experiments at Witchlets, Vermont, & Loreley Camps

by George Franklin

Written in 2009 – references to camp years are relative to 2009. This was after about half-dozen years of Witchlets Teens Path, and just as we launched Teen Earth Magic.

Our experiences at this point were with younger teens. As we've grown a community of older teens and young adults, we've developed new practices and woven these folks into organizing our camp. See Organizing: Mentors.

I stand on the edge of a four-foot porch with my back to the group of teenagers. My heels are at their eye level. They are arrayed in two lines behind me, arms outstretched to form a web six feet long. Exactly my height.

Whose idea was this? Oh, yeah – mine. I had this idea that our Youth Path at Loreley WitchCamp might form tighter bonds if we did some trust exercises.

Of course, the Reclaiming teacher (Riyana) who taught me this "trust fall" emphasized that if I asked the teens to do the exercise, they'd expect the same of me.

So here I am, trusting a bunch of teenagers to catch me. We're talking about young folks age 10-15, none taller than my shoulders, backed up by two adult teachers.

I steady myself and glance back. Petra, my co-teacher, recites the final instructions for forming the web. I can feel the teens' energy brace behind me.

Summoning a breath from above and below, I recite my mantra, which I honed earlier in the Spring when I accompanied some kids to Great America amusement park (a daredevil I am not): "Where there's fear there's power!"

"Ready when you are," speaks Petra. I suck in one more breath, remembering to keep my body stiff. Then I drop backward.

The fall begins in slow motion, gaining momentum as I plunge toward the Earth. Suddenly, in a whoosh of air, I tumble into the line of teens. Their line wavers and dips, then holds. With a shout of joy I come to rest, cradled in a web of arms.

   *   *   *

Months later, it is one of my favorite memories from Loreley WitchCamp – being held by the teens in our Youth Path – and feeling how our path was held by the larger circles of Loreley Camp and all of Reclaiming.

Teaching Magic to Teens?

Teaching magic to teenagers? I didn't think that would be my vocation in my 50s. But teaching Teens Paths and workshops has been my richest experience in recent years. It is amazing to see the young people of Reclaiming, who have been raised with such awareness and openness, growing and stepping into leadership in camps and in the wider world.

For me, this work is very part-time. I'm not a parent or real-world teacher. I've co-taught Teens Path at Witchlets (CA) for seven years, Loreley Camp (Northern Europe) for two, Vermont Camp in '08, and Pixie Path at Free Activist Camp one Summer. Before that – 30 years ago – I worked in a Presbyterian youth camp for several summers. And I cut my teeth at Boy Scout camps in my own teens.

My goal – that teens come to a spiritual retreat with their families, go through personal changes they never imagined – and want to come back. I figure if we can pull off this feat, the rest will follow in due course.

What does it mean to teach magic to teens? Well, to date, none of our students has successfully levitated anyone, no one has been transmogrified via magic wands, and no additional appendages have been grown due to curses or spells.

When working with teens, I'd consider "magic" a synonym for self-awareness, transformation, and empowerment. The skills we teach help young folks to be more grounded and authentic in their daily lives, to be more open and trusting with one another, and fearlessly to pursue their dreams.

What sorts of skills? Not everything works. Grounding seems like a useful talent, but I haven't had much luck teaching it to young teens. Experienced adults can do a five-minute grounding (I admit, I lose focus after that...). But few younger teens make it to the 60-second point without looking bored and agitated – not exactly the mindset we're trying to foster.

Similarly, circle casting and invoking elements and deity – the core of my daily practice – seem like formalities to some younger teens, who may learn the correct motions and correspondences, but seem mostly uninspired by these practices.

continued on next page

ORGANIZING & RESOURCES

Teaching Magic to Teens (pg 2)

Early Experiments at Witchlets, Vermont, & Loreley Camps

Tangible Magic

Our experience is that younger teens are drawn to tangible magic – tarot, labyrinths, cauldrons. They like physical workings more than interior processes such as grounding or invoking. Rather than fight against this tendency, we've looked for ways to work with it.

Tarot – we use tarot as a mirror for self-reflection. Our approach is intuitive, encouraging teens to look at the cards and develop their own stories and meanings (Rider-Waite-Smith and Inner Child are good decks for this). Tarot is a tangible, visual tool for young folks who are starting to ask questions such as, "Who am I?" and, "What is my life about?" As much as anything, the cards slow us down for a moment so we have space to reflect.

Labyrinths – labyrinths have provided the basis for more complex workings. Teens walk partway into the labyrinth, where they are met with a challenge which they must exit and undertake. On returning, they circle further into the labyrinth and receive another challenge, until after several challenges they reach the center. We have built entire workshops around this sort of structure (see Rituals: Labyrinth Challenges).

Fire – as a rule of thumb in Teens Path: when in doubt, burn something. Write down personal blocks and burn them to release the block. Write down a pledge and burn it to raise energy. Place a stick in the fire to signify a commitment. And it's hard to go wrong with the drama of a flaming cauldron.

Animal allies – inspired by the teachings of Michael Harner, we've done "animal ally" work at our camps. Animal allies may be a stepping stone toward working with deities as allies. When one of the teens told me her favorite deity is Bast, an Egyptian Goddess often portrayed as a cat, I could see the possibilities.

Trust games – group-building games and trust exercises have worked well. As ways to include play, physical contact, movement, and laughter, they form part of each day's flow. Cumulatively these exercises have helped build group cohesion.

Ecology and nature awareness – this is great material for teens, and we incorporate it into our paths, particularly in connection with the elements.

Handfasting invocation at Witchlets 2018 – photo by Alla Irwin.

Autonomous Teens Space

How integrated are the teens in camp, and especially in all-camp rituals – the core of the magic for many adults? This has been an ongoing discussion.

My sense is, many teens want and need separate space at WitchCamp and other Reclaiming events. This was certainly true for me as a young person, active in a Congregationalist (liberal Protestant) church. Our Youth Room, which we painted and decorated ourselves, was off limits to adults other than our young-adult advisors. While we were not allowed to hang out there during church services, it was still our retreat space during coffee hour, Sunday evening activities, etc.

As I will recount below, a separate teens space at Witchlets developed because many teens were skipping the all-camp rituals and campfire anyway. It's not as if the teens were taking part and we somehow whisked them away.

continued on next page

ORGANIZING & RESOURCES

Teaching Magic to Teens (pg 3)

Early Experiments at Witchlets, Vermont, & Loreley Camps

At Loreley Camp, the teens have an option to leave evening rituals after the invocations and go to their own campfire. Most do, and some nights it's a mass exodus at that point. One adult called it peer pressure, but that misses what's happening. It isn't pressure – it's a desire on the part of teens to be with each other in a space that feels like their own. If we want teens at WitchCamps and other activities, I think we have to provide this sort of "autonomous space" option.

Does this mean giving up all-ages activities? I don't think so. When we find the right event, integration happens naturally. At the 2009 Faerie Ball fundraiser in Berkeley, we set up a teens chill space (which the young folks had requested) – but during most of the evening, the teens were on the dance floor along with the adults (it didn't hurt to have a youth DJ for part of the evening).

From some parents and organizers, I hear a desire to have the teens more integrated into rituals and the wider workings of camp. I'd encourage interested adults to organize workshops and other activities and invite teens to participate. Experiment and see what will work with specific groups of young folks.

My experience is that most of our all-ages rituals don't speak to a lot of young people after about age 10. And that's not going to change by tinkering with a few parts of the ritual.

If I wanted a typical 13-year-old to take enthusiastic part in a Reclaiming ritual, I would plan it for about five years from now, when they're 18. Some young adults are excited by what we do in ritual. A lot of younger teens are not. We can go with this flow and develop autonomous teen activities, or we can fight it and drive teens away.

Witchlets in the Woods (California)

Although Witchlets sounds like a kids' camp, we have had a large and vibrant Teens Path for years.

Teens Path at Witchlets grew out of a perceived need in the first couple of years of camp (2001-02) – workshop

offerings attracted mainly younger kids. The dozen or so kids over age 10 didn't take much part. So for 2003, organizers invited Jonathan, Seed, and me to create a morning path for ages 10-up.

Our first year was spotty. Trying to cater to a wide range of ages, interests, and attention spans, we at least succeeded in holding the group together for the three mornings of path. But I wouldn't say that it was a big success.

In the evenings that year, we again saw the familiar dynamic – adults and younger kids gathered around the

continued on next page

Photos

At Witchlets 2018, one of our longtime Witchlets / Redwood Magic / Teen Earth Magic young adults asked the camp, and especially the youth, to co-create a handfasting ritual for her and her partner. Photos by Alla Irwin.

ORGANIZING & RESOURCES

Teaching Magic to Teens (pg 4)

Early Experiments at Witchlets, Vermont, & Loreley Camps

night campfire for singalongs, story-telling, and general camaraderie. Meanwhile, the teens were seldom to be seen, preferring to hang out in their cliques of two or three.

We were wondering what we might do to bring the teens together, when they did our job for us. We heard a rumor that on the final night of camp some of them were going off into the woods to experiment with "fireballs." Seeing as how this was California in the peak dry season, it didn't seem like a great idea. But we hated to squelch their plans.

Our solution was to ask if a couple of the teen teachers could come along. Co-teacher Jonathan knew what fireballs were – a cigarette lighter trick – and we wound up hiking into the woods with the entire teen group to find a gravel island in the middle of the creek where we could play with lighters.

A good time was had by all, and thus was born the teens night campfire. The following year, we proposed to camp organizers that the teens have a separate evening fire at a smaller fire circle about 50 yards through the woods from the main lodge and campfire. Since the teens weren't taking part in the main evening fire anyway, we got the go-ahead.

To make a long story short – the evening fire became the center of the teens' experience. It became a place where all teens could gather, where no one was left out. Teachers were present, but didn't guide all the activities. The group spirit that developed at the night fire carried over and made our morning path more cohesive. It's my sense that this separate space played a key role in the teens' feeling that Witchlets is "their" camp.

After six years, the Witchlets teens have bonded strongly, yet the group remains porous enough that each year new campers are welcomed into the circle (in recent years we've had about two dozen teens, with five to six new folks each year).

Our magical work has grown from doing short, simple elemental invocations to doing deep trances and oracle work. One year, the teens did a tarot salon where they offered readings to adults at camp.

The Witchlets teens are spread across Northern California, and it takes parental driving to bring folks together. When I see them at events like Spiral Dance and the Faerie Ball, I know they have made a real effort to attend, and I am struck by the emotional charge at these mini-reunions.

In recent years, a mid-year teens class has been offered – Labyrinths one year, Pearl Pentacle and a nonviolent activism prep in others. We plan to do more classes, beginning with a tarot workshop this Fall. One of our goals is to get a variety of Bay Area teachers involved in offering classes for teens.

Witchlets has grown from a family retreat to become a cornerstone of the Northern California Reclaiming community. The teen

Handfasting ceremony at Witchlets 2018 – photo by Alla Irwin.

continued on next page

ORGANIZING & RESOURCES

Teaching Magic to Teens (pg 5)

Early Experiments at Witchlets, Vermont, & Loreley Camps

presence at the Faerie Ball in 2009 showed the sort of multi-generational community the Bay Area has become, largely thanks to Witchlets.

In recent years there has been more involvement of older teens in all-camp rituals at Witchlets, although many teens still skip the rituals.

Witchlets is still a large and vibrant camp – and in 2013 spawned a second family camp, Redwood Magic.

Vermont WitchCamp

I co-taught Youth Path with Hannah at Vermont Camp in 2008. This path, for ages 10-16, was in its third year (Charles and Alphonsus taught in previous years). Vermont Camp is all-ages, and in addition to Youth Path also offers a Pixie Path for younger kids. There were about 10 kids in each path, in a camp of 120 people.

Our 2008 youth path was similar to those described above. We added an overnight camping expedition, which taught me that I need to learn more campfire games. And we worked with a myth – Ariadne and Theseus – through the entire week.

Vermont teens were more involved in all-camp rituals than at other camps I've seen. We offered a separate campfire, as at Loreley and Witchlets, but it was only sporadically attended. I think this is partly a matter of personalities, and could be different in other years. But I'd say as of 2008, Vermont ritual-organizers had learned how to work with all ages in ways I hadn't seen at other camps.

The Vermont teens tended to clump together at rituals (true also at Bay Area rituals such as the Spiral Dance). I think this is related to the "autonomous space" issue above, and we might look at how to anticipate and work with this dynamic at rituals involving youth.

At Vermont, this clumping had an occasional drawback – when an adult decided to play "Puck" at a ritual, they found a convenient audience for their antics. Nothing like a game of "Sausage" during a trance to spice up a ritual.

Before camp started, organizers told me that the Youth Path was originally (after much discussion) consensed as a three-year experiment, and 2008 was the "year of decision."

In the final camp feedback circle, the agenda set aside a good bit of time for evaluation of youth participation in future Vermont camps. While I knew most people were supportive, I went into the meeting feeling apprehensive.

My worries were unfounded. Several teens spoke strongly about their experiences at camp. Numerous adults spoke in support.

The deal was clinched when an older camper spoke in a choked voice about how he had originally opposed including youth in the camp, but had come to see how much richer his experience had become because of their presence – a sentiment echoed by many in the circle.

Vermont Camp welcomes young people with their families.

Loreley WitchCamp (North Europe)

Loreley WitchCamp, in Northern Europe, began as an adults-only camp. Heading into its third year (2006), organizers decided to add a Youth Path for folks age 10 and up. I came over to help teach, along with two Loreley organizers, Petra and Anje.

To a small camp with about 30 adult campers, we added a dozen kids age 10-15. Unlike Witchlets, the young people were not the focus of the camp, but simply a sub-group of the larger circle.

The beauty and magic that youth added to the camp was undeniable. As we've seen at Witchlets in the Woods, the sheer presence of young people at a camp adds an "historical" dimension – our future is literally underfoot.

Having teens at WitchCamps has raised issues of how much and when teens would participate in various activities. For instance, teens under 16 have their own morning path, and their own affinity group (support group). There have been concerns about youth presence at rituals dealing with "adult" material such as abuse, death, or sex.

But concerns also come from the teens themselves. The first year, we talked with the Loreley youth about taking part in the evening rituals. It was clear that given the option, most would prefer going to their own campfire once the invocations were over. In other words, they mostly

continued on next page

ORGANIZING & RESOURCES

Teaching Magic to Teens (pg 6)

Early Experiments at Witchlets, Vermont, & Loreley Camps

opted out of the "core working" of the rituals. As with Witchlets, the evening fire became an important venue for group bonding.

We have tried a couple of all-camp rituals where we asked the teens to take full part. These have been shorter, and involved things like small groups (the teens formed their own group) or "roving meditations" that let folks move around at will for most of the working. These rituals had some success in engaging teens in the ritual workings, and they have taught us some lessons for future years.

The lack of interest in rituals doesn't show an indifference to magic. The morning Youth Path was very magically focused. Several participants had strong magical backgrounds, so we weren't starting from scratch. Also, Loreley is a full-week camp, and I have been amazed at how much deeper we are able to go with five days of path (versus three at Witchlets). As discussed above, tarot, labyrinths, and animal allies have been successful ways of engaging the young Loreley teens.

Language has presented a special problem. Loreley Camp was conducted in English, but not all of the teens were fluent, meaning that we had to express everything in three or even four languages. This made discussions, check-ins, and other full-group sharing practices nearly impossible. A particular challenge was coming up with games and exercises that didn't depend on language skills. We found silent trust-exercises powerful with this group.

Considering that including teens was an experiment in 2006, Teens Path took solid root after two years. It's impossible to imagine Loreley WitchCamp without young folks.

Sadly, Loreley Camp is no longer active.

Conclusion

What's next? More of the same, if I'm lucky.

Here in California, local / regional workshops are possible, thanks to the support of parents and allies. For other places, WitchCamp may be the one opportunity each year to gather. A challenge is how to support teens in pursuing solitary or small-group magic in between camps.

To anyone with ideas for teaching magic to teens, I'd say start talking to the teens and parents. I've been amazed how responsive young folks are when they realize that we really want to share magic with them. Our paths at Witchlets and Loreley evolved because a few people took a leap and announced plans. May it happen elsewhere!

Drop us a line if you have feedback or want to share experiences and thoughts from other camps, classes, Pagan home schooling, etc.

Contact us at ReclaimingQuarterly@gmail.com.

Thanks for inspiration and support to my co-teachers and planners in these early years – Petra, Anje, Seed, Lyra, Jonathan, Riyana, April, Rebecca, Jason, Lucy, Allison, Hannah.

And thanks to the Weavers and Spinners (organizers) at the family-inclusive Reclaiming camps!

Otters (young adults) share deep magic at Witchlets 2018 – photo by Alla Irwin.

ORGANIZING & RESOURCES

Teen Earth Magic: Our Story

Notes for a Future History

Teen Earth Magic began when teachers, parents, and campers who had been part of Witchlets in the Woods family camp decided to organize an Earth-based teen retreat in late 2007.

We started with a one-day labyrinth workshop at a site near Nevada City, CA. Five teens attended, and we felt inspired to try an overnight retreat the following Summer.

The first year, a dozen teens explored Earth magic (including a composting ritual – see Workings: Shadow: Composting Headlines), visited the Yuba River, did daily rituals, and built group bonds.

We also learned important lessons such as how hot Nevada City is in July!

The Early Years

In 2009, 24 teens and young adults gathered in mid-June and worked with the life story of the Salmon, native inhabitants of Northern California's rivers and creeks.

A core teaching team developed that helped carry the camp through the next half-dozen years.

2010 again drew two dozen teens and young adults for the Pentacle of the Great Turning, inspired by the work of Joanna Macy (see pages 252-254). Older teens began assisting with leading exercises and ritual planning.

2011-2016 worked with themes such as the Journey of the Bard, the Life of the Butterfly, and Sweet Magic of the Beehive (see page 98).

Teens Take Over

Beginning around our fourth year, we felt a shift away from a teaching team that planned most of the paths and rituals to increasing camper involvement in creating and offering workshops, optional offerings, and even entire rituals.

This gradually grew into our Mentors program for young people age 18-24 (see next article).

A notable area of growth around this time (2010ff) was young people's awareness of the complexities of gender, including multi-gender workshops and rituals. Some teachers had to work hard to keep pace with the rapid evolution of gender ideas and practices among our campers (read more about this in Intro: Gender Issues).

Current Topics

As we go to press in Spring 2019, here are some of the issues that we're discussing at TEM meetings:

- Relations to the specific land we are on and its ownership / relations with First People of that land.

Nurturing our seeds – a magical working at Teen Earth Magic 2010.

- Bringing more practical training into morning paths, and then using new skills in evening rituals.
- Space to talk about mixed race / people of color (POC) identity at camp.
- Develop Mentor Path more / student-teaching plan.
- Hearth – integrating hearth (kitchen) more with camp.
- Opening up space for teens to explore why stuff is important instead of just saying, "this is important."
- Incorporating animism / the aliveness of all things / listening to the land.
- Teaching team – decide ahead of time who's taking a break on what day – and bring back morning of repose!

ORGANIZING & RESOURCES

Mentors: Young Adults & Student Teachers

Creating a Post-Teen Path

When we began Older Kids' Path at Witchlets in 2003, our oldest teen was 14. The next year, with kids ages 10-15, we had a 17-year-old as part of our teaching team.

Over the years, Teen Earth Magic has helped grow a group of older teens and young adults which has opened new possibilities for our camps and for the wider community.

As teens aged out of TEM, we invited them to return as "mentors" and help create the camp. Some of these folks also help teach younger kids at our family camps.

Eventually some of the mentors were ready – or rather demanded! – to be part of the teaching team. As we pass our tenth year of TEM, several former campers are part of our teaching and organizing team, and several middle teens are helping organize TEM and Witchlets.

The latest step – TEM "graduates" have begun student teaching in Bay Area Reclaiming core classes.

Supporting young adult leadership

One TEM teacher says: "Our job is to teach ourselves out of a job." Our goal is that young people learn to organize camp, teach workshops, lead rituals, anchor the kitchen, dig the trench toilets, etc.

Each year we see new ways that young people are taking leadership and responsibility, bringing power and depth to the camp – and by extension to our other camps and the wider Reclaiming community.

What is a mentor?

A mentor is a young adult age 18-24 who is part of Teen Earth Magic, Witchlets, or Redwood Magic camps and takes on responsibilities of priestessing, planning, vibes-watching, and/or mentoring for younger campers and the wider community. Mentors might be student teachers, help in the hearth, plan and take notes in rituals, run an awesome workshop or game during optional offering time, or many other roles.

The word "mentor" is a recognition of the power that older teens / young adults hold in setting the tone of camp, and the responsibilities that come with that power. It's also a reflection of our desire to support people in their transition toward adulthood.

Mentors participate in all aspects of camp. For some activities they circle with their own age group.

How are mentors different from campers?

Like teachers, mentors are "on-call" to help with camp work. Whether it's improvising an invocation or taking an extra dishwashing shift, mentors help the camp happen.

How do people become mentors?

Mentors are mainly recruited by invitation among past participants in Witchlets and Teen Earth Magic. The role was created partly as a way for post-teens to continue to participate in our camps.

People can also be recommended by TEM teachers and organizers, other Reclaiming organizers, and/or parents.

What requirements are there for mentors?

Age 18-up. Prior experience in Reclaiming or at a similar camp. Recommendation of a TEM teacher or organizer, another Reclaiming teacher or organizer, or a TEM parent. Short interview with a current teacher. Willingness to work within group process and boundaries, and to give legal contact information on camp registration form. No past legal or disciplinary issues regarding minors.

Mentors are welcome to attend meetings through the year as organizers, but it's not required. All mentors are expected to attend the final pre-camp meeting to discuss roles and ethics.

Mentor Training & Ethics Agreement

Our teacher / mentor training prior to camp includes an ethics component. The training was created in consultation with Alexis Lezin, a therapist and youth-camp consultant. It is still possible for a mentor to withdraw at this point, or for organizers to express concerns and/or ask someone to withdraw before camp begins.

Mentors (as well as teachers and all adults on site) read and sign an Ethics Agreement stating that they understand and will abide by camp policies and California law as it pertains to our camp and community (see Ethics Agreement on page 337).

The pre-camp training has a section specifically devoted to explaining camp policies and California law. Mentors are informed and agree that boundaries with younger campers (under 18) extend beyond the dates of camp.

Contact us at TeenEarthMagic@gmail.com

ORGANIZING & RESOURCES

TEM Teachers: A Roundtable

Why do post-teens spend their vacations volunteering with TEM?

What calls you to this work?

Vesper: I keep coming back to TEM and Witchlets because of how loving, supportive, and amazingly creative the community is! TEM inspires me to step more fully into who I am.

Lyra: I grew up in Reclaiming, and I see how deeply ritual and camp experiences have impacted my growth as an individual. I want to perpetuate this work and add to it as I learn and collect ideas, tools, and sacred truths from the wider world. The experimental nature of our working and teaching process is exciting and expansive – it allows me room to come and go, to grow frustrated and inspired, as needed in my life. I feel free to be myself, and I feel my self is valued.

Jason: Seeing a group of boys at Witchlets who were not engaging, I could see the discontinuity in Reclaiming. I like the idea of continuity through all stages of life.

Penskee: Working with teens is fun (and not as stressful as working with adults). With TEM, the process – how we decide the structure of camp or rituals – feels like part of the work and the magic. We're learning together how to make decisions, share ideas, and communicate. I am a teacher, yet I am continuously taught by our camp.

Briar: I'm drawn by overlapping visions for our communities and the Earth. I'm drawn by the intimate scale of TEM. Navigating 30 people's needs is more sustainable than 100-plus!

What gives you hope in your wider life?

Lyra: People give me hope. Despair is available to me everywhere, but people continue to surprise me when we make ourselves vulnerable, when we perceive and break old patterns, when we create together, when we love with abandon. The longer I live and the more I grow, the broader my perspective becomes, allowing me to catch sight of hope in more and more surprising places.

Penskee: I am continually awed and inspired by the teens and young adults I work with. My wonder and interest in the world has grown through my involvement with TEM. I have seen again and again that science and magic do not have to be at odds, and that truth and guidance lie somewhere there between. This fuels my optimism for the future not only for our tradition but also humanity. It's going to be one wild ride, and I can hear our teens laughing along the way!

George: Pop music. Just when I think I've heard everything and it's all boring, along comes a sound that is so perfect for that moment. It's a reminder that new and amazing things are continually happening.

Vesper: Every act of loving service gives me hope. Every kind thought, every kind word. Every time someone is inspired to do the hard work to overcome challenges and make their dreams happen. These actions plant seeds for a better way to live and breathe and be on this planet.

Briar: The Earth gives me hope! And the stars, and kids, and faith – that sense of something generously connecting everything. Working with people, with the inevitability of surprise, while sometimes very challenging, gives me hope.

Jason: Young people. I feel a lot of sorrow, too. I talk with my kids, and they often don't understand how dire the situation is. I feel like it's my responsibility to remain hopeful. I need to be able to be there for them, to believe that there is a better future ahead of us.

TEM Weavers busting out – camp organizers and teachers for 2019!

ORGANIZING & RESOURCES

Ethics Agreement

Code of Ethics & Agreements for Facilitators, Mentors, & Onsite Adults

Teen Earth Magic includes a Mentors program for ages 18-24, to weave a new generation of teachers and organizers.

Our training for mentors and facilitators (teachers) includes a discussion of ethics, boundaries, and legalities when working with young people, following which people are asked to sign this agreement.

Facilitators and teachers in the Reclaiming Tradition are people who take on a sacred responsibility – the mantle of nurturing the spiritual development of individual youth and creating a healthy container for the youth community as a whole.

Whether we take on mentorship in active roles as teachers and facilitators, or whether we help "priestess from the sidelines" by providing one-on-one counseling or providing service with our hands and hearts to the camp, our position of being adults within the youth community carries with it a special energy that can help our younger friends develop a strong sense of self and a spirit of independence and pride. This special energy is power.

One of the most important areas of growth for young people is their sense of self-worth and the development of a healthy identity as a sexual being. In order to help cultivate these beautiful and important qualities in a young person, we must allow them to grow and develop in ways that are healthy for them in the long term.

The relationship between young people and the adults in their lives must be one of power-with and mutual respect if the positive potential of that relationship is to be realized. Facilitators, teachers, and adults who abuse that power and engage in inappropriate relationship dynamics with young people -- especially where sexuality is involved -- hurt not only the individuals involved, but the whole community.

Our camp expects that facilitators, mentors, and on-site adults understand:

- There are federal and state laws that prohibit sexual intimacy between people of some ages, and if those laws are broken, it puts the entirety of our camp at risk of permanent closure. California has some of the strictest laws about this in the nation: legally, people age 18 and over are not allowed to engage in sexual activity with anyone under the age of 18.

- Above and beyond what California state law requires of us, it is important that all facilitators, mentors, and on-site adults be in their integrity in regards to sexual behavior, physical and / or verbal abuse, the use of adulterating substances, and their power as a role model within the youth community. We expect strict adherence by all adults to our "no drugs or alcohol" agreements.

Our intention is to create a container that is sex-positive and healthy for everyone in our camp community – one that is empowering for people of every age, sexual preference, and gender. We do not in any way want to bolster the sexual oppression that is so prevalent in our dominant culture, nor do we want anyone to feel repressed in expressing their healthy sexuality or the power that comes from deep within us all. As witches and Pagans, we embrace both sexuality and power as our sacred birthrights and as a guiding force in our lives.

We challenge ourselves to take the good road as we examine issues of power, sexuality, and integrity. At times the good road is rocky, unclear, and requires slow and careful navigation. If at any point you have a question about what is the most positive and healthy action for yourself, for the camp, and for our younger comrades in a given circumstance, we strongly encourage you to find an ally or group of allies to talk to. If for some reason you do not feel like you can talk to us about the situation you are in, that's a pretty good sign that there are issues of integrity involved and it's especially important that you find someone to talk to right away.

By signing below, I agree that I have read and understand and agree to abide by the Code of Ethics for Facilitators, Mentors, and On-Site Adults. I understand that if my behavior is such that my adherence to this Code of Ethics is called into question, appropriate action will be taken. This may include mediation, being asked to leave, or legal recourse if necessary.

Legal Name: _____

Legal Signature: _____

Date of Birth: _____

Today's Date: _____

Social Security or CDL Number: _____

Magical Name or Camp Name: _____

ORGANIZING & RESOURCES

TEM Organizing Wheel of the Year

Initially organized by a small group of teachers, TEM is now co-created by a circle of teachers, young adult mentors (some of whom are also teachers – it gets complicated!), and older campers. This calendar shows how we try to get the organizing done. It's based on a camp held in June.

Meeting 1 (July)
Post-Camp Feedback – hopes and changes
Post-camp financial report
New weavers volunteer / community consenses

Meeting 2 (September)
Invite new people interested in weaving or spinning
Organizing structure and roles (go over summaries, decide what roles to use, fill those roles)
Review wheel of the year / annual timeline
Site options and dates – schedule if possible
Spiral Dance planning and teen outreach
Set date for Spring retreat and/or fundraiser if possible

Meeting 3 (November)
Fill roles – weavers, spinners, specific year-round tasks
Retreat and fundraiser planning – determine focus of event(s) – set intentions
Outreach – plan timeline for TEM and events
Hearth (kitchen) – find anchor(s); review responsibilities
Confirm or discuss site and date / make deposits
Ideas for new / returning teachers and mentors
Teacher / mentor curriculum – coming year and long-term

Meeting 4 (January)
Decide on theme / story – choose anchors for ritual-arc team
Outreach to possible new teachers and mentors
Outreach and registration, materials
Send out reg pamphlet / announce to Reclaiming lists
Finances check-in / forming a budget
Retreat / fundraiser check in
Plan conversations re teaching ethics / power dynamics (to be held at future meetings)

Retreat and/or Fundraiser – February-March?

Meeting 5 (March)
Finalize story arc, brainstorm re: paths and rituals – decide how morning paths and evening rituals will relate
Plan camp schedule aka "The Grid" (see next page)
Hearth (kitchen) – anchors, finances
Finalize teaching team and mentors to extent possible
Divide days for teaching path / leading ritual
Discuss – how much is each of us capable of doing? Plan at-camp breaks, teacher-circles, communications.
Begin filling at-camp roles
Organizer conversations before and at camp:
• Teaching ethics and power dynamics
• How to exercise compassionate authority
• Flow from camper / mentor / spinner / weaver?
• Issues such as racism, supporting diversity, appropriation
• Communications and connections with local Indigenous people – possible pre-camp or at-camp workshop?

Meeting 6 (May) – main camp business meeting
Create feedback form
Finalize path and ritual teams, new teachers and mentors
Big chart – each person sign up (not for too much!)
Having gaps in the chart is okay – leave room for mentors, campers, and for spontaneity at camp
Finalize grid – times for ritual and path planning at camp
Brainstorm additional at-camp activities, optional offerings and workshops, possible guest teachers
Plan at-camp conversations with whole group:
• Race and Reclaiming
• Power dynamics
• Why do we care about the things we care about?
• Boundaries and allies
• Engaging with the land
Finalize camp roles – including youth weavers / spinners / mentors

Meeting 7 (June) – everyone age 18-up
Final pre-camp planning – small groups plan opening day, evening ritual, and first morning path
Ethics & boundaries discussions / training
Roles at camp – rituals, path, hearth, logistics – all help!
Review grids and charts of schedule and signups

At camp (June)
Brainstorm with campers re: feedback, future themes
Final circle – who wants to be involved in coming year?

ORGANIZING & RESOURCES

Camp Grid / Timeline

Thursday	Friday	Saturday
7:00-9:00 BREAKFAST	7:00-9:00 BREAKFAST	7:00-9:00 BREAKFAST
9:30 All-camp Meeting		
10-12 MORNING PATH	10-12 MORNING PATH	10-12 MORNING PATH
12:30-1:30 LUNCH 1:15 childcare 1:15 Ritual Planning 2-4 PM Activities/Offerings Archery Swimming Hole	12:30-1:30 LUNCH 1:15 Childcare 1:15 Ritual Planning 2-4 PM Activities/Offerings 1:30 Archery - kids 2:00 Archery - Teen/Adult 3:15 Sacred Sculpy 4 PM Ritual	12:30-1:30 LUNCH 1:15 childcare 1:15 Ritual Planning 2-4 PM Activities/Offerings 1:30 Archery - kids 2:00 ~~Archery - Teen/Adult~~ 2:45 Tie Dye 3:15 Favorite Fairy Picture Books 4:30 PM All-camp meeting
5:30-6:30 DINNER 6 PM start cleanup (6:15)	5:30-6:30 DINNER 6 PM start cleanup (6:15)	5:30-6:30 DINNER 6 PM start cleanup (6:15)
7 PM-ish Ritual Night Hike	7 PM-ish ~~Ritual~~ it's in the afternoon (Probably 7:30) Talent Show	7 PM Ritual-ish Dance Party get your groove on!

This sample grid is from Redwood Magic Family Camp (hence the "Childcare" line). A written grid shows us the flow of each day, reminds us what's next when we're lost between the worlds – and gives us an overview of where we're coming from and where we're going.

ORGANIZING & RESOURCES

Gaining Key Skills: The Hearth

Young Adults Anchor Kitchen at TEM 2017!

For many years, young adults have helped anchor rituals and path-work at TEM, Witchlets, and Redwood Magic.

In 2017, several of our TEM "graduates" stepped up to create the hearth for our camp – ie, to prepare our meals for five days.

In the past we've always had an experienced adult who cooked for camp. Sometimes the cook was also a teacher (how did they do it?). Other years we paid someone a small stipend to keep us fed and happy.

For 2017, several of our early-20s folks expressed interest in creating the hearth.

We knew they could cook – but doing it for 25 people (and, as it turned out, in 100-degree heat!) seemed like a stretch. But what is TEM about if not stretching?

To add to the challenge, the hearth team decided they wanted each evening's dinner to correspond to the point on the Pentacle of the Great Turning that we were exploring that day – so the opening dinner was "Desire," the first point on the pentacle, and so on.

See the next page for our complete menu with Great Turning correspondences!

(For more on the Great Turning, See Workings: Pentacle of the Great Turning – page 252.)

The TEM 2017 Kitchen Team – three young adults who've been part of camp for many years supported by a parent – lovingly serve lunch to appreciative campers.

ORGANIZING & RESOURCES

Gaining Key Skills: The Hearth (pg 2)

Our 2017 Menu – with Pentacle of the Great Turning points!

Saturday Dinner: Desire
Pasta & sauce
Garlic bread
Salad

Saturday Dessert: Desire
Something with roses

Sunday Breakfast: Desire
Cereal & milk
Toast
Fruit
Hardboiled eggs
Protein
Coffee & tea
Oatmeal
Yogurt

Sunday Lunch: Desire/Surrender
Sandwiches
Cucumber salad
Chips
Lavender lemonade

Sunday Dinner: Surrender
Curry rice
Chicken
Tofu
Collard greens

Sunday Dessert: Surrender
Mango & coconut sticky rice

Monday Breakfast: Surrender
Cereal & milk
Toast
Fruit
Coffee & tea
Oatmeal
Yogurt

Monday Lunch: Transformation
Sandwiches
Pasta salad
Nettle pesto
Chips
Iced tea

Monday Dinner: Transformation
Burrito bar
Fixings
Green salad

Monday Dessert: Transformation
Cookies (ginger? chocolate chip?)

Tuesday Breakfast: Transformation
Cereal & milk
Fruit
Tofu scramble
Scrambled eggs
Potatoes
Yogurt

Tuesday Lunch: Solidarity
Sandwiches
Bean salad
Chips
Honey & ginger popsicles

Tuesday Dinner: Solidarity
Falafel bar
Turkey meatballs
Homemade hummus
Quinoa tabbouleh
Pita

Tuesday Dessert: Solidarity
Peach cobbler

Wednesday Breakfast: Solidarity
Oatmeal, cereal, & milk
Toast
Fruit
Coffee & tea
Yogurt

Wednesday Lunch: Manifestation
Sandwiches
Rice salad / egg salad
Vegetable soup
Chips

Wednesday Dinner: Manifestation
Chili
Meat on the side
Cornbread
Fixings
Red cabbage salad

Wednesday Dessert: Manifestation
Kettle corn

Thursday Breakfast: Back to Desire
Leftovers!

ORGANIZING & RESOURCES

Reclaiming Resources

Ten Pages of Marvelous Magical Miscellany!

Reclaiming Chants Albums

Books by Reclaiming Authors

Reclaiming Archives & Back Issues

Following Pages:

- Reclaiming WitchCamps & Earth Activist Training
- Reclaiming chants albums
- Activist resources
- Books by Reclaiming authors
- Archives: Reclaiming Newsletter & Quarterly – free downloads
- Getting involved with Reclaiming

ORGANIZING & RESOURCES

Reclaiming WitchCamps

Magical Intensives in Europe, Australia, & North America

Reclaiming WitchCamps are intensive retreats for the study of magic, ritual, and for building and renewing our commitment to world change.

WitchCamps include all levels of experience. Newcomers learn basic magical skills. Advanced paths offer chances to apply these tools and skills.

Camps are currently offered in Europe, Australia, and around North America. Some camps are family-friendly, and offer programs for various ages.

Early WitchCamps were teacher-training intensives. In the 90s the idea blossomed into broader retreats. Reclaiming Collective teachers traveled and trained others, gradually building a large network of WitchCamp teachers.

Many camps are geographically based, and help anchor Reclaiming communities in their region.

Family camps have included Tejas Web, Witchlets in the Woods, Redwood Magic, and Wild Ginger.

Others are built around a particular theme or constituency, such as Free Activist WitchCamp, JeWitch Camp, and Teen Earth Magic. There have also been camps for women, and Queer Camp met twice in the 2000s.

Several camps focus on seasons or sabbats: Winter WitchCamp (Minnesota and Spain) and Mysteries of Samhain (Northern California).

WitchCamp.org – visit our website for a current schedule of Reclaiming WitchCamps.

Earth Activist Training
With Starhawk & Earth Activists

Starhawk's Earth Activist Trainings (EAT) helped inspire Teen Earth Magic. EAT can set your life on a new path... or show you how to save the world.

EAT is practical Earth-healing with a magical base of ritual and nature awareness, integrating mind and heart, with lots of hands-on practice and plenty of time to laugh.

Permaculture has many tools to address the problems of climate change and environmental degradation, and EAT's courses focus on solutions and positive approaches to the grave problems which confront us today.

Experiential courses include: hands-on projects, songs, exercises, discussions, and rituals, as well as classes.

EAT practices Social Permaculture – the application of ecological principles to designing beneficial human relations.

EAT teachers are deeply involved in organizing around climate change, anti-racism, and social justice as well as environmental issues. They work with the Black Permaculture Network, and have a commitment to share these skills and tools with the communities most impacted by injustice.

Planting seedlings with intention, magic, and micorrhizal fungi. Teen EAT mini-intensive, 2015. Photo by Luke Hauser.

EAT Contacts

EarthActivistTraining.org and Starhawk.org

EarthActivistTraining@gmail.com

ORGANIZING & RESOURCES

Campfire Chants – Our Latest Album!

Join us around the WitchCamp bonfire for inspirational chants and songs perfect for rituals, circles, marching for peace and justice – and singing along!

Featuring chants written by Starhawk, Suzanne Sterling, T. Thorn Coyle, Alphonsus Mooney, Laurie Lovekraft, Seed, Max Ventura, Meg Yardley, and more, these are among our most-sung chants from WitchCamps, classes, and rituals.

Several are among our favorite activist chants – perfect for rituals, rallies, and direct actions.

Recorded by a homespun, all-ages chorus accompanied by conga, guitar, flute, fiddle, clarinet – and even harmonica and ukulele.

Listen free at youtube, spotify, google, etc. Downloads at CDBaby, iTunes, and other usual sites.

Proceeds support Redwood Magic and Reclaiming's family camps.

CampfireChants.org – links and more info.

WeaveAndSpin.org/playlists – links to all of our chants on youtube and spotify.

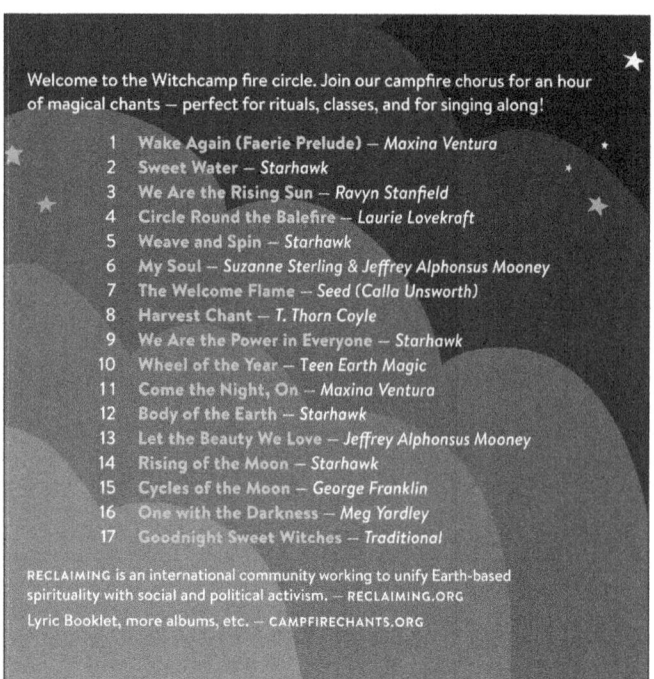

Lyrics & Lore Book – free online!
(or full-color print edition at amazon)

Enjoy this 50-page book of interviews, history, and stories about the chants – plus complete lyrics and guitar / ukulele chords.

Hear from Ravyn Stanfield (We Are the Rising Sun), Suzanne Sterling (My Soul), Laurie Lovekraft (Circle Round the Balefire), Seed (The Welcome Flame), Starhawk (five of her most-loved chants!), and more.

Plus sections on past Reclaiming music, WitchCamps, activism, the Spiral Dance ritual, and more.

There's even a Pagan Workers Vanguard satire page!

Perfect for your coffeetable, bookshelf, or altar.

Free download at CampfireChants.org.

Full-color print edition just $15 at amazon – search <Campfire Chants> for album and book. Proceeds benefit future recordings, publications, and archives.

ORGANIZING & RESOURCES

More Chants Albums from Reclaiming

Songs, chants, and meditation music from the Reclaiming network:

Chants: Ritual Music – 19 classic chants from the early days, recorded by a chorus and drum.

Second Chants: More Ritual Music – more chants and songs from the early years, recorded by soloists, chorus, and folk accompanists.

Let It Begin Now: Music from the Spiral Dance – chants and songs from our annual Samhain ritual.

Witches Brew: Songs & Chants from the Reclaiming Cauldron – greatest hits from teachers and musicians around Reclaiming – including Labyrinth Meditation Music.

Campfire Chants: Songs for the Earth – post-2000 Reclaiming hits, recorded by chorus and folk ensemble.

Way to the Well – a 45-minute trance journey ritual with Starhawk.

WeaveAndSpin.org/playlists – links to our chants on youtube and spotify.

ORGANIZING & RESOURCES

Magical Activist Resources

Direct Action: An Historical Novel

by Luke Hauser

"Affinity groups, consensus decision-making, and solidarity come alive. These are engaging stories of real people – stories that can be laughed at, cried over, and treasured."

– Karen Pickett, Earth First!

More than 7000 people were arrested in nonviolent protests in California during the early 1980s, developing the art of direct action in the U.S. to a peak not reached again until Seattle in 1999, and perhaps never surpassed.

Luke Hauser narrates the back-story of Reclaiming – the history of a community of activists who helped lay foundations for today's resistance movements.

Direct action is more than getting arrested. It's solidarity. It's affinity groups and collective process. It's nonhierarchy and respect for diversity. It's coalitions and alliance building.

It's not just a political tactic – it's a whole new practice.

Free download or read online – DirectAction.org.

Print edition at amazon.

Magical Activist Websites

Starhawk.org – workshops, writings, and resources.

EarthActivistTraining.org – intensive retreats with Starhawk and others.

DirectAction.org – free downloads of Luke Hauser's activist novel, plus handbooks, music, and more.

WeaveAndSpin.org – current Reclaiming posts.

ReclaimingQuarterly.org – includes photo-coverage of Pagan Cluster actions from about 2005-2016.

Reclaiming's Activist Elist

The Living River is the Pagan Cluster's international activist listserve. Learn about upcoming actions, workshops, and more. Contact others and join the actions.

Questions or to join the list:
ReclaimingQuarterly@gmail.com.

Activist Handbooks

Free PDF downloads of classic direct action handbooks. Practical discussions of consensus, nonviolence, affinity groups, feminism, confronting oppression, and much more.

DirectAction.org/handbook/

TeenEarthMagic.org

ORGANIZING & RESOURCES

Books & Resources from Starhawk

Books by Starhawk

- The Spiral Dance: A Rebirth of the Ancient Religion of the Goddess – the basic text from the early years of Reclaiming
- Dreaming the Dark: Magic, Sex, & Politics – visionary activist tools
- Truth or Dare – the personal and the political
- The Earth Path – building relations with our home
- The Empowerment Manual: A Guide for Collaborative Groups
- The Twelve Wild Swans: A Journey to the Realm of Magic, Healing, and Action

Novels
- The Fifth Sacred Thing – the troubled birth of a new world
- Walking to Mercury – activism-infused prequel to FST
- City of Refuge – creating the new world
- The Last Wild Witch – an eco-fable for children and everyone

With Others
- Circle Round: Raising Children in Goddess Traditions – with Anne Hill & Diane Baker
- The Pagan Book of Living & Dying – with M. Macha NightMare

Audiobooks by Starhawk
- Fifth Sacred Thing – the troubled birth of a new world
- Earth Magic: Sacred Rituals for Connecting to Nature's Power
- Wiccan Meditations – a short introduction to Pagan spirituality
- Wiccan Blessings & Rituals: Celebrating the Traditions of Earth-Based Spirituality
- The Beginner's Guide to Wicca

Pagan Chants from Starhawk
Recorded by Reclaiming

Albums with Starhawk's chants on all streaming and download services. Listen free at spotify and youtube.

For a Starhawk & Reclaiming playlist of all these songs and more, visit: WeaveAndSpin.org/playlists.

from the album Campfire Chants
- Sweet Water
- Rising of the Moon
- Weave and Spin
- We Are the Power in Everyone
- Body of the Earth

from Chants: Ritual Music
- Rise with the Fire
- Kore Chant (She Changes Everything She Touches)
- Where There's Fear There's Power
- We Are Alive

from Second Chants
- Barge of Heaven
- When We Are Gone (with Anne Hill)

from Witches Brew
- Who Is the Goddess (with D J Hamouris)

from Let It Begin Now
- No End to the Circle
- The God Song (with Michael Charnes)
- Set Sail (with Mara June Quicklightning)
- Let It Begin Now (with L. Gale & A. Khan-Engel)
- Demeter's Song (I Am the Wealthy One)
- No End to the Circle (Devocation)

Drum Trance Ritual with Starhawk
- Way to the Well (on all streaming services)

Starhawk.org
- Starhawk.org – all Starhawk, all the time!
- EarthActivistTraining.org – Permaculture intensives with Starhawk and others

ORGANIZING & RESOURCES

More Books from the Reclaiming Network

T. Thorn Coyle
- Evolutionary Witchcraft
- Kissing the Limitless
- The Witches of Portland (novels)

Gerri Ravyn Stanfield
- Revolution of the Spirit: Awaken the Healer: An Invitation to Radical Healing

Suzanne McAnna
- Tarot Through the Witch's Eye

M. Macha NightMare
- Pagan Pride: Earth & Goddess

Jone Salomonsen
- Enchanted Feminism: The Reclaiming Witches of San Francisco

David Miller
- I Didn't Know God Made Honky Tonk Communists: A Memoir About Draft Card Burning & Witchcraft

Phoenix LeFae
- Hoodoo Shrines and Altars
- Cash Box Conjure: Hoodoo Spells
- What Is Remembered Lives

Jane Meredith & Gede Parma
- Magic of the Iron Pentacle
- Elements of Magic (editors – plus many Reclaiming contributors!)

Jane Meredith
- Journey to the Dark Goddess
- Aspecting the Goddess
- Rituals of Celebration
- Circle of Eight

Gede Parma
- By Land, Sky, & Sea: Shamanic Witchcraft
- Ecstatic Witchcraft: Shamanic Craft
- Spirited: Beyond the Circle

Margo Adair
- Working Inside Out: Tools for Change

Candace Savage
- many titles on Bird Wisdom, the Prairie, Wolves, Bees, and more

Alex Iantaffi
- Life Isn't Binary
- How to Understand Your Gender (with Meg-John Barker)

Sea Raven
- The J'Argon (novel)

Cynthia Lamb
- Brigid's Charge (novel)

Dixie W. Franklin
- The Hardy Girls Mystery Series

The Magical Writer
A do-it-yourself online course!

A dozen sessions to inspire your writing and creativity:
- magical writing space
- invoking characters and allies
- integrating your inner critic
- plot, story, and myth

Course booklet – free download

DirectAction.org/magicalwriter

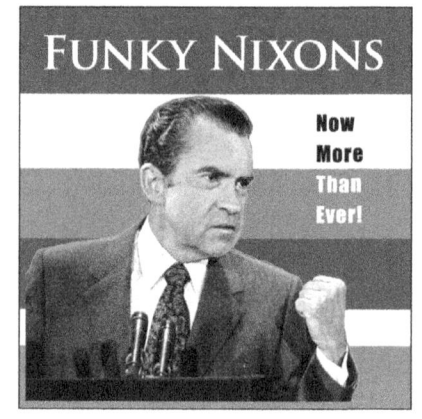

Funky Nixons

Straight Outa Berkeley – garage-based rock, rap, and country music.

Timeless tunes to lift your political blues and set those revolutionary toes tapping. Proceeds benefit Reclaiming publishing.

On all streaming and download sites.

ORGANIZING & RESOURCES

Reclaiming Newsletter & Quarterly – free!

Catch up on 40 years of Reclaiming news & views!

From 1980 through 2011, Reclaiming published more than 100 issues of our Newsletter and later the Quarterly.

The publications appeared quarterly until around 2004, and sporadically afterward. Escalating costs and diminishing demand for print finally turned the magazine into ReclaimingQuarterly.org (and more recently WeaveAndSpin.org).

Get all 100+ issues free online – find single issues or a zip file of the entire collection at:

WeaveAndSpin.org/back-issues/

Featuring writers, artists, poets, and photographers from around the Reclaiming network – magic, activism, humor, poetry, recipes, history, tradition, and much more!

Free downloads – WeaveAndSpin.org/back-issues/

ORGANIZING & RESOURCES

Teachers, Classes, & Starting a Camp

Reclaiming Core Classes Online!

World Tree Lyceum Offers Reclaiming classes

World Tree Lyceum offers basic and advanced magical classes online, including many Reclaiming classes.

Here's a chance to connect with folks studying and working magic in our tradition.

Visit WorldTreeLyceum.org.

Important – if you are under age 18, please tell the teachers your age when you contact them, and inform your parent or legal guardian.

Bring TEM Teachers to Your Event

Whether it's a retreat or a workshop, a conference or a class, TEM teachers can anchor offerings for youth or adults and bring inspiration and Earth magic to your event.

Email us – see below.

Starting a Reclaiming Camp

Want to start a Reclaiming camp in your area, or link your camp to our network?

Look through the early pages of this chapter and download the Witchlets Manual (see page 327).

Gather a team. Share your visions. Look for a site.

To be a Reclaiming camp, you'll need a couple of Reclaiming-trained teachers (who in turn can help train local teachers for your community). Maybe you already know them. Or contact us to find teachers in your area.

Email us – see below.

Who Can Attend Teen Earth Magic?

Teen Earth Magic is a retreat for young people from Reclaiming Tradition and their guests.

We welcome new folks at our family and all-ages camps – a great place for young people to get involved and meet TEM participants and teachers.

Visit WitchCamp.org for camp contacts, or contact us with questions – see below.

Who Can Teach TEM Workshops?

This book is designed for young people working alone or with friends, or for teachers at Reclaiming WitchCamps.

We're honored to have other teachers adapt these exercises for use at their retreats and workshops.

Q: How many TEM teens does it take to set up a tent? (Answer at bottom of page.)

However – unless you are formally trained in our tradition, please do not teach this material under the name "Teen Earth Magic" or "Reclaiming."

Reclaiming has a teacher-development process. Teen Earth Magic also has its own process.

No Grooming or Recruiting

No Grooming or Recruiting – this book is not to be used to recruit youth for circles or classes apart from knowing and communicating with their families. No Reclaiming material is ever to be used to groom young people. Contact us with any questions – email below.

Contact Teen Earth Magic & Reclaiming

TeenEarthMagic@gmail.com

Quarterly@Reclaiming.org

Quiz Answer

A: How many are in camp? It's a group effort!

ORGANIZING & RESOURCES

How to Get Involved with Reclaiming

Reclaiming Websites

Reclaiming.org – portal site with basic info about Reclaiming, links to local groups, etc.

WitchCamp.org – dates and links to our WitchCamps and family camps in Europe, North America, and Australia.

BayAreaReclaiming.org – local rituals and events in the San Francisco Bay Area.

ReclaimingSpiralDance.org – information, tickets, and volunteer opportunities for our biggest annual gathering in the Bay Area, each year around Samhain.

ReclaimingQuarterly.org – archival website of our former newsletter and magazine (1980-2011) – hundreds of articles, publications, downloadable files, etc.

WeaveAndSpin.org – new Reclaiming Quarterly-sponsored site with current posts, archive highlights, links to music and videos, and much more.

WeaveAndSpin.org/playlists/ – youtube and spotify playlists for chants and other recordings.

CampfireChants.org – links to our latest album and past chants albums.

DirectAction.org – free downloads of activist handbooks and other resources.

TeenEarthMagic.org – information about TEM, our book, and other resources.

Facebook – many local Reclaiming groups, camps, and circles have pages – visit Reclaiming.org/worldwide for current contacts.

Reclaiming Listserves/Elists

Any interested person can ask to join these lists.

To join, email us: ReclaimingQuarterly@gmail.com.

RIDL – Reclaiming International Discussion List – keep up with classes (including online), WitchCamps, activism, and more from around the Reclaiming network.

LivRiv – the Living River is the listserve of the Pagan Cluster – keep up with international activist organizing and find out how you can take part and/or support.

BARD – Bay Area Reclaiming's elist, open to all who are interested. Local rituals, classes (online too), music and nature circles, activist gatherings, and more.

Reclaiming Magic Classes – local, retreats, & online

Various Reclaiming communities offer classes and workshops in ritual, activism, personal growth, and more.

Some offer classes such as Elements of Magic. Others host intensive retreats. For current offerings, join our elists – see info on this page – and visit our international website:

Reclaiming.org/worldwide.

Online – Reclaiming classes online – see top of page 350.

In the Bay Area for Halloween? Join us for

The Spiral Dance

First held in 1979 to celebrate the release of Starhawk's book, the ritual is danced each year around Samhain – the New Year of the witches and the Bay Area's biggest magical gathering.

This participatory pageant has become a central event in the wheel of the year for the Reclaiming community and beyond.

Dozens co-create the event, and hundreds gather to dance the sacred spiral.

If you are in the Bay Area in late October, join us!

Tickets are available online. Many volunteers are also needed to create this wonderful community ritual. Visit our website for more information.

ReclaimingSpiralDance.org

ORGANIZING & RESOURCES

Ye Olde Index

a mostly helpful guide to the complete contents of this book!

Activism, Magical
Activist Chants 113, 155
Reclaiming's Pagan Cluster 148, 155
Introduction 148, 152
Teens Roundtable 149
Student Activism 151
Activism & the Internet 154
Nonviolence: Our Commitment 156
Finding Your Activism 158
Salt & Apple Activism Ritual 159
Street Theater, Chalking, Banners 166-169
Shadow Work: Headlines & Oppressions 262-265
Activist Resources & Handbooks 346

Affirmation & Commitment
An Affirmation Ritual 121
Workings: Words of Affirmation 180
Workings: Bead Ceremony 197
Workings: Flaming Cauldron 219

Agreements
Working Together: TEM Agreements 32
Reclaiming's Principles of Unity 37

Alcohol & Drugs 30

Altars 184
Ancestor Altar 85
Workings: Altars: Scavenger Altars 187
Workings: Altars: Youth Visions 189

Ukulele – the perfect accompaniment for learning chants! Complete guitar / uke chords for songs on our Campfire Chants album are available in the full-color Lyrics & Lore booklet. Visit CampfireChants.org for free PDF or print info.

Allies
Invoking Allies 86, 90
Discovering My Allies 92
Workings: Allies Circle 181
Workings: My Own Best Ally 183

Ancestors 85

Auras 190
Workings: Sensing Auras 190
Workings: Auras & Boundaries 192
Workings: Aura Carwash 194

Automatic Writing 196

Bead Ceremony 197

Blessings
Workings: Bead Ceremony 197
Workings: Elemental Blessing 199
Workings: Blessing Line 200
Workings: Blessing: Star Goddess 201
Workings: Circle Blessing 208
Workings: Mirror Goddess 242

Books by Reclaiming Authors 346-348

Book of Shadows 202

Boundaries & Shielding
Shielding & Negative Energy 29
Workings: Auras & Boundaries 192
Workings: Boundaries: Collage Shields 203
Workings: Boundaries: Scrub-Jay Lines 204
Workings: Mirror Shielding 243

Brass Liberation Orchestra 171

Breathing 205

California WitchCamp 57, 104, 187

Campfire Activities 206

Chants & Music
How To Teach Chants 110
Resources & Online Chants 111-113
Reclaiming Albums 111, 344-345
Online Playlists 112, 345
Chants for Each Ritual Role 112
Activist Chants 113
Let It Begin Now: A Music Ritual 124
Around the WitchCamp Bonfire 147

Charging & Empowering
Workings: Overflowing Cup Spell 248
Workings: Spell: Charging with Fire & Flour 278
Workings: Zap (Quick Charging) 324
Charging a Magical Tool 305

Circles & Covens 26

Circle Casting & Workings 68-76
Teens Roundtable 68
Circle Casting Intro & Exercises 70
Ye Olde Circle Casting ("By the Earth that is...") 71
Workings: Circle Blessings 208
Workings: Circle: Pass the Knot 209
Workings: Circle: Yarn Web 210

Classes: Local & Online 350

Collages 211

Commitments (making commitments)
An Affirmation Ritual 121
Workings: Bead Ceremony 197
Workings: Flaming Cauldron 219
Workings: Spell: Charging with Fire & Flour 278

Cone of Power 108

Consensus & Group Process 93, 160, 346

Cooperative Games 221

Correspondences, Magical
Water (Example) 137
Workings: Tools of Magic 303

Costume Magic 212
Workings: Costume Shadows 266

Covens & Circles 26

Cultural Appropriation
Interview: Diversity & Cultural Appropriation 40
Myths, Deities, & Appropriation 90, 91

Curses & Hexes 28, 273

Daily Practice 115

Deity / Goddesses & Gods
Gender Issues 38, 89-90
Cultural Appropriation Issues 40, 90-91
Invoking 86, 90

Devocations / Devoking 79

ORGANIZING & RESOURCES

Ye Olde Index (pg 2)

Dia de los Muertos (Day of the Dead) 171

Direct Action: An Historical Novel 154, 346

Discernment (figuring stuff out)
Workings: Divination 214-218
Workings: Tarot 285-302

Diversity Issues
Interview: Diversity & Cultural Appropriation................40
Myths, Deities, & Ritual...90, 91

Divination
Workings: Divination: Nature Readings.......................214
Workings: Divination: Oracles......................................216
Workings: Divination: Scrying 218
Workings: Tarot 285-302

Drugs & Alcohol...30

Earth Activist Trainings with Starhawk 343

Earth First! 163-165, 171, 346

Elemental Practices
Invoking Elements..84
Correspondences & Tools..84, 303
Book: Elements of Magic (2018)...................................102
A Water Ritual..133
Creating Elemental Rituals...139
Workings: Altars: Scavenger Altars..............................187
Workings: Elemental Blessing......................................199

Energy-Raising Workings
Workings: Flaming Cauldron 219
Workings: Lifting Each Other Up..................................236
Workings: Spell: Charging with Fire & Flour 278

Ethics Agreement 337

Etiquette in Circles & Rituals 27
Magical Tools Etiquette 304

Final & Climactic Workings (end of class or ritual)
Workings: Flaming Cauldron 219
Workings: Overflowing Cup Spell 248
Workings: Trust Falls..312
Workings: Lifting Each Other Up..................................236

Fashion, Witchy Etc 212-213

Fire Skills & Spells
Fire Safety 9, 31
Firetending..103
Workings: Spell: Burning Putdowns 275
Workings: Spell: Charging with Fire & Flour 278
Workings: Spell: The Wicker One 281

First People: On Indigenous Land 15
Cultural Appropriation Issues 40, 90-91
Honoring First People..59
Solidarity Actions...170

Outline of Ye Booke

The book consists of five chapters. See Table of Contents for complete outline.

Introduction introduces the voices of our campers and our camp culture.

Ritual Skills follows the order of a Reclaiming ritual – index on page 58.

   Rituals shares a dozen different types of rituals – index on page 114.

Activism is a bit anarchic, and there's not a separate index – starts on page 148.

Workings chapter is alphabetical – complete index on page 172.

Organizing & Resources chapter is just plain fun to look through!

Full-Color PDF – Download at Our Website

The outline of the book is easy to see in the full-color PDF version – each section has its own color (and most of the photos are in color, too).

The PDF version is also handy if you want to print selected pages for a workshop.

Visit TeenEarthMagic.org or WeaveAndSpin.org/resources for this and more.

Flaming Cauldron 219

Food Not Bombs... 170

Forest Activism 163-165, 171

Free Activist WitchCamp.................. see Free Cascadia

Free Cascadia WitchCamp 16, 20, 41

Funky Nixons..348

Games, Cooperative 221
Games, April's Book... 174, 222

Gender Issues
Interview: Gender Complexities 38
Circle Casting & Gender Issues............................... 71-72
Invoking Deities & Allies: Gender Issues 80, 89-90
Ritual, Myths, & Gender 97

Getting Involved with Reclaiming.......... 36, 350-351

Goddesses & Gods .... see Deity

Goddess, Mirror Working..242

Great Turning, Pentacle of the 252, 254, 341

Grounding.. 62-67
Grounding: Tree of Life 53, 115
Teens Roundtable..62
Ritual Skills: Grounding 64
Pentacle Grounding..66
Online Tree of Life Grounding with Starhawk 115
A Grounding Ritual..116
During Activism 162
Workings: Grounding: Red Cord Spell 225

Gun Control (Student Activism)............................151

Handbooks, Activism 155, 346

Hauser, Luke
This Book... 1-358
Other Books 7
Direct Action: An Historical Novel 154, 346

Hearth (Kitchen)..340

Hexes & Curses 28
Hexes & Negative Spells 273

Indigenous People .... see First People

continued on next page

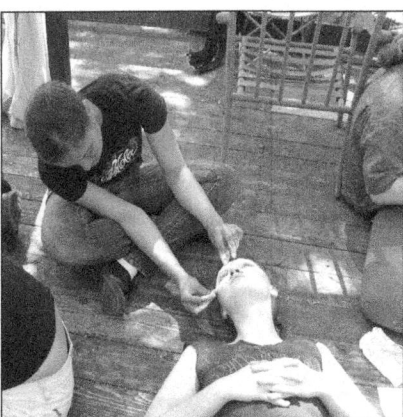

A mask workshop lets us explore different identities.

ORGANIZING & RESOURCES

Ye Olde Index (pg 3)

Intuitive Practices 229
Workings: Auras 190
Workings: Divination: Nature Divination 214
Workings: Divination: Oracles 216
Workings: Divination: Scrying 218
Workings: Tarot, Intuitive 289

Invoking 77-92
Invoking: Example of Ritual Invocations 54-56
Invoking Pentacle (How to Draw) 72
Teens Roundtable 77
Ritual Skills: Invoking 79
Invoking & Gender Issues 80, 89
Ways of Invoking 83
Invoking Elements 84
Invoking Ancestors 85
Invoking Deities & Allies 86-91

Journey of the Spirit (Tarot) 299

Labyrinths
Ariadne, Theseus, & the Minotaur 97, 231
Labyrinth Challenges Ritual 125
How to Draw 129, 232
Labyrinth Workings 230
Finger Labyrinths 231

Law of Threes / Threefold Return 28
Law of Threes & Spellwork 273

Letter to Myself 233

Liberation Circle 234

Lifting Each Other Up 236

Listening
Listening Stations Working 132
Non-Judgmental Listening 246

Listserves & Elists for Reclaiming 351
Listserve: Pagan Cluster (Living River) 155

Loreley WitchCamp 16, 224, 332

Macy, Joanna (& The Great Turning) 252, 254

Magic
What Is Magic 17
What Is Earth Magic 20
Beliefs 23, 80
Magical Correspondences 303

Magical Activism .... see Activism

Magical Writing .... see Writing

Meditative Workings
Ritual Skills: Grounding 65
Way to the Well (Online ritual with Starhawk) 115
Workings: Nature Sit & Night Sit 244
Workings: Trance: Place of Power (Online) 309

Mentors (Young Adults) 335

Milling Exercises 179

Mirror Magic
Workings: Mirror Affirmations 241
Workings: Mirror Goddess 242
Workings: Mirror Shielding 243
Workings: Voice Magic: Mirror Singing 320

Motherpeace Tarot Deck 285

Mysterious Ones 90

Myths & Stories
Cultural Appropriation Issues 40, 90-91
Gender Issues 89, 97
Ritual Themes & Stories 96
Ariadne, Theseus, & the Minotaur 97, 231
Themes & Stories from Our Camps 98

Native Americans .... see First People

Occupy (2011 Protests) 107, 148-153

Online Classes with World Tree Lyceum 350

Online Trances & Meditations 115, 309

Opening Workings (start of class or ritual)
Workings: Purification: Bridge Challenge 255
Workings: Aura Carwash 194
Workings: Non-Judgmental Listening 246
Workings: Spectrums 268-269

Oracles .... see Divination

Organizing
Family & Youth Camps 326, 350
Camp Organizing Resources 327
Organizing Timeline & Camp Grid (Schedule) 338-339

Overflowing Cup Spell 248

Parents: A Word To Parents 9

Pearl Pentacle 249, 289

Pentacle Magic 249-254
Invoking Pentacle (How to Draw) 72
Workings: Blessing: Star Goddess 201
Workings: Pearl Pentacle 249
Running Pentacles 250
Workings: Pentacle of the Great Turning 252, 254

Permaculture
Permaculture Stations Working 131
Earth Activist Training (EAT) 343

Place of Power Trance (Starhawk online) 309

Purification 60
Workings: Purification: Bridge Challenge 255
Workings: Purification: Star Purification 256

Reclaiming
About Reclaiming 34-37
Principles of Unity 37
Getting Involved, Website, Contacts 36, 350-351
Reclaiming Chants 111, 344-345
Classes: Local & Online 350

Can you count the Teen Earth Magic folks in this whirl? The Spiral Dance 2007. Photo by Michael Rauner – michaelrauner.com.

ORGANIZING & RESOURCES

Ye Olde Index (pg 4)

Reclaiming Newsletter (1980-1996).................6, 349
Reclaiming Quarterly (1996-2011)...........6, 251, 349
Recorded Trances & Meditations..................115, 309
Redwood Magic Family Camp
Diversity Issues...41-42
Magical Themes..98
Camp Organizing Resources.........................327
Resources... 342-351
Activist Resources...155
Camp Organizing...327
Revolutionary Pagan Workers Vanguard............357
Rituals
Complete Index to Rituals Chapter..............114
Create Your Own Rituals................................145
Activism: Salt & Apple (A Ritual of Concern)...............159
Harvest Stations..227
Ritual Skills
Complete Index to Rituals Skills Chapter........58
Ritual Outline..45
Creating Sacred Space...............................49, 52
Ritual Planning..92
Ritual Roles...95
Ritual Themes & Arcs.......................................96
Ritual Skills Stations Working..............131, 257
Sacred Space: Quick Ways..............................49
Speed Space..51
Sacred Space: A Longer Example............. 52-57
Salmon, Journey of................................. 99-101
Salmon Journey Brainstorm..........................101
Scrying...218

One last hug before camp ends!

Shadow Work
Intro: Curses, Hexes, & Boundaries................29
Workings: Pentacles & Shadows...................251
Workings: Shadow Work...................... 259-267
Workings: Composting Headlines................262
Workings: Composting Oppressions............264
Workings: Costume Shadows.......................266
Shielding...see Boundaries
Shoes, Witchy..212

Solitaries & Solo Work..................................26
Solo Workings..................see Workings Chapter!
Solstice in the Streets...........23, 88, 148-153, 166-169
Handmade Posters................................ 168-169
Spectrums of Belief & Practice.............268, 269
Spells & Spellcrafting...................................271
Curses, Hexes, & Negative Spells............28, 273
Grounding: Red Cord Spell...........................225
Overflowing Cup Spell...................................248
Breaking a Commitment...............................274
Burning or Composting Putdowns..............275
Spell Candles..276
Charging with Fire & Flour............................278
Temperance Pouring......................................279
Waters of the World.......................................280
The Wicker One..281
Yarn Binding Spell..283
Tarot: Journey of the Spirit...........................299
Spiral Dance: Book by Starhawk................102
Other Books by Starhawk..............................347
Spiral Dance: How to Lead........................106
Cone of Power..108
Spiral Dance: Good Chants.................. 112-113
Spiral Dance: Occupy Oakland 2011.........107

continued on next page

Seven Key Reclaiming Resources

- **Chants Online** – pages 111-113 & WeaveAndSpin.org/playlists
- **Books & Downloads** – pages 347-349 & WeaveAndSpin.org/books
- **Join an Elist or Contact Reclaiming** – pages 350-351 & Reclaiming.org
- **WitchCamps** – page 343 & WitchCamp.org
- **The Spiral Dance (SF Ritual)** – page 351 & ReclaimingSpiralDance.org
- **Download PDF of this Book** – TeenEarthMagic.org
- **Teen Earth Magic** – pages 16, 334-341, & TeenEarthMagic.org
- **Contact TEM** – TeenEarthMagic@gmail.com & Quarterly@Reclaiming.org

ORGANIZING & RESOURCES

Ye Olde Index (pg 5)

Spiral Dance Annual Ritual 35, 114, 351, 354
Let It Begin Now: Musical Ritual Online 124
Spiral Dance Altar Photos 184-186

Spirits of the Land 91

Star Goddess Blessing 201

Star Purification 256

Starhawk Resources
Foreword: An Interview 12
Online Trances 115
Earth Activist Training 343
Books & Chants 347

Stories of the Land 99

Student Activism 151

Tarot Workings 285-302
Tarot: A Key Magical Practice 285
Good Decks for Intuitive Reading 285
Tarot Jargon 286
Intuitive Reading & Exercises 288
Reversals & Difficult Cards 293
Tarot: Living Tableaux 295
Tarot Speed Readings 296
Tarot: Journey of the Spirit 299

Teaching
TEM Teachers Over the Years 6
Teaching Teen Earth Magic 9, 174, 350
Teacherly Tips & Toolkit 175
Teaching Younger Teens 323, 328
TEM Teachers for Your Event 350
Reclaiming Classes, Camps, & Contacts 350
Online Classes with World Tree Lyceum 350

Teen Earth Magic
About 8, 16, 98, 334
Who Can Attend 16, 350
Teaching This Material 9, 174, 350

TEM Teachers' Voices 336
TEM Organizing Calendar 338
Camp Grid (Schedule) 339
Hearth (Kitchen) 340
TEM Teachers for Your Event 350
Teens Interviews .... see Teens Roundtables

Teens Roundtables & Interviews
Foreword: An Interview with Starhawk 12
What Is Magic? 17
What Is Earth Magic? 20
What Do We Believe? 23
Gender Complexities (Mykel Mogg) 38
Diversity & Cultural Appropriation (Rahula Janowski) ... 40
Ritual Skills: Rituals 47
Ritual Skills: Grounding 62
Ritual Skills: Casting a Circle 68
Ritual Skills: Invoking 77
Ritual Skills: Deities & Allies 86
Activism: Magical Activism 149
Activism: Student Activism 151
TEM Teachers: What Calls Us? 336

Temperance Pouring Spell 279

Threefold Return / Law of Threes 28, 273

Tools of Magic 303-308
Workings: Book of Shadows 202
Elemental Tool Correspondences 303
Workings: Tools Cakewalk 307
Workings: Wand Crafting 322

Trance
Online: Way to the Well with Starhawk 115
Online: Place of Power with Starhawk 309

Transformational Tableaux 310

Transitions (Techniques) 175, 176

Trust Exercises 312-316
Workings: Trust Fall 312
Workings: Trust Run 315
Workings: Trust Walk 316

Vermont WitchCamp 16, 332

Voice Magic 317
Workings: Singing With Support 318, 320
Singing In Tune 321

Wagon Wheel Technique 178

Wand Crafting 322

Water: An Elemental Ritual 133

Waters of the World Spell 280

Websites & Elists for Reclaiming 351

Wheel of the Year Rituals 46

Wicker One Spell 281

Witch 22, 23
Witchy Shoes 212

WitchCamp: About & Contacts 35, 343

Witchlets In the Woods Family Camp 330
Diversity Issues 40-42
Magical Themes 98
Opening Night Teens Ritual 140
Camp Organizing Resources 327
Early Teens Paths 330
Photos 325-333

Workings: Complete List 172
Workings: Introduction 173
Workings: Tips for Teachers 175
Workings: Teacherly Toolkit 175
Workings: Handy Techniques 176

World Tree Lyceum (Online Classes) 350

Writing
Workings: Automatic Writing 196
Workings: Book of Shadows 202
Workings: Magical Writing 239

Yarn Binding Spell 283

Young Adults (Mentors) 335

Younger Teen Groups
Sacred Space: Quick Ways 49
Workings: Ideas for Younger Groups 323
Organizing: Teaching Magic to Teens 328

Yuba River 19

Zap (Quick Charging & Empowering) 324

That's all, folks!

After camp – waiting for a ride home (and catching up on a week's worth of texts!).

TeenEarthMagic.org

Revolutionary Pagan Workers Vanguard

Issue #38 — *The Voice of the Pagan Proletariat* — Mid 2019

Teens Affinity Group Seizes Beltane Maypole

Youth In Perpetual Motion affinity group caught Beltane traditionalists napping at this year's Reclaim May Day ritual, and in a daring maneuver seized and made off with the maypole just as the celebration peaked.

Inspired by legendary accounts of the Peoples Pagan Party's expropriation of the maypole in the mythical era of the 1990s, YIPM cadre infiltrated the Beltane crowd, and at a key revolutionary juncture grabbed the pole and absconded before other celebrants could recover from the cone of power.

Maypole guardians from Wisdom of the Ancient Ones coven publicly expressed dismay at the action.

But several secretly smiled afterward, noting that whoever leaves the ritual with the maypole is responsible for storing it until next year.

Teen Earth Magic Announces Upcoming Theme: Mud Mysteries

Teen Earth Magic has revealed the ritual theme for next summer's camp: The Mystery of Mud.

Not satisfied that the recent Mushrooms & Fungi theme got down to essentials, organizers dug deeper and came up with the ultimate Earth Magic theme:

continued on page D-359

RPWV Archives at RQ.org

This is issue #38 of the Revolutionary Pagan Workers Vanguard, Reclaiming's all-purpose satire page created around 1997 by Reclaiming Quarterly magazine. Find reprints of past editions of the RPWV at our archives site:

ReclaimingQuarterly.org/web/rpwv

Ex-Teens Launch Geezer Earth Magic!

Decrying petit-bourgeois ageist tendencies rampant in Reclaiming, a cabal of former teens has seceded from the Teen Earth Magic organizing cell and declared their intention to form a new camp: Geezer Earth Magic.

"We're getting a mite bit tired of the constant emphasis on the voices of youth and new inspirations and all that," said elderly spokeswitch Lucifer "Larry" Hieronymous. "It's time we give heed to the weary voices of aged wisdom."

The breakaway faction formed after Hieronymous was found to have lied about his age in order to be a camper for the first eleven years of TEM.

When it was discovered that he was actually 47, he was immediately removed as a camper and transferred to the Young Adult Mentor Program.

Hieronymous, no stranger to controversy, responded by announcing plans to form a new spiritual tendency based around a WitchCamp for revolutionary old people and their allies.

Proto-Ancestors Make Demands

Among the changes demanded by the Provisional Revolutionary Council of Geezers, Aged Ones, Old Folks, & Beloved Proto-Ancestors, are:

• Every day of camp is Morning of Repose. Rituals begin when we get there.

• Cushioned, reclining seating at all bonfire rituals.

• Paved walkways through the woodlands with rustic restrooms every 25 feet.

• Teens and young adults to act as sherpas.

Initiation Ritual Raises Concerns

Some applauded, but as details of the initiation ritual for Geezer Earth Magic began to emerge, others in Reclaiming expressed concerns.

"We're hearing all sorts of complaints from campers, from reduced mobility to hearing loss to aching bunions," said Reclaiming spokeswitch Sunshine MoonBeam. "If they can't find a way to age more gracefully, we may have to ban this sort of organizing!"

A young adult mentor rushes to the aid of a TEM camper whose air invocation has gone awry.

TeenEarthMagic.org

TEEN EARTH MAGIC

AN EMPOWERMENT WORKBOOK

Welcome to our book – here's a few ways to get started!

- **Read** the Teens Roundtables and hear directly from TEM campers – (pages 17-24, pages 86-89, and more).
- **Skim** the Table of Contents (pages 10-11) or Ye Olde Index (pages 352-356) for an overview of the book.
- **Play** Reclaiming chants while flipping through the book (see pages 111-113 for online links).
- **Jump** to the chapter on Magical Activism for some quick inspiration (page 148).
- **Listen** to an online ritual with Starhawk while reading (see page 115).
- **Do Bibliomancy** (divination from a sacred text) – open the book at random and start reading!

Want to do a ritual without reading the whole book?

- Read the Ritual Skills intro and outline (pages 44-45) and Sacred Space: Quick Ways (pages 49-51).
- Select a core working from the Workings chapter or another that interests you.
- Choose a few chants that fit your theme and mood (pages 111-113).
- Let the magic begin!

A word to parents & other teachers

Please see page 9 for a special welcome and more information about Reclaiming and Teen Earth Magic.

You can contact us at: TeenEarthMagic@gmail.com and Quarterly@Reclaiming.org.

Made in the USA
Las Vegas, NV
28 September 2023

78276707R00197